W9-ACQ-550

A Concise History of Brazil, Second Edition

The second edition of *A Concise History of Brazil* offers a sweeping yet accessible history of Latin America's largest country. Boris Fausto examines Brazil's history from the arrival of the Portuguese in the New World through the long and sometimes rocky transition from independence in 1822 to democracy in the twentieth century. In a completely new chapter, his son Sergio Fausto, a prominent political scientist, brings the history up to the present, focusing on Brazil's increasing global economic importance as well as its continued democratic development and the challenges the country faces to meet the higher expectations of its people.

Boris Fausto is a renowned Brazilian historian and political scientist. He is a retired professor of political science at the University of São Paulo.

Sergio Fausto is a political scientist and executive director of the Fernando Henrique Cardoso Institute, a Brazilian think tank.

A Concise History of Brazil, Second Edition

BORIS FAUSTO

Universidade de São Paulo

With contributions by

SERGIO FAUSTO

Instituto Fernando Henrique Cardoso

Translated by Arthur Brakel

CAMBRIDGE
UNIVERSITY PRESS

CAMBRIDGE
UNIVERSITY PRESS

University Printing House, Cambridge CB2 8BS, United Kingdom

One Liberty Plaza, 20th Floor, New York, NY 10006, USA

477 Williamstown Road, Port Melbourne, VIC 3207, Australia

4843/24, 2nd Floor, Ansari Road, Daryaganj, Delhi - 110002, India

79 Anson Road, #06-04/06, Singapore 079906

Cambridge University Press is part of the University of Cambridge.

It furthers the University's mission by disseminating knowledge in the pursuit of education, learning and research at the highest international levels of excellence.

www.cambridge.org
Information on this title: www.cambridge.org/9781107635241

First edition published 1999
Second edition published 2014

A catalogue record for this publication is available from the British Library

Library of Congress Cataloging in Publication data
Fausto, Boris, 1930–
[Historia concisa do Brasil. English]
A concise history of Brazil / Boris Fausto ; translated by Arthur Brakel. – Second edition.
pages cm
Includes bibliographical references and index.
ISBN 978-1-107-03620-8 (hardback) – ISBN 978-1-107-63524-1 (pbk.)
1. Brazil – History. I. Brakel, Arthur. II. Title.
F2521.F33213 2014
981–dc23   2014006977

ISBN 978-1-107-03620-8 Hardback
ISBN 978-1-107-63524-1 Paperback

To Cynira Stocco Fausto, in memoriam

CONTENTS

LIST OF MAPS

PREFACE

Writing a synthetic history of Brazil for an English-language readership entails a set of challenges that I feel I must make explicit.

Beginning with the presupposition that there is scant familiarity with Brazilian history in the English-speaking world, I chose to emphasize historical narrative and introduce my readers to a body of knowledge which I consider fundamental. This choice has obvious advantages. Among them, it avoids taking gaps in readers' knowledge for granted. However, at the same time, to lead readers along a path in a historical narrative is methodologically outdated and could result in a superficial understanding of important events.

I tried to minimize this shortcoming by combining narrative with discussions of central themes in the Brazilian historical process: e.g., the nature of Brazilian slavery, Brazil's remaining united once it became an independent country, and the characteristics of its recent transition from an authoritarian government to a democratic one.

I have also sought to inform readers about the more significant historiographical controversies when such controversies make way for different interpretations of the past as well as when they demonstrate that history is a body of knowledge subject to constant reappraisal and refinement.

As they get into the book, readers will become more aware of my working premises, but there is at least one more that should be made clear. I have rejected two opposing tendencies in discussing the Brazilian historical process. On the one hand, I have rejected the tendency to consider Brazilian history as an evolutionary trend characterized by constant progress. This is a simplistic point of view that events in recent years have belied. On the other hand, I have also rejected the point of view that emphasizes inertia – that suggests, for example, that problems caused by political patronage, by corruption, and by the state's impositions on society have been the same and have not changed over the years.

Oddly, the latter proclivity has been associated both with revolutionary ideologies and with conservative outlooks. For revolutionaries, their view of political and social domination as, for all intents and purposes, one and the same leads them to the notion that efforts in the interest of gradual change are useless. They prefer abrupt cuts. Conservative thinkers who share this inertial point of view tend to be skeptical of change; or, in their more elaborated thinking, they are in favor of intervention by an authoritarian government whose objective is to impose new directions on the country.

My exposition takes a position contrary to both points of view. On a step-by-step basis, I have attempted to show that in the midst of continuity and accommodation, Brazil changes – sometimes in the political sphere, sometimes socioeconomically, and at times in both arenas.

I should also point out that strictly speaking, cultural manifestations are not the object of this text. This deliberate omission is not meant to slight culture. I have decided to leave out culture because the interrelatedness of sociopolitical and cultural phenomena, owing to their complexity and importance, deserves to be dealt with in a book wholly on that subject.

Taking into account the purpose of this book, I have not included any notes containing marginal observations and references to sources. If this has made the text lighter reading, it has, simultaneously, presented me with a problem. Much of this book is indebted to the work of other authors which I have selected and incorporated for my own purposes. How can I not quote them without being unjust and without running the risk of being accused of plagiarism? I have tried to solve this dilemma in the Bibliography at the end. My references do not exhaust all the sources I consulted and do not mention all the basic bibliography. I have included only those texts I consulted in the writing of this book. Of course, my using them indicates that I consider them important.

Finally, I would like to thank my friend and colleague Herbert S. Klein, whose suggestions and considerations encouraged me to write this book.

Map 1 Brazil. Reprinted with permission from *The Cambridge History of Latin America*, ed. Leslie Bethell, vol. 5 (Cambridge: Cambridge University Press, © 1986).

Fr.
N A

Belém
Bragança
São Luís
Rosário
Fortaleza

MARANHÃO
CEARÁ RIO GRANDE DO NORTE
Natal

PARÁ

PIAUÍ
PARAÍBA
PERNAMBUCO
Recife

ALAGOAS

SERGIPE

R. São Francisco

GOIÁS
BAHIA
Salvador

ATLANTIC

MINAS GERAIS

Belo Horizonte
ESPÍRITO SANTO
OCEAN

Ribeirão Preto
Victória

SÃO PAULO
Campinas
Campos
RIO DE JANEIRO

São Paulo
Rio de Janeiro

PARANÁ
Santos

Paranaguá

SANTA CATARINA

RIO GRANDE
DO SUL
Porto Alegre

Rio Grande

0 _____ 800 km
0 _____ 500 miles

I

Colonial Brazil (1500–1822)

The Portuguese reached the coast of what today is Brazil in April 1500. This occurrence was but one of the many episodes of Portuguese overseas expansion, which began early in the 15th century.

Why did a tiny country such as Portugal begin its expansion at the beginning of the 15th century, almost 100 years before Columbus, sailing for Spain, reached the Americas? There is more than one answer to this question, and, to answer it, a number of factors should be taken into account. In the first place, Portugal had distinguished itself among the European nations as an independent country with a tendency to look beyond its borders. Even though they were still no rivals for Venetians and Genoese, whom they would eventually surpass during the 13th and 14th centuries, the Portuguese had accumulated considerable experience in long-distance trade. Besides, before the Portuguese took control of their own international trade, Genoa had invested in their expansion and had made Lisbon a major center of its commercial endeavors.

Also, Portugal's economic involvement with the Islamic world in the Mediterranean facilitated this commercial experiment, and its rising trade can be measured by the growing use of money as a means of payment. Doubtlessly, the affinity of the Portuguese for the sea was abetted by their country's proximity to islands in the Atlantic and to the coast of Africa. Owing to the technology of the time, mariners relied on specific ocean currents, which favored Portuguese ports as well as those situated in southwest Spain.

But there are other factors of Portuguese political history which are at least as important as those already mentioned. Portugal did not escape the crisis affecting all of western Europe. However, the nation faced it under political circumstances that were better than those of other kingdoms. During the entire 15th century, Portugal was a united kingdom and less subject to internal upheaval and dispute. This was not the case in France, England, Spain, and Italy – all of which were involved in wars and in dynastic complications.

The Portuguese monarchy had been consolidated in the revolution of 1383–1385, a very significant episode in the country's history. Beginning with a dispute over who should succeed as king of Portugal, the bourgeoisie in Lisbon revolted. A popular uprising followed, called "the revolt of the common folk" by the chronicler Fernão Lopes. This revolution was similar to other events which shook western Europe at the same time, but its denouement was different from those of the peasant revolts which in other countries were crushed by powerful lords. When the king of Castile, who was supported by the Portuguese nobility of highest rank, entered the country to take control of the throne, the problem of dynastic succession became, in addition, one of national independence. When the two sides met, both Portuguese independence and Dom João's claim to the throne had been secured. Dom João, the central figure in the revolution, was an illegitimate son of King Pedro I. He is known as the Master of the Order of Aviz.

Even though some historians consider the revolution of 1383 to be a middle-class uprising, it ended up reinforcing and concentrating power in the king owing to the policies undertaken by the Master of Aviz. Different influential sectors of Portuguese society – the nobility, the merchants, and the nascent bureaucracy – gathered around the crown. This is a fundamental point in any discussion of the reasons for Portuguese expansion. At that time the state, or better yet the crown, was the only entity capable of great undertakings – provided it had the power and stability necessary for such endeavors.

Finally, one should not forget that at the beginning of the 15th century, overseas expansion served the varied interests of the diverse classes, social groups, and institutions that constituted Portuguese society. For the merchants, expansion offered the prospect of wealth. For the king it was an opportunity to create new sources of income at a time when crown revenues had greatly diminished. It was also a good way to keep the nobles busy, and it was a source of prestige. For the nobles and for the church, to serve the king or to serve God by bringing Christianity to the heathen entailed rewards and jobs that were more and more difficult to obtain within Portugal's narrow framework. For the common people, going to sea meant emigrating and searching for a better life. It was a flight from an oppressive state of affairs. The only ones left out of these converging interests were the large landowners, for whom the departure of men meant a rise in the cost of labor.

This is why overseas expansion became a sort of great national venture which everyone or almost everyone joined and which went on for centuries.

The search for adventure was not just a search for wealth. Five centuries ago there were continents that were scarcely known or totally undiscovered. There were oceans that had yet to be crossed. The so-called unknown regions captivated Europeans' imaginations. In those regions they foresaw, in different cases, fantastic kingdoms, monstrous creatures, and the locus of earthly paradise.

For example, when he discovered America, Columbus thought that further inland he would find men with only one eye and others who looked like dogs. He saw three mermaids leap from the sea, but was disappointed with their faces – they were not as beautiful as he had imagined. In one of his letters he referred to people further west who were born with tails. In 1487, when Afonso de Paiva and Pero da Covilhã left Portugal in search of an overland route to India, they carried orders from Dom João II to locate the kingdom of Prester John. According to legend, Prester John was a descendant of the Wise Men and an entrenched enemy of the Muslims. From at least the middle of the 12th century, Prester John was part of Europeans' fantasy world. The legend derived from reality, from the existence of Ethiopia, in east Africa, where blacks had adopted a form of Christianity.

The dreams associated with the oceanic adventure should not be seen as scornful fantasies used to hide material interest. But beyond doubt material considerations prevailed, especially when the world's contours became better known and practical matters of colonization entered center stage.

Two final points should be noted when one analyzes Portuguese expansion in general. On the one hand, this expansion constituted an important renovation of the so-called seafaring techniques. When Lusitanian ships set out for Guinea, navigation charts still did not include latitudes and longitudes, only routes and distances. Improved quadrants and astrolabes allowed navigators to use the stars to pinpoint their ships' positions. This was an important innovation. With the caravelle, which was used beginning in 1441, the Portuguese had also developed a more appropriate type of ship design. The caravelle was, for its time, a light and rapid vessel. Its draft was shallow, which allowed it to come quite close to dry land and still avoid running aground. The caravelle was the apple of Portuguese eyes, and they made full use of these ships in their voyages to Brazil during the 16th and 17th centuries.

The other point has to do with a gradual change in outlook notable among Portuguese humanists such as Duarte Pacheco Pereira, Diogo Gomes, and Dom João de Castro. Overseas exploration showed over and over how mistaken the old notions were. For example, the description of the world in Ptolemy's *Geography* was refuted by firsthand experience. Given cases such as this, ancient authorities began to be doubted.

Gold and spices were the goods most sought by the Portuguese. Their interest in gold is easy to understand. It was used as a reliable means of exchange, Asian aristocrats decorated their temples and palaces with it, and they used it in their clothes. But why spices, or rather condiments?

The high price of seasonings can be explained by the era's limited techniques for the preservation of food and also by people's eating habits. Medieval western Europe was a "carnivorous civilization." Huge quantities of cattle were slaughtered at the beginning of summer, when they could no longer forage in the countryside. Meat was stored and precariously preserved by salting it, smoking it, or drying it in the sun. Fish was also preserved in these ways. However, these processes often made the food unpalatable.

Seasonings were required, and adding pepper helped to disguise rot. Condiments were also used in stylish food of the time, just like coffee, which much later ended up being consumed in grand scale all over the world. Gold and spices were always in high demand during the 15th and 16th centuries, but there were other sought-after goods as well: fish and meat, wood, dyes, medicinal herbs, and, little by little, instruments endowed with speech – African slaves.

The 1415 conquest of Ceuta, in northern Africa, is usually considered the starting point for Portuguese overseas expansion, which progressed methodically down the west coast of Africa and out to the islands in the Atlantic Ocean. Exploration of the African coast did not happen overnight. It took 53 years, beginning with Gil Eanes's passing Cape Bojador in 1434 to Bartolomeu Dias's rounding of the fearsome Cape of Good Hope in 1487. Once he was in the Indian Ocean, it was possible for Vasco da Gama to reach India, the elusive land of spices and dreams. After this, the Portuguese went all the way to China and Japan, where their influence was considerable. Japanese historians have called the period between 1540 and 1630 the "Christian century."

Without going far into the African continent, the Portuguese set up a series of fortified trading posts or *feitorias* along the coast. The Portuguese crown regulated African trade. It established a royal monopoly on gold transactions and required money to be coined in the Casa da Moeda or Mint. Around 1481 it also created the Casa da Mina or Casa da Guiné, which was a special customs house for African trade. From the west coast of Africa the Portuguese brought back scant quantities of gold dust, ivory (which up to then had come from Egypt and had been controlled by Arab merchants), and a pepper known as *pimenta malagueta*. After 1441 their specialty became slaves. In the beginning slaves were sent to Portugal, where they were employed as domestic servants and urban workers.

The history of Portuguese occupation of the Atlantic islands is quite different. There they carried out significant experiments in large-scale agriculture using slave labor. After disputing and losing the Canary Islands to the Spaniards, the Portuguese managed to hold on to other islands: Madeira (ca. 1420), the Azores (ca. 1427), Cape Verde (1460), and São Tomé (1471). On the Isle of

Madeira two parallel farming systems vied with one another. Traditional wheat farming attracted a considerable number of small, rural landowners. Sugar plantations arose simultaneously. They were financed by Genoese and Jewish merchants and commercial agents and relied on slave labor.

The sugar economy ended up winning out, but its success was short-lived. Its rapid decline came from internal factors as well as from competition with sugar from Brazil and São Tomé. In fact, on the Isle of São Tomé the Portuguese set up a system of large-scale sugar plantations very similar to the system they would use in Brazil. São Tomé could count on an abundant supply of slaves because it was close to the African coast and to the trading posts at São Jorge da Mina and Axim. It had plantations or *engenhos* which had as many as 150 to 300 slaves, according to an account written in 1554. São Tomé was always a way station for slaves brought from the continent. From there they were sent to America or to Europe. In the 17th century the sugar industry fell on hard times, and slave distribution became the main activity on São Tomé.

The first ship to return from Vasco da Gama's expedition reached Portugal in July 1499. It produced great enthusiasm. Months later, on 9 March 1500, a fleet of 13 ships set sail from Lisbon. This was the most grandiose of all expeditions so far. It was apparently destined for the East Indies and was under the command of Pedro Alvares Cabral, a nobleman scarcely more than 30 years old. The fleet, after passing the Cape Verde Islands, headed west, away from the African coast. On 21 April it sighted what would become Brazilian land. On that day a landing party went ashore briefly. On the following day the fleet anchored at Porto Seguro, on the coast of the present-day state of Bahia.

Beginning in the 19th century, scholars have debated whether the Portuguese arrival in Brazil was a chance happening brought about by ocean currents or whether there was prior knowledge of the New World, and Cabral had set off on a sort of secret mission toward the west. Everything suggests that Cabral's expedition was directed to India. This does not rule out the probability that European navigators, especially Portuguese navigators, might have visited the coast of Brazil before 1500.

I.2 THE INDIANS

When the Europeans reached the land that would someday be Brazil, they found an Amerindian population living along the coast and in the basin of the Paraná and Paraguay Rivers. This population was linguistically and culturally quite homogeneous.

Notwithstanding their homogeneity, they can be divided into two large groups: the Tupi-Guarani and the Tapuia. The Tupi-Guarani lived along almost the entire Brazilian coast – from at least Ceará in the North to Lake Patos in the far South. The Tupi, who were also known as the Tupinambá, dominated the coastal strip from the North down to Cananéia, in the southern part of the present-day state of São Paulo. The Guarani were located in the basin of the Paraná and Paraguay and along the coast, from Cananéia down to the southern reaches of present-day Brazil. In spite of their different geographic locations, the two subgroups are known as Tupi-Guarani because of their similarity in language and culture.

At points along the littoral, the Tupi-Guarani population was interspersed with other groups: the Goitacá at the mouth of the Paraíba River, the Aimoré in southern Bahia and the northern part of present-day Espírito Santo State, the Tremembé along the strip between Ceará and Maranhão further north. These groups were called Tapuia, a generic word used by the Tupi-Guarani to indicate Indians who spoke a language different from theirs.

It is hard to analyze this indigenous society and its customs because their culture was so different from ours, and there was and still is considerable prejudice against Brazilian Indians. This prejudice can be seen in greater or lesser proportions in the writing of chroniclers, travelers, and priests – especially in Jesuit writings.

These accounts differentiate between Indians with positive and negative characteristics according to their greater or lesser degrees of resistance to the Portuguese. The Aimoré, outstanding for their military prowess and their rebelliousness, were always portrayed in a negative light. According to various descriptions, Indians usually lived like "human beings," in houses. The Aimoré lived like animals in the forest. The Tupinambá ate their enemies out of vengeance; the Aimoré ate them because they liked the taste of human flesh.

When the crown passed its first law prohibiting Indian slavery (1570), only the Aimoré were specifically excluded from this prohibition.

There is also a shortage of data, deriving neither from faulty understanding nor from prejudice, but from their difficulty in being obtained. No one knows how many Indians lived in the territory which comprises present-day Brazil and Paraguay 500 years ago, when the Portuguese came to the New World. Estimates range from a low of two million for the entire territory to five million for the Amazon region alone.

The Tupi groups hunted, fished, gathered fruit, and raised crops. When the soil gave out, they migrated to different areas, temporarily or permanently. To plant crops they cut down trees and burned the vegetation. The colonists employed the same techniques. They planted beans, corn, squash, and especially manioc. Manioc flour became a staple food in the colony. The Indian economy was at a subsistence level, and people consumed what they produced. Each village was self-sufficient, and there was little trading of foodstuffs between villages.

There were, however, contacts among villages for the exchange of women and luxury items such as toucan feathers and stones for making labrets. From these trading contacts, alliances formed and groups of villages attacked other groups. War and the capture of enemies who were later killed during celebrations of cannibalistic rites were essential elements in Tupi society. Prestige and fresh supplies of women were the products of these activities, which were reserved for men.

The arrival of the Portuguese was a veritable catastrophe for the Indians. Coming from afar, in tremendous ships, the Portuguese, and especially the priests, were associated in the Tupi mind with great shamans who traveled the land going from village to village. These shamans cured people; they prophesied and spoke of a land of plenty. Whites, as men endowed with special powers, were at the same time respected, feared, and hated.

On the other hand, since there was no Indian nation, only scattered groups of Indians who were often in conflict with one another, it was possible for the Portuguese to find native allies in their struggles against groups who resisted. Without Tupi allies, the town of São Paulo de Piratininga (today the capital of São Paulo state) would have been conquered by the Tamoio Indians during its first years of existence. This is not to say that Indians did not ferociously resist the colonists, especially when the latter made attempts to enslave them. One exceptional form of resistance amounted to self-isolation, which they achieved by constant migration toward poorer regions. Within extremely narrow bounds, this strategy preserved their biological, social, and cultural heritage.

The Indians who gave in, or who were conquered, experienced cultural violence, epidemics, and death. From their contact with Europeans sprang a mixed population whose silent presence in the formation of Brazilian society can be seen even now.

But all in all, the word "catastrophe" is the most appropriate for describing the fate of the Amerindian population. Millions of Indians lived in Brazil at the time of conquest, and only some 270,000 are with us today.

1.3 COLONIZATION

The so-called discovery of Brazil occasioned none of the enthusiasm that Vasco da Gama's arrival in India had. Brazil appears as a land whose profit potential and geographic features were unknown. For several years people believed it was nothing more than a huge island. It was known mainly for its exotic lures: Indians, parrots, and macaws. Some informants, especially the Italians, began to call it the Land of the Parrots. King Dom Manuel first named it Vera Cruz and later called it Santa Cruz. The name "Brazil" began to appear in 1503. This word is associated with brazilwood, from a tropical tree that was the main resource of the land during the early days. Its duramen was very red and was used to make dye. Its sturdy wood was used to make furniture and in ship-building. Curiously, the "Brazil Islands" or something similar were mentioned in medieval Europe's tales of fantasy. Three islands with this name appear in a 1367 map. They are strewn among the Azores, at the latitude of Brittany (France), and along the coast of Ireland.

The first attempts at trading on the Brazilian coast relied on the same feitoria system that was used on the African coast. Brazil was leased for three years to a commercial consortium in Lisbon.

The group was headed by the New Christian Fernão de Noronha (or Loronha), who had obtained a monopoly. In exchange for his monopoly, he was obliged, so it seems, to send out six ships per year to explore 300 leagues (around 2,000 kilometers) of coastline and to set up a trading post. This consortium sent out a few expeditions, but when its lease expired in 1505, the Portuguese crown apparently assumed the responsibility of exploring the new land.

During these early years, from 1500 to 1535, the chief economic activity was the extraction of brazilwood, which was obtained mainly by trading with the Indians. Brazilwood trees did not grow in clusters or groves, but were scattered everywhere. As the supply gave out along the littoral, Europeans started relying on the Indians to furnish it. Collective work, especially in felling trees, was a common task in Tupinambá society, which meant that harvesting brazilwood would be relatively easy to integrate into traditional patterns of indigenous life. Indians supplied wood and to a lesser degree manioc flour. They traded them for pieces of cloth, knives, pen knives, and baubles – cheap items as far as the Portuguese were concerned.

In the beginning, Brazil was often mentioned along with India, either as a stop-off on the way there or as the location of a new route to India, which the Spaniards (mainly) sought. When he discovered America in 1492, Columbus, reaching the Antilles, thought he had reached the China Sea. Portugal contested the ownership of the new land, which gave rise to a series of negotiations and in 1494 produced the Treaty of Tordesillas. The world was divided into two hemispheres separated by an imaginary line 370 leagues west of the Cape Verde Islands. The land discovered west of the line would belong to Spain; that east of it would belong to Portugal.

This division lent itself to controversy, since it was never possible to establish exactly where the Line of Tordesillas was. (Only at the end of the 17th century did the Dutch devise a technique for measuring longitude accurately.) In whose territory lay the mouth of the Amazon or the mouth of the River Plate? Were these northern and southern points Portuguese or Spanish? Both rivers were seen as potential westward routes to India. Several expeditions from both countries succeeded one another southward down the coast of Brazil. Finally a Portuguese, Ferdinand Magellan, sailing under the Spanish flag, traversed the strait which today bears his name. He sailed across the Pacific Ocean and reached the Philippines in 1521. This spectacular feat of navigation was, at the same time, a letdown for the Spaniards. The westward route to India had been found, but it was too long and difficult to be economically viable. Spanish eyes fixed on the riches in gold and silver that were being found in the American lands under their domain.

The greatest threat to Portugal's hold on Brazil came not from Spain but from France. France did not recognize the Treaty of Tordesillas, but it supported the principle of *uti possidetis*, which maintained that whoever effectively occupied an area owned it. Since Brazil's coast was too long to be defended by Portuguese patrols, the French began to trade for brazilwood, and they practiced piracy. Later on, at different times (1555–1560, 1612–1615), they would found settlements in Guanabara Bay (Rio de Janeiro) and in the North, in the present-day state of Maranhão.

Political considerations convinced the Portuguese crown that it was necessary to colonize this new land. Martim Afonso de Sousa's expedition (1530–1533) marks the moment of transition between the first and second phase of this endeavor. The expedition was to patrol the coast and to explore the land while keeping in mind the need to occupy it effectively. A colony was established (São Vicente, 1532), but the colonists accompanying Martim Afonso would not be able to pass their lands on to their descendants.

There are indications that Martim Afonso was still in Brazil when Dom João III decided to create hereditary captaincies. Brazil was divided into 15 sections by a set of lines running parallel to the equator and toward the Line of Tordesillas. Each section would be awarded to a so-called donatary captain. These donataries were a diverse group of people: bureaucrats, merchants, and members of the petty nobility. What they had in common was some connection to the crown.

Martim Afonso, an expert navigator, was one of the donataries. Another was Duarte Coelho, a soldier of modest means who had distinguished himself in the Orient and whose stay in Brazil would be recognized owing to his success in Pernambuco. Jorge Figueiredo Correia, a scribe of the Royal Treasury and a great businessman, became a donatary. He was an associate of Mem de Sá and Lucas Giraldes, himself a member of the Giraldi family of Florentine merchants and bankers. One more donatary was Pero do Campo Tourinho, who sold his land in Portugal and set off for Brazil with 600 colonists. After conflicts with his colonists and after being reported to the Inquisition, Tourinho was sent back to Portugal. Before 1532, Fernão de Noronha had received the first Brazilian captaincy, São João Island, known today as Fernão de Noronha. There was no one from the high nobility on the list of original donataries because at that time dealings in India, in Portugal, and on the Atlantic islands were more attractive.

Donataries received an endowment from the crown which entitled them to take possession but not ownership of the land. They could not sell or partition their captaincies. Only the king had the right to change or nullify a captaincy. Possession of the land gave donataries extensive rights in the economic sphere, in the collecting of fees, and in the administration of their captaincies. To set up sugar mills or water mills or to exploit salt deposits required the paying of fees. A percentage of the fees or tribute owed the crown for the right to brazilwood, precious metals, and fishing derivatives was owed to the donatary captains as well. In the administrative sector donataries had a monopoly on the system of justice; they could found towns, mete out plots of land, enlist colonists for military purposes, and form militias under their command.

The right to award individuals plots of land is important because it gave rise to the formation of vast *latifúndios*, or estates. In Brazil, these land grants, called *sesmarias*, were understood to be tracts of virgin land for a single individual who was obliged to cultivate the land within five years and to pay a fee to the crown. Grantees or *sesmeiros* rarely fulfilled this obligation. On founding these hereditary captaincies, the crown did not limit its privileges to managing them. The king retained his monopoly over raw materials and spices, as well as his entitlement to a part of the tribute paid for use of the land. He also retained the right to administer the law in cases of death penalties or corporal punishment for people of noble lineage. On top of this, he appointed a battery of officials to guarantee collection of the crown's income.

When it instituted the captaincies, the crown adopted a system whose origin can be found in the medieval society of Europe. One instance of this is the donataries' right to obtain payment for permission to set up sugar mills. This is analogous to the "banalities" farmers paid feudal lords. However, in their essence, even in their original form, captaincies were a transitory and still tentative attempt at colonization and at integrating the colony into the European mercantile economy.

With the exception of those of São Vicente and Pernambuco, the captaincies, to a greater or lesser extent, failed owing to a lack of resources and experience, to internal rifts, and to Indian attacks. It was not by chance that the most successful captaincies combined their sugar economy with a less aggressive relationship with Indian tribes. Over the years the crown bought the captaincies back. They survived as administrative units, but their character was changed because they belonged to the state. Between 1752 and 1754, the Marquis of Pombal for all intents and purposes finished the process of removing captaincies from the private domain and placing them in the public one.

Dom João Ill's decision to set up an overall government (*governo geral*) for Brazil came at a time when the Portuguese crown was struggling with significant events in the international sphere. Business in India had faced its first serious crises. Even though the dream of an African empire had not died, Portugal had suffered several military defeats in Morocco. In the same year (1549), Tomé de Sousa was sent to Brazil as its first royal governor, and the Portuguese commercial emporium in Flanders was shut down because it had failed to make a profit. Finally, in contrast to how things were going in Brazil, in their American colonies the Spaniards had experienced growing success in their search for precious metals. And in 1545 they had discovered the great silver mine in Potosí. While all these factors may have influenced the crown's decision, it must be remembered that the captaincies' failure made the problems of Portuguese America's precarious administration clearer to the Portuguese themselves.

Tomé de Sousa, a nobleman with experience in Africa and India, arrived in Bahia in the company of more than 1,000 people. Of them 400 were deportees. The governor-general brought with him a long list of written instructions which show the crown's intent to guarantee occupation of the new land, to colonize it, and to administer the crown's income. To these ends some new administrative positions were created. The most important of them were the *ouvidor*, who would administer justice; the *capitão-mor*, whose job it was to patrol the coast; and the *provedor-mor*, who would oversee and increase the collection of fees.

However, throughout the 16th century, Brazil did not provide much in the way of riches for the royal coffers. Indeed, according to Vitorino Magalhães Godinho, in 1558 the revenue from tribute coming from Brazil amounted to something like 2.5 percent of the crown's income. Trade with India supplied 26 percent.

With the governor-general came the first Jesuits – Manuel da Nóbrega and five companions. Their mission was to catechize the Indians and to discipline the scanty but ill-reputed clergy already in Brazil. Later on, in 1552, the first episcopate (under the archbishopric of Lisbon) was founded in Salvador. This was a step toward establishing a close relationship between church and state. The beginning of the colonial overseas administration (i.e., *governos gerais*) entailed the establishment of an executive pole in the colony's organization. Tomé de Sousa followed his instructions and immediately began the long task of constructing Salvador, the capital of Brazil up to 1763.

The institution of an overseas administration attempted to insure governmental centralization, but the governor-general was not all-powerful, nor, in the early years, could he undertake wide-ranging initiatives. Links among the captaincies were quite precarious, which limited the governors' radii of action. Correspondence among the Jesuits gives clear indication of their isolation. Father Francisco Pires, writing from Salvador in 1552 to his brothers in Coimbra, complains of only being able to operate locally because "at times a year goes by, and we know nothing of one another owing to the weather and the few ships that go up and down the coast. We often see more ships from Portugal than from the other captaincies." A year later, off in the backlands of São Vicente, Nóbrega says practically the same thing: "in this captaincy, one is more likely to have news from Lisbon than one is likely to hear from Bahia."

After the first three decades, which were marked by efforts to secure Portuguese possession of the land, colonization patterns began to emerge. As was the case in all of Latin America, Brazil became a colony whose essential role was one of supplying highly important foodstuffs or minerals for European commerce. Portugal adopted a policy consisting of incentives for commercial endeavors with massive holdings. It exported a few products on a large-scale basis. This directive must have been aimed at making wealthy merchants, the crown, and the crown's dependents even wealthier. Since Portugal did not dominate European commercial circuits, which were controlled by Spain, Holland, and England, the policy must have helped Europe's economy in general.

The preference for large landholdings was linked to the notion that large-scale production was beneficial. In addition, small-scale, autonomous landowners would tend to produce enough for their own subsistence and to market only small surpluses, all of which would be contrary to a mercantilistic undertaking.

In addition to commercial objectives and the system of large landholding, came a third element: compulsory labor. Notwithstanding local variations, this was another feature common to all of Latin America. Different forms of servitude prevailed in Spanish America, while slavery was dominant in Brazil.

Where was the appeal in such an odious and apparently moribund form of labor, especially at a historical juncture pompously called the Dawn of the Modern Era? One can formulate an answer by saying that there was an insufficient supply of men who could emigrate as indentured or salaried workers, and wage labor was not convenient for the goals of colonization. There was a tremendous amount of available land because the immense sesmarias or land grants were not always effectively occupied by the donataries. For this reason, it was no simple matter for ranchers to keep free workers on their properties. They could try to make their living in another manner, which would create fluctuations in labor supply for the mercantile endeavor.

However, if the introduction of slave labor can be explained in this way, why then did the Portuguese opt for black slaves rather than for Indian slaves? Lest one forget, there was a period of transition from Indian to black slaves. Its dates and places varied, however. It was shorter in the more dynamic and profitable central portion of the colony. That is, the sugar economy had the means to purchase black slaves, who were more expensive than Indian slaves. The transition period was longer in the periphery. Only at the beginning of the 18th century, with the discovery of gold, would São Paulo begin to use black slaves regularly and in large numbers.

Several factors explain the choice of African slaves. Indian slavery collided with a series of nuisances as far as the goals of colonization were concerned. The Indians' culture was incompatible with intensive, regular toil and was much less compatible with the compulsory labor Europeans had in mind. Indians were not loafers or even lazy. They simply did what was needed to get by, which was not much, given that fish, fruit, and animals abounded at that time. Much of their energy and imagination were spent on rituals, celebrations, and wars. Notions of constant work, or what today is known as productivity, were totally alien.

The Portuguese attempted to subject Indians in two basic ways. One method of subjection was carried out in a ruthless economic venture by the colonists, who, purely and simply, enslaved Indians. The other was tried by religious orders, principally by the Jesuits. Their motives were based on their concept of missionary work. They tried to turn Indians into "good Christians" by gathering them into small towns or villages. To be a "good Christian" also meant acquiring European work habits, which would create an indigenous and pliable labor force to serve the needs of the colony.

The two methods were not the same. Religious orders had the merit of trying to protect Indians from being enslaved by colonists, which gave rise to considerable friction between colonists and priests. But the fathers had no respect for the indigenous culture either. Indeed, they went so far as to doubt the Indians' status as people. Father Manuel da Nóbrega maintained that "Indians are dogs who kill and eat one another. And in their vices and dealings with one another, they are pigs."

Indians resisted the different forms of subjection by waging war, by fleeing, and by refusing to perform forced labor. Comparatively speaking, Indians were in better positions to resist than African slaves were. Africans faced unknown territory into which they had been forcibly transplanted, whereas the Indians were on native ground.

Another factor which put Indian slavery at a disadvantage was the demographic catastrophe. Indians fell victim to diseases such as measles, smallpox, and the common cold – against which they had no biological defenses. In 1562 and 1563, two epidemic waves were exceptionally virulent. They appear to have been responsible for 60,000 deaths among Indians, without counting any victims in the backlands. The death of indigenous people, who in part were employed in raising foodstuffs, caused a terrible famine in Brazil's Northeast, as well as a shortage of workers.

It was not by chance, then, that beginning in the 1570s, the importation of Africans was encouraged, and the crown began to take measures and pass laws which tried to stop the wholesale slaughter and enslavement of Indians. These laws had exceptions and were easily flouted. Indians were enslaved after "just wars" – that is, wars considered to have been fought in self-defense. Slavery was a punishment for cannibalism. And Indians captured by other tribes were ransomed and enslaved rather than being eaten in cannibal rituals. Only in 1758 would the crown proclaim definitive freedom for indigenous peoples. But, essentially, Indian slavery had been abandoned long before, owing to the difficulties suggested above and the existence of an alternative solution.

As they explored the African coast during the 15th century, the Portuguese had begun their slave trade, which was helped along by their contact with societies which, to a large extent, were familiar with the market value of slaves. By the last decades of the 16th century, African slave trade was not only reasonably developed, but it had also demonstrated how profitable it could be. Colonists knew about blacks' abilities, especially about how lucrative their labor had been in the sugar industry of the Atlantic islands. Many slaves came from cultures which regularly worked with iron implements and in which cattle were raised. Because of this, their productive capacity was significantly higher than the Indians'. It has been estimated that during the first half of the 17th century, during the peak years of the sugar economy, the purchase price of a black slave was recovered after 13 to 16 months of work. Even after a huge rise in slave purchase prices after 1700, slaves paid for themselves in 30 months.

The flow of Africans brought from the so-called black continent varied in its intensity. And the estimates of the number of people brought over as slaves vary considerably. It is said that between 1550 and 1855 four million slaves came in through Brazilian ports. Most of them were young males.

Where they came from depended on how the slave trade was organized, on the local conditions in Africa, and, to a greater extent, on the preferences of Brazilian slave owners. During the 16th century Guinea (Bissau and Cacheu) and the Mina Coast, indeed four ports along the Dahomey littoral, provided the bulk of African slaves. Beginning in the 17th century, regions farther south on the African coast such as Angola and the Congo became the most important exportation centers. They used the ports of Luanda, Benguela, and Cabinda. Angolans were brought in greater numbers during the 18th century and seem to have made up 70 percent of all slaves transported to Brazil during that century.

Historians customarily divide African peoples into two large ethnic groups: the "Sudanese," who came from western Africa, the Egyptian Sudan, and the north coast of the Gulf of Guinea; and the "Bantus" from equatorial and tropical Africa, that is, from part of the Gulf of Guinea, from the Congo, Angola, and Mozambique. Within these two large groups, black slaves of many different ethnicities came to Brazil. The "Sudanese" included Yorubas, Iwes, Tapas, and Haussas; the "Bantus" Angolas, Bengalas, Monjolos, and Mozambicans.

The two great import centers for slaves were Salvador and later Rio de Janeiro. Each had its own way of doing business, and each rivaled the other. The slave traders in Salvador used tobacco as a valuable means of exchange on the African coast. This tobacco was grown in the Bahian Recôncavo, a humid, fertile region surrounding Salvador. They were always more closely associated with the Mina Coast, Guinea, and the Bight of Benin – in the latter case even more so after mid-1770, when the Mina slave trade began to decline. Rio de Janeiro received slaves mainly from Angola. It surpassed Salvador once gold mines were discovered, as the sugar industry worked its way southward, and when the city of Rio began its considerable growth in the first part of the 19th century.

It would be wrong to think that while Indians opposed slavery, blacks accepted it passively. From the very beginning, individual or mass flight, attacks on masters, and daily resistance were part of the relationship between masters and slaves. Hundreds of maroon communities, known locally as *quilombos*, were formed by runaway slaves during colonial times. In these Brazilian communities, Africans created social organizations similar to what they knew in Africa. One of these communities, and certainly the most important of them, was known as Palmares. It was a network of settlements situated in a region which today corresponds to the state of Alagoas, in the Brazilian Northeast. It was formed in the beginning of the 17th century and withstood attacks from the Portuguese and the Dutch for almost an entire century, only to fall in 1695.

Little is known of the Palmares quilombo. It is mentioned in some Portuguese sources, which toward the end of the community's existence announce the imprisonment and hanging of the rebels' leader – a black by the name of Zumbi. Recent archeological research in the vicinity of the quilombo suggests that Palmares was a socially diverse community which took in ex-slaves as well as whites who were wanted by the crown because of religious or other infractions.

Notwithstanding the different forms of resistance, which continued until the last decades of the 19th century, African slaves as well as Afro-Brazilians were not able to overthrow forced labor. For better or worse, they adapted to it. Among the different factors that limited their potential for collective rebellion, it must be remembered that contrary to the Indians, blacks had been uprooted, arbitrarily separated, and brought in successive waves to an alien land.

On the other hand, neither the church nor the state opposed the enslavement of blacks. Religious organizations such as the Benedictines even became large-scale slave owners. They maintained that the institution of slavery already existed in Africa and that they had merely transported slaves to the Christian world where they would become civilized and saved, once they knew true religion. On top of this, blacks were considered racially inferior. In the course of the 19th century, "scientific" theories reinforced this prejudice. The size and shape of blacks' skulls, the weight of their brains, and other factors "demonstrated" that blacks were a race of people with low intelligence, that they were emotionally unstable and biologically destined to subjection.

One should also remember how laws affected blacks. The contrast with Indians in this matter is blatant. The latter group could rely on laws protecting them from slavery – of course few of these laws were enforced, and they all had many exceptions. Black slaves had no rights whatsoever: as far as the law was concerned, they were considered things rather than people.

To look at demography for a moment, even though estimates vary, data show that, compared to slave mortality in the United States, there was a higher mortality rate among black slaves in Brazil. Children and new arrivals were especially vulnerable. At the beginning of the 19th century, observers estimated that the slave population in Brazil declined at a rate of 5 to 8 percent per year. Recent data reveal that the life expectancy of a male slave born in 1872 was somewhere around 20 years. That of the population at large was 27.4 years. A male slave born in the United States around 1850 had a life expectancy of 35.5 years.

In spite of these shocking numbers, it cannot be said that black slaves suffered a demographic catastrophe as great as the one that decimated the Indians. Blacks who came from the Congo, from northern Angola, and from Dahomey (present-day Benin) were less susceptible to contagious diseases such as smallpox. At any rate, even with the premature physical destruction of blacks, slave owners always had the possibility of renewing their supply by bringing more in. Brazilian slavery became totally dependent on this source. With rare exceptions, there were no attempts at stimulating the growth of the slave population already in Brazil. Slave women had low fertility. On top of this, to raise a child for 12 or 14 years was considered a risky endeavor if one kept in mind the high mortality rates owing to slaves' living conditions.

For several centuries the Portuguese crown tried to insure the greatest profit from the colonial endeavor through strategies closely related to the then prevailing notions of mercantilist economic policy. This policy maintained that colonies should contribute to the mother country's self-sufficiency. Colonies were supposed to be reserves belonging to colonizing powers, which, internationally, were in competition with one another. To this end each metropolis established a system of norms and practices designed to keep competitors from exploiting the colonies within its particular colonial system. The basic goal was "exclusivity" – colonies should trade with their imperial capital and with no one else.

As far as possible, they attempted to prohibit foreign ships from transporting merchandise from a colony, especially if those ships were to sell the merchandise in other European countries. They likewise sought to prohibit merchandise, especially merchandise not produced in Portugal, from being brought to a colony by foreign vessels. Put very simply, mother countries tried to depress prices they paid their colonies for local products as much as possible; they tried to sell those products at the highest possible prices in the metropolis. They also tried to profit as much as they could from the sale of goods to their colonies, without having to compete with other suppliers. Colonial exclusivity took different forms: leasing, direct exploitation by the state, and the creation of privileged trading companies which benefited specific groups in the mother countries.

In the Portuguese case, mercantile precepts were not always consistently applied. The Portuguese crown made exceptions to mercantilist principles mainly because it had no means of enforcing them. This is not a matter of smuggling, because to smuggle was, purely and simply, to break the rules of the game. It is, rather, a matter of Portugal's position within the entirety of European nations. While the Portuguese were in the vanguard of overseas exploration, they had no means of monopolizing their colonial trade. By the 16th century, the great commercial centers were not in Portugal but in Holland. And the Dutch were important commercial partners with Portugal. They transported salt, Portuguese wine, and Brazilian sugar. In turn, the Dutch supplied manufactured products: cheese, copper, and cloth.

Later on, throughout the 17th century, Portugal would be forced into an unequal relationship with England, at that time an emerging power in Europe. For these reasons, Portuguese colonial exclusivity vacillated according to the circumstances. At times, trade was relatively open, at times it was regulated by a centralized and controlled system combined with special concessions. These concessions meant, deep down, that other countries profited from the Portuguese colonial system.

Without going over all the advances and retreats, what follows are some typical examples. The period between 1530 and 1571 was one of relative freedom of trade. But in 1571 the king, Dom Sebastião, decreed that Portuguese ships had exclusive right of trade with the colony. This measure coincided with the beginning years of the great expansion in the sugar economy. The years between 1580 and 1640, known as the Crown Union, was a time in which the king of Spain also occupied the Portuguese throne. It was characterized by growing restrictions on other countries' participation in colonial trade. More than any other country, Holland was ruled out because it was at war with Spain. Even so, there is evidence of regular and direct traffic around 1590 between Brazil and Hamburg, Germany.

After the end of the Crown Union, when Dom João IV was proclaimed king of Portugal, a brief period of "free trade" followed, and there was little regulation and an absence of control on the colonial import market. However, in 1649, a new, centralized and controlled system of trade was established which used fleets. With capital obtained primarily from New Christians (Jews or descendants of Jews forced in 1497 to convert to Catholicism), the Companhia Geral de Comércio do Brasil (the General Brazilian Trading Company) was created. This company had the responsibility of maintaining a fleet of 36 armed ships which twice a year would escort merchant ships leaving and reaching Brazil. In exchange for its colonial monopoly on wine, flour, olive oil, and salt cod, the company had the right to set prices for these items. Beginning in 1694 the company was turned into an arm of the government.

Nonetheless, this enterprise did not stop Portugal from offering concessions to Holland and, especially, to England. Succinctly speaking, the crown sought political protection from England and offered England commercial advantages. One good example is the treaty imposed by Cromwell in 1654. It gave the English the right to deal directly with the Brazilian colony. England could not, however, buy or sell products under the monopoly of the Companhia Geral. The system of fleets was abandoned in 1765, when the Marquis of Pombal decided to stimulate trade and restrict the growing power of the English in Brazil. He accomplished this by creating new companies (Companhia do Grão-Pará e Maranhão, Companhia de Pernambuco e Paraíba). These were the last manifestations of mercantilism in Brazil.

The two institutions naturally suited for organizing the colonization of Brazil were the state and the Catholic church. They were closely linked to one another, since Catholicism was recognized as the state religion. In principle, there was a division of labor between these two institutions. The state had the fundamental role of guaranteeing Portuguese sovereignty over the colony, of administering it, of developing a settlement policy, of solving basic problems such as the supply of labor, and of establishing the sort of relationship that should obtain between Lisbon and the colony. This task presupposed that settlers in Brazil recognized the authority of the state – because they were forced to, because they agreed to, or for both reasons.

This is where the church came in. Since it was in charge of people's behavior and "in control of their souls" in daily life, it was a very efficient means for conveying the idea of obedience and, strictly speaking, obedience to the power of the state. But that was not all the church would do. It was present throughout people's lives – in the decisive episodes of their birth, marriage, and death. Membership in a particular community, being able to live a decent life, and having a sinless departure from this "vale of tears" depended on ceremonies monopolized by the church: baptism, confirmation, matrimony, confession, extreme unction in the hour of one's death, and burial in a cemetery known by the weighty term *campo santo* or "holy field."

As everyone knows, in the history of Western civilization relations between church and state have varied from country to country. Over time, they have not even been constant within particular countries. In the Portuguese case, the church had been subordinated to the state by a mechanism known as *padroado real* or "royal patronage." This patronage entailed an ample concession from the Roman church to the Portuguese crown. In exchange for this, the state guaranteed it would promote and safeguard the clergy and their rights in all the territory it discovered. The king kept his right to receive the tribute or tithe owed by the church's subjects – that is, a tenth of their earnings from whatever endeavor. The church had the right to create dioceses and to name its bishops.

At least in theory, many of the crown's duties made the church even more subordinate to the state. This was the case in the state's commitment to pay the clergy and to construct and preserve church buildings. To supervise these goings-on, the Portuguese government created a sort of religious department of state. It was known as the Mesa da Consciência e Ordens (Council of Conscience and Orders).

Crown control over the church was restrained in part by the fact that, up to the time of the Marquis of Pombal (1750–1777), Jesuits were very influential in the court. In Brazil, state control suffered from other restrictions. On the one hand, it was very difficult to monitor the activities of the secular clergy, who were dispersed throughout the territory. On the other hand, religious orders were able to acquire a greater degree of autonomy. The greater autonomy enjoyed by Franciscans, Fathers of Mercy, Benedictines, Carmelites, and, especially, Jesuits was the result of several different circumstances. Each institution obeyed its own laws and had a definite policy with respect to vital colonial matters such as the Indian question. On top of this, once they acquired vast tracts of land and began to farm, they no longer depended on the crown for their survival.

Secular priests endeavored to flee the weight of the state and of the church itself whenever they could. They preferred to act on their own. The presence of priests can be documented in practically all rebel movements beginning in 1789 and continuing beyond Brazilian independence up to the middle of the 19th century. It would, however, be a mistake to consider all the clergy rebellious in nature. Rebels were visible, but exceptions to the rule. In its day-by-day activity, the church, either silently or with pomp, tried to carry out its mission of converting Indians and blacks and to convince people to obey its rules, as well as those of the state.

At the time of colonization, Portugal was an absolutist state. In theory, all power was concentrated by divine right in the king. The kingdom (i.e., the territory, his subjects, and their possessions) belonged to the king as part of his patrimony. Notwithstanding his power, the king had to consider the interests of social classes and social groups: nobles, merchants, clergy, and common folk. Nor does "absolutist" mean that he alone ruled. The preference for the word "crown" rather than "king" as a designator of the Portuguese monarchy and its power reflects this last assertion. If the king's word was decisive, a bureaucracy, a branch of government the king himself had created, weighed heavily in his decisions. A series of primarily fiscal measures designed to restrict the king's power had set up some distinctions between what was private and what was public. The notion of "common good" arose as a new idea which justified restricting royal power to demand loans or to usurp private property.

The establishment of a colonial administration fractured and weakened the crown's power. Of course all important decisions were made in Lisbon. But the administrators in Brazil had their own prerogatives. They at times had to improvise solutions for unexpected situations. And they often maintained a delicate balance between the immediate pressures they felt from the colonists and their orders emanating from far-off Lisbon.

1.4 COLONIAL SOCIETY

Within the colony's social structure, "purity of blood" was a criterion used to segregate people, at least up to 1773. Those of impure blood were New Christians, free blacks, and, to an extent, Indians and different types of racially mixed people. This racial dividing line ruled out certain jobs, titles of nobility, and membership in prestigious brotherhoods for many people. The charter of 1773 abolished the distinction between Old and New Christians; but this does not mean that from that time on prejudice ceased to exist.

This discriminatory criterion applied essentially to persons. There was, however, a deeper cleavage which separated persons and non-persons – that is, free people from slaves. As far as the law was concerned, slaves were things. Whether one was free or enslaved was closely linked to color and ethnicity. Slaves were mainly black, or Indians and mixed-bloods. There was a special nomenclature for racial mixtures: people were known as mulattos; *mamelucos*, or mixtures of Indian and white; *curibocas* or *caboclos*, "near whites or descendants of white men"; and *cafusos*, or mixtures of Indians and blacks.

One must distinguish, however, between Indian slavery and black slavery. From the beginning of Brazil's colonization up to the time indigenous slavery was formally extinguished, there were enslaved Indians and Indians known as freed or "administrated." These Indians had been captured, but had been placed under colonists' tutelage. Their situation was not much different from the slaves'. However, if in general the Indian's lot was a sad one, it was nothing compared to that of blacks. The protection offered by religious orders to their Indian settlements put limits on outright exploitation of Indians. And the crown itself tried to establish a less discriminatory policy.

For example, a 1755 decree went so far as to encourage marriages between Indians and whites and maintained that there was "nothing wrong" with such unions. The issues of these marriages were to be preferred for "jobs and honors," and it was against the law to call them caboclos or other similar names that might be taken as "injurious." Years later, the viceroy of Brazil dismissed a militia chief (who was an Indian) because he "displayed sentiments so low as to marry a black woman, staining his blood with this union and making himself unworthy of the office of militia chief."

The importance of Africans and Afro-Brazilians in Brazilian society can be confirmed by population statistics from the end of the colonial period. In the four largest provinces (Minas Gerais, Pernambuco, Bahia, and Rio de Janeiro), blacks and mulattos made up nearly 75 percent, 68 percent, 79 percent, and 64 percent of the respective populations. Only São Paulo had a majority (56 percent) of whites in its population. Slaves worked in the fields, in the sugar mills, in the mines, and as servants in their masters' houses. In the cities they were given unpleasant jobs: as bearers of people and goods, as bearers of foul-smelling garbage and sewage, or as construction workers. They were also employed as artisans, vegetable stand operators, street vendors, and messenger boys.

Slaveholding did not always add up to a direct relationship between master and slave; it involved other people. Some slaves were rented to perform services for third parties, and, in the cities, there were "slave earners" (*escravos de ganho*). In the latter case, masters permitted their slaves to be self-employed, either offering services or selling merchandise. The masters received a fixed percentage of slaves' daily or weekly earnings. Slave earners were common in Rio de Janeiro during the early decades of the 19th century. They were used in small- or large-scale operations – sometimes masters had only one slave earner, other times they had as many as 30 or 40. While the majority of these slave earners worked out of doors, and some of them, with their masters' approval, became prostitutes or beggars, others worked in barber shops or as laborers.

Even among the slaves there were social distinctions, some of which were made according to slaves' occupations. There was a difference between working in the master's house and in the fields, and likewise a difference between working on some huge estate and being a slave earner in the city. Other distinctions were made according to their origins, to the length of time they had been in Brazil, and to their skin color. Slaves recently arrived from Africa were called *boçais* (singular: *boçal*) because they did not know the language or the local customs. Those who had, relatively speaking, "adapted" and spoke and understood Portuguese were known as *ladinos*. Those born in Brazil were called *crioulos*. Colorwise, one extreme was the "pitch black," the other the light mulatto. In general, mulattos and crioulos were preferred for domestic service, as artisans, and as supervisors. The darker slaves, especially the Africans, were given the heaviest work.

Besides the distinctions within the enslaved masses, one should remember that in colonial Brazil there were many free or manumitted Africans or Afro-Brazilians. Data from the end of the colonial period indicate that nearly 42 percent of the black or mulatto population was free. Their freedom was ambiguous, however. While they were formally considered free, in practice they ended up being arbitrarily enslaved, especially when their color or their features identified them as black. They could not be members of town councils or of prestigious lay brotherhoods like the Ordem Terceira de São Francisco. Ex-slaves' liberty could even be revoked if they acted disrespectfully toward their former masters.

Slavery was a national institution. It permeated the whole of society and conditioned Brazilians' way of acting and thinking. The desire to be a slave owner and the effort to obtain slaves ran from the ruling class all the way down to the humble urban artisan. There were plantation and mine owners with hundreds of slaves, small farmers with two or three, and urban households with only one slave. Prejudice against blacks transcended slavery and has survived in a different form up to today. At least until the time that masses of European workers came to central and southern Brazil, manual labor was socially scorned as "something just for blacks."

In theory, free people in the colony belonged to a hierarchical order. This division into nobility, clergy, and folk was typical of the *ancien régime* in Portugal. Its transfer to Brazil had few practical repercussions. The white elite avidly vied for titles of nobility, but there was no hereditary aristocracy. There were few true nobles (*fidalgos*), and common people with noble pretensions were in the majority.

All this does not mean that Brazil's colonial society was made up only of masters and slaves. Backwoodsmen, small farmers, and workers lived in the countryside. The few cities had their share of street vendors, small merchants, and artisans. And this picture was not static. The discovery of gold and diamonds in Minas Gerais, Goiás, and Mato Grosso early in the 18th century and the arrival of the royal family in Rio de Janeiro at the beginning of the 19th century contributed, each in its own way, to social diversification and changes in the relationship between the city and the country. As far as the mining regions and cities like Salvador and Rio de Janeiro are concerned, one can speak of an administrative bureaucracy, of men of letters, and of people engaged in the professions, especially in law.

Different undertakings were unequal in their prestige. The most prestigious, especially in the early days, was not so much the activity associated with planting as merely "being a plantation owner." In the famous words appearing in Father Antonil's *Cultura e opuléncia do Brasil por suas drogas e minas,* which he wrote at the beginning of the 18th century:

plantation owner is the title to which many aspire because it brings with it the idea of being served and respected by many people. And...being a plantation owner in Brazil is as esteemed as the titles of nobility are esteemed in Portugal.

Commerce was considered to be a less worthy profession, and, theoretically, businessmen were excluded from town councils and from receiving special honors. The fact that many merchants were New Christians added another element of discrimination. Artisans were also undervalued since working with one's hands was thought to be an inferior activity. Because they were almost always not represented in the town councils, these people sometimes made themselves heard through the *juízes de fora* – professional magistrates appointed by the crown. In addition to their regular duties, these judges presided over town councils in major cities.

At the top of the social pyramid were the wealthy rural landowners and merchants engaged in foreign commerce. This was typical of settlements on the northeast coastline and later on of Rio de Janeiro. Since they played a strategic role in the life of the colony, these wealthy merchants were not subject to the discrimination that was theoretically applied to their livelihood. Quite to the contrary, by the middle of the 17th century they were on a course of social and political upward mobility. They were more and more regularly included in the city councils and in the prestigious brotherhoods. They also obtained high ranks in the militia.

Between the two factions at the top, there were meeting points and issues of rivalry. On the one hand, they combined to form the colonial dominating block which presided over the masses of slaves and freemen of lower social standing. Their rising wealth eased merchants' entry into the colonial elite. Through marriage and the purchase of land, many merchants also became plantation owners in the Northeast, and the distinction between merchants and planters was sometimes blurred.

On the other hand, there were reasons for potential conflicts. Wealthy merchants were able to manipulate prices for import and export goods, especially when they worked for the privileged commercial concerns set up by the crown. On top of this, they lent resources to wealthy rural landowners to finance their planting and to buy slaves and equipment, but these loans were guaranteed by mortgages the planters took out on their land. Matters of debt and controversies over petitions for moratoriums were commonplace in the sugar-producing regions of the Northeast. The disputes grew bitter when they were exacerbated by the different origins of the opposing parties: when the rural landowners were native-born and the merchants were Portuguese.

One extreme example of opposing sides was the so-called Peddlers' War (Guerra dos Mascates) in Pernambuco (1710–1711), in northeast Brazil. The rivalry between the two cities, Olinda and Recife, was a superficial reflection of a more profound rift between the old plantation aristocracy in Olinda and Recife's "peddlers," who were not peddlers at all. They were, in fact, wealthy merchants, some of whom had seen their power grow when they acquired, in auctions sponsored by the crown, the right to collect taxes.

A social division directly related to the notion of purity of blood concerned religion. Portuguese subjects living in Brazil were by definition Catholic. But some were more Catholic than others. The less Catholic were New Christians. They were scorned by Old Christians, who believed they practiced Judaism in secret. From the very start, however, New Christians played important roles in the colony as traders, artisans, and plantation owners. They also worked for the government and the church. In spite of these relevant roles, indeed perhaps because of them, New Christians were the object of discrimination, and some of them were arrested and killed at the hands of the Inquisition. Comparatively speaking, however, persecution of New Christians was not carried out with the same efficiency as it was in the Spanish American colonies. The Inquisition was never a permanent fixture in Brazil, and its terrifying visitations, with the exception of the one to the state of Grão Pará in 1763–1769, occurred during the time the Portuguese crown was in the hands of Spanish kings. The Holy Office visited Bahia and Pernambuco between the years 1591 and 1595. It returned to Bahia in 1618.

Lastly, in analyzing the family, one should remember the division between men and women. Traditionally, owing especially to the work of Gilberto Freyre, the idea of family during colonial times is intimately linked to the patriarchal model. In the Northeast, the family was extended and consisted of blood relatives and in-laws, hangers-on (*agregados*) and godchildren. It was indisputably headed by a male figure. The patriarchal family was of great importance and prefigured the relationship between society and state. It was typical of the ruling class, especially of the ruling class in the Northeast. Among people of lower social standing, the extended family did not exist, and women tended to have more independence, especially when they had no husband or male companion. In Ouro Preto, for example, in 1804 only 93 of 203 households were headed by males.

Even among the elite families there are exceptions to the general rule that women were submissive. In certain circumstances, women played relevant roles in economic activities. This was the case in the region around São Paulo, where women, described by a governor of the captaincy as "beautiful and virile," supervised their households and their possessions while the men spent years off on expeditions in the backlands.

The great bulk of the colonial population lived in the country-side. Cities grew slowly and were dependent on the rural population. Even the colonial capital, Salvador, was described in the 16th century by Friar Vicente do Salvador as a

weird city, with empty houses, because the owners spend more time at their rural properties and only come to town for the holiday season. The urban population is made up of craftsmen who ply their trades, merchants, officers of the law, of public finance, and of war – all of whom are obliged to live there.

During the 17th century, a Jesuit father alluded to the poverty of the tiny city of São Paulo owing to the constant absence of its inhabitants. Except for the three or four main holidays, *Paulistas* spent their lives on their rural properties or tramping through forests and over grasslands in search of Indians.

This situation changed somewhat thanks to the growing influence of wealthy merchants and to the increase in administrative offices, which increased cities' influence. Events such as the Dutch invasion and, especially, the arrival of the royal family in Rio de Janeiro were also important factors in cities' growth.

In Brazilian historiography, there are two basic, diametrically opposed interpretations of the relationship between state and society. One interpretation considers the state to have been dominant. Supposedly, the origin of its dominance can be found in Portugal, which, since the 14th century, was characterized by an early centralization of power. In the colony, the state bureaucracy purportedly had begun as a centralizing agent and increased its mechanisms of power and repression. Its authority reached far into the backlands thanks to local strong men (*caudilhos*) and to slavehunters and prospectors (*bandeirantes*), who, after all, acted on behalf of the state.

The other, older, point of view maintains that a particular sector of colonial society reigned over a weak, unassertive state. The dominant pole is held to have been the large landowners. It was they who governed, who legislated, who administered justice, and who waged war against backland Indian tribes. They defended the people who lived around their ranches, which were like feudal castles and courts of their domains.

There are two main reasons why one cannot join either interpretive camp. Neither model takes into account the specific historical times or the geographic location in which the relationship obtained. Beyond this, putting the state at one extreme and society at the other tends to exclude the possibility of their being mutually entwined. On the one hand, the state was in fact absent in certain areas where its role was assumed by private groups. This was the case in the northeastern cattle-raising regions. Still, such circumstances did not obtain in the colony as a whole.

On the other hand, the Portuguese state cannot be made to look like an overwhelming bureaucratic machine that was successfully transposed to the colony. Colonial government was severely hampered by the size of the colony, by its distance from the capital, and by the unprecedented problems the administration had to face in its attempt to transpose Portuguese administrative processes to Brazil. Over time (i.e., over centuries) the state extended its power.

It was a greater presence in the regions which formed the fundamental nuclei of the colony's export economy. Until the middle of the 17th century, people in charge efficiently exercised their power at the seat of the colonial government (*governo geral*) and in the surrounding captaincies. In other regions, religious orders, especially Jesuits, ruled as states within the state. In different areas, larger rural landowners or bandeirantes held forth.

With the discovery of gold and diamonds at the beginning of the 18th century, the state tightened its control. Its objective was to organize a rapidly growing society and to insure that tribute was paid on the new wealth. But even in this case, it was only in the diamond region of Minas Gerais that the state appeared to overwhelm society and removed any member who challenged its supremacy.

This does not mean that it is impossible to establish a general pattern of the relations between state and society in colonial Brazil, taking into account differences in time and space. To begin with, when referring to the highest levels of state activity, one will almost always be able to distinguish between the state's activities and the overriding interests of society. The crown and its agents in Brazil took on the role of general organizer of life in the colony, and this role did not necessarily correspond to colonial society's interests. For instance, measures intended to restrict enslavement of Indians or to guarantee the supply of foodstuffs by obliging ranchers to plant crops occasioned rebellions among Indian hunters and rural landowners.

But state and society are not two alien worlds. To the contrary, there was a reciprocal movement of the state toward society and society toward the state, which ended up blurring the boundaries between public and private space. If on the one hand private interests influenced the state, on the other hand the state's domain was not clearly drawn. Indeed, people (or subjects) had no rights as individuals. The traits of the Portuguese patrimonial state, where everything, after all, belonged to the king, were readjusted to the needs of a colonial society. There, family solidarity was more relevant than class interests.

The family or the allied families of the ruling class appear as networks formed not just by blood relatives, but by godfathers and godchildren, as well as supporters and friends. As far as the crown was concerned, the state was a royal patrimony, and the governors should be chosen from men loyal to the king. Conversely, the dominant sectors of colonial society tried to break through the state machinery or they tried to curry the governors' favor to benefit the family network.

Through different routes, the end result was a government run not according to impersonal criteria based on obedience to the law, but according to loyalty.

1.5   ECONOMIC ACTIVITIES

Regional diversity characterized economic life in Portugal's biggest colony.

The northeast coast was the first center of colonization and urbanization in the new land. The situation of Brazil's Northeast today is not a product of fate but of a historical process. Up until the middle of the 18th century, the Northeast was the center of the most significant economic and social goings-on in the colony. During that time the South was peripheral. It had fewer cities and no direct link to the export economy. Salvador was the capital of Brazil until 1763, and for a long time it was Brazil's only important city. Although there are no accurate population data for that city until the middle of the 18th century, it probably had 14,000 inhabitants in 1585; 25,000 in 1724; and around 40,000 in 1750 – half of whom were slaves. These numbers might seem modest, but they become quite significant when compared to other populations. The city of São Paulo, for example, had fewer than 2,000 inhabitants in 1600.

The sugar industry was the nucleus of socioeconomic activity in the Northeast. Sugar has a long and contradictory history, both with respect to its use and as far as where it was grown. During the 15th century it was still a rare commodity (*especiaria*) used as medicine or as an exotic condiment. Cookbooks from the 16th century indicate that it was gaining ground in European aristocratic cuisine. It would soon go from being a luxury item to one of mass consumption.

It was during the 1530s and 1540s that sugar production was firmly established in Brazil. In his 1532 expedition, Martim Afonso brought along an expert in the manufacture of sugar. In addition to Portuguese, there were Italians and Flemings who acquired experience in the sugar industry on the island of Madeira. Cane was planted and sugar mills were set up in all the captaincies, from São Vicente to Pernambuco. One of the main objectives in the creation of the royal government (*governo geral*) of Brazil, with its capital in Salvador, was to encourage sugar production in the abandoned Captaincy of Bahia. The instructions Tomé de Sousa brought with him contained a series of orders destined to stimulate the planting and milling of sugar cane. Among the advantages given to cane planters was an exemption from taxation for a stipulated period. In addition, the royal governor built a sugar mill for the crown, in Pirajá, not far from Salvador.

In the São Vicente captaincy, Martim Afonso entered into partnership with some Portuguese and foreigners, and their sugar mill may have been the largest in southern Brazil. It was known as São Jorge dos Erasmos, a name derived from a German, Erasmus Schetz, who bought the mill from the original partners. The production of sugar cane in Rio de Janeiro, especially in the area around Campos, was noteworthy. Until the 18th century, however, white rum or *cachaça* instead of sugar was the main product produced there. It was used as a medium of exchange in the Angolan slave trade.

The great sugar-producing centers in colonial Brazil were Pernambuco and Bahia. This can be explained by climatic, geographic, political, and economic factors. The two captaincies along the coast had a combination of high-quality topsoil and an adequate supply of rain. They were closer to the European importing centers, and they could easily count on their production being bought, especially once Salvador and Recife became important ports.

To set up a sugar mill was a mighty undertaking. As a rule, each mill had its own cane fields. Each needed equipment to process the cane, as well as buildings, slaves, cattle, pasture land, carts for transportation, and a big house. Making sugar from sugar cane was a complicated process. From the early days, the administration of and the techniques for sugar production were all-important. Over the years they were perfected. There were various steps in the process. It began with the extraction of the liquid, its purification, and purging. Cane was ground by a system of gears powered by water or by animals. The mills run by water, owing to their greater size and productivity, ended up being known as royal sugar mills.

There were no sugar refineries set up either in Brazil or in Portugal during the colonial period. Brazilian sugar was called *barreado* or "clayish" because clay was used to make it. This does not mean that it was of poor quality. Brazilian sugar was made into white sugar, which was highly prized in Europe. It was also made into *mascavo* or brown sugar, which was considered inferior. The technique of obtaining white sugar by using clay made up, in part, for the lack of refineries.

To set up and run a sugar mill was also an expensive venture which required credit. During the 16th century, at least part of that credit came from foreigners – Flemings and Italians, or from Lisbon. Later on, during the 17th century, these sources appear to have become unimportant. At least in Bahia, the two main sources of credit were religious or charitable institutions and merchants. Merchants maintained a special relationship with the plantation owners. They financed the building of mills, they advanced resources to get the business going, and, owing to their position, they had the means to purvey imported consumer goods to the plantations. Credits and debits were adjusted between the two parties once the harvest was in. Merchants would often take sugar in exchange for planters' debts, but they took it below market price. The last chapter of the sugar story was out of local hands, as well as out of Portuguese hands. The great importing centers were Amsterdam, London, Hamburg, and Genoa. Notwithstanding Portugal's efforts to retain a monopoly over the most profitable product from its American colony, foreign importers had tremendous influence and the power to fix prices.

It was in the sugar business that the gradual passage from Indian to African slavery occurred. Between the years of 1550 and 1570, there were practically no Africans on the sugar plantations of the Northeast. The labor force consisted of Indian slaves or, to a lesser degree, of Indians coming from Jesuit villages and working for miserable wages. By examining Sergipe do Conde, a large plantation in Bahia, whose records have survived down to the present, we can gain an idea of how the transition took place. In 1574 Africans made up only 7 percent of the slave work force. In 1591 they were 37 percent. And, around 1638, Africans and Afro-Brazilians made up the entire labor force.

Slaves worked at a great array of jobs, but were mostly concentrated in heavy work in the fields. The situation of those working at the mill and around the ovens and kettles could even have been worse. It was not uncommon for slaves to lose a hand or an arm in the grinder. The ovens and kettles were unbearably hot and often caused workers' burns. Many slaves were trained early on for this work, which was also considered apt punishment for anyone who rebelled. In spite of all this, there were exceptions. Some slaves rose in the hierarchy of occupations and became "bankers" (aides to the sugar master), or they even became sugar master of a particular mill. The master was a skilled worker who was responsible for the final stages in sugar production and, after all, for the final quality of the sugar.

Plantation owners wielded considerable economic, social, and political power in the life of the colony. They formed an aristocracy based on wealth and power, but they never became a hereditary nobility of the sort that existed in Europe. The king meted out titles of nobility for services rendered or for money paid. However, these titles were not handed down to the nobles' heirs. One should be careful not to exaggerate plantation owners' social stability or their wealth. What was true of a few families did not obtain for the entire class. Sugar was a risky business. It was susceptible to price fluctuations. It needed good administrators and masses of well-controlled slaves. Plantations and mills often outlasted their owners. They kept their names for hundreds of years, while often changing hands.

Who were the plantation owners early on? Some were families of noble background or with important positions in the Portuguese government. Others were wealthy immigrants or merchants who engaged in trade and sugar production. Very few were real nobles, and not all of them were Old Christians. Among the first plantation owners in Bahia, in the period between 1587 and 1592, many were New Christians. Of 41 plantations with owners whose origins could be identified, 12 of them belonged to New Christians. As time went by, and with the many marriages taking place among the same families, the planter class became homogeneous. The more prestigious planters then tried to trace their family trees back to noble roots in Portugal.

Between the two extremes (masters and slaves), freed slaves and white workers specialized as artisans (blacksmiths, carpenters, sawyers, etc.) and sugar masters. The largest group of free men involved in sugar production were independent cane planters who did not have the resources to build a mill. They were dependent on the wealthier mill owners, but at times they had the power to strike deals with them when cane production waned on the bigger plantations. Mulattos or freed blacks were rarely cane planters. Given this racial barrier, planters' economic power varied greatly. There were humble individuals cultivating small plots of land with two or three slaves while others had 20 or 30 slaves and were the next thing to being true-blue *senhores de engenho*.

One can distinguish some basic phases in sugar's history during the colonial period. These phases are set off by wars, foreign invasions, and competition. Between 1570 and 1620, there was an opportunity to expand sugar production since demand had grown in Europe and because there was practically no competition. Toward the end of that period, however, things became complicated because of the beginning of the Thirty Years' War in Europe (1618) and, later on, because of the Dutch invasion of Brazil's Northeast.

The invasions had a very negative effect in general. Still, one must make a few distinctions. The Dutch occupation of Salvador in 1624–1625 was disastrous for the sugar economy in the Bahian Recôncavo (a humid area surrounding Salvador), but not for Pernambuco. Later on, between the years of 1630 and 1637, when Pernambuco was suffering from the consequences of struggles associated with another Dutch invasion, Bahia reaped the benefits from sugar's scarcity on the international market and from its inevitable rise in price.

Competition began between 1630 and 1640. On the small islands of the Caribbean Antilles, England, France, and Holland began the planting of cane on a large scale. This unleashed a series of negative effects on the sugar economy in northeast Brazil. Setting prices for sugar was even farther out of the hands of Portuguese merchants and colonial producers in Brazil. Caribbean sugar, which was also produced by slave labor, created an increase in the price of slaves, which brought Dutch, English, and French competitors into the slave trade along the African coast. Brazil's sugar economy would never relive the "good old days." Still, during the colonial period, the highest income came from sugar exports. Even at the height of gold exports, sugar continued to be Brazil's most important product, at least in legal trade. In 1760 sugar made up 50 percent of the total value of Brazilian exports, and gold 46 percent. Beyond this, at the end of the colonial period, sugar production revived, and not just in the Northeast. Measures taken by the Marquis of Pombal and a series of international events favored its expansion. Among these events, one should mention the great slave rebellion in Saint Dominique, or Haiti, then a French colony in the Caribbean. During ten years of war, Saint Dominique, a great source of sugar and coffee, was absent from the international scene. At the beginning of the 19th century, in order of their importance, Bahia, Pernambuco, and Rio de Janeiro all produced sugar. São Paulo had begun its production, but it was still a modest exporter.

From a social and economic point of view, the colonial Northeast was not just a producer of sugar, precisely because, within certain confines, sugar engendered diverse activities. The tendency toward specialization in cane planting created a continuous scarcity of foodstuffs, which then gave rise to their production, especially the growing of manioc. Cattle raising was also linked in part to the needs of a sugar economy.

Although it was far behind sugar, tobacco was Brazil's second most important export product. It was mainly planted in the Bahian Recôncavo. Several different types of tobacco were grown – fine export tobaccos for Europe all the way down to coarse types which were important as a means of exchange along the African coast. Tobacco's limited viability allowed a class of small landowners to emerge. They were ex-planters of manioc or Portuguese immigrants with scant resources. Over the years mulattos became common among tobacco planters. A sample of 450 Bahian tobacco farmers between the years of 1684 and 1725 shows that only 3 percent were mulattos, whereas a similar study carried out at the end of the 18th century shows their percentage to have risen to 27.

Cattle began to be raised near the sugar mills, but the tendency of cattle to monopolize the most fertile land pushed cattlemen into the backlands. In 1701 the Portuguese administration outlawed cattle ranches within 80 kilometers of the coast. Cattle ranching was responsible for taming the immense backlands or *sertão*. Ranchers made their way into Piauí, Maranhão, Paraíba, Rio Grande do Norte, and Ceará, and, starting out from the area around the São Francisco River, they reached the Tocantins and Araguaia rivers. The backlands, more so than the coastal areas, were characterized by immense individual properties or *latifúndios* in which cattle roamed out of sight. By the end of the 17th century, individuals in the Bahian sertão owned tracts of land bigger than Portugal. One powerful rancher's property totaled over one million hectares of land.

1.6 THE IBERIAN UNION AND ITS IMPACT ON BRAZIL

One change of direction in the Portuguese monarchy had important consequences in the colony. In the wake of a crisis that left the Portuguese throne vacant, in 1580 the Portuguese nobility and wealthy bourgeoisie proclaimed Philip II of Spain king of Portugal. This ended the Aviz dynasty. The presence of Spanish Bourbons on the Portuguese throne would last until 1640. In addition to the intimate ties between the Portuguese and Spanish nobilities, interests linked to the colonial world also carried weight. With the two crowns united, the Portuguese merchant class expected and hoped for greater access to Spanish markets in America. They also hoped to trade slaves and foodstuffs for silver.

The Iberian Union brought about a temporary disregard for the Line of Tordesillas. It opened territory and allowed Portuguese trailblazers into the Amazon region as well as into what today is central Brazil (the states of Mato Grosso and Goiás).

From an institutional point of view, one of the period's most important measures was the promulgation of the Philippine Ordinances in 1603. These laws consolidated and widened Portuguese laws. With considerable modifications, they remained valid in Brazil until 1917, when they were replaced by the Civil Code.

The most significant consequence of the union of the two crowns occurred on the international level. Portugal's close relationship with the low countries came to an end. It was followed by a period of open confrontation – a natural consequence of the already existing feud between the low countries and Spain. In the American colonial world, the struggle was centered around control of the sugar business and the slave trade.

This was the setting that brought about the Dutch invasions of Brazil, the greatest political and military conflict of the colonial era. The Dutch began by pillaging the African coast in 1595 and by raiding Salvador in 1604. But the Twelve Years' Truce between Spain and the low countries (1609–1621) left Portugal in a relatively calm state. The end of the truce and the creation of the Dutch West Indies Company changed the picture. Created from state and private capital, the company aimed mainly at occupying the sugar-producing regions of Portuguese America and at controlling the supply of slaves.

The invaders began by occupying Salvador in 1624. It took the Dutch a little more than 24 hours to take the city, but for all intents and purposes, they never got beyond its limits. The so-called *homens bons*, "good [well-to-do] men," took refuge in the ranches near the capital. There they organized a resistance movement under the new governor they had chosen, Matias de Albuquerque, as well as under Bishop Dom Marcos Teixeira. Using guerrilla tactics and aided by reinforcements from Europe, they halted the invaders. A fleet of 52 ships and more than 12,000 men then joined the combatant forces. After fierce battles, the Dutch surrendered in May 1625. They had been in Bahia for a year.

The attack on Pernambuco began in 1630 with the conquest of Olinda. Beginning with this episode, the war can be divided into three distinct periods. Between 1630 and 1637, a war of resistance was waged. It ended with Dutch hegemony over the entire area from Ceará down to the São Francisco River. During this period, from the Luso-Brazilian point of view, a negative figure stands out – Domingos Fernandes Calabar. Calabar was born in Porto Calvo,

Alagoas. He had perfect knowledge of the terrain where the battles would be fought. He defected from the Luso-Brazilian forces and joined the Dutch, with whom he collaborated efficaciously until he was captured and executed.

The second period, from 1637 to 1644, is characterized by relative peace, owing to the governorship of Prince Maurice of Nassau. His name is associated with a series of important political initiatives and undertakings. With the goal of ending economic paralysis and of establishing links with the local society, Nassau had the abandoned sugar plantations sold on credit. These plantations' owners had fled to Bahia. He also took on the problem of foodstuffs and had rural landowners plant the "local bread," manioc. They were to plant it in proportion to the number of slaves they held.

The prince, himself a Calvinist, was tolerant as far as Catholics and, according to all indications, Jews were concerned. The so-called cripto-Jews, that is, New Christians who practiced their old religion secretly, were authorized to profess Judaism openly. Two synagogues were opened in Recife during the 1640s, and many Jews came from Holland. When the Dutch left Brazil, one of the terms of their surrender allowed the Jews who had been on their side to emigrate. They left for Suriname, Jamaica, or New Amsterdam (New York), or they went back to Holland.

Nassau looked favorably on artists', naturalists', and men of letters' coming to Pernambuco. One of the artists was Frans Post, the earliest painter of Brazilian landscapes and domestic scenes. The prince's name was linked to improvements made in Recife, which the Dutch elevated over Olinda to capital of the captaincy. Next to old Recife he built Mauristaad. It was geometrically laid out and had canals which tried to replicate distant Amsterdam in the tropics. Owing to disagreements with the West Indies Company, Nassau returned to Europe in 1644.

The third period, between 1645 and 1654, is known as the reconquest. The end of the Iberian Union did not occasion peace. Relations between Portugal and Holland had changed after Spanish domination. The peaceful relationship both countries enjoyed prior to 1580 was not automatically reestablished. The Dutch now occupied a part of Brazil and they did not wish to leave.

The main center of rebellion against Dutch presence was in Pernambuco, where André Vidal de Negreiros and João Fernandes Vieira stood out. Vieira was one of the wealthiest landowners in the region. He and Vidal were joined by Henrique Dias, a black, and by Felipe Camarão, an Indian. After a few initial victories by the Luso-Brazilian forces, the war reached an impasse and dragged on for several years. While the rebels controlled the countryside, the Dutch held onto Recife. The impasse was broken in the two battles of Guararapes (1648, 1649), which the insurgents won. In addition, a series of circumstances made life difficult for the occupiers. The West Indies Company had run into difficulties, and no one wanted to invest in it. There was a faction in Holland that was in favor of peace with Portugal. Its members alleged that the salt trade with Setúbal was essential to the Dutch fish industry and that it was more important to the economy than the dubious profits from the overseas colony. Finally, in 1652, the start of war between Holland and England made resources for military operations in Brazil scarce. During the following year, a Portuguese squadron besieged Recife by sea, and the Dutch capitulated in 1654.

The history of the Dutch occupation is a clear example of the relations between colonial production and the slave trade. As soon as they were able to stabilize, to a reasonable extent, the sugar industry in the Northeast, the Dutch sought to guarantee the supply of slaves by controlling sources in Africa. In truth, they fought on two very distant but interconnected fronts. Several places along the Mina Coast were occupied in 1637. A truce established between Portugal and Holland right after the restoration of the Portuguese monarchy was broken by Nassau with the occupation of Luanda and Benguela, in Angola (1641). Luso-Brazilian troops under the command of Salvador Correia de Sá were responsible for retaking Angola in 1648. It was not an accident that men like João Fernandes Vieira and André Vidal de Negreiros headed the Portuguese administration of that African colony.

The resources gathered locally for the war in the Northeast amounted to two-thirds of the money spent in the resistance phase and almost the entire amount spent during the reconquest. Likewise, during the first phase of the war, the great bulk of the troops were Portuguese, Spanish, and Neapolitan mercenaries. During the second phase, local soldiers and especially soldiers from Pernambuco were in the majority. The same situation obtained in the command sector. These men waged "Brazilian" or "mobile" war instead of "European war." Their guerrilla tactics won decisive victories over the Dutch.

To emphasize the role of local force in the Dutch war is not to say that the local forces formed a democratic, model army of "three united races." Because of his importance, Calabar has been recognized as the great traitor of the first phase of the war. But he was not alone. In fact, the Dutch could always count on local support – from different plantation owners and cane growers, as well as from people poorly integrated into Portuguese colonial society or from those totally outside it. New Christians, black slaves, Tapuia Indians, and poor, destitute mixed-bloods aided the Dutch. It is true that Camarão's Indians and Henrique Dias's blacks sided with the Luso-Brazilians. However, these mobilizations were relatively small. For example, in 1648 Henrique Dias's contingent contained 300 soldiers. That amounted to 10 percent of the armed resistance and 0.75 percent of the region's slave population.

The role of Pernambucans in expelling the Dutch gave momentum to Pernambucan nativism. For the next 200 years, up to the Praieira revolution of 1848, Pernambuco would be a rallying point for autonomy and independence, as well as a center of open revolt. Up until Brazil's independence, Pernambucans' main target was Lisbon. After independence, they sought autonomy for their province, and this sought-after autonomy was tinged with demands for social justice. Pernambucan nativism changed in content over the years according to specific contexts and the particular social groups involved, but nativism was a permanent trait of the region.

1.7 COLONIZATION OF THE PERIPHERY

Far from the main centers of the colony, life in northern Brazil was very different from that of the Northeast. Colonization proceeded slowly. Economic integration with European markets remained precarious until the end of the 18th century. Indians were regularly enslaved. To simplify matters, one speaks of the region as a whole, but one should never forget the profound differences between Maranhão on the one hand and Amazônia on the other.

Until 1612, when the French settled in Maranhão and founded the city of São Luis, the Portuguese had not shown much interest in or likelihood of settling that region. The risk of losing land caused them to expel the French and, in 1616, to found Belém. Belém was the point of departure for the gradual exploration of the Amazon River, whose entire length, all the way to Peru, was navigated in 1637 by Pedro Teixeira. In 1690, the Portuguese set up a small frontier post at the mouth of the Rio Negro, near present-day Manaus. The crown set up a separate administration for northern Brazil and created the State of Maranhão and Grão Pará, whose governor and administration were separate from the State of Brazil. Maranhão remained at least formally and intermittently a separate state until 1774.

Indigenous influence was clear, both numerically and culturally. In the middle of the 18th century, the dominant language was a pidgin variety of Tupi. There was widespread racial mixing owing especially to the scarcity of white women – notwithstanding efforts to send Azorean emigrants to São Luis.

If all regions of Brazil suffered from a scarcity of currency, the northern region suffered more. Until the mid-18th century, direct barter was frequent. Sometimes cotton cloth or cocoa beans were used as money. Attempts to set up an agricultural export economy based on sugar and cotton largely failed until the last decades of the 18th century, at which time Maranhão quickly became an important cotton-producing region. Then cotton spread to the Northeast. Mainly, however, northern products came from the forests. They were the so-called backland drugs (*drogas do sertão*): vanilla, sarsaparilla, and, especially, native cacao, which was harvested along the rivers and brought to Belém by Indians and mestizos.

The large Indian population made the North one of the main fields of missionary activity for the religious orders, with Jesuits taking the lead. Around 1740, some 50,000 Indians may have been living in Jesuit and Franciscan villages. The work of Father Antônio Vieira was important here. He arrived in Brazil in 1653 as a Jesuit provincial. He developed an intensive preaching campaign to put a stop to abuse of the Indian population. There were constant conflicts among representatives of the crown, colonists, and clergy in the

North. The Jesuits were in the public eye because they had plans for acculturating and controlling Indians, and their plans were very different from the colonists'. On top of this, they had large cattle ranches, cotton plantations, and sugar plantations (with mills), and they actively traded in forest products (the "back-land drugs"). They encountered many problems and were expelled from Maranhão in 1684. With the crown's support, they returned two years later, but the balance between missionaries and colonists would always be precarious – up to 1759, when the Jesuits were expelled once and for all.

When, in 1627, Friar Vicente do Salvador wrote the first history of Brazil, he bemoaned the predatory nature of Portuguese colonists, who, up to that point, had been incapable of populating the hinterland. They merely "clawed the coast like crabs." What he said was largely true, but he was being contradicted in some areas, especially in south central Brazil.

Colonization of the captaincy of São Vicente began as it did in the Northeast, along the coast, where cane was planted and sugar mills were constructed. This activity did not last long. Local sugar was at a disadvantage to that of the Northeast, because of the quality of soil and because of the region's distance from the ports of Europe.

On the other hand, the great numbers of Indians in the region attracted the first Jesuits. Priests and colonists, with different objectives, set off on a grand adventure in the backlands. First they scaled the Serra do Mar, the coastal mountain range. They made their way along Indian trails up to the Piratininga Plateau, 800 meters above sea level. In 1554, Fathers Nóbrega and Anchieta founded São Paulo on the plateau. In 1561 it became a *vila* (town), and a Jesuit school was set up. Separated from the coast by a natural barrier, the early colonists and missionaries set their sights more and more on the backlands. They found their way with help from the Indians and took advantage of the river network formed by the Tietê, the Paranaíba, and other rivers.

There were some similarities between this region in its earliest times and the northern periphery. They both were weak in export crops. They had large Indian populations. Colonists and missionaries fought over control of the Indians. Currency was scarce. Barter was frequently used. And indigenous influence was especially noticeable. Extensive interbreeding owing to the small number of white women gave rise to white and Indian mixtures which were called *mamelucos*. Tupi was the dominant language until the 18th century. The Portuguese in São Paulo adopted many of the Indians' habits and practices. They were able to fight equally well with bows and arrows and with firearms.

Once again, missionaries and colonists were at loggerheads given their diverse methods and objectives in subordinating the Indians. Crown and papal decisions (1639–1640) confirming the limits to Indians' enslavement occasioned violent reactions in Rio de Janeiro, Santos, and São Paulo. The Jesuits were expelled from the region, and returned to São Paulo only in 1653.

In spite of its early similarities with the North, the area around São Paulo was to have a unique history beginning at the end of the 16th century. Settlers combined viniculture, cotton planting, and especially wheat farming with other activities that took them far into the totally unknown or scarcely explored Brazilian hinterland. Paulista cattle ranchers spread northward into the São Francisco River valley all the way to Piauí. To the south, Paulistas tried their hand at mining – in the present-day state of Paraná, which was at that time an extension of São Paulo. Cattle spread down through Santa Catarina, Rio Grande do Sul, and into the "Banda Oriental," or what today is Uruguay.

Individual initiative worked hand in hand with crown endeavors to secure the area and to push the border with Spanish America as far back as possible. Immigrants brought from the Azores archipelago as well as from São Paulo founded Laguna, Santa Catarina, in 1684. A few years earlier, in 1680, the Portuguese had set up Colônia do Sacramento along the River Plate, across from Buenos Aires. They planned to use this outpost to trade with Upper Peru. They especially wanted to trade for silver, which came down the river on its way overseas.

1.8 *BANDEIRA* EXPEDITIONS AND PAULISTA SOCIETY

Paulistas' greatest influence on colonial life during the 17th century was exerted through the *bandeira* or "flag" expeditions, which at times entailed hundreds of enslaved Indians marching off into the backlands, spending months and sometimes years hunting Indians to enslave or searching for precious metals.* It is not hard to understand why enslaved Indians might join these expeditions. War, as opposed to agriculture, was an activity worthy of men in indigenous society. The number of Indians and mamelucos on these expeditions was always larger than the number of whites. The great 1629 expedition into the Guaíra region, led by Manuel Preto and Raposo Tavares, consisted of 69 whites, 900 mamelucos, and 2,000 Indians.

The bandeiras went in different directions: toward Minas Gerais, Goiás, Mato Grosso, and into the regions containing Guaraní Indian villages run by Spanish Jesuits. Among these villages Guaíra stood out. It was located in western Paraná, between the Parana-panema and Iguaçu Rivers. The bandeirantes regularly sacked and destroyed Indian villages when they took Indian prisoners from this region. Some bandeiras entailed immense journeys in which the search for adventure melded with economic objectives. As an experienced bandeirante, Raposo Tavares undertook a 12,000-kilometer journey. Between the years of 1648 and 1652, he traveled toward Paraguay and reached the foothills of the Andes. Then he headed northeast and crossed the present state of Rondônia, after which he traveled down the Mamoré and Madeira Rivers to the Amazon, which he followed all the way to Belém.

The relationship between crown interests and bandeirantes' interests was complex. Some expeditions received direct incentives from the Portuguese administration while others did not. In general, the search for precious metals, the capturing of Indians during specific periods, and territorial expansion were compatible with Lisbon's objectives. Bandeirantes also aided in repressing and subordinating peoples in north and northeast Brazil. Domingos Jorge Velho fought in the battles of Rio Grande do Norte during the Indian rebellion known as the Barbarians' War, which lasted from 1683 to 1713. And between 1690 and 1695, in Alagoas, Domingos Jorge Velho also led the final campaign which defeated the Palmares maroon community.

---

* These were called flag expeditions because a flag bearer marched at the front of them. This was an Indian custom adopted by the Portuguese. – Trans.

Jesuit observers estimated that 300,000 Indians were captured in their Paraguayan missions alone. These numbers could be exaggerations, but all other estimates are also high. What did they do with these Indians? The strongest indicators suggest that they were sold as slaves in São Vicente and especially in Rio de Janeiro, where sugar production had developed during the 17th century. According to data from the Congregation of São Bento, Indians constituted from a fourth to a third of the work force at the Benedictine sugar plantations in Rio de Janeiro. There was a shortage of African slaves between 1625 and 1650 owing to the Dutch presence in Brazil and Africa. It was not a mere coincidence that during those years bandeirantes were active.

A considerable portion of the captured Indians were employed in the Paulista economy, especially in wheat farming. This was particularly apparent during the 17th century and was linked to the Dutch invasions. With the Portuguese fleet destroyed, wheat importation was touch and go. At the same time, the presence of large numbers of foreign troops in the Northeast increased the demand for wheat. At the end of the war, wheat farming went into decline and ended entirely – owing to the dwindling number of Indian reserves and to foreign competition.

In their travels through the backlands, Paulistas were to fulfill an old dream of the Portuguese colonists. In 1695, on the Velhas River (Rio das Velhas), near the present-day towns of Sabará and Caeté, in the state of Minas Gerais, gold was discovered in significant quantities. Tradition links these early discoveries to Manuel Borba Gato, a son-in-law of Fernão Dias, himself known as the "Emerald Hunter." During the next 40 years, gold was found in Minas Gerais, in Bahia, Goiás, and Mato Grosso. Along with gold, people found diamonds in northern Minas Gerais (Serro Frio), around 1730. Diamonds were never as important economically as gold was, however.

Mining of precious metals had important effects in Lisbon and in Brazil. The gold rush brought about the first large wave of Portuguese immigration to Brazil. During the first 60 years of the 18th century, nearly 600,000 people came to Brazil from Portugal and the Atlantic islands. Yearly, an average of 8,000 to 10,000 people of all stripes made the journey: small proprietors, priests, merchants, prostitutes, and all sorts of adventurers.

On the other hand, the precious metals momentarily eased Portugal's financial burdens. The trade imbalance between Portugal and Britain had become a fact of life. Beginning in the early 18th century and for several years thereafter, this imbalance was offset by the gold coming from Brazil. Precious metal took three different routes. Part of it stayed in Brazil, where it contributed to the relative wealth of the mining regions. Another part went to Portugal, where it was consumed throughout the reign of Dom João V (1706–1750). It was spent on the royal court and on works such as the gigantic convent-palace at Mafra. The third part was directly or indirectly smuggled into British hands and accelerated the accumulation of finance capital in England.

The precious metal boom had repercussions on the Northeast's sugar economy, which was undergoing hard times 20 years prior to the discovery of gold, but which did not die. It was, however, affected by population shifts out of the Northeast, and especially by a rise in the price of slaves owing to an increase in demand for them. For administrative purposes, the axis of colonial life also shifted toward the Center-South and especially toward Rio de Janeiro, where slaves and supplies entered the country and where the gold from the mines left. In 1763 the capital of the Viceroyalty of Brazil was transferred from Salvador to Rio. Both cities had approximately the same population (around 40,000 inhabitants), but it was one thing to be the capital and something else to be merely the largest city in the Northeast.

The mining economy tended to link distant parts of the colony. Cattle and foodstuffs were sent to Minas from Bahia, and a reciprocal trade pattern was established. From the South came both cattle and the mules which were absolutely necessary for transporting merchandise. In São Paulo's hinterland, Sorocaba and its fair became an obligatory stop for the cattle drives heading mainly for Minas Gerais.

The extraction of gold and diamonds gave rise to the most overreaching supervision the Portuguese crown established in Brazil. The Portuguese government made a great effort to collect its tribute. It took various measures aimed at regulating daily life in the mining areas as well as elsewhere in the colony – so as to benefit the crown and to avoid having the gold rush turn into chaos. In an attempt at reducing smuggling and increasing its own receipts, the crown set up systems of collecting tribute which would vary over the years.

In general there were two basic systems. There was the royal fifth or *quinto* and the head tax or *capitação*. The first simply decreed that one-fifth of all metal taken out should belong to the king. The quinto was deducted from all the gold dust and nuggets taken to the foundries. Capitação, which the crown initiated in search of greater income, was, in comparison to the quinto, more all-encompassing. As far as miners were concerned, it was a tax imposed for every slave, male or female, over the age of 12 – whether they were productive or not. Independent gold panners, that is, miners who had no slaves, also paid the head tax – on themselves. This same tax was also imposed on businesses such as workshops, stores, inns, and slaughterhouses.

The crown also sought to set limits on how many people could enter the mining region. In the early days, São Paulo's town council petitioned the king of Portugal and requested that only citizens of the town of São Paulo be given mining concessions, because they had discovered the gold in the first place. The facts themselves demonstrated how unviable this request was. Waves, not only of Portuguese but also of Brazilians, especially Bahians, rolled into the mining area. This gave rise to the civil war known as the *Emboabas* (an epithet for "Portuguese") from 1708 to 1709. On one side there were Paulistas, on the other foreigners and Bahians. The Paulistas did not succeed in their undertaking, but they succeeded in having the captaincy of São Paulo and Minas do Ouro created. They were separated from Rio de Janeiro in 1709. The Paulistas' efforts also led to São Paulo's being officially declared a city in 1711. In 1720, Minas Gerais became a separate captaincy.

The Paulistas did not succeed in gaining a monopoly over the mines, but the crown sought to keep the mining region from becoming open territory. It also tried to stop Portugal's depopulation by regulating emigration. Friars were prohibited from emigrating, and a 1738 regal order to the governor of Minas Gerais called for the imprisonment of any cleric who was there "illegally or without a job." Early in the history of the mines, friars were suspected of smuggling. Goldsmiths were also closely monitored because of the nature of their profession. They were obliged to change their occupation or be banished from the mining areas.

Other crown efforts were aimed at avoiding an imbalance between the mining region and other parts of the country. Transfer from Bahia to Minas Gerais of merchandise imported from Portugal was prohibited. Measures were taken to guarantee a supply of slaves for the Northeast by establishing quotas for their entry into the mining area.

In an attempt at insuring "law and order," the crown created tribunals and appointed trial judges or *ouvidores*. The ouvidores were often given the duties of judges and of supervisors in charge of collecting the quinto. The latter occupation, in principle, should have gone to the chief purveyor (*provedor-mor*). To control the slaves, to escort the gold, and to put down disturbances, Portugal sent two companies of dragoons (professional military forces) to Minas Gerais in 1719.

The Portuguese administration did not attain its basic objectives in the mining region. The Portuguese government's mission was difficult because of the great distances, the corruption of local authorities, the authorities' precarious position between the crown and the colonial world, and the conflicts between government employees' rights. On top of this, the orders coming from Lisbon did not add up to a coherent policy. Doubts, delays, and changes in direction contributed to widening the gap between intentions and reality.

From a mixture of all sorts of people, a heterogeneous society sprang forth. It consisted not only of miners, but also of businessmen, lawyers, priests, ranchers, artisans, bureaucrats, and soldiers. Many of these individuals' interests were closely linked to the colony's, and it is not by chance that there were many revolts and conspiracies against colonial authorities in Minas Gerais. Even though the richest sectors of the population were often ranchers who invested in faraway mining endeavors, social life was centered in the cities, themselves hubs of commerce, population, and commemorative festivals. In the cities of Minas Gerais there were remarkable manifestations of culture: in the arts, letters, and music. The laws prohibiting religious orders from entering Minas Gerais gave rise to religious lay associations – the brotherhoods and Third

Orders (*Ordens Terceiras*). They financed the building of baroque churches in Minas. And in the decoration of these churches the mulatto sculptor known as Aleijadinho, "the Little Cripple," stood out. Aleijadinho, or Antônio Francisco Lisboa, was the illegitimate son of a Portuguese house builder and a slave woman.

Slaves were at the base of society. The hardest work was mining, especially when the riverbed deposits were spent and gold had to be dug underground. Illnesses such as dysentery, malaria, and pulmonary infections, as well as accidental deaths, were commonplace. There are estimates suggesting that the slaves could only be worked some seven to 12 years. Continuous importation of slaves kept the mining economy going and was necessary just to replace workers who were worn out. Between the years 1720 and 1750, the number of slaves imported to Brazil grew, notwithstanding the sugar crisis. Population data from the captaincy of Minas Gerais in 1776 indicate an overwhelming majority of blacks and mulattos. Of the nearly 320,000 people there, blacks made up 52 percent, mulattos 26 percent, and whites 22 percent.

Over the years miscegenation was intense. The female population grew and in 1776 made up nearly 38 percent of all inhabitants. There was, in addition, a phenomenon whose interpretation is controversial: many slaves were freed. To appreciate the extent of manumission, one need only look at the following data. Between 1735 and 1749, freed slaves made up 1.4 percent of the African population. Around 1786, they constituted 41 percent of that population and 34 percent of all people in Minas Gerais. The most plausible explanation for these numbers, which were greater than those for Bahia, is that as the mines petered out, it was either unnecessary or impossible for many slave owners to hold onto their property.

Mining society, owing to the gold, is associated with riches. Seen up close, there were many restrictions on that wealth. One must make an initial distinction between the early days of the gold rush and the second phase. In the beginning period, the last decade of the 17th century and the beginning of the 18th, the search for gold without support from other endeavors created a shortage of foodstuffs and an inflationary spiral that affected all of Brazil. There was severe famine, and many campsites were abandoned. As time passed, plots were cultivated and a diversified economy emerged from what had been utter poverty. Society in Minas Gerais accumulated wealth whose vestiges can still be seen in the buildings and works of art in what today are its historic cities (Ouro Preto, Congonhas do Campo, Sabará, Caeté).

Still, this wealth ended up in a few select hands. It belonged to a group of people employed not only in the somewhat tenuous extraction of gold, but also in the many businesses and opportunities that sprang up around gold mining. Some of these people worked for the government as independent contractors. Below them on the social scale was a wide layer of free individuals who were poor or who were low-level government employees or merchants. All of them had meager economic prospects. Of course, mining society was more open and more complex than sugar society. But even so, in its entirety, it was never more than a society made up largely of poor people. The high point of gold mining came between 1733 and 1748. After that it began to decline. By the beginning of the 19th century, gold production was no longer an important part of the Brazilian economy. Clearly, the region had regressed. Cities, with their once intense goings-on, became historical sites, which also means they stagnated. Ouro Preto had 20,000 inhabitants in 1740 and only 7,000 in 1804.

But this reversal did not affect the entire captaincy of Minas Gerais. It was not just a mining region. Even in its golden heyday, Minas Gerais had ranches which often combined cattle raising, sugar planting and milling, flour milling, and gold mining. As far as cattle, cereals, and later on manufacturing are concerned, Minas did not retreat entirely. To the contrary, during the 19th century it would expand these activities and import a constant flow of slaves. Minas Gerais would be a curious blend: a slaveholding society whose economy was not a plantation economy nor was it mainly an export economy.

1.9   THE CRISIS IN THE COLONIAL SYSTEM

The last decades of the 18th century were characterized by a series of transformations in the Western world, and these transformations occurred both on an ideational level and on a factual level.

The *ancien régime*, Europe's absolute monarchies, had ruled since the beginning of the 16th century. These governments, which were linked to specific notions and practices, entered a period of crises. Beginning with the French philosophers and the British economists, enlightened thought and liberal points of view took root and spread. A few significant facts set off the transformations of the Western world. In 1776 the British colonies in North America declared their independence. Beginning in 1789, the French Revolution put an end to the *ancien régime* in that country. There were repercussions which entailed the use of force throughout Europe. At the same time, a silent revolution was underway in England: the Industrial Revolution. The use of new sources of energy, the use of machines, especially in the textile industry, the development of agriculture, and the control of international commerce are factors which would turn Britain into the greatest world power of the time.

In the search for wider markets, the British started to impose free trade and the abandoning of mercantilistic principles on everyone. At the same time, they tried to protect their own market and those of their colonies by imposing protective tariffs. In their relations with Spanish and Portuguese America, the British made bigger and bigger cracks in the colonial systems. They made use of trade agreements, smuggling, and alliances with local merchants. The colonial world felt the effect of another important factor. A movement toward limiting or abolishing slavery appeared first among the great powers of the time, in Britain and France. In February 1794 revolutionary France declared an end to slavery in its colonies. Britain did the same in 1807. One should not forget, however, that Napoleon revoked the French measure in 1802.

The international state of affairs affected the relationship between the Portuguese crown and its largest colony. In the middle of the 18th century, Portugal would become a backward nation as far as the great powers of Europe were concerned. It was dependent on Britain, and in exchange for its dependency Britain would protect Portugal from France and Spain. Even so, the Portuguese monarchy tried to maintain its colonial system and limit the growing British presence in Brazil.

An important milestone during this period is the ascension of Dom José I to the Portuguese throne in 1750. However, Dom José was not as important as his minister, Sebastião José de Carvalho e Melo, the future Marquis of Pombal. Until he was appointed minister, aged over 50, Pombal had had a relatively obscure career as a Portuguese representative in England and as a diplomat in Vienna. During his term of office, which ran from 1750 to 1777, he worked to make the Portuguese government more efficient and to change Portugal's relationship to its colonies. Pombal's reforms would be a singular mixture of the old and new, which is explainable given Portugal's peculiarities. Pombal took enlightened absolutism and attempted to apply it to mercantilistic doctrine. This overall formula came together in a series of measures. Those important to Brazil will be examined here.

In tune with mercantilistic notions, Pombal created two privileged commercial companies: the Companhia Geral do Comércio do Grão-Pará e Maranhão in 1755 and the Companhia Geral de Pernambuco e Paraíba in 1759. The task of the first company was to develop the northern region by offering attractive prices for export products coming from that area. Its cacao, clove, cinnamon, and more recently cotton and rice would be transported exclusively by company ships for consumption in Europe. Pombal had black slaves brought to the North. However, given the region's poverty, most of these slaves were reexported to the mines in Mato Grosso. The second company was supposed to revive the Northeast using similar tactics.

Pombal's policies worked against Brazilian merchants, who were displaced by the privileged companies. The policies were not, however, intended to make life difficult for the local elite. Quite the opposite: members of the elite were given administrative and fiscal responsibilities in the government, in the courts, and in the military.

Pombal's economic program was, to a large extent, frustrated because in the middle of the 18th century Brazil experienced an economic depression which lasted through the 1770s. The sugar crisis and the declining gold production were mainly responsible for this depression. At the same time that Portugal's income was falling, its expenditures rose. It had to spend extraordinary amounts of money to rebuild Lisbon and wage war with Spain. Lisbon had been destroyed by an earthquake in 1755, and Spain was vying for control of the large area extending from southern São Paulo all the way to the River Plate.

Pombal attempted to reduce gold and diamond smuggling and tried to improve the collection of tribute. In Minas Gerais, the capitação was replaced by the old royal quinto. The government required a yearly minimum of 100 *arrobas* or 1,500 kilos (an arroba was equal to 15 kilos) of gold. After a series of bankruptcies, in 1771 the crown itself took charge of the diamond mines. At the same time, Pombal sought to make Portugal less dependent on manufactured imports by offering incentives for setting up factories in Portugal and even in Brazil.

One of the most controversial measures of Pombal's government was the 1759 expulsion of the Jesuits from Portugal and all its territories. He also ordered the expropriation of all their wealth. These measures can be understood best in the context of Pombal's objectives. He wanted to centralize Portugal's authority and to restrict autonomous areas run by religious orders, whose goals were different from those of the state. Besides the Jesuits, the Brothers of Mercy were expelled from Amazônia and had their possessions confiscated. They had been the second most important order in the region. But Pombal's main target was the Jesuits, who were accused of forming a "state within the state."

According to Pombal, Brazil's northern and southern boundaries could be secured by integrating the Indians into Portuguese civilization. If there were no reliable inhabitants born in Brazil who identified with Portugal and its objectives, it would be impossible to assure Portugal's control over the vast, semi-populated regions of that colony. This explains the adoption of a whole series of measures concerning native peoples. Indian slavery was abolished in 1757. Many of the religious villages in the Amazon region were turned into towns with civil administrations. Laws were passed encouraging marriages between whites and Indians. This assimilationist policy collided head-on with Jesuit paternalism and was a major bone of contention.

At the same time, Spanish Jesuits were accused of fomenting an indigenous rebellion at the missions in the Seven Peoples region of

Uruguay. The accusation that they were against Portugal's taking
that territory gave rise to the so-called Guarani War, which lasted
from 1754 to 1756. One should also not forget that the Jesuits' vast
properties had become coveted objects for the colonial elite and the
crown.

The greater part of the rural and urban property confiscated from
the Jesuits was auctioned off to large landowners and wealthy merchants. Its biggest churches fell into the hands of bishops who did
not belong to religious orders. Many Jesuit schools were turned
into governors' palaces or military hospitals. All in all, there was
widespread waste, especially of cultural assets such as Jesuits'
libraries, which colonials considered of little worth.

The Jesuits' expulsion created a vacuum in the colony's already
impoverished colonial system of education. The Portuguese crown,
contrary to the Spanish crown, feared the appearance of a lettered
colonial elite. In the 16th century, Spain had created several universities in the Americas: one in Santo Domingo in 1538, one in Lima,
and another in Mexico City in 1551. Nothing similar occurred
in Portuguese America during the entire colonial period. It was
the same for the press. During the 16th century, newspapers also
appeared in the major colonial cities of Spanish America. With the
exception of one press opened in Rio de Janeiro in 1747 and immediately shut down by a royal order, in Brazil there would be no
printing presses until the Portuguese crown took refuge in Rio.

The crown took some measures to compensate for the prob-
lems created in education owing to its expulsion of the Jesuits.
A special tax known as the literary subsidy was created to finance
state-supported education. The bishop of Olinda created the Olinda
Seminary, which specialized in natural sciences and mathematics.
Small intellectual clubs were formed in Rio de Janeiro and Salvador.

Pombal's measures against religious orders were part of the policy
of subordinating the church to the Portuguese state. The state tried,
however, to avoid direct conflicts with the pope. The church, for
its part, accepted the expulsion of the Jesuits. Even more, in 1773
Pope Clement XIV, believing that they were more trouble than they
were worth, abolished the Jesuits. They were resurrected in 1814.

Among Portuguese historians, the great controversy over Pombal
has led to the notion that there was an abrupt change between

Pombal's administration and the one that followed, under Queen Dona Maria I. Many things changed. The commercial companies were dismantled, and Brazil was prohibited from maintaining its factories and from making cloth, except for the crude cotton cloth slaves wore. This fact and the punishment of the men involved in the Inconhdência Mineira (see below) made Brazilian historians take a negative view of the period after Pombal's fall.

It is, nonetheless, the case that between 1777 and 1808 the crown went on trying to carry out reforms and adapt to the new times, as well as to preserve mercantilistic colonialism. Contrary to the previous reign, the reign of Dona Maria I and prince regent Dom João VI benefited from a situation which favored reviving agriculture in Brazil. Sugar production became worth the effort and expanded, thanks to the slave rebellion in Saint Dominique. On top of this, a new culture had become viable. Cotton had been developed by Pombal's commercial company and was given an added impulse by the United States' war of independence. And for a time cotton turned Maranhão into the most prosperous part of Portuguese America.

1.10   REBEL MOVEMENTS AND NATIONAL CONSCIOUSNESS

At the same time that the Portuguese crown's policy was to reform absolutism, there appeared, in the colony, several anti-Portuguese conspiracies and attempts at independence. They were related to new ideas and new facts present on the international level, but they also reflected the local reality. They were, in fact, regional rebellions rather than national revolutions. Regional issues were the common trait of diverse episodes such as the Inconfidência Mineira in 1789, the Tailors' Conspiracy in 1798, and the 1817 revolution in Pernambuco.

When did Brazilian-born members of colonial society, as well as a few Portuguese living in Brazil, begin to think of Brazil as a unit different from Portugal? In other words, when did it occur to people that they were Brazilians?

There is not a single nor a standard answer for a question of this nature. National consciousness became apparent as sectors of the colony's society began to have interests different from those of the motherland – or when they began to see the motherland as the source of their problems. Far from being a homogeneous group, these sectors were made up of diverse entities, from wealthy rural landowners on the one hand to artisans and poorly paid soldiers on the other. In between these extremes, there were graduates of foreign universities and men of letters. None of these people thought exactly alike, even though the "French ideas" and the liberalism of the American revolution were their sources of inspiration. Of course, the dominant sectors of native society tried to dampen these ideas and were very circumspect when it came to the abolition of slavery, which was contrary to their interests. On the other hand, for the poor the idea of independence went hand in hand with egalitarianism and social reform.

The Peddlers' War in Pernambuco (1710), the rebellions in Minas Gerais beginning with that of Felipe dos Santos in 1720, and, mainly, the plots and revolutions during the last few decades of the 18th century and the first two of the 19th are often pointed out as positive examples of national consciousness. While rebellions might be seen as manifestations of a national consciousness, in Brazil they were manifestions of regional consciousness. At least as often as rebels claimed to be Brazilians, they called themselves Mineiros, Bahians, Pernambucans, and in some cases poor folk.

The most important manifestation of rebellion in Brazil, beginning at the end of the 18th century, was the so-called Inconfidência Mineira of 1789 in Ouro Preto, Minas Gerais. Its importance does not come from its occurrence; it comes, instead, from what people made it symbolize. The movement was directly related to the worsening plight of regional society of the time. At the same time, conspirators had been influenced by new ideas coming from Europe and North America. Many members of the Mineiro elite were world travelers and had studied in Europe. José Joaquim da Maia, a student who had studied at the University of Coimbra, in Portugal, went to medical school in Montpelier, France, in 1786. During 1786 and the following year, he was in contact with Thomas Jefferson, at that time the United States' ambassador to France. He requested support for a revolution that, according to him, was being planned in Brazil. One of the members of the Inconfidência, José Alvares

Maciel, graduated from the University of Coimbra and spent a year and a half in England. There he studied manufacturing techniques, and with English merchants he discussed the possibility of support for a Brazilian independence movement.

The *inconfidentes* were, largely, an elite group of colonials. They were miners and ranchers, priests also involved in business, prestigious government workers and lawyers, as well as one high-ranking military officer. All of them had ties with the colonial authorities in the captaincy, and, in some cases, they were members of the judicial apparatus.

José Joaquim da Silva Xavier was to some extent an exception. Handicapped by his parents' premature deaths, as one of seven children he had lost his property because of debts. He had tried his hand at business with no success. In 1775, he joined the army at the rank of second-lieutenant (*alferes*) which was the lowest rank among officers. During his free time he practiced dentistry. This is how he got the somewhat derogatory nickname of Tiradentes, or "tooth-puller."

During the late decades of the 18th century, Minas Gerais society was in decline. The decline was marked by lower and lower gold production and government initiatives aimed at securing the royal quinto. Along with this, the close relationship between the local elite and the administration of the captaincy was ruptured when Governor Luis da Cunha Meneses arrived in Minas. Cunha Meneses set aside the most important members of the local elite and showered favors on his friends. Although he did not belong to the elite, even Tiradentes suffered when he lost the command of the military detachment patrolling the strategic highway through the Mantiqueira Mountains, which form the gateway to the mining region.

The situation worsened with the nomination of the Viscount of Barbacena to replace Cunha Meneses. Barbacena had received orders from the Portuguese minister Melo e Castro. He was to guarantee the government's annual tribute of 100 arrobas in gold. To make this quota, the governor had the right to all the gold available, and, if this were not enough, he could call for a *derrama*, a head tax levied on every inhabitant in the captaincy. He was further instructed to investigate everyone in debt to the crown, as well as all contracts signed between government officials and private citizens. These instructions cast a widespread threat over the captaincy. It fell most directly on the local elite, among whom were those most in debt to the crown. Anticipating a derrama, the inconfidentes began to prepare their rebel movement during the last months of 1788. However, they never actually set their plans in motion. In March 1789, Barbacena issued a decree suspending any derramas, and at the same time the conspirators were denounced. They were immediately jailed – Tiradentes in Rio de Janeiro, the rest in Minas. A long trial in the colonial capital finally ended on 21 April 1792. In a scene typical of executions during the *ancien régime*, Tiradentes was hanged as a leading character. Soldiers, speeches, and cheers for the queen were some of the scene's ingredients. Afterward, Tiradentes's body was cut to pieces. His severed head was displayed in the main square of Ouro Preto.

What were the inconfidentes after? The answer is not simple. It is largely derived from what the prisoners and witnesses had to say during the trial staged by the crown. For the prisoners this was literally a matter of life and death. It appears that the majority's intention was to declare Brazil a republic with a constitution modeled on that of the United States. The diamond mining region would be freed from the restrictions weighing on it. Debts to the crown would be forgiven. Incentives would be offered for setting up factories. There would be no permanent army. Instead, citizens would bear arms and serve in the national militia when necessary. The most interesting of their many proposals concerns slavery. Divided between ideological coherence and their own interests, the inconfidentes opted for a middle route. They apparently supported freeing all slaves born in Brazil.

The Inconfidência Mineira is an example of how historical occurrences of seemingly limited scope can have an impact on a country's history. As a material fact, the rebel movement did not get off the ground. Its likelihood of success was almost nil. As far as military success is concerned, the 1817 revolution was more important: it spread from Pernambuco over an extensive area of the Northeast. But the relevance of the Inconfidência comes from its symbolic force. Tiradentes became a national hero. The scenes of his death, the quartering of his body, and the displaying of his head have ended up being emotionally and horrifically evoked in Brazil's classrooms. This did not happen from one day to the next. It took a long time to form this myth, which has its own history. At first, while Brazil was still a colony, the colonists' version prevailed. The very expression "Inconfidência Mineira" demonstrates this. It was coined at the time, and tradition has maintained it up to the present. "Inconfidência" is a word with negative connotations, meaning "lack of fealty, the failure to do one's duty," especially to the sovereign or the state itself. During the empire, the episode made the elite uncomfortable, since the conspirators had little sympathy for the monarchical form of government. On top of this, the two emperors of Brazil were direct descendants of Queen Dona Maria I, who was responsible for the sentencing of the revolutionaries.

The proclamation of the Brazilian republic favored a change in status for the movement and a transformation of Tiradentes into a national martyr. And there was a real foundation for this. There are indications that the great spectacle the Portuguese crown staged to intimidate the colonial population had the opposite effect. It kept the memory of the event alive and made people sympathize with the inconfidentes. At a certain point in the trial Tiradentes assumed complete responsibility for the conspiracy. His final sacrifice facilitated his rise in stature to national hero right after the proclamation of the republic. The 21st of April became a national holiday. In every painting made of him, Tiradentes's face more and more resembled the most popular portraits of Christ. This man has thus become one of Brazil's few national heroes. He is celebrated as a martyr by the right, by the left, and by the common folk.

Brazil's independence was not to come from a revolutionary break with the motherland, but from a process which occasioned a few changes from and much continuity with the colonial period. The history of this process begins with the transfer of the Portuguese royal family to Brazil and the opening of Brazilian ports to foreign commerce, which put an end to the colonial system.

The war with Britain which Napoleon was waging in Europe in the beginning of the 19th century ultimately had an impact on the

Portuguese crown. Once Napoleon controlled almost all of western Europe, he imposed a commercial blockade between Britain and the continent. Portugal was an opening in the blockade that needed to be closed. In November 1807 French troops crossed into Portugal from Spain and marched toward Lisbon.

Prince Dom João VI had ruled the kingdom as regent since 1792, when his mother Dona Maria was declared insane. He very quickly opted to transfer the entire court to Brazil. Between 25 and 27 November 1807, some 10,000 to 15,000 people set sail for Brazil in Portuguese ships. They were escorted by a British fleet. The entire bureaucratic apparatus headed for the colony: ministers, counselors, Supreme Court justices, Treasury officials, army and navy officers, and members of the high clergy. They took with them the royal treasury, governmental archives, a printing press, and several libraries which would form the basis of the National Library in Rio de Janeiro.

Shortly after he arrived, and still during his brief stay in Salvador, on 28 January 1808 Dom João opened Brazil's ports to friendly nations. Even if one acknowledges that at that time "friendly nations" meant Great Britain, Dom João's decree put an end to a 300-year-old colonial system. In April 1808, having reached Rio de Janeiro, the prince regent revoked decrees that prohibited setting up factories in Brazil. He exempted from tariffs those raw materials imported for industrial purposes. He offered subsidies to the wool, silk, and iron industries. And he encouraged the invention and introduction of new machinery.

The opening of the ports was a historically predictable act, but was triggered by the circumstances at hand. Portugal had been taken over by French troops so no business could be done there. As far as the crown was concerned, it was preferable to legalize the already existing contraband between Britain and Brazil so the government could collect tariffs.

Great Britain was the chief beneficiary of this measure. Rio de Janeiro became the port of entry for British manufactured products – not only for Brazil, but also for the River Plate region and the Pacific coast of South America. By August 1808, there was a nucleus of between 150 and 200 British merchants and commercial agents in Rio. The opening of the ports also favored rural land-owners growing export crops, mainly sugar and cotton. This freed them from the metropolis's commercial monopoly. From then on, they would be able to sell to whomever they pleased, with no more restrictions imposed on them by the colonial system.

On the other hand, this measure sparked such great protests from merchants in Rio de Janeiro and Lisbon that Prince Dom João had to make some concessions to them. In a decree of June 1808, free trade was limited to the ports of Belém, São Luis, Recife, Salvador, and Rio de Janeiro. What was known as *cabotagem*, or trade among colonial ports, was reserved for Portuguese ships. The tariff on import goods, which had been set at 24 percent, was reduced to 16 percent for goods brought in on Portuguese ships. Only the last decision was of any real importance, but even it would be scuttled.

Britain's effort to control the Brazilian colonial market culminated in the Treaty of Navigation and Commerce, which was signed in 1810 after protracted negotiations. The Portuguese crown had little leeway because recovering the motherland depended on Britain and its winning the war against Napoleon. In addition, Portugal's colonies were being protected by the British navy. The 1810 treaty set the tariff on British merchandise exported to Brazil at 15 percent. This gave British products an advantage, even over those from Portugal. Even when a short time later both tariffs were made the same, Britain's advantage was immense. Without protective tariffs, products from Portugal could not compete, in price or in variety, with those from England. Portugal was by this time a backward country compared to those of capitalistic Europe. Dom João's measures favoring incipient industry became, with a few exceptions, dead letters.

One point in British policy would be a matter of concern for the dominant sectors of Brazil's colonial society. After having benefited greatly from the slave trade, England, beginning in the late 18th century, turned against slavery. In the Treaty of Alliance and Friendship, which was signed along with the Treaty of Navigation and Commerce in 1810, the Portuguese crown agreed to limit its slave trade to its own territories, and it promised, vaguely, to take measures to restrict its internal slave trade. A few years later, in 1815, when the victors of the Napoleonic wars gathered at the Congress of Vienna, the Portuguese government signed another treaty and agreed to cease all slave trade north of the equator. In principle, this treaty should have stopped the slave trade between the Mina Coast and Brazil. An additional clause in the treaty gave Britain the "right to board" ships suspected of transporting slaves on the high seas. They could apprehend any slave ships. None of these measures stopped the traffic, which, quite to the contrary, was greater during the 1820s than it had been at the turn of the century. But on the horizon one could see a dispute forming between the British and Brazilian governments. This dispute would become crucial once Brazil was independent.

The transfer of the seat of the Portuguese monarchy to Brazil changed the structure of international relations, at least as far as South America was concerned. Portugal's foreign policy was being decided in its colony once the Ministry of War and Foreign Affairs was set up in Rio de Janeiro. In addition to sending an expedition to French Guiana, which the British had requested, the crown focused its attention on the River Plate, specifically on the Banda Oriental – where Spaniards and Portuguese had clashed since the final decades of the 17th century.

With the objective of annexing Banda Oriental to Brazil, Dom João sent out two military expeditions, one in 1811 and another in 1816. Artigas, the main figure in the struggle for Uruguayan independence, was defeated. This guaranteed Portuguese possession of the region; in 1821, Banda Oriental was incorporated into Brazil. It was called the Cisplatine Province. However, conflicts in the River Plate region were far from over.

The arrival of the royal family was the final step in the transferal of the colony's administrative axis to Rio de Janeiro. It also changed the face of the city. Some of the changes included an incipient culture. Books became available and, relatively speaking, ideas began to circulate. In September 1808 the first colonial newspaper started publishing. Theaters and libraries also opened. Literary and scientific academies attended to the needs of the court and of a rapidly expanding urban population. During Dom João VI's stay in Brazil (1808–1821), Rio's population doubled, going from 50,000 to 100,000 people. Many of the new inhabitants were immigrants – and not just Portuguese, but also Spaniards, French, and

Britons who would become middle-class professionals and skilled artisans.

In addition, scientists and foreign travelers came to Brazil. Among them were John Mawe, an English naturalist and mineralogist; the Bavarian zoologist Johann Baptist von Spix; Karl Friedrich Philipp von Martius, a Bavarian botanist; and the French naturalist Étienne Geoffroy Saint-Hilaire. Their works are indispensable for understanding the early 19th century. In March 1816, a French artistic mission reached Rio de Janeiro. With it came the painters Félix Émily Taunay and Jean Baptiste Debret and the architect Grandjean de Montigny, who designed urban buildings. Taunay and Debret left behind sketches and watercolors depicting landscapes and customs in Rio de Janeiro.

After coming to Brazil, the Portuguese crown did not stop favoring Portuguese interests in Brazil. One of the principal focuses of discontent was in the army. Dom João brought troops from Portugal and garrisoned them in the main cities of Brazil. He organized the army and reserved the best posts for Portuguese noblemen. In addition, the tax burden increased since now the colony alone had to bear the court's expenses, as well as the expenditures for the military campaigns the king sent to the River Plate.

In addition, there was a problem of inequality among Brazil's regions. The reigning sentiment in the Northeast was that, with the royal family in Brazil, political control of the colony had gone from one foreign city to another; that is, from Lisbon to Rio de Janeiro. The revolutionary explosion in March 1817 in Pernambuco fused this sentiment with several other complaints arising from economic conditions and the privileges given to the Portuguese. The revolution included a wide cross section of the population: military men, rural landowners, judges, artisans, merchants, and a large number of priests – so many, in fact, that it became known as the "priests' revolution." Especially noteworthy was the participation of important Brazilian businessmen involved in foreign trade. They had begun to compete with the Portuguese in an area that up to then had been the latter's private domain.

Another important characteristic of the 1817 revolution was its scope. It began in Recife and spread to the backlands – into Ala-goas, Paraíba, and Rio Grande do Norte. The government's slighting of the entire region along with strong anti-Portuguese sentiment made up the common denominator of this generalized revolt in northeast Brazil. The different social groups did not have the same objectives, however. For the urban poor, independence was associated with the notion of equality. The main objective of the large rural landowners was to do away with the central government, which had been forced on them by the crown. They wanted to take matters into their own hands, at least as far as the Northeast was concerned.

The revolutionaries captured Recife and set up a provisional government based on an "organic law" which announced the founding of a republic and established equal rights and religious tolerance. It did not address the problem of slavery. In search of aid and recognition, emissaries were sent to other captaincies as well as to the United States, Britain, and Argentina. The revolt spread through the backlands, but the Portuguese forces soon attacked, blockading Recife and landing in Alagoas. Battles raged in the hinterland and revealed despair and disagreement among the revolutionaries. By May 1817 Portuguese troops had taken Recife. Then came the sentencing and execution of the movement's leaders. It had lasted over two months and would make a deep impression on the Northeast.

Around 1817 whoever might have said that within five years Brazil would be an independent country would be making a very dubious prediction. The Pernambucan revolution was confined to the Northeast and was defeated. The crown then took the initiative to try to make Portugal and Brazil integral parts of a single kingdom. The war in Europe had ended in 1814 with Napoleon's defeat. There seemed to be no more reasons for the court to stay in Brazil. However, Dom João decided to stay and in December 1815 raised Brazil to the status of a kingdom united with Portugal and the Algarves. A few months later, after the queen's death, the prince regent would become the king of Portugal, Brazil, and the Algarves. His title was Dom João VI.

Brazil's independence can be explained by a series of factors, both internal and external. But it was the wind from without that set the events on an unforeseen course as far as most of the participants were concerned. An effort that began as a means to defend Brazil's autonomy turned into a movement for independence.

In August 1820 a liberal revolution inspired by ideas from the Enlightenment broke out in Portugal. The revolutionaries sought to face head-on a moment of profound crisis in Portuguese life. It was a political crisis caused by the king's absence as well as the absence of the organs of government. It was an economic crisis due in part to free trade, which benefited Brazil. And it was a military crisis owing to the presence of British officers in high places in the army and the passing over of Portuguese officers for promotion. During Dom João's absence, Portugal was governed by a regency council run by the British Field Marshal Beresford. After the war, Beresford became commander of the Portuguese army.

The Portuguese revolution of 1820 had internal contradictions. It could be considered liberal because it regarded absolute monarchies as out of date and oppressive. It also tried to give some life to organs such as the Cortes which would represent society at large. At the same time, when it promoted the interests of the Portuguese bourgeoisie and tried to limit British influence, it was also trying to get Brazil to submit to the motherland once more.

At the end of 1820, the revolutionaries set up a provisional junta in Portugal and governed in the name of the king, while demanding his return. They decided to call a meeting of the Cortes, which would be elected throughout the Portuguese world, for the purpose of writing and approving a constitution. The revolutionaries planned to create loyal governing juntas in the different captaincies of Brazil, which would then be called provinces.

Unrest within the armed forces prompted the 1820 movement in Portugal. It was also within the Brazilian military, which included Portuguese officers and men, that the movement's first repercussions were felt. Troops rebelled in Belem and Salvador, giving rise to government juntas. In Rio de Janeiro civil and military protests forced the king to reform the ministry and create juntas where they did not exist. He was also forced to prepare for indirect elections to the Cortes.

At this juncture, dividing lines were drawn over the question of Dom João's return to Portugal. His return was urged in Rio de

Janeiro by the "Portuguese faction," made up of high-ranking military officers, bureaucrats, and businessmen interested in subordinating Brazil to Lisbon – if possible within the lines of the colonial system. The "Brazilian party" was opposed to his return for the opposite reasons. This group was made up of large rural landowners in the captaincies near Rio de Janeiro, as well as of Brazilian-born bureaucrats and members of the legal profession. They were joined by Portuguese whose interests had become linked to the colony's, by businessmen who had adjusted to free trade, and by investors in urban and rural real estate who were often linked by marriage to people in the colony. The "Brazilian party" is mentioned in quotes because it does not exactly refer to a party but to a segment of public opinion. Political declarations during this period were made through Masonic lodges, whose most radical members were in favor of independence.

The matter of Dom João VI's return was soon decided because he feared that he might lose his throne should he fail to come back. Along with 4,000 Portuguese, he set sail in April 1821. In his place he left behind as prince regent his son Pedro, who would become Dom Pedro I, emperor of Brazil. In the months after his departure, elections were held for the Brazilian representatives to the Cortes. Almost everyone elected had been born in Brazil. Among them there were several radical or once-radical defenders of Brazil's independence: Cipriano Barata of Bahia, Muniz Tavares of Pernambuco, and Antônio Carlos Ribeiro de Andrada of São Paulo. They had all taken part in the 1817 revolution.

The Cortes convened in January 1821, months before the arrival of the Brazilian delegates. It passed a series of measures that produced profound discontent in Brazil. Provincial governments were to be independent from Rio de Janeiro, but directly subordinate to Lisbon. There were attempts to revoke the trade agreements with Britain that favored the British as well as the wealthy rural landowners and urban consumers in Brazil. On top of this, the leaders of the liberal revolution in Portugal added fuel to the fire by making disdainful remarks about the colony. As far as many of them were concerned, Brazil was "a land of monkeys, bananas, and darkies plucked from the coast of Africa" and in need of a watchdog to keep it in line.

In 1821, around the end of September and during October, the Cortes took more measures that would buttress Brazil's option for independence, which up to then had been little more than a vague projection. The Cortes decided to bring back to Lisbon the more important government offices Dom João had set up in Brazil, and to send more troops to Rio de Janeiro and Pernambuco. The last straw was a measure requiring the prince regent to return to Portugal.

The Brazilian party put all its effort into getting Dom Pedro to stay in Brazil. The prince's decision to stay, solemnized on 9 January 1822, the *Dia do Fico*, "I Shall Stay Day," was a choice from which there was no turning back. The prince regent's acts after that day were acts of breaking away. The Portuguese troops who refused to swear their loyalty to Dom Pedro were obliged to leave Rio. From that point on, Brazil's army began to be built. Dom Pedro created a new ministry that was made up of Portuguese but headed by a Brazilian, José Bonifácio de Andrada e Silva.

The Andrada brothers – Antônio Carlos, Martim Francisco, and, especially, José Bonifácio – were central figures in Brazilian politics of the time. They came from one of the richest families in Santos, where their father had worked as a sugar exporter. José Bonifácio studied in Coimbra and lived in Europe from 1783 to 1819. He held several important administrative posts in Portugal and had been a professor at the University of Coimbra. Returning to Brazil, he was called to preside over the provisionary junta of São Paulo in March 1821. It is not an easy matter to apply a label to this man's thought. In the social realm, he espoused progressive ideas such as the gradual extinction of the slave trade and of slavery. He also supported agrarian reform and the free entry of immigrants. Politically, he was a liberal conservative and an adversary of the "ragged banners of filthy and chaotic democracy," as he once put it. He believed that a monarchical form of government was right for Brazil if supported by citizen representatives drawn from the dominant and enlightened classes.

As the events which culminated in Brazil's independence unfolded, the conservative and radical wings of the Brazilian party became clearly defined. During the years immediately before independence, the conservative wing had supported greater Brazilian autonomy from Portugal. Only later did it embrace the idea of independence. According to the conservatives, a constitutional monarchy with limited representation would be the desirable form of government and would guarantee order and social stability. It is harder to define the radical wing because it included monarchists who wanted greater popular representation and greater freedom, especially freedom of the press. It also included the so-called extremists, for whom independence was linked to the idea of a republic, popular suffrage, and, in some cases, social reform.

Once the agreement to call a constitutional convention had been made, steps toward breaking away accelerated. One had to swear to support the union and Brazil's independence to enter the civil service. The provincial governments were told not to accept employees sent from Portugal. In August 1822, the prince regent declared that troops coming from Portugal should be considered enemies. Gonçalves Ledo and José Bonifácio sent manifestoes to friendly nations.

The arrival from Lisbon of dispatches which revoked the prince regent's decrees, which called once more for his return to Portugal, and which accused Brazilian ministers of treason, strengthened the idea of a definitive break. Princess Dona Leopoldina and José Bonifácio quickly forwarded the news to the prince, who was on his way to São Paulo. The news caught up with him on 7 September 1822. He was near the banks of Ipiranga Brook. There Dom Pedro delivered the so-called cry of Ipiranga: *"Independência ou morte!"* ("Independence or Death!"), which formalized Brazil's independence. On 1 December, at the age of only 24, the prince regent was crowned emperor and received the title of Dom Pedro I. Brazil had become independent, but with the monarchical form of government maintained. Beyond this, the new country would have a Portuguese king on its throne.

1.11   BRAZIL AT THE END OF THE COLONIAL PERIOD

From a territorial and demographic point of view, what was this newly independent Brazil?

Since the beginning of the 18th century, Brazil's borders had nothing to do with the blurry Line of Tordesillas. The spread of São Paulo's bandeira expeditions westward and that of the cattle

Map 2 Brazil before and after the Treaty of Madrid, 1750. Reprinted with permission from *The Cambridge History of Latin America*, ed. Leslie Bethell, vol. 1 (Cambridge: Cambridge University Press, © 1984).

ranchers and the armed forces in a southwesterly direction extended the country's frontiers. The mining expeditions beginning in the 18th century produced another westward movement. Brazil's territorial appearance was, in fact, quite similar to its present shape.

The new borders still had to be legally recognized, and this was a matter to be taken up mainly with Spain. In the Treaty of Madrid, which was signed by both the Spanish and the Portuguese crowns, the principle of *uti possidetis* was accepted, to the benefit of the Portuguese. There was one exception pertaining to the southern boundaries. Portugal gave up Sacramento Colony on the banks of the River Plate, next to Montevideo, in what today is Uruguay. In exchange, it received some land on the left bank of the Uruguai River. This area, called the Seven Missions Territory, had been occupied by Indians and Jesuits.

In spite of the agreement, controversies concerning the southern boundaries did not cease. A 1761 agreement annulled the Treaty of Madrid. Afterward, the Treaty of São Ildefonso in 1777 gave the Seven Missions region back to Spain. The Portuguese held onto their claims to Sacramento Colony because it was a strategic base for smuggling out silver, which was brought down from Bolivia and Peru on the Paraná River.

In spite of the well-defined borders, vast regions of Brazil were for all intents and purposes unknown or occupied only by Indians who still had no contact with the colonists. There are no reliable figures for Brazil's population at the end of the colonial period. The censuses ordered by the crown often excluded children under the age of seven, as well as Indians and sometimes even slaves. It is believed that in 1819 there were some 3,600,000 people living in Brazil – mainly in the provinces of Minas Gerais, Rio de Janeiro, Bahia, and Pernambuco. Southern Brazil was still peripheral.

This was, in general, how Brazil looked at the end of the colonial period, as far as its territory and population were concerned. Its inhabitants no longer crawled along the coast like crabs, but 74 percent of them still lived around the main ports of export and in the rural parts of the coastal captaincies: Rio de Janeiro, Bahia, Pernambuco, and Paraíba.

2

Imperial Brazil (1822–1889)

2.1 CONSOLIDATING INDEPENDENCE AND BUILDING THE STATE

Independence was consolidated in a few years. Portuguese troops resisted in the Cisplatine Province, but they left it in November 1823. At that point, a long war for Uruguayan independence began, but now it was a war against Brazil rather than against Portugal. Another center of confrontation was Bahia, where Brazilians finally defeated the Portuguese.

Internationally, the United States recognized Brazil's independence in May 1824. It had been informally recognized by Britain, which wanted order maintained in the old Portuguese colony. Thus Britain preserved its commercial advantage in a country which, at that time, was its third largest foreign market. Formal recognition was delayed because the British tried to get Brazil to put an immediate end to its slave trade. Still, directly or indirectly, the British were present during the consolidating phase. They were also intermediaries in Portugal's recognition of the new nation.

That occurred in August 1825, in a treaty whereby Brazil agreed to pay Portugal 2,000,000 British pounds sterling for the loss of its old colony. It also agreed not to unite with any other Portuguese colony. The need to compensate the Portuguese crown occasioned Brazil's first foreign loan, which it took out in London. The second clause, which might seem strange, can be explained by the fact that

Brazilian interests linked to the slave trade were strongly ensconced at different places along the coast of Africa. When news of Brazil's separation reached Angola, pamphlets printed in Brazil appeared inviting Benguela to join the "Brazilian cause." Portugal's worry was, it seems, not baseless.

It is traditional in Brazilian historiography to contrast the relative ease with which Brazil became independent with the complicated process of emancipation in Spanish America. In addition, people point out that while Brazil remained united, Spanish America broke up into many different nations. Both observations are interrelated. They will be treated separately here since the way in which Brazil maintained her territorial unity will be clearer once the events between 1822 and 1840 are analyzed.

One should ask right at the beginning if this traditional interpretation can still be sustained. There is no dearth of objections to it. Its critics point out that independence, in the form of a union centered in Rio de Janeiro, was the result of a struggle and not of a general consensus. In that struggle, both the movements for local autonomy and those favoring a continued union with Portugal, as the one in Pará did, were defeated.

These objections have the merit of pointing out that Brazilian independence was not the result of a peaceful transition. But at the same time they do not invalidate the fact that, notwithstanding the use of force and the consequent deaths, independence was consolidated in a few years and without wreaking havoc on the nation. Indeed, Brazil's emancipation did not produce great alterations in the social and economic order of the time, or in the form of government. As a unique entity in Latin America, Brazil became a monarchy among republics.

One of the main reasons for this relative continuity between the two periods is the royal family's presence in Brazil. Another is how the process of independence was carried out. Dom João VI's opening of the ports made a bridge between the Portuguese crown and the dominant sectors of the colony – especially those living in Rio de Janeiro, São Paulo, and Minas Gerais. The benefits brought to the area around Rio de Janeiro, owing to the king's presence, created incentives for economic expansion in that area, linked as it was to the sugar and coffee business – as well as to slave trade.

Of course, there still remained much discontent with the court in Rio, but it was nothing compared to the dissatisfaction in some regions of the Northeast, where ideas of a republic first appeared. The political elite behind the independence movement had no interest in furthering breaks that might threaten the old colonial ways as they knew them. One must also remember that movements for autonomy, which became a movement for independence, targeted the king and later the prince regent. In the first years after independence, the monarchy was to become a symbol of authority, even during those times when the emperor himself was challenged.

In the international sphere, Britain guaranteed and accelerated the recognition of Brazil's independence by other European countries. Brazil imposed no restrictions on British commerce. It established a direct, dependent relationship with the British financial world, and, in contrast to "the fractious republican tendencies" of the rest of the continent, it adopted a monarchical regime.

The claim that independence was achieved in a short time and without great setbacks should not lead one to draw the wrong conclusions. One of these erroneous conclusions would be that nothing had changed, since Brazil had gone from being indirectly dependent on Britain, through Portugal, to being directly dependent. Another would be to take for granted the existence of a homogeneous political elite with a solid social foundation and a clear set of aims for the new nation.

There are several reasons why the first conclusion would be wrong. The new, dependent relationship which had been growing stronger and stronger since 1808, when the ports were opened, was more than just a mere change in names. It signified a change in how the ex-colony would fit into the international economic system. In addition, independence required Brazilians to build a nation, organize the country, and keep it united.

The second conclusion would be equally incorrect because even within the nucleus of people who were in favor of independence, with José Bonifácio at their helm, there was no agreement on the basic structures on which the state was to be organized. Indeed, the years between 1822 and 1840 would be marked by enormous political fluctuation, by a series of rebellions, and by contradictory attempts at consolidating power.

The central political debate of the first two years after the country's independence dealt with devising a constitution. Elections for a constituent assembly had been foreseen months before independence. They were held after the 7th of September, and the constituent assembly began to meet in Rio de Janeiro, in May 1823. Discord immediately arose between the assembly and Dom Pedro, who was at first supported by his minister, José Bonifácio. Their discord centered on which powers to bestow on the executive branch (in this case the emperor) and which to give the legislative branch.

The assemblymen did not want the emperor to have the power to dissolve the Chamber of Deputies and, by this measure, to be able to call new elections whenever he thought them necessary. They also did not want him to have the power of absolute veto, that is, the right to deny the validity of whatever law the legislature might approve. As far as the emperor and his supporters were concerned, they needed a strong executive who could face down "democratic and fractious" tendencies. This is how they justified giving the emperor greater powers. It was a time of political uncertainty. Less than one year after independence, in July 1823, José Bonifácio was removed from his post as minister. He had been squeezed out by critical liberals and dissatisfied conservatives. They did not look kindly on that minister, who blocked their direct access to the throne.

The dispute over power brought about Dom Pedro's dissolution (with support from the military) of the constituent assembly. Several deputies, including the Andrada brothers, were jailed. Immediately thereafter, a constitutional project was undertaken which produced the constitution ratified on 25 March 1824. It was not much different from the one the previous constituent assembly had proposed before its dissolution. But one difference must be pointed out. The first Brazilian constitution came from the top and was imposed on the "folk" by the king. However, one should understand "folk" to mean the minority of whites and mixed-bloods who voted and who in some fashion participated in political activities.

Slaves, a significant contingent of the population, were excluded from all constitutional guarantees. They were not even considered, except by implication, when freedmen were discussed. Also, there was a considerable gap between principle and practice. The constitution represented progress by organizing jurisdictions (branches of government), allocating powers, and guaranteeing individual rights. Problematically, however, especially as far as individual rights were concerned, the constitution would be applied in a relative manner. Individual rights were overshadowed by reality: Brazil was still a country where the great bulk of the free population depended on the large rural landowners. Among them only a small minority had any schooling, and they had been brought up in an authoritarian tradition.

The 1824 constitution, with a few modifications, remained in effect until the end of the empire. It defined the political system as monarchical, hereditary, and constitutional. The empire would have a nobility without an aristocracy. That is, there would be nobles thanks to titles the emperor might confer on people, but these titles would not be passed on, so as not to give rise to a "blood aristocracy." The Roman Catholic church continued to be the official religion. Other religions could only be practiced privately.

The legislative branch consisted of a Chamber of Deputies and a Senate. Both houses would be elected, albeit with basic differences. Election to the Chamber was temporary whereas election to the Senate was for life. On top of this, the electoral process for the Senate required three candidates to be elected from each province, and the emperor would then chose which of them would actually serve. In practice this meant that the Senate was made up of the emperor's lifelong appointees.

Voting was indirect and restricted. It was indirect because voters, corresponding to today's electoral masses, in what were considered primary elections, voted for an electoral body or college. The electoral college then elected the deputies. The vote was restricted because voters in primary elections were those Brazilian citizens whose yearly income in rents, industry, commerce, or salary was at least 100 milreis. They voted for the electoral college, that is, the electors. These people, in addition to the above requirements, had to have an annual income of 200 milreis. And they could not be ex-slaves. To be a deputy, among other requirements, one had to have 400 milreis of annual income and be a Catholic. There was no explicit reference to women, but they were excluded from political rights by the mores of the time. Curiously, up to 1882, a large number of illiterates were allowed to vote, since the constitution had nothing to say about their right as voters.

The country was divided into provinces whose presidents would be named by the emperor. Individual rights were guaranteed. Brazilians had the right to equal treatment before the law, religious freedom (with the aforementioned restrictions), freedom of thought, and freedom of assembly, among others.

An important organ in the governmental structure was the Council of State (Conselho de Estado). It was made of counselors who were appointed for life by the emperor. They had to be Brazilian citizens and at least 40 years old (which was old for the time). Their income could not be less than 800 milreis per annum, and they needed to be "people of knowledge, ability, and virtue." The Council of State was to be heard in "grave matters and in general measures pertaining to public administration." These included declarations of war, pay adjustments, and dealings in which the emperor intended to exercise his moderating power.

The notion of instituting moderating power is owed to the French writer Benjamin Constant, whose books were read by Dom Pedro and by many contemporary politicians. Constant defended a separation between executive power and what could rightly be called imperial power. Executive power would be exercised by the king's ministers, whereas imperial power was held to be neutral or moderating. The king would not intervene in politics and day-to-day administration, but he would have the right to moderate more serious and overarching disputes, where he would determine what "the nation's will and interests" were.

In Brazil, moderating power was not clearly distinguished from executive power, and this lack of distinction concentrated power in the emperor. Thanks to the constitutional principles behind moderating power, the emperor was considered to be an inviolable and sacred individual who was not beholden in any way. It was his prerogative, among others, to appoint senators, to dissolve the Chamber of Deputies, and to call elections for new deputies. He had the right to approve or veto decisions coming from the Chamber of Deputies or from the Senate.

The emperor's dissolving the constituent assembly and passing a constitution of his own were marks of his supremacy, as well as that

of the bureaucrats and merchants who made up his inner circle –
most of whom were Portuguese. In Pernambuco these acts added
fuel to the fire that had been burning even before 1817.

There was new impetus to propagate republican, anti-Portuguese,
and federative ideas in that restless province. Friar Joaquim do
Amor Divino stood out as a central figure in criticizing the empire.
His nickname, Frei Caneca (Friar Mug), came from his humble
origins; as a boy he sold mugs on the streets of Recife. He was
educated in a seminary in Olinda, itself a focus of liberal ideas.
He became a learned intellectual and a man of action. The distress
caused by the appointment of an undesirable governor for Pernambuco set the stage for the revolt. Its ostensible leader, Manuel de
Carvalho, announced the formation of the Equatorial Confederation (Confederação do Equador) on 2 July 1824. Carvalho was a
curious figure. He had married an American woman and was a
great admirer of the United States. On the day the constitution was
delivered, in 1824, that is, before the rebellion, Carvalho had sent
official correspondence to the American secretary of state. He had
asked that a small squadron be sent to Recife as a check against
the threats to freedom posed by the presence of British and French
battleships. In his letter, he invoked President Monroe's recently
articulated doctrine against foreign intervention in the Americas.

In addition to Pernambuco, the Equatorial Confederation was
intended eventually to include the provinces of Paraíba, Rio Grande
do Norte, Ceará, and possibly Piauí and Pará in a federal republic.
This uprising was notably urban and popular in content – in contrast with the 1817 revolution, whose wide front was led by rural
landowners and a few businessmen. The English traveler Maria
Graham was in Recife trying to reach an accord between the con-
tending parties. Keeping things in proportion, she likened the atmosphere in the governmental palace (occupied by the rebels) to that
of the National Convention of the French Revolution. She claimed
the lower posts in the palace were occupied by common folk, real
sans culottes whose eyes were peeled and ears were pricked in anti-
cipation of traps and betrayals.

The Equatorial Confederation did not have the means to take root
and defeat governmental forces on the battlefield. It was defeated
in different provinces of the Northeast and came to an end in

November 1824. The revolutionaries were punished beyond all expectations. A court under the influence of the emperor sentenced Frei Caneca and other revolutionaries to death. On the gallows, Frei Caneca was shot because the hangman refused to carry out the sentence.

The revolution's basic traits would not disappear easily. In fact they can be seen as having contributed to a series of rebellions and revolts carried out in Pernambuco between 1817 and 1848, which made the province a center for spreading dissatisfaction throughout the Northeast.

The recently created Brazilian empire inherited the problems generated by Portugal's occupying Banda Oriental. In 1825 a rebellion in that region declared its independence from Brazil. The rebels incorporated what would someday be Uruguay into the United Provinces of the River Plate. This caused war to break out between Brazil and Argentina in December 1825.

The war was a military disaster for Brazilians, who were defeated at Ituzaingó in 1827. It was a financial catastrophe for both nations. Peace was achieved by mediation from Britain, which sought to reestablish the normal commercial relations the conflict had annihilated. The peace treaty ending the conflict guaranteed the emergence of Uruguay as an independent nation, and it guaranteed open navigation on the River Plate and its tributaries. The latter point was of interest to Brazil and to European powers, especially Britain. In Brazil's case, geopolitical motives were mixed with economic ones because rivers were the chief means of reaching the western province of Mato Grosso.

Within Brazil this war occasioned an unpopular and feared military conscription which was carried out by force. The emperor also contracted foreign troops to fill the army's ranks. In the main, these troops were poor men who bore no resemblence to professional soldiers. They were recruited in Europe and enticed by the prospect of becoming small landowners in Brazil. As one would expect, they contributed nothing toward swinging the war in Brazil's favor. On top of this, a few hundred disillusioned German and Irish mercenaries rebelled in Rio de Janeiro in July 1828. The situation became dangerous, and the government found itself in the humiliating position of seeking protection from some British and French ships.

Military expenditures made the already existing economic and financial problems worse. While some products such as coffee were exported in much greater volume during the 1820s, the prices of cotton, leather, cacao, tobacco, and even coffee were on the decline. Government income, which was largely dependent on import tariffs, was insufficient. In August 1827, Britain imposed a commercial treaty on Brazil, which kept the tariff on its products at 15 percent. This tariff was later extended to other nations' products.

The Bank of Brazil, which Dom João VI had founded in 1808, encountered difficulties beginning in 1821, when the king left for Portugal taking the gold he had deposited there. The bank was closed in 1829. Dom Pedro had a large quantity of copper coins minted, and these were copied by counterfeiters. The cost of living soared, especially in urban centers. The term "inflation" was not yet current, but people spoke of something similar and called it *inchação* or "swelling" of the means of exchange.

Even paper money issued by the Bank of Brazil and by the Treasury was poorly received outside Rio de Janeiro. In 1829, in São Paulo, paper money was accepted at 57 percent of its official value. On the other hand, all through the 1820s, the value of Brazilian money fell in relation to the British pound. This favored exports, but at the same time it increased the price of those imported consumer goods so in demand among the elite and the incipient urban middle classes.

Discontent exacerbated the friction between Brazilians and Portuguese. The Portuguese, who controlled the bulk of the retail market, became a favorite target of the natives. The political struggle was derived from but also transcended their different nationalities. During Dom Pedro's time, the political elite was divided into liberals and absolutists. Absolutists defended order and property, which, according to them, would be vouchsafed by a strong and respected emperor. They feared that "excessive freedom" would put their privileges at risk, and in the name of order they accepted unlawful imperial acts. Like the absolutists, liberals lined up in defense of order and property, but order and property were to be guaranteed by the constitution. They were in favor of "novelties," especially the great novelty of being able to oppose the government and the monarch himself.

Many members of the Brazilian elite sided with Dom Pedro because they were wary of liberalism, or because they had positions in the government and had received honorary titles generously conceded by the emperor. However, as events unfolded, more and more Brazilians joined the ranks of the liberal critics, while the Portuguese closed ranks around the emperor. Among the urban population and in the army, anti-Portuguese sentiment had a strong mobilizing force. People suspected that Dom Pedro might try to return to the time of the United Kingdoms, especially because once Dom João had died, in 1826, there was a possibility that Dom Pedro, as the oldest son, could succeed to the Portuguese throne.

The army began to distance itself from the emperor. Its recruits came from the poorest sectors of the urban centers. Soldiers were mainly mulattos who suffered from the wretched garrison life, from delays in pay, and from the discipline that was imposed on them. The officer corps was unhappy with its military defeats and with the presence of Portuguese officers in command posts.

Beginning in the middle of 1830 things snowballed. The fall of Charles X in France and the beginning of the July Monarchy, which was considered liberal, had repercussions in Brazil. They were even debated in the Council of State. In March 1831, political heat was on in Rio de Janeiro. The emperor was on his way back from Minas Gerais, where he had been received with supreme indifference. Under the auspices of the secret society known as the Coluna do Trono (Throne's Column), the Portuguese decided to meet him with a party and show their support. Brazilians reacted. For the next five days Rio was in a tumult. There were attempts at forming a new ministry and there were more protest demonstrations. Brazilian military commanders of the highest prestige, such as the Lima e Silva brothers, one of whom was the future Duke of Caxias's father, joined the revolt. In the end, on 7 April 1831, Dom Pedro was forced to abdicate in favor of his son, Dom Pedro II.

Brazilians could look forward to crowning a king born in their own country, but a decade would go by before this would come to pass. Young Pedro was only five years old when his father abdicated the throne and left for England with dreams of recovering another throne, that of Portugal, which was occupied by his brother, Dom Miguel.

The period after Dom Pedro Fs abdication is known as the Regency, because during that time Brazil was run by politicians acting in the emperor's name until his premature coming of age in 1840. In the beginning there were three regents, but by 1834 only one was in control.

The Regency was one of the times of greatest unrest in Brazil's political history. During those years, the country's territorial unity was at risk. Matters such as centralization or decentralization of power, the degree of autonomy provinces would enjoy, and the organization of the armed forces assumed center stage in political debate. The reforms enacted by the regents are also a good example of the difficulties they experienced in devising a liberal modus operandi that avoided the evils of absolutism. Because of the nature of Brazil's society and culture at the time, many measures aimed at making the political system more flexible and at guaranteeing individual rights ended up creating violent clashes among the elites. Often the interest of local cliques won out over the central government. Not everything was resolved during the Regency. Indeed, only around 1850 would the centralized monarchy be consolidated after the final provincial rebellions were quelled.

One important point worthy of emphasis in order to understand the difficulties of this period is that among the dominant classes, there was no consensus over what institutional arrangement served their interests best. Even more, it was not clear what the state's role should be in organizing the dominant, overall interests, since to do this it would sometimes have to sacrifice the specific interests of some sector of society.

The political tendency that prevailed after 7 April was that of the moderate liberals who were organized, according to Masonic tradition, into the "Society for Defense of Liberty and National Independence." In their midst was a high proportion of politicians from Minas Gerais, São Paulo, and Rio de Janeiro. There was also a significant number of priests and graduates from the University of Coimbra. Many were landowners and slave holders. Names that stood out among them were: Bernardo Pereira de Vasconcelos, a Mineiro judge who had studied in Coimbra; Father Diogo Feijó, a Paulista and future regent; and Evaristo da Veiga, in charge of Rio de Janeiro's *Aurora Fluminense*, the most important liberal newspaper of its time.

The opposition had two factions: the "Exalteds" and the "Absolutists." The Exalteds were in favor of federalism, individual freedom, and in some cases the republic. The Absolutists were known as Caramurus. Many of them were Portuguese who had important posts in the bureaucracy, in the army, and in business. They wanted Dom Pedro I back on the throne. Their dreams of his restoration were short-lived, as Dom Pedro I died in Portugal in 1834.

The reforms of the Regency period were aimed at eliminating or diminishing the power of monarchical governmental organs and at creating a different type of military organization where the army's role would be minimal.

In 1832, the Criminal Justice Code went into effect and established norms for the application of the Criminal Code of 1830. The Criminal Justice Code gave greater power to justices of the peace. These locally elected justices existed during Dom Pedro I's reign. Now they had the power to arrest and try people accused of minor infractions. At the same time, the Code, following the American and English models, created the jury system for judging the great majority of criminals. It also established the right of habeas corpus for people who had been illegally jailed or for those whose freedom was in danger.

A law passed in August 1834 is known as the Additional Act because it added to and altered the 1824 constitution. This law prohibited the use of moderating power during the Regency. It also eliminated the Council of State. Provincial presidents were still appointed by the central government, but provincial assemblies with greater powers were created to replace the old General Councils (Conselhos Gerais).

It contained additional legislation concerning the division of income among the central government, provinces, and municipalities. Provincial assemblies could determine municipal and provincial expenditures. They could collect the taxes necessary for these expenditures provided they did not interfere with the central government's tax collection. This vague formula for splitting taxes allowed the provinces to obtain their own resources, and it weakened the central government. One of the most important powers given to provincial assemblies was to appoint and remove public servants. This put a mighty weapon into the hands of local politicians.

They could both get votes in exchange for favors and harass their enemies.

When the Regency began, the army was a poorly organized institution which the government distrusted. Even after Dom Pedro's abdication, the number of Portuguese officers in the army was high. The biggest worry, however, concerned the men at the bottom. They were poorly paid, unhappy, and given to joining the local populace in urban rebellions.

A law of August 1831 created the National Guard to replace the old militias. This law was a copy of a French law passed the same year. Its intent was to create an armed corps of trustworthy citizens. On the one hand, these citizens would counter the excesses of a centralized government; on the other they would stand guard against threats from the "dangerous classes." In practice, this new institution was charged with maintaining order in specific municipalities. In special cases, it was called out to put down rebellions outside their municipalities and to protect the country's borders. In these cases it was under the army's command.

All male citizens between the ages of 21 and 60 who could vote in primary elections were obliged, as a general rule, to join the National Guard. Obligatory enlistment in the National Guard devastated the ranks of the army because membership in the National Guard exempted people from the military draft. Until 1850, the lower officers in the National Guard were chosen by its members in elections presided over by a justice of the peace. National reality and the need to establish a hierarchy overrode the elective principle, and National Guard elections were a dead letter even before the law was changed.

Revolts during the Regency do not fit into a single framework. They were related to the difficulties of daily life and to the state of flux in the organization of the government. But each rebellion was the result of specific conditions in the provinces or in specific localities. Many rebellions, especially those in the middle 1830s, took place in the most important capitals. Their protagonists were soldiers and the common folk. In Rio de Janeiro, there were five uprisings in 1831. In 1832 the situation had gotten so bad that the Council of State was consulted concerning what measures should be taken to save the young emperor in the event the city were overtaken by anarchy and the northern provinces were to declare their independence from the South.

In contrast with these uprisings, the Cabanos War (1832–1835) broke out in Pernambuco. This was an essentially rural movement which in content was also different from the other Pernambucan insurrections. The Cabanos were small landowners, rural workers, Indians, and slaves – as well as a few plantation owners at the beginning. In several ways these rebels foreshadowed the backland rebellion at Canudos during the early years of the republic. The Cabanos fought on behalf of religion and for the emperor's return, as well as against what their leaders called the Jacobite Carbonari – a reference to French revolutionaries and members of Europe's 19th-century liberal secret societies.

In this manner, people from the poor strata of the rural population expressed their complaints against far-off changes they did not understand. Given the specific objectives of this revolt, the Cabanos had counted on unprecedented help from Portuguese businessmen in Recife and from Rio de Janeiro's politicians favoring Dom Pedro I's return.

At the end of a guerrilla war, the rebels were finally defeated. Their victors were led, ironically, by Manuel Carvalho Pais de Andrade, the same person who in 1824 had announced the Equatorial Confederation and who now was the president of Pernambuco.

After the Additional Act, the Cabanagem War broke out in Pará in 1835 and lasted until 1840. This conflict should not be confused with the Cabanos War in Pernambuco. Also worthy of mention are the Sabinada Revolt in Bahia (1837–1838), the Balaiada in Maranhão (1838–1840), and the War of the Farrapos in Rio Grande do Sul (1836–1845).

Knowing that many of the old provincial complaints were directed at the central monarchy, it might seem strange that so many rebellions occurred during the Regency, which, after all, attempted to give some autonomy to provincial assemblies and to organize a division of funds between the central government and the provinces. It happened, however, that by moving in this direction, the regents ended up fueling local disputes among regional elites vying for control of their provinces now that provinces were more important. On top of this, the government had lost the aura of legitimacy it had had when, for better or worse, the emperor was on the throne. The last straw was the naming of the wrong man as provincial president.

The Cabanagem War shook Pará, already a region with tenuous ties to Rio de Janeiro. Its social structure was not as stable as other provinces', nor did it have a well-established class of rural landowners. Pará was a world of Indians, mixed-bloods, dependent or slave workers, and a white minority made up of Portuguese businessmen as well as a few Englishmen and Frenchmen. This minority was concentrated in Belém, at that time a small town with some 12,000 inhabitants. The province's modest exports of tobacco, cacao, rubber, and rice left from that settlement.

A dispute among various members of the local elite over the appointment of the provincial president opened the way to a popular rebellion. Pará proclaimed its independence. A force made up mainly of blacks, mixed-bloods, and Indians attacked Belém and conquered the city after several days of fierce battle. After that, the revolt spread into the countryside. While the fight was on, Eduardo Angelim stood out among the rebel leaders. He was only 21 years old and had migrated to Pará from Ceará in 1827, after a great drought. Angelim tried to set up a government. He appointed a priest as his secretary since he was one of the few people in the revolt who could write with any fluency.

The Cabanos never got around to providing an alternative government for Pará. Instead they concentrated on attacking foreigners and Masons while defending the Catholic church, Brazilians, Dom Pedro II, Pará, and liberty. Even though there were many slaves among them, they did not abolish slavery. Angelim even put down one slave insurrection.

After a blockade of the mouth of the Amazon River and a series of extended and devastating battles, the rebellion was vanquished by loyalist troops. Belém was almost entirely destroyed, and its economy was crushed. Deaths on both sides are believed to have totaled 30,000, which is tantamount to 20 percent of Pará's population at that time.

The Sabinada gets its name from its principal leader, Sabino Barroso, a newspaperman and professor in Bahia's medical school. Since independence, Bahia had been the scene of several urban revolts, including slave revolts or revolts in which slaves took part. The Sabinada gathered wide support, which included Salvador's middle and merchant classes. It espoused federalist and republican ideas.

By dividing slaves into native- and foreign-born, the movement sought to compromise on that matter. Native-born slaves who took part in the rebellion would be manumitted. The rest would remain slaves. The "Sabines" were not able to enter the Recôncavo because there the planters supported the government. After besieging Salvador by land and by sea, government forces took the city in hand-to-hand combat which left nearly 1,800 people dead.

The Balaiada in Maranhão began with a series of disputes among rival groups of the local elite and became a popular uprising. Its action occurred mainly in the southern part of the province near the border with Piauí. This was an area of small cotton farmers and cattle ranchers. One of the movement's leaders was a cafuso, a mixture of black and Indian, named Raimundo Gomes. Gomes was involved in local politics. Another was Francisco dos Anjos Ferreira, whose profession of basket making gave the rebellion its name (*balaio* means "basket"). Ferreira joined the rebellion to avenge his daughter, who had been raped by a police captain. In addition, a black leader known in all the historical accounts only as Cosme commanded 3,000 runaway slaves.

The rebels were able to occupy Caxias, the second largest city of the province. From the few written proclamations of this rebellion, people have found declarations supporting the Catholic church, the constitution, Dom Pedro II, and "the holy cause of freedom." Matters of a social or economic nature cannot be found, but it is hard to imagine that Cosme and his men were not fighting for the personal cause of freedom, be it holy freedom or whatever.

The Balaios' diverse orientations led to dissension among them. Conversely, government troops acted quickly and efficiently. The rebels were defeated halfway through 1840. Their defeat was followed by an amnesty contingent on rebel slaves' being returned to their masters. Cosme was hanged in 1842. At the head of the imperial troops was an officer by the name of Luiz Alves de Lima e Silva. During the Second Empire, he would be a constant figure in many political confrontations and battles. He became the Duke of Caxias.

In 1835, thousands of miles from the North and from the Northeast, the War of the Farrapos or Farroupilhas broke out in Rio Grande do Sul. The words *farrapos* and *farroupilhas* are synonyms meaning "poorly dressed, ragged people." The Farrapos of Rio Grande do Sul got their scornful moniker from their adversaries. But even if the foot soldiers dressed in rags, their leaders did not, because they were part of the cattle-raising elite from that southern province.

Ever since colonial times, Rio Grande do Sul has been a special case within Brazil. Owing to its location, its economic makeup, and its social ties, its inhabitants, known as Gaúchos, were closely linked to the area around the River Plate, especially to Uruguay. The leaders, the war lords or *caudilhos* of military groups along the border, were also cattle ranchers who had extensive intercourse with Uruguay. They owned land there and were linked by marriage to many of Uruguay's elite families.

On the other hand, Rio Grande do Sul's economy, as far as its products were concerned, was traditionally linked to the internal market. Mule raising was important because before the railways mules were used to transport merchandise throughout the south central section of Brazil. During the agricultural renaissance of the late 18th century, colonists came from the Azores. They planted wheat, which was consumed mainly in Brazil. When Brazil became independent, wheat farming also came to an end owing to blights and to competition from American wheat.

Cattle raising spread over the land, and meat was dried and made into jerky. Jerky was all-important. It was eaten by poor folk and by slaves in the South and Center-South. Cattle ranchers and jerky makers were two different groups. The ranchers were situated in the Campanha region, near the border with Uruguay. The jerky makers had their industry set up along the coastal lagoons, near cities such as Rio Grande and Pelotas. Both ranchers and jerky makers employed slave laborers as well as dependent workers.

Rio Grande had had long-standing complaints with the central government. Gaúchos felt that despite their province's contributions to Brazil's economy, they were being exploited by a system of heavy taxes. Their demands for autonomy and even separation were long-standing and often caused liberals and conservatives to join forces.

The Regency and the Additional Act did not mollify Gaúchos' complaints. Those provinces that could not meet all their expenses were subsidized by the central government, and this meant those provinces received money from wealthier ones. This was the case before and after the Additional Act. Rio Grande do Sul continually sent money to cover the expenses of Santa Catarina and other provinces.

Still, the revolt did not bring all sectors of Rio Grande do Sul together. It was begun by ranchers along the border and by some members of the urban middle class, and these were its two main sources of support. The jerky makers were dependent on Rio de Janeiro, which was the largest Brazilian consumer of jerky and leather. They sided with the central government.

Besides the general complaints pointed out above, ranchers had their own reasons for being upset. They wanted to do away with or at least to reduce taxes on the cattle raised on the border with Uruguay. They wanted the cattle raised on either side to traverse the border freely. On top of this, since they were already set up militarily with their small private armies subservient to absolute leaders, ranchers considered the founding of the National Guard to be a dangerous novelty, especially since its officers were elected.

The rebels counted on the cooperation of some army officers who had recently arrived in Rio Grande do Sul. In their ranks at least two dozen Italian refugees exiled in Brazil stood out. The most famous of them was Giuseppe Garibaldi. The movement's most important figure was Bento Gonçalves, the son of a wealthy rancher. Gonçalves had plenty of experience in wars of the region. He organized Masonic lodges along the border and used the Masons' postal service for his secret correspondence.

This was a long struggle based on cavalry movements. Garibaldi and Davi Canabarro carried the war to the northern part of the province and for a while occupied Santa Catarina. In the region dominated by the rebels, the Republic of Piratini was proclaimed in the city of the same name, in 1838. Bento Gonçalves was named president.

The government's position in dealing with the rebels was to mix battles with concessions. The Farrapos' leadership was made up of members of the elite, and the region where they fought was of great strategic importance. At the beginning of 1840, for example, the government gave in to one of the Farrapos' principal demands and declared a 25 percent import tariff on salt meat coming from the River Plate and competing with the local product.

An important step toward ending the conflict occurred in 1842, when Caxias was named president and military commander of the region. He devised a clever strategy which mixed military attacks with pacifying measures.

Finally, in 1845, after making individual agreements with different rebel chieftains, Caxias and Canabarro signed a peace treaty. It was not a case of unconditional surrender. Rebels were given general amnesty; Farroupilha officers were integrated into the Brazilian army according to their ranks; and the imperial government assumed the Piratini Republic's debts.

It cannot be firmly claimed that the Farrapos wanted their independence from Brazil so they could form a separate country with Uruguay and the River Plate provinces. However it was, one common point among all the rebels was at least to make Rio Grande do Sul an autonomous province with its own income and to make it free from the centralizing power imposed by Rio de Janeiro.

The Farrapo revolution forced Brazil to adopt a very different, nontraditional foreign policy for the River Plate region. For years on end, Brazil was obliged not to be aggressive there. It had to appease Buenos Aires so as to deal with the revolution along its borders.

The end of the rebellion rekindled Brazil's desire to exert strong influence over Uruguay as well as its fear that a single power might come to control both banks of the River Plate. These fears increased as Juan Manuel de Rosas, heading Buenos Aires and other Argentine provinces, tried to consolidate his power.

An anti-Rosas coalition was formed among Brazil, the Uruguayan "Colorado" faction traditionally allied with Brazil, and the Argentine provinces of Corrientes and Entre-Ríos, which were up in arms against Rosas. Brazilian presence was dominant in the war begun in 1851, with Dom Pedro II already on the throne. Around 24,000 Brazilian soldiers mainly recruited in Rio Grande do Sul took part in the conflict. With the control of Uruguay guaranteed by the Colorados, Rosas's troops were defeated at Monte Caseros, Argentina, in February 1852.

While rebellions shook Brazil, political tendencies in its center became more and more defined. The two great imperial parties, the Conservatives and the Liberals, began to emerge. The Conservatives consisted of magistrates and bureaucrats, some of the rural landowners, especially from Rio de Janeiro, Bahia, and Pernambuco, and wealthy merchants, among whom many were Portuguese. Liberals included the small urban middle class, a few priests, and rural landowners from the less traditional areas – especially São Paulo, Minas Gerais, and Rio Grande do Sul.

The political system had not become stable, however. In the April 1835 elections for the one-man regency, Father Feijó defeated his main rival, Holanda Cavalcanti, a rural landowner from Pernambuco. A little more than two years later, in September 1837, Feijó quit. He had endured pressure from the Congress and was accused of not employing sufficient energy in suppressing the Farrapos. (One of Feijó's cousins was a Farrapo leader.) The following elections were won by Araújo Lima, the future Marquis of Olinda. He was a former president of the Chamber of Deputies and a plantation owner in Pernambuco.

Araújo Lima's victory hailed the beginning of what is known as the *regresso*, the activation of the conservative current which wanted to return to a centralized government with strong (central) authority. One of the first laws favoring this return was a May 1840 interpretation of the Additional Act. It took away several of the provinces' powers, especially those dealing with the appointment of government employees.

2.2   THE SECOND EMPIRE

Owing to one of those paradoxes common to politics, it was not the Conservatives but the Liberals who hastened Dom Pedro's ascension to the throne. They had been bettered by the initiatives of the "regressionists," so, through one more interpretation wrung from the Additional Act, they argued for the king's premature adulthood in Congress. Thus, while still an adolescent, Dom Pedro II (at age 14) assumed Brazil's throne in July 1840.

Regressive measures continued after 1840. The Council of State was reestablished, and the Criminal Justice Code was modified in 1841. The entire administrative and legal apparatus (except for the justices of the peace) returned to the hands of the central government. The justices' importance was diminished, however, while that of the police increased.

Now, in each provincial capital, there was a chief of police appointed by the Ministry of Justice. The offices of deputy and sub-deputy were created in all parishes and municipalities. These men took over many of the duties of the justices of the peace, including those of judging petty crime cases. The police in some instances had the job not only of investigating crimes but also of trying individuals and sentencing them.

The centralization process and that of strengthening the emperor (two main objectives of the regresso) were completed with the reform of the National Guard. The elective principle, which already in practice did not work, disappeared completely. The Guard's officers were now chosen by the central government or by provincial presidents, and the income requirement to assume those posts was increased. The hierarchy was established, and officers would be recruited from more restricted milieus. From that time on, instead of the army and the National Guard competing with one another, their labor would be divided. The National Guard was charged with maintaining order and defending the ruling groups at the local level while the army was to mediate disputes, guarantee borders, and maintain general stability throughout the country.

Even though Liberals benefited from the centralizing measures while they were in power, their lot was not a tranquil one. In the early 1840s, the imperial government still lacked a solid base of support among the people. Liberal revolts had occurred in May and June 1842 in Minas Gerais and São Paulo. Large rural landowners were split between the two camps in this struggle. In Rio de Janeiro, the rebel leader was Joaquim de Sousa Breves, a coffee planter and the richest man in the province. Breves opposed the government and tried to dodge coffee taxes and measures against the slave trade.

A few years later, in 1848, the Praieira revolution was launched in Pernambuco. The name for this revolution comes from a liberal newspaper, *Diário Novo*, located on Rua da Praia ("Beach Street") in Recife. A series of democratic revolutions also swept Europe in 1848, hardly a humdrum year. In Olinda and Recife people breathed what an anonymous, anti-revolutionary author some years before had called "the malignant Pernambucan vapor." This vapor was now made up of social critiques and socialist ideas. One example of bruising social criticism was Antônio Pedro de Figueiredo's pointing out great evils in the pages of his magazine, O *Progresso*, published from 1846 to 1848. Figueiredo claimed the great social evils in Pernambuco included its agrarian structure, with the bulk of the land in the hands of a few proprietors, as well as the monopoly foreigners had on business. Socialist ideas were given voice by people as diverse as Louis Vauthier, a French architect hired by the president to make Recife more beautiful, and General Abreu e Lima, who years later would publish a book called O *Socialismo*. This was not Marxian socialism, which was scarcely known at that time, even in Europe. It was, rather, a brand of socialism based on the work of Proudhon, Fourier, and Owen.

The Praieira revolution was not socialistic, however. It was preceded in Recife by several deaths during anti-Portuguese demonstrations. In the countryside, its support came from plantation owners belonging to the Liberal Party. Their complaints stemmed from having lost the province to the Conservatives. Standing out from within the Praieira urban nucleus was the old Republican Borges da Fonseca. The urban faction espoused a program favorable to federalism. They were also in favor of abolishing moderating power, the expulsion of the Portuguese, and the nationalization of retail commerce, which the Portuguese largely controlled. A new feature was their defense of universal suffrage, which would have a few restrictions. There would be a minimum voting age, as well as a minimum age for holding office. But there would be no minimum income requirements. Around 2,500 men attacked Recife, but were defeated. The struggle went on in the form of guerrilla warfare until 1850, but never upset the imperial government.

The Praieira was the last of the provincial rebellions. At the same time it marked the end of the Pernambucan revolutionary cycle, which had begun during the war with the Dutch. Pernambuco was brought under the imperial order.

Well in advance of the Praieira revolution, imperial elites had been trying to set down the rules of the political game. The great agreement that was finally attained had strengthening the emperor as its basic pillar. Moderating power as well as the Council of State were restored, along with a set of written and unwritten norms. These norms made up the deliberately vague "spirit of government." A system was set up similar to but not exactly like parliamentary government in the true sense of the expression. In the first place, the 1824 constitution was not at all parliamentary. According to its provisions, executive power was under the emperor's command, along with that of the ministers of state, whom he had nominated at will. The First Empire and the Regency were not parliamentary governments, but there was activity in Brazil's Congress. A parliamentary government was only to begin, and even at that in an unusual and restricted form, in 1847. In that year, by decree, the position of president of the Council of Ministers was created. He would be appointed by the emperor. This political agent would appoint the ministry, which all together formed the Council of Ministers or the cabinet. They controlled executive power. For the system to work, it was presumed that the cabinet would need the confidence of the Chamber of Deputies as well as that of the emperor to stay in power. There were times when the Chamber forced the Council of Ministers to change its composition. But the emperor held on to a considerable sum of power through his ability to moderate, and this is what made the imperial system less than totally parliamentary, even between 1850 and 1889. The emperor exercised his moderating prerogatives when the Chamber did not support the cabinet he preferred. On those occasions, after hearing from the Council of State, he would use his power to dissolve the Chamber and call for new elections. The government had tremendous influence on elections, and the emperor was able to get deputies elected who were in tune with the cabinet he wanted.

Owing to this mechanism, in a government that lasted 50 years, there was a succession of 36 cabinets, each lasting an average of fifteen months. At first glance, this might suggest great instability. But in spite of the crises, this political state of affairs permitted turns in power for the two main parties. For members of the opposition, there was always a chance that they might be called to govern. It was, thus, unnecessary to resort to arms.

The two principal parties, the Conservative Party and the Liberal Party, had formed by the end of the 1830s. Were their differences social or ideological? Might not they have been two almost identical groups of people split by personal rivalries? Back then that is what many people believed. A sentence in that regard attributed to Holanda Cavalcanti has become famous. He said that nothing looked more like a *Saquarema* than a *Luzia* in power. Conservatives were known as Saquaremas during the early years of the Second Empire. The nickname comes from a municipality in the state of Rio de Janeiro. The Viscount of Itaboraí, one of the party's leaders, had a ranch near Saquarema. In an allusion to the town of Santa Luzia, where the revolution of 1842 began, Liberals were called Luzias. The idea that the parties were undifferentiated would seem to be confirmed by the frequent passage of politicians from one camp to the other.

When considering this matter, one should keep in mind that back then, and in general, one did not go into politics to attain great ideological objectives. To rise to power meant to gain prestige and benefits for oneself as well as for one's friends. In elections, no one expected candidates to be faithful to party programs; they were expected to fulfill their promises to their fellow party members. Both Liberals and Conservatives resorted to the same means to win elections: they gave their friends favors and used violence to sway fence-sitters and to vanquish enemies. The split between Liberals and Conservatives was thus very similar to a dispute between different clienteles seeking advantages or crumbs of power.

At the same time, however, politics was not merely a matter of personal interest. On a broader plane, the political elite was charged with dealing with larger issues such as the organization of the state, individual freedom, representation, and slavery. Is it the case that the dividing lines on these issues corresponded to party lines? And if that was true, what did these dividing lines mean? For the time being, the matter of slavery will not be addressed, since it deserves separate treatment.

The theme of centralization or decentralization of power divided Liberals and Conservatives. This division was more relevant, however, during the early 1830s, before these two tendencies had become parties. The regressive measures and Dom Pedro's "adulthood," which Liberals supported, were victories for the centralist model. Thereafter, the two parties accepted the central government's authority – notwithstanding Liberals' outward insistence that they were in favor of decentralization.

Defense of individual freedom and wider political representation for citizens were two flags raised by the Liberal Party. It was only after 1860 that these themes gathered strength, along with another spate of propositions for decentralization. The so-called New Liberal Party was founded in 1870 with the support of Conservatives such as Nabuco de Araújo and Zacarias de Góis. It supported direct elections in the larger cities, a periodically elected Senate, the reduction of the power of the Council of State, guarantees of freedom of belief, education, business, and industry – as well as the gradual abolition of slavery.

If there were ideological differences between the two parties, one must ask why this was. When he analyzed the makeup of the imperial ministries, the historian José Murilo de Carvalho derived some significant conclusions. According to him, especially during the 1840s and 1850s, the Conservative Party represented a coalition of rural landowners and government bureaucrats joined by some wealthy merchants worried about urban disturbances. The Liberal Party consisted mainly of rural landowners and trained professionals.

There is an important distinction regarding the two parties' regional bases. While Conservatives received their greatest backing in the provinces of Bahia and Pernambuco, Liberals were stronger in São Paulo, Minas Gerais, and Rio Grande do Sul. The union between bureaucrats (especially magistrates) and wealthy landowners in Rio de Janeiro State made up the heart of the centralizing policy supported by Conservatives.

The notion of a stable and unified empire, which originated in the government bureaucracy, was embraced by the *Fluminense* landowners (i.e., inhabitants of Rio de Janeiro province), who were closely tied to the court owing to geography and business. The rural landowners in Bahia and Pernambuco who belonged to the Conservative Party had lived through and were still experiencing the struggles for local autonomy. These struggles were supported by the common folk, which was why landowners would support a powerful and authoritarian central government.

On the one hand, at least in the beginning, liberal proposals for decentralization came from areas such as São Paulo and Rio Grande do Sul, where the regional ruling class enjoyed a tradition of autonomy. Liberalism, in the case of Minas Gerais, came as much from the rural landowners as it did from the urban population in the old mining cities.

On the other hand, the introduction of the theme of greater representation and the emphasis on the role of public opinion came from the urban professionals in the Liberal Party. Their presence became significant beginning in the 1860s, as cities developed and more and more people had better educations.

Finally, it should be remembered that around 1870, mainly in São Paulo, socioeconomic transformations had created a class based on coffee production, the so-called coffee bourgeoisie. With all its consequences, this class embraced one of the main features of decentralization: it defended provincial autonomy. At the same time, another conviction arose among groups with different social bases, which included the coffee bourgeoisie and the urban middle class. They doubted that decentralizing reforms or reforms in favor of greater political representation could occur within the monarchical framework. This is how the republican movement began.

Why did Brazil maintain its territorial unity inherited from colonial times? Why did it not break up? The provincial rebellions described here and the uncertainty concerning how to regard central power suggest that the country's unity was not a foregone conclusion when its independence was declared. Brazil's unity was the product of forceful and apt resolution of conflicts and of leaders' efforts to construct a centralized state. But there is no doubt that within that process the likelihood of the provinces' going their separate ways was always less than the probability of their remaining united.

In Brazilian historiography this topic is quite controversial. There are conflicting explanations for unity, and they range from those emphasizing sociocultural factors to those emphasizing the nature of Brazil's elite. But it is not impossible to combine all the explanations. From the structural point of view, the explanation lies in slavery. The interest in maintaining slavery led the most important provinces to discard the possibility of leaving the empire because that would have weakened them enormously in the face of international anti-slavery movements headed by Britain. At the same time, Britain was in favor of keeping together the country which constituted its greatest Latin American market. Brazil was a relatively stable monarchy surrounded by turbulent republics.

In turn, the formation of a homogeneous elite that was educated in hierarchical, conservative law schools in Coimbra, and later on in Olinda-Recife and São Paulo, favored the implementation of a policy that aimed to build a centralized empire. Because members of that educated elite assumed administrative posts in different provinces, their distribution throughout the country weakened their ties with specific regional interests while it made them advocates of centralized power.

2.3 SOCIOECONOMIC STRUCTURE AND SLAVERY

The greatest novelty in the Brazilian economy during the early decades of the 19th century was the emergence of coffee as an export commodity. Francisco de Melo Palheta is responsible for introducing coffee bushes to Brazil. He brought the first seeds to Pará in 1727. Used for domestic consumption, coffee began to be planted in Rio de Janeiro around 1760. It was grown among other plants in little orchards and gardens around the capital.

It was, however, the vast Paraíba River valley, which crosses a part of Rio de Janeiro and São Paulo, that had all the conditions for coffee's first great expansion to commercial proportions. The Paraíba River valley was known territory. It was traversed by roads and trails which, since the high point of mining, led to Minas Gerais. There was virgin land available and the climate was favorable. Besides, even though transportation was touch and go, the valley's proximity to Rio de Janeiro made the product easier to export. It also made contacts for obtaining credit and the purchase of merchandise more available.

Ranches were set up in the traditional mold, with the work being done by slave labor. It would not have been impossible to have produced exportable coffee from small, productive tracts of land, as Colombia would someday demonstrate. Nonetheless, given the

Brazilian state of affairs, with access to the land and a system and supply of slave labor, the large-scale model won out.

The history of how the land was occupied followed a pattern that came from the past and would be repeated over and over throughout Brazil's history. There was a total lack of defined property lines and much unused land. Property titles, when they existed, could be contested because, among the many reasons, there was often more than one title for the same tract of land. In this type of framework the strongest contenders won. And the strongest ones were those who could use force to keep their land. They could eject resourceless squatters, hire good lawyers, and influence judges. This is how they legalized their claims.

To set up a coffee plantation, a rancher had to make significant investments which included felling trees, preparing the ground, planting, building slave quarters, and buying slaves. On top of this, even though the coffee bush is a perennial plant, and even though it would not have to be renewed on a short-term basis, it only produced its first crop after four years. In the beginning, resources to set up coffee plantations appear to have come from savings garnered from the great commercial expansion once Dom João VI came to Brazil. With the passage of time, profits from coffee growing and, after 1850, capital freed by the extinguished slave trade became sources of investment.

During the entire monarchical period, coffee was produced with very simple techniques. Some of these techniques, such as soil depredation, are still being used. There was extensive planting, which means that there was no interest in or worry about the soil's productivity. When the soil was spent owing to the lack of fertilizer or attention, coffee bushes were planted elsewhere. The old area was either abandoned or used to grow foodstuffs.

The basic and almost exclusive work instruments used in this massive coffee-growing region were the hoe and the sickle. Slaves had become accustomed to these traditional farm implements in Brazil, and the topography of the Paraíba Valley favored their use. Coffee planters only started using plows around 1879, in the new coffee areas of São Paulo.

Leaving out exceptional cases, coffee growing developed in the following way. Once the trees were felled, part of the wood was used and the rest was burned. Cuttings were planted; in the beginning, planters did not even line them up. According to a Caribbean custom, crops such as beans, corn, and manioc were planted in the land between each coffee bush. This practice furnished the necessary shade for the growing saplings as well as food for the owners, their dependents, and slaves.

The care of coffee groves was limited to weeding the land. When the bushes began to produce, slaves picked them by hand. On average, one slave tended between 4,000 and 7,000 coffee plants on the Fluminense farms. This ratio suggests there was little maintenance. The production and processing techniques were preindustrial. Transporting coffee to an export dock after it was put in sacks was characteristically precarious. Before the railways were built, coffee was carried to the ports by mule trains led by a guide and slave muleteers. These caravans would travel the roads from the valley to Rio de Janeiro several times a year. On their way to Rio they bore the produce; on the way back they carried supplies like codfish, jerky, salt pork, and tools. As time went by, farmers started buying furniture and luxury items such as crystal and porcelain.

Commissioners were important personages in the commercialization of coffee. They first worked in the port of Rio de Janeiro and later on in Santos. They were middlemen working among producers and exporters. They received the merchandise and sold it to exporters at the time they considered right. In exchange for the coffee they received or were going to receive, commissioners supplied, at a profit, those consumer goods and implements the planters ordered. A relationship of trust was built up between planters and commissioners. The latter opened accounts for planters and maintained records of their credits and debits. In some cases, their relationship was so close that commissioners would give their clients guided tours of the capital or they would look after planters' children when they came to Rio to study. Planters and commissioners were as a rule Brazilians. But coffee exportation was, right from the beginning, controlled by large American and British concerns.

Even though coffee drinking was a widespread habit in Brazil, the internal market could not absorb large-scale production. The coffee business depended then and depends today on the export market.

Coffee production advanced hand-in-hand with the North American and European middle class's increasing coffee consumption. The United States became the biggest buyer of Brazilian coffee, which was also exported to Germany, the low countries, and Scandinavia. Britain, where the custom of drinking tea was firmly rooted, was never a good customer. What little coffee they drank came from Britain's Caribbean colonies, from Central America, and from southern Asia. This coffee paid lower tariffs to enter the British market, which made Brazilian coffee even less viable there. An important characteristic of Brazil's international economic and financial relations during the 19th and part of the 20th century is encapsulated here. The country depended on England for credits and loans. Its foreign debt was mainly with English bankers. But Brazil's business dealings with Britain were not sufficient to pay for the products it imported from there, or to service its debt.

The rise of coffee production and its importance for Brazil's foreign trade can be measured by one datum. Between 1821 and 1830, coffee made up 18 percent of the total revenue from Brazil's exports. Between 1881 and 1890, it made up 61 percent.

From the socioeconomic point of view, the coffee complex opened a fan of activity and established the country's dynamic axis in the Center-South once and for all. Thanks to coffee, ports were outfitted, new credit mechanisms were set up, jobs were created, and transportation was revolutionized. But this did not happen from one day to the next. There was a relatively long process of decay in the Northeast and of invigoration in the Center-South. By 1870 the trend was irreversible.

Wealthy planters in the Paraíba Valley benefited from centralized power. Their vanity was appeased by titles of nobility the emperor bestowed on them. Political stances of people like Joaquim de Sousa Breves, the great Fluminense planter who led the liberal rebellion of 1842, had become ancient history. In the middle of the 19th century, the empire had secured a base of support among wealthy businessmen and rural landowners, among whom the coffee barons from Rio de Janeiro stood out. This assertion should not be understood to mean that these elements had taken over the state. There were differences between the state and the dominant social groups. One indication of this is that provincial presidents were normally not chosen from members of the local elite. This practice avoided a nominee's straightforward identification with specific regional interests. And this is how the central government kept itself apart from local politics and applied its policies in every province.

By safeguarding order in general and by dealing with slavery on a step-by-step basis, the emperor and the bureaucracy attended, in essence, to the interest of the ruling class. But in doing this, they sometimes went against the points of view of their supporters. The Law of the Free Womb, which the emperor proposed in spite of planters' almost total opposition, is one example of this tendency. Within the nucleus of the statist vision of Brazil were the lifelong members of the Council of State. José Murilo de Carvalho depicted the situation as follows: as far as the imperial councilmen were concerned, Brazil was like a solar system. For its sun it had the state, around which whirled the larger planets otherwise known as the conservative classes. Beyond them lay a myriad of stars – the great bulk of the population.

Brazil is coffee and coffee is the Negro. This sentence, common in the ruling circles of the first half of the 19th century, was only true in part. Brazil was not just coffee, just as it had never been only sugar. On top of this, coffee production would go on in the future without slave labor. Still, there is no doubt that during this period a large part of the expansion of the slave trade was to meet the needs of coffee growers.

After independence, the Brazilian government found itself in a difficult situation. Except for a few isolated voices, almost everyone, from large landowners to slave traders as well as the free population at large, was convinced that to end the slave trade would, on a short-term basis, wreak havoc on Brazilian society. However, Britain, on whom Brazil depended, pressed for an end to the trade. The disagreements and accords between Brazil and Britain on this matter show that in spite of Brazil's dependence on that nation, things could not go as Britain wished, at least immediately.

During the first decade of independence, the slave trade picked up, compared to the previous decade. According to official statistics, the average yearly rate of slave entry into Brazil was 32,700 for the years 1811–1820. It was 43,100 between 1821 and 1830. The numbers of slaves entering through ports south of Bahia grew tremendously, with Rio de Janeiro as the most prominent port of entry. Southern ports accounted for 53 percent of the total number of slaves brought in between 1811 and 1820 and 69 percent of the total between 1821 and 1830. The majority of slaves were sent to the coffee plantations in the Paraíba Valley, or they stayed in Rio de Janeiro. It was slave importation rather than slave transfer from Minas Gerais, as historians believed a few years ago, that accounted for the supply of slaves during this phase of the coffee economy.

In 1826 Britain exacted a treaty from Brazil. According to the treaty, three years after its ratification slave traffic to Brazil, from whatever source, would be declared illegal. Britain reserved the right to inspect ships on the high seas, if they were suspected of carrying slaves. The accord was ratified in March 1827, which meant that it would take effect beginning in March 1830. A law of 7 November 1831 sought to support the treaty by assigning severe penalties to slave traffickers and by declaring free any slave who entered Brazil after that date. The law was approved during a fleeting moment when the flow of slaves into the country had ebbed. Soon the flow increased and the law's provisions were, for all intents and purposes, not applied.

Slave traders were not yet the object of scorn among the ruling classes. In fact, slave traders also benefited from the decentralizing reforms made during the Regency. Local juries, which were controlled by wealthy landowners, absolved the few people accused of slave trafficking when they went to court. The law of 1831 was considered one "to show the Englishmen." From that time on, the expression *para inglês ver* has been commonly used to indicate something that is done for the sake of appearance, but that means nothing.

There are various reasons why the dominant groups were committed to slave labor. One reason was that there was no viable alternative to slave labor on large plantations; another was that there had been no widespread slave rebellions. One partial exception to this rule occurred in the Bahian Recôncavo and the city of Salvador. From the beginning of the 19th century, slave unrest was present in that region. It had become part of daily life. However, blacks born in Brazil were as a rule absent from the different movements, which indicates those movements' limited nature. The most significant revolt occurred in 1835, when hundreds of black Africans (slaves and freedmen) rose up in Salvador. These rebels were Muslims and known as *Malês*, and that is how the rebellion got its name. The Malê Uprising was put down with violence. Seventy participants died. More than 500 Africans were sentenced: a small number to death, others to terms in prison, whiplashes, and deportation.

Bahia's situation was exceptional, and, even so, it experienced no more significant rebellions after 1835. In Rio de Janeiro, where slaves constituted over 40 percent of the population, nothing like the Malê Uprising occurred. Repression, hopes of being freed, divisions among slaves who were better off than others, divisions among freedmen and slaves, and differences between native-born and African slaves were several factors which contributed to the lack of uprisings.

Britain did not remain passive in the face of the Brazilian government's inertia. Many slave ships were apprehended. In 1846 the agreement giving Britain the right to inspect ships would end, and Brazil was not inclined to extend it. In the face of this, the British Parliament passed a bill which in Brazil was known as *Bill Aberdeen* – a reference to Lord Aberdeen, the British minister of foreign affairs. This bill authorized the British navy to deal with slave ships as if they were pirate ships. This gave them the right to apprehend them and to try slave traffickers in British courts. In Brazil the Aberdeen Bill was the target for ultra-nationalistic attacks. Even in Britain, many voices were raised against the role the country was taking as the "world's moral guardian."

In September 1848, a conservative cabinet had come to power. Beginning in October, it was presided over by the Marquis of Porto Alegre. The cabinet represented an alliance of bureaucrats, magistrates, and wealthy landowners – especially Fluminense coffee planters. Eusébio de Queiroz was named minister of justice. The son of a Portuguese-Angolan judge, Eusébio de Queiroz had been born in Angola and had married a woman from a family with ties to the commercial world of Rio de Janeiro. The Ministry of Justice issued a proposal to the Parliament. The proposed law would reinforce the law of 1831 with more efficacious measures against the slave trade. Among the law's other points, Brazil was to acknowledge that the slave trade was tantamount to piracy. Special courts would judge the perpetrators. This proposal became a law in September 1850. This time the law stuck. The entry of slaves into Brazil fell from nearly 54,000 in 1849 to less than 23,000 in 1850, and down to around 3,300 in 1851. After that, for all intents and purposes, no more slaves entered Brazil from Africa.

What could have happened between 1831 and 1850? Why did the second law stick while the first one failed? The answer lies in the prevailing conditions at the end of the 1840s, especially in the increased pressure from Britain. Supported by Aberdeen's bill, the British navy did not restrict itself to apprehending suspected slave ships on the high seas. British ships entered Brazilian territorial waters and even threatened to block the main ports. Britain's escalation provoked incidents all along the coast. The most serious one consisted of shots fired back and forth between a ship in a British squadron and Fort Paranaguá, in Paraná. The imperial government had little likelihood of resisting the British onslaught – especially since Brazil was wary of a different threat from the south, an invasion from Argentina. Brazil needed Britain's protection.

Outside pressure was, then, a key element in ending transatlantic slave trade. At the same time, after so many years of intensive importation of slaves, the Brazilian market was well stocked with them at the end of the 1840s. Fluminense planters had mortgaged their properties to large-scale traffickers. Their objective was to obtain money to buy slaves. Traffickers, many of whom were Portuguese, began to be the object of resentment. The internal anti-British front had broken.

On top of this, reinforcement from the central government, which was obtained through conservative initiative, aided the repressive action. Nabuco de Araújo (the father of Joaquim Nabuco), minister of justice from 1853 to 1857, went so far as to replace the president of Pernambuco with a stickler after one of the last attempts at landing slaves in Brazil occurred in that province.

Once effective measures were taken against the slave trade, slavery was destined to end. Slave owners in Brazil never worried about slaves' reproduction. Masters always depended on the flow from abroad. Once imports were cut off, the number of slaves tended to become insufficient for the many tasks to which they were destined.

On top of this, the end of the slave trade would also be a political and ideological watershed. If Brazil made the importation of slaves illegal, maintaining slavery within the country lost its legitimacy. But, from that premise, various questions arose. How and how long would it take for slavery to be abolished in Brazil? Who would replace the slaves?

The beginning of an answer can be found in the Law on Land, which was approved in 1850, two weeks after the ending of the slave trade. This law tried to put an end to the existing confusion concerning rural property. It stipulated that from then on public land would be sold and not given away, as had been the case with the old *sesmarias* or land grants. It established norms to legalize possession of property, and it sought to force people to register their property. This legislation was conceived to be a way to deter future immigrants from acquiring property. Public land should be sold at prices high enough to frustrate squatters and poor immigrants. Foreigners whose passage to Brazil had been subsidized by Brazil were prohibited from acquiring land for three years after their arrival. In sum, wealthy planters wanted to attract immigrants to substitute for the slaves, but they tried to stop these immigrants from becoming landowners. Massive immigration was, however, still far in the future. The most widely used means of securing workers in the Center-South was to buy slaves on the internal market, from regions of declining prosperity.

2.4 MODERNIZATION AND THE EXPANSION OF COFFEE

The year 1850 in Brazil did not merely mark the half century. That was the year the slave trade ended; the Law on Land was passed; the National Guard was centralized; and the first Commercial Code was approved. The Commercial Code entailed some innovations, and at the same time it brought together various texts handed down from the colonial period. Among other things, it defined the types of companies that could be set up in the country, and it regulated their operations. As was the case with the Law on Land, its reference point was the ending of the slave trade.

The end of the slave trade liberated capital, which gave rise to intense business activity and speculation. Banks, industries, and steamship companies arose. Thanks to a rise in the tariffs placed on imported products owing to a decree of 1844, governmental revenues increased. In 1852 and 1853, they were twice what they had been in 1842 and 1843.

In the political arena, Liberals and Conservatives devised a provisional national accord by forming the Ministry of Reconciliation (1853–1856), which was led by the Marquis of Paraná. Somehow, this agreement remained in effect among the later ministers until 1861.

In the country's more dynamic areas, changes toward capitalist modernization began to appear: the first attempts to create a labor market, a land market, and a market for the available resources were made.

Modernization should begin by improving the precarious system of transportation. In the middle of the 19th century, modern transportation was synonymous with steamships and, mainly, railways. Even so, an important highway, the so-called Estrada União e Indústria (Union and Industry Highway), was built on the initiative of Mariano Procópio. It linked Petrópolis, in the province of Rio de Janeiro, to Juiz de Fora, in Minas Gerais. Begun in 1856, it reached Juiz de Fora in 1861. It was 144 kilometers long, paved with crushed rock – "macadamized," as they said back then, since the system had been invented by the British engineer John McAdam. This highway was impressive thanks to its metal bridges and its way stations for a line of stagecoaches that regularly traversed it. The Union and Industry Highway had been very expensive to build and was hard to maintain. It would soon be vanquished by competition from the railway.

The major incentives for building railways came from the need to improve the transportation of the principal export merchandise to the country's most important ports. It was imperative to improve on inconvenient, precarious roads and the mule trains which made for high expenditures and an inadequate flow of products.

In the Northeast, the most important activity took place in Pernambuco, whose basic function was to export sugar. Business ventures financed with English capital appeared: the very early Recife-São Francisco rail line, begun in 1855; and, much later, during the 1880s, the Great Western line. In the Center-South, the main objective of the railways would be to transport coffee, whose shipping became more and more problematic as plantations spread farther and farther inland, away from Rio de Janeiro and into the Forest Zone (Zona da Mata) of Minas Gerais and then off into the area of western São Paulo, which was known as the Oeste Paulista. The construction of railways and steamship lines revolutionized Britain's economy between 1840 and 1880. It increased heavy industry's production of iron, steel, and coal. The accumulation of surplus capital made foreign loans and investments possible. And railways were a favorite investment. Many of Brazil's railways were built by British contractors with British financial resources, material, and equipment.

Around 1850, the coffee economy in the Paraíba Valley reached its pinnacle. The transportation problem was in great part solved with the building of the Dom Pedro II Line, later known as the Central do Brazil, or the Brazil Central Railway. Its construction began in 1855. Over the years, successive stretches of rails were opened, and in 1875 the line finally reached Cachoeira, in São Paulo. After this, a São Paulo firm would connect Cachoeira to the provincial capital, and this completed the rail connection between Rio and São Paulo.

While this was going on, coffee began to take root in a new area, in the backlands of São Paulo, the Oeste Paulista. Coffee bushes were planted in part to substitute for sugar cane on the old plantations. Considering Brazil's economy as a whole, São Paulo had always been a marginal producer of sugar. Sugar's tendency to decline in price, in contrast to coffee's stability, motivated the change from sugar to coffee. The success of coffee-producing endeavors in Oeste Paulista in essence depended on transportation and a viable port for exportation, since Rio de Janeiro was far away. The biggest problem was crossing over the Serra do Mar, a coastal mountain range that extends to the littoral. This was accomplished with the construction of the rail line from Santos to Jundiaí. It was built by an English concessionary company named the São Paulo Railway Co. Limited, or SPR, which began to operate in 1868. Santos had been exporting small quantities of coffee harvested along the coast since the end of the 18th century. Once the railway reached it, the city became an export center.

The SPR had the right to extend its line from Jundiaí to Rio Claro. It declined to do this because of alleged difficulties in the London finance market. Strategic considerations may have prevailed, however, since in practice the company had a monopoly on the interior's access to the port of Santos. Consequently, taking its first steps in 1868, the Paulista Company was formed. This company was backed by Brazilian capital linked to the coffee business. After it came the Mogiana, the Ituana, and the Sorocaba lines. Sorocaba was an exception because it was not built with coffee money but by money from cotton, which began to be planted around Sorocaba during the 1860s.

The coffee economies of the Paraíba Valley and the Oeste Paulista were headed in opposite directions. Beginning in the last decade of the empire, it was possible to see that the Paraíba Valley economy was in decline, whereas in Oeste Paulista the economy was plainly expanding. Large-scale agriculture was being used both in the valley as well as in São Paulo. However, in the latter area, there were vast tracts of available land, which allowed new areas to be opened continuously. The Paraíba Valley had clear geographical limits, and planters had few places to go. Consequently, with the land spent and eroded, their productivity went down, and so did the price of that land. On the eve of Abolition, the Paraíba Valley planters' biggest investment was their slaves, which alone shows the impact of ending slavery in that region.

Besides the availability of land, other factors contributed to Oeste Paulista's rising star. They included the physical surroundings, technology, and the specific time in history. The best soil and climate for growing coffee were on the high plateau of rural São Paulo. The soil is red there, highly productive, and it would go on producing coffee for 30 years, while other soil never produced coffee for longer than 25 years. In Portuguese, this soil is called *terra roxa*, or "purple land," because Brazilians heard Italians call it *terra rossa*.

While one should not exaggerate the role of technological advancements, it was in Oeste Paulista that plows and hulling machines were first used. The huller represented a revolution in the way in which coffee beans were cleaned.

The moment in history, too, was important to Oeste Paulista's success. In the new region, accumulation of capital took place at a time when it was obvious that alternatives to slave labor were necessary. The Paraíba Valley coffee culture had emerged earlier, when slavery seemed to be the only option. Only when that economy had reached its pinnacle was the slave trade abolished. As the valley's productivity declined, the difficulty of finding a source of substitute workers became greater, but could not be solved.

Out of this situation, two regional classes were formed – with different fates. The Paraíba Valley planters had supported the monarchy, but had distanced themselves from the emperor as laws were passed that tended to abolish slavery gradually. This distancing process was complete once slavery was abolished, in 1888. However, by that time, the Paraíba Valley coffee barons were no longer important socially or politically.

The economy of Oeste Paulista gave rise to a new class commonly known as the coffee bourgeoisie. In the last decades of the 19th century, São Paulo began to change into a region where socioeconomic transformations would make capitalism possible. This required a little time. In some ways, the shift to capitalism has only recently been completed. Over many decades, capital has been accumulated, the economy has diversified, and land, production, and consumption markets have been formed.

The accumulation of capital first occurred because of coffee production. It then combined with the railway investments, with banks, and with business. Coffee's expansion gave rise to a network of urban nuclei which became centers of small-scale production and consumption, with incipient and diverse economies. The massive entry of immigrants beginning in the 1880s would bring about the formation of production, consumption, and labor markets.

It would be an illusion to think that the social groups of the Paraíba Valley and Oeste Paulista were totally different, with one being the "old," decadent aristocracy and the other the "new," entrepreneurial bourgeoisie. Both groups based their beliefs (and modus operandi) on the same premises, but they changed owing to the differences in their physical and social surroundings. Both were engaged in large-scale agriculture, and both used slave labor extensively. The São Paulo planters did not turn to immigrants because they believed in the virtues or in the greater productivity of free labor. They did it because there was a labor problem, and there was no one else to turn to. In 1887, less than a year before Abolition, of all the provinces São Paulo had the third highest number of slaves – 107,000. In first place was Minas Gerais with 192,000, in second Rio de Janeiro with 162,000.

After 1850, slaves were bought and sold internally. Brazil's internal migrations began sadly, with the forced transference of slaves from one region to another. New slave traders appeared, as did a new profession – the itinerant slave buyer who would roam the provinces persuading poor ranchers or urbanites to sell one or two of their slaves. Slaves were transported to the coffee region not only by sea, but also by land. Possibly to avoid paying the proper embarkation tax in the ports, many slaves were obliged to travel overland through the Bahian and Minas Gerais countrysides all the way to the coffee region.

There are no good data on the size of the interprovincial slave trade. Rough estimates suggest that between 1850 and 1888 some 100,000 to 200,000 slaves were removed from the sugar-producing areas of the Northeast and sent to the Center-South. Between 1864 and 1874, the number of slaves in the Northeast declined from 774,000, or 45 percent of all the slaves in Brazil, to 435,000, or 28 percent of the total. During the same period, in the coffee regions, the slave population rose from 645,000, or 43 percent of the total, to 809,000 or 56 percent. São Paulo alone more than doubled its slave population, going from 80,000 to 174,000.

With the rise in slaves' prices owing to the end of slave importation, even traditionally productive areas such as Bahia and Pernambuco exported large quantities of slaves. Beginning in 1874, the slave population dropped all over Brazil. This tendency accelerated after 1885. Even so, the drop in numbers was much more obvious in the Northeast than in the Center-South. While the overall average decline was 19 percent between 1874 and 1884, it was 9 percent in the Center-South and 31 percent in the Northeast. The South also evinced a strong drop in the number of slaves; Rio Grande do Sul led the way, with a drop of almost 39 percent during that period.

2.5   THE BEGINNING OF LARGE-SCALE IMMIGRATION

A region's greater or lesser dependence on slave labor had important repercussions on advancing abolitionist causes. But the possibility of achieving an alternate solution to the labor problem, which arose in São Paulo, also played a relevant part. The alternative consisted of attracting European workers to come and work on coffee plantations. Why was no attempt made to turn slaves into free workers? And why weren't people enticed to move southward from the poor areas of the Northeast?

The first question has a mixed answer. On the one hand, large-scale planters' prejudices made even the thought of transforming slaves into free workers difficult or, quite likely, impossible. On the other hand, it is doubtful that after years of servitude, ex-slaves would have been inclined to stay in a situation that was not much different from slavery. In this vein, it should be remembered that immigrants were forced to pressure planters for better treatment than slaves got, especially when slavery still existed.

The answer to the second question has one point of contact with the first one. Racist thought had won the minds of the empire's rulers. Influenced by the writings of Buckle and Gobineau, leaders not only considered slaves and ex-slaves inferior; they also considered racially mixed people born during the entire Portuguese colonization of Brazil to be inferior. The only hope for Brazil seemed to be to make it European as quickly as possible. Along with this cultural factor, others should be taken into account. The sugar and cotton planters of the Northeast had lost part of their slave labor force and would not look kindly on further transferal of their supply of labor toward the Center-South.

It is true that drought periodically afflicted some provinces in the Northeast and created a mass of refugees. Still, many of them were left to fend for themselves, while others were either recruited to harvest rubber in the North or to work in the cacao plantations of Bahia. During the last years of the 19th century, the dream of wealth or at least of a better life did not focus on the distant Center-South; it focused on Amazônia and on certain areas of the Northeast itself.

The history of large-scale immigration into the coffee regions of São Paulo transcends periodization of Brazilian political history. It began during the Second Empire, but its major impact came after the proclamation of the republic. Getting immigrants to come was a process of trial and error. In 1847, Nicolau de Campos Vergueiro first experimented with immigration. Vergueiro had been an imperial regent and a planter whose fortune came largely from the business of importing slaves. With resources from the imperial government, he brought German and Swiss immigrants to work as partners on his plantations in Oeste Paulista. This experiment created much friction. Even though they had come from regions of Europe that had suffered from food shortages, these tenant farmers would not put up with the living conditions they found in Brazil. They were subjected to strict discipline which included censoring their correspondence and restricting their movements on plantations. Finally a revolt broke out in 1856, on one of Vergueiro's plantations. From then on such schemes ceased.

Efforts to attract immigrants were once more made beginning in 1871, the year of the Law of the Free Womb. This time the initiative came from the provincial government as well as from planters. A law of March 1871 authorized the government of São Paulo to acquire funds by selling bonds to private citizens. The funds would be lent to planters who would use them to bring in farm laborers. To attract immigrants, they planned to subsidize their passage. This was the beginning of state-subsidized immigration to São Paulo. Over the years subsidies varied. They sometimes included an eight-day stay in a government building in the capital as well as transportation to the plantations.

The number of people coming to São Paulo as immigrants was tiny until the early 1880s. Between 1875 and 1879 only 10,455 people are registered as having entered. This number was well below the needs of coffee producers. The Italians, who little by little had begun to arrive in 1874, would not settle for the sort of life awaiting them in Brazil, and many returned to Italy. In 1885 the Italian government published a handbill which described São Paulo as an inhospitable and unhealthy region; it advised people not to emigrate to Brazil.

The most preeminent figures of the Paulista elite reacted to this state of affairs at a crucial moment, when it was obvious that the slave-holding system was unraveling. The Society for Promotion of Immigration (Sociedade Promotora de Imigração) was formed in 1886 at the initiative of, among others, the brothers Martinho Prado Jr. and Antônio da Silva Prado. It proposed a series of measures designed to attract immigrants to coffee plantations.

This society published pamphlets in Portuguese, German, and Italian emphasizing the advantages of coming to São Paulo. They made favorable comparisons with other, more attractive countries such as the United States and Argentina, which also received immigrants. These pamphlets did not mention the existence of slavery or other drawbacks of Brazil. Martinho Prado Jr. traveled to northern Italy to study ways of enticing immigrants. An office of the Society for Promotion of Immigration was opened in Genoa.

Finally, several factors, from both sides of the Atlantic, began to favor a large flow of immigrants. The crisis arising from Italy's unification and its switch to capitalism hit poor people hardest and was fundamental to emigration. Likewise, paid transportation and the possibility of subsidized lodging upon arrival were, for better or for worse, other incentives.

Until the early years of the 20th century, most immigrants who reached São Paulo were rural workers or small-scale rural landowners from northern Italy. They came especially from Veneto and Lombardy, where they could not survive just cultivating their own fields.

During the last years of the empire, immigration from all sources to São Paulo leaped from 6,500 people in 1885 to almost 92,000 in 1888. During 1888, Italians made up almost 90 percent of all immigrants. Significantly, the 1888 coffee harvest, which followed Abolition (May 1888), was completed with no problems in the availability of labor.

2.6 THE PARAGUAYAN WAR

While coffee marched westward in São Paulo, and while early proposals for a gradual abolition of slavery were being made, an international "incident" would leave a deep mark in the history of the Second Empire. This was the Paraguayan War, which lasted over five years, from 11 November 1864, when the first hostile act was perpetrated, to 1 March 1870, when the war ended.

In order to put the conflict into perspective, it is necessary to give a general outline of the traits of the nations involved in the war as well as their relationships with one another.

The Viceroyalty of the River Plate did not survive as a political entity once Spanish colonialism ended early in the 19th century.

After protracted conflicts, that area split into the nations of Argentina, Uruguay, Paraguay, and Bolivia. The Argentine Republic only emerged after many fits and starts, as well as wars, in which Federalist and Unitarian factions fought one another.

The Unitarians were made up mainly of Buenos Aires businessmen who advocated a centralized state under the command of the capital, like the old Viceroyalty. From the port of Buenos Aires, the business community could control Argentina's foreign commerce and keep the revenue from import tariffs.

The Federalists consisted of regional elites, large landowners, small manufacturers, and businessmen whose interests were local. They advocated a decentralized state so that their incomes would be protected and not be submitted to taxes imposed on them by the business bureaucracy in Buenos Aires.

Uruguay was born in 1828 after three years of struggle involving Argentines, Brazilians, and an independence faction. Britain looked favorably on the creation of a country that would stabilize the area around the Plate estuary, where Britons had financial and commercial interests. However, Uruguay's history during the 19th century was anything but peaceful. The *Blanco* and *Colorado* factions vied for power with iron and lead. The Colorados were linked to business and to European powers, and they sympathized with liberal ideals. The Blancos were mainly rural landowners who had inherited the old Spanish authoritarian tradition and were suspicious of gains made by new European powers in their country.

The inhabitants of the old province of Paraguay, in large part descendants of Guarani Indians, would not submit to the Buenos Aires bourgeoisie and began to govern themselves during the second decade of the 19th century. Their independence was not recognized in Buenos Aires, which, in 1813, for all intents and purposes stopped Paraguayan commerce with the outside world. Buenos Aires blocked the Plate estuary, the natural route to the sea, which Paraguayans reached by sailing the Paraguay and Paraná Rivers. This blockade led the Paraguayan leader José Gaspar de Francia to isolate Paraguay and become its dictator. The state expropriated lands belonging to the church and to a sector of the elite which favored an accord with Buenos Aires and became the principal agent of production and commerce in Paraguay.

The characterization of Paraguay as a country made up of small landowners under the command of a clairvoyant state was common in leftist historiography of the 1970s, which focused especially on Francia's dictatorship. It is true that, in the South American context, he took exceptional measures. But to call them progressive simplifies their content. The government set up *Estancias de la Patria*, or Estates of the Fatherland, on the land it confiscated. These estancias were run by the government or by government lessees, and slaves or convicts worked them. The Paraguayan economy ceased to be based on money. Both rent on the land and taxes were paid in kind, with no exchange of money.

After Francia's death, Carlos Antonio López was named president. He declared Paraguay's independence in 1842. Trying to end his country's isolation, he set up a rail system and stimulated foreign trade. His son Francisco Solano López was sent to England, where he purchased war matériel and recruited European technicians to come and modernize Paraguay. In stages, Paraguay attempted to grow by making connections with outside markets. Its interest in controlling navigation along the Paraguay and Paraná Rivers grew, as did its interest in free transit through the port of Buenos Aires. This was the state of affairs in Paraguay when Solano López ascended to power in 1862, after his father had died.

During the first half of the 19th century, Brazil's position vis-à-vis its neighbors can be quickly summed up. The imperial government was chiefly concerned with Argentina. It feared a unified country that might become a strong republic capable of checking Brazil's hegemony and bringing over to its side the restless province of Rio Grande do Sul.

As far as Uruguay is concerned, there was always Brazilian influence in that country. As cattle ranchers, the Gaúchos of Rio Grande do Sul had economic interests in Uruguay. They looked unfavorably at measures designed to stop smuggling along the border. Brazil supported the Colorados, whose political aims were compatible with Brazilian interests. The imperial government even reached a secret accord with the Colorados, Rosas's adversaries, and agreed to subsidize them on a monthly basis.

During the first half of the 19th century, Brazil's relations with Paraguay depended on how it was getting along with Argentina.

When rivalry between the two countries increased, the imperial government tended to favor Paraguay. When things cooled off, differences of opinion between Brazil and Paraguay came to the surface. Their diverging wills involved border matters and Brazil's insistence on free access to the Paraguay River, which was the main way to reach the province of Mato Grosso.

To all appearances, there was scant likelihood of an alliance among Brazil, Uruguay, and Argentina against Paraguay. But that is what happened. The future allies first approached one another in 1862, when Bartolomé Mitre defeated the Federalists and took over in Argentina. The country unified under the name of the Argentine Republic, and Mitre was elected president. His policies were seen as favorable by Brazilian Liberals, who had also come to power that year. Mitre approached the Uruguayan Colorados and became a defender of free access to the rivers.

These approximations set the stage for conflict between Brazil and Paraguay. Even though both countries competed for the yerba mate market, their disputes, from the Brazilian government's point of view, were primarily geopolitical: they quarreled over borders and access to the rivers. With the idea of ending Paraguay's isolation once and for all, and expecting to carry some weight in the region, Solano López joined the Blancos in Uruguay and Mitre's adversaries – leaders in the Argentine provinces of Entre-Rdíos and Corrientes.

Brazil was far from acting as an instrument of British interests at the beginning of the 1860s. Indeed, the imperial government got enmeshed in several incidents with Britain known as the Christie Controversy or *questão Christie*, after the British ambassador to Brazil. Early in 1863, when a British naval detachment stationed in Rio de Janeiro apprehended some Brazilian merchant marine ships, Brazil broke off diplomatic relations with Britain. Patriotic exuberance spread throughout the country owing to this and to the news that Brazilian citizens were being attacked in Uruguay, where the Blancos were in power. In September 1864, the imperial government invaded Uruguay with the goal of putting the Colorados in power.

Solano López likely believed that Brazilian and Argentine expansionism had been set in motion and would end up suffocating

Paraguay. So he decided to take the initiative. On 11 November 1864, a Paraguayan gunboat captured the *Marquês de Olinda*, a Brazilian ship on the Paraguay River. After this act, diplomatic relations were cut off between the two countries. War operations effectively began on 23 December 1864, when Solano López launched an offensive into Mato Grosso. Immediately afterward, Solano López asked Argentina for permission to send troops through Corrientes Province, after which they would attack Brazilian forces in Rio Grande do Sul and Uruguay. His request was denied.

There is much speculation about why Solano López was moved to begin the conflict, seeing that it could bring about a union against Paraguay of two old rivals, Brazil and Argentina. He appears to have wanted to neutralize the threats from his powerful neighbors and to turn Paraguay into an active participant in the continent's political game. For this he counted on a victory in defenseless Mato Grosso. This would bring Brazil into line. He also counted on the support of Uruguay's Blancos and on backing from the Argentine provinces opposed to Mitre.

But his hopes were dashed. His support from the Argentine provinces never materialized. In Uruguay Brazil had put Venancio Flores, a Colorado, in power. In March 1865, Paraguay declared war on Argentina, and on 1 May 1865 the Brazilian, Argentine, and Uruguayan governments signed the Treaty of the Triple Alliance. Argentine President Mitre took command of the allied forces.

The economic and demographic weight of the three allies was greatly superior to Paraguay's. As often happens at the outset of a conflict, in Brazil and Argentina people thought the war would be a lark. It was anything but that. Solano López, unlike his adversaries, was well prepared militarily. Seemingly, since there are no reliable statistics, at the war's beginning there were 18,000 career soldiers in Brazil, 8,000 in Argentina, and 1,000 in Uruguay. Paraguay had around 64,000 soldiers plus a reserve force of 28,000 veterans. For battles on the river, however, Brazil enjoyed ample naval superiority.

As the years passed, the Triple Alliance's forces grew; and Brazilians predominated, contributing at least two-thirds of the total number of allied soldiers. The number of Brazilians mobilized is estimated to have been between 135,000 and 200,000, out of a total male population of some 4,900,000 in 1865. The troops were selected from men in the regular army, from men in the National Guard, and from men who in the main were recruited in the old colonial style – by force. That is, many who fought with the Patriotic Volunteers (*Voluntários da Pátria*) were hardly volunteers.

Slave owners offered slaves who would fight as soldiers. An 1866 law appealed to "the Nation's Slaves" and offered freedom to any who would serve in the army. The law applied to Africans who had been brought in illegally, after the slave trade had ended. They had been caught and were being detained by the imperial government.

The Brazilian army solidified its position during the Paraguayan War. Up to then, the empire had relied on a small professional officer corps. It had experienced great difficulty in increasing the number of military careerists. There was no obligatory military service, but there was a very restricted lottery which chose people to serve in the army. The National Guard was made up largely of white men who were exempt from serving in the army. Until the Paraguayan War, the militia in Rio Grande do Sul had managed Brazil's military campaigns along the River Plate, but it was incapable of taking on a modern army like Paraguay's.

In the history of the war, military feats on both sides are combined with deprivation and death in combat and from disease, especially cholera. At the beginning of the conflict (June 1865), in the battle of Riachuelo, the Brazilian navy crushed Paraguay's navy in Argentine territory. With the Paraguayan navy defeated, the allies blockaded the Paraná River, Paraguay's only access to the world. This advantage was not pressed to the limit. Fearful of enemy fortifications along the Paraguay, especially around Humaitá, the allies remained at an impasse for several years. They were immobilized by the Paraguayans' system of land defense.

Also in June 1865, Paraguayan forces already in Corrientes invaded Rio Grande do Sul, but were soon defeated. Beginning in November 1865, the conflict was waged on Paraguayan soil. (Mato Grosso, by then a secondary front, was the only exception.) In May 1866, the major battle of the war was fought in Tuiuti. In spite of the Paraguayans' defeat, the allies could not press their advantage and soon suffered a serious setback in Curupaiti. The object of these battles was to take the fortress at Humaitá.

An important factor in the war's execution was Caxias's appointment as commander of Brazilian forces, in October 1866. He was appointed owing to pressure from the Conservative Party, then the opposition, which blamed Liberals for the uncertain outcome of the war. At the beginning of 1868, Caxias also took command of the allied forces. Mitre had been obliged to return to Buenos Aires to deal with matters of internal politics. Among these problems, provinces' opposition to sending troops to Paraguay stood out. From then on, Brazil carried on practically single-handedly.

Before attacking Humaitá, Caxias worked on establishing an adequate infrastructure in the army. Then he took the offensive. Humaitá capitulated in August 1868 and in January 1869 Brazilians entered Asunción. Sick and wanting peace, Caxias resigned his command. By this time the only point of the war was to destroy Paraguay. Caxias was replaced by Count d'Eu, Princess Isabel's husband. The princess was next in line to the imperial throne.

After several battles, Brazilian troops defeated the last remnant of the Paraguayan army. It consisted of old and sick men and some boys. Solano López was finally surrounded in his encampment and killed by Brazilian soldiers on 1 March 1870.

Paraguay was devastated by the conflict and lost parts of its territory to Brazil and Argentina. It also lost its future. Its process of modernization became a thing of the past, and Paraguay itself became an exporter of products of scant value. The most reliable estimates suggest that half of Paraguay's population died in the struggle. The population fell from 406,000 in 1864 to 231,000 in 1872. Most of the survivors were old people, women, and children.

Brazil ended the war even deeper in debt to Britain. (Diplomatic relations had been reestablished when hostilities began.) But the greatest consequence of the war was the army's emergence as an institution with a definite form and a set of objectives all its own. Among other points, its longtime grievances with the imperial government were expressed in a different manner. After all, in success and failure, the army had stood firm on the battlefront. While soldiers were fighting, the elite civilians, the "tail coats" as they came to be called with scorn, had been out of danger and, in certain cases, had gotten rich dealing in supplies for the troops.

2.7   CRISES OF THE SECOND EMPIRE

Beginning in the 1870s, a series of symptomatic crises began to emerge. They included the republican movement and the friction between the imperial government and the army and church. On top of this, the resolution of the problem of slavery weakened the relationship between the state and its base of support. These factors did not have equal weight in bringing about the end of the monarchy, which can be explained by an array of reasons including socioeconomic transformations which gave rise to new social groups and made notions of reform more appealing.

Abolition of slavery proceeded in a step-by-step manner and was fully achieved in 1888. The major controversy concerning legal measures pertaining to slavery did not occur at its end, but in 1871, when the imperial government proposed the so-called Law of the Free Womb. The law proposed to make children of slave women born after 1871 free. These children would be controlled by their mothers' masters until age eight. Once the children were eight, their masters could chose between receiving an indemnity from the state or utilizing the children's services until they reached age 21.

This project originated in a conservative cabinet led by the Viscount of Rio Branco, who had snatched the abolitionist banner from the Liberals. What could have led the government to propose a law that, without being at all revolutionary, would create problems for the government? Indeed, the government created problems within its base of support – those Brazilians who could vote.

The most reasonable explanation is that the initiative came from the emperor and his council. Even though there were no slave uprisings after the Paraguayan War, the ruling elite concluded that Brazil suffered from a basic weakness on its internal front since it could not count on the loyalty of a sizable part of its population. Resolution of the "servile question," even if it were to wound important economic interests, was seen as the lesser evil in the face of the problem of slaves' loyalty and the potential risk of slave revolts.

The ruling class, on the other hand, felt the project posed a great risk to social order. They believed that when masters freed their slaves in acts of generosity, the former slaves would be grateful and would continue to be obedient. For the government to pass a law freeing them would give slaves the idea they had rights and would lead the country into a race war.

The deputies' positions concerning the project, which was finally approved, are quite revealing. While the representatives from the Northeast voted overwhelmingly in favor of the project (39 to 6), those from the Center-South inverted this tendency (30 against, 12 in favor). These votes reveal in part that interprovincial slave traffic had reduced the Northeast's dependence on slave labor.

There is one other important datum. In significant numbers, deputies were also public servants, especially magistrates. This group, largely Northerners and Northeasterners, was allied with the government and threw its weight behind the project. As far as parties were concerned, there was no clear division of votes between Liberals and Conservatives. Deputies from both parties, on individual bases, voted for or against the proposal.

In practice, the 1871 law had few repercussions. Few children were turned over to the state, and slave owners continued to use children's services.

Beginning in the 1880s, the abolitionist movement gathered momentum. New associations and newspapers appeared and supported the propaganda. People from different social backgrounds and standings as well as people with different points of view participated in the abolitionist campaign. Joaquim Nabuco stood out among the different elite figures. He was an important parliamentarian and writer who came from a family of politicians and large landowners in Pernambuco. Blacks and mulattos of humble origins, José do Patrocínio, André Rebouças, and Luiz Gama were also central figures in the movement.

Patrocínio was the son of a slave-holding planter, who was also a Catholic priest. His mother was black and made her living as a street vendor. Patrocínio owned the *Gazeta da Tarde*, an abolitionist newspaper in Rio de Janeiro, and was famous for his exciting, emotional speeches.

Rebouças was completely different. He was an engineer, an introvert, a teacher of botany, calculus, and geometry at the Escola Politécnica in Rio de Janeiro. He associated the end of slavery with the establishment of "rural democracy" and argued for giving land to freed slaves and for creating a territorial tax which would force large estates or *latifúndios* to be divided up and sold.

Luiz Gama's life reads like a soap opera. His father belonged to a wealthy Portuguese family in Bahia, and his mother, Luiza Mahin, according to her son's proud affirmation, "was a free black African who always rejected baptism and Christian doctrine." Gama was illegally sold as a slave by his impoverished father. He was sent to Rio and then to Santos. Along with 100 other barefoot and hungry slaves he climbed the Serra do Mar mountains. He fled his master's house and became a soldier and later on a poet, lawyer, and journalist in São Paulo.

As the abolitionist movement grew, provinces in the North became uninterested in maintaining the slave system, and Ceará on its own ended slavery there in 1884. In this vein, the Sexagenarian Law, also known as the Saraiva-Cotegipe Law, was approved in 1885. The law was proposed by a liberal cabinet headed by José Antônio Saraiva, known as Conselheiro Saraiva. The measure was approved in the Senate when the Conservatives, under the leadership of Baron Cotegipe, had returned to power. This law set slaves over the age of 60 free and established norms for gradual manumission of all slaves with indemnities to be paid to owners. The law was supposed to offer a means of detaining radical abolitionists, but it was unsuccessful.

Between 1885 and 1888, after a brief halt, the abolitionist movement again gained momentum. At that time, the most important fact was disarray on São Paulo plantations; it had been caused by massive flights of slaves. Activists would leave São Paulo for the plantations and rural towns and incite slaves to rebel. They were led by Antônio Bento, a member of a wealthy São Paulo family. In a short time, Santos became a center for sheltering runaway slaves. While this was going on, the Paulista coffee elite stepped up the pace of their immigration plan because they understood that the slave-holding system was coming apart at the seams.

By 1888, the only ones in favor of slavery were the representatives from the old coffee areas in the Paraíba Valley, where declining fortunes were measured by the number of slaves people held. Antônio Prado, a Conservative senator from São Paulo with ties in Oeste Paulista, proposed a measure to delay matters. It provided for the immediate freeing of all slaves. Indemnities would be paid, and slaves would be obliged to work for three months, to bring in the next harvest. In the face of Liberal opposition, the Council president João Alfredo, a Conservative, opted for unrestricted Abolition. His initiative was approved by a large parliamentary majority and was ratified on 13 May 1888 by Princess Isabel, who was on the throne for her father. Of the nine deputies who voted no, eight were from Rio de Janeiro. In the Senate Baron Cotegipe led the faltering opposition. He gave voice to the following threat: "In a short time they'll be asking for the land to be divided and the state will declare it expropriated with no indemnities."

The slaves' fate varied from region to region. As a rule, in the Northeast they became dependents of the large landowners. Maranhão was an exception to the rule, since in that province freedmen left the plantations and settled on unoccupied land, as squatters.

In the Paraíba Valley, ex-slaves became sharecroppers on the coffee plantations, and later they worked as small farmers or as cowhands. In Oeste Paulista, massive flight characterized the last few years before Abolition. Even so, the flow of blacks into the city of São Paulo and other areas lasted at least ten years. In the São Paulo and Rio de Janeiro urban areas, the situation varied. Whereas in São Paulo stable jobs went to European immigrants (and former slaves were relegated to poorly paid temporary work), the picture was somewhat different in Rio de Janeiro. Given that there had been a tradition of employing free blacks as well as slaves in artisans' workshops and in manufacturing, and given that fewer immigrants stayed in that region, black workers had, relatively speaking, greater opportunities there. In 1891, 30 percent of the industrial employees in Rio were black while in 1893 immigrants occupied 84 percent of the jobs in Paulista industry.

In Rio Grande do Sul, like São Paulo, for regular work slaves and ex-slaves were replaced by foreign immigrants.

In spite of differences in specific regions of Brazil, the abolition of slavery did not end blacks' problems. Bosses' preference for immigrant workers in the economy's most dynamic regions and the scanty opportunities available to former slaves in other areas put the black population at a tremendous social disadvantage. Especially in areas of large-scale immigration, blacks were considered inferior beings, useful when subservient, dangerous by nature. They were thought of as idlers and criminally inclined.

Few historic themes in Brazilian history have been studied the way slavery has. There are passionate controversies over slaves' death rates as they crossed the Atlantic; over the possibilities of establishing slave families; over the meaning of manumissions, that is, freeing of slaves before 1888; over the so-called *brecha camponesa*, or "rural opening"; and over slave life in different work situations.

These controversies have supported the affirmation that the slave system was not sustained only by open violence, even though violence was basic to the system. Slavery had a long life because it pervaded private and public domains, because of the differences among slaves, and because of slaves' real or imaginary expectations of getting their freedom. Two themes stand out: the "brecha cam-ponesa" and manumissions.

The existence of a rural opening is sustained by a group of authors led by Ciro Flammarion Cardoso. They emphasize the importance of the sector of the economy dedicated to the internal market during Brazil's colonial period and during the 19th century. Their thesis is based on the fact that both on sugar and especially on coffee plantations, slaves had permission to grow gardens near their quarters or on small plots of land. There they grew foodstuffs for their own consumption as well as to sell. This practice eventually became widespread and almost customary. By this reasoning, those scholars maintain that once slaves were growing crops on their own to sell on the open market, slaves were also peasants, and had made an opening in the system of slavery. They also claim that, legally speaking, while slaves were still things, in practice, and owing to this custom, they began to have rights.

The problem of manumission arose because of the large number of slaves manumitted in the Spanish colonies and in Brazil, when compared to manumission rates in British and French colonies. Indeed, in spite of the unreliable statistics, researchers are sure that at the end of the colonial period, 42 percent of the people of African descent (blacks and mulattos), which was 28 percent of the country's population, were free or had been freed. Slaves still made up 38 percent of the total population. According to the 1872 census,

73 percent of the Afro-Brazilian population was free or had been freed. This was 43 percent of the total population; slaves made up only 15 percent of the total.

Manumissions occurred when slaves bought their freedom; when third parties bought it for them; or when masters decided to let them go. The fact that more manumissions were purchased in the cities indicates that cities offered slaves greater possibilities for saving money.

A facile explanation for masters' liberating slaves is that only old and sick ones were manumitted, and then for economic reasons. However, some studies challenge this explanation. A study of 7,000 freedmen in Salvador between 1684 and 1785 shows that the average age of most of the beneficiaries was 15.

This does not mean that financial considerations should be struck from the list of causes for the large number of manumissions. When one compares zones of economic expansion to others in decline, the latter had more manumissions than the former. But reasons of the heart may have weighed heavily on many liberating acts, since when one looks at the sex of people freed, women are in the majority. In Rio de Janeiro between 1807 and 1831, 64 percent of all manumitted people were women. This percentage is especially significant considering that the proportion of men in the slave population was considerably higher than that of women.

Lastly, it should be remembered that being manumitted did not mean that one was free. Until 1865, a paid manumission could be revoked if an ex-master merely claimed the person was ungrateful. On top of this, on paper or in practice, being freed was often contingent on a set of restrictions, especially that of continuing to serve the old masters. Legislation after 1870 maintained this custom when it conditionally freed children and old people.

While some freedmen were involved in black rebellions, these people were halfway between being slaves and being free. Their social status was close to that of poor whites. Manumission softened the head-on racial opposition. In addition, where there were large concentrations of blacks, freedmen played an important role in community preservation. The most typical case is that of Bahia, where 19th-century freedmen safeguarded the existence of a community combining African and European cultures.

2.8 THE REPUBLICAN MOVEMENT

Republicanism played a role in the movements for independence. At the end of the 18 th century, republicanism was associated with revolution and with ideas of social reform. Some members of the republican movement which began in 1870 in Rio de Janeiro inherited these concerns. Men like Lopes Trovão, who signed the Republican Manifesto of 1870, and Silva Jardim (during the last years of the empire) advocated a popular revolution as a way of creating a republic. However, the vast majority was of the same opinion as Quintino Bocaiuva, who favored a peaceful transition from one type of government to another and who favored waiting, if possible, until after Dom Pedro II died.

Besides the military, the social base for urban republicanism was made up mainly of professionals and newspaper people, whose numbers had grown owing to the growth of cities and greater numbers of schools. The republicans in Rio de Janeiro wanted a federal republic with greater representation for its citizens, with individual guarantees and rights, and without slavery.

The novelty of the 1870s was the appearance of a conservative republican movement in the provinces. Its major proponent was the Partido Republicano Paulista (PRP), founded in 1873. The party's directives came mainly from the coffee bourgeoisie. The basic point of their program consisted of federalism; they wanted to assure ample autonomy for all provinces. Whereas Tavares Bastos, one of the leading advocates of federalism, argued in favor of a federative monarchy, the São Paulo republicans had become convinced that an empire would be incompatible with a federation. Among other reasons for this, for them a federation meant that provinces would control their finances and admission of immigrants. It also meant that government revenue would be decentralized.

In São Paulo, republicanism differed from that of Rio de Janeiro because it emphasized the notion of federalism. It was less interested in defending civil and political liberties. And it addressed the problem of slavery in a different manner. If one considers its social makeup, it was not by chance that the PRP avoided taking a clear-cut position on slavery. Indeed, its members failed to discuss the matter until Abolition was practically upon them. Paulista republicans' complaints against the central government had to do, among other things, with São Paulo's underrepresentation in Parliament and in the offices of the executive branch. They also criticized the way government revenues were spent. They emphasized that São Paulo with its expanding economy was contributing more and more to the government's receipts, but that it did not receive benefits commensurate with its payments.

In spite of being an active campaigner and publisher of newspapers, the republican movement in Rio de Janeiro never managed to become a political party. The significant republican parties up to the end of the empire were those in São Paulo and Minas Gerais, especially the PRP. In 1884, the PRP, allied with the opposition Conservatives, sent Prudente de Moraes and Campos Sales to the Chamber of Deputies. These men would be the first two civilian presidents of the Brazilian republic. According to some estimates from 1889, one-fourth (3,600 people) of the Paulista electorate were republicans. This was, however, less than the Liberals and Conservatives, who numbered 6,600 and 3,900 respectively.

During the 1870s, the relationship between the church and state became tense. The union of "throne and altar" in the 1824 constitution was in itself a potential source of conflict. While Catholicism was the official religion, the constitution actually gave the state the right to approve or deny ecclesiastic decrees.

The conflict began with the Vatican's new guidelines of 1848, during the pontificate of Pius IX. The pontiff condemned "modern liberties" and tried to assert the church's worldwide spiritual authority. In 1870, the pope's power was strengthened when a Vatican Council proclaimed the dogma of papal infallibility. This position had repercussions in several countries. In the United States, it coincided with the arrival of huge numbers of Irish Catholic immigrants. Within the Protestant ruling class, people feared that the United States would become a Catholic country. In Brazil, the Vatican policy occasioned a more rigid attitude from priests as far as religious discipline was concerned. The church also asserted its independence from the state.

The conflict arose when the bishop of Olinda, Dom Vital, in obedience to the pope's decree, decided to prohibit Masons from joining religious brotherhoods. In spite of their small numbers,

Masons exerted influence in the ruling circles. The Viscount of Rio Branco, president of the Council of Ministers, was a Mason. When misunderstandings arose, Dom Vital was treated as a "rogue civil servant." He was arrested and sentenced to jail. After him another bishop received the same fate. The tempest only abated after an agreement (1874–1875) in which Rio Branco's cabinet was replaced, the bishops were granted amnesty, and the pope revoked his prohibitions against Masons.

The participation of army officers in government was significant up to Dom Pedro I's abdication. From that point on, their participation dwindled. Soldiers' presence in public uprisings after independence made the army suspect. During the Regency, Liberals, headed by Feijó, reduced the number of career servicemen and created the National Guard. They argued that a large standing army would give rise to little Napoleons, as had been the case in Argentina and Mexico. The navy, on the other hand, was indulged. It was seen as a noble organization, perhaps because it had taken in some British officers during the first few years after independence.

In spite of the unequal treatment, up to 1850 the army officer corps had elitist traits. But that changed considerably during the following years. The low pay, the shabby life, and the slow promotions tended to dissuade the sons of important families from opting for a military career. On the other hand, the numbers of military men's and bureaucrats' offspring who aspired to officer-hood grew.

Regionally speaking, the majority of the new officers came from backlands towns in the Northeast or from Rio Grande do Sul. As a rule, those from the Northeast were from traditional families whose fortunes had declined and who could not send their sons to school. In Rio Grande do Sul, a border region where military detachments were concentrated, a career in the army was thought to be relatively prestigious. One sign of this is that the government, in 1853, founded a military academy for training infantry and cavalry officers there.

The army's changing social composition helped drive a wedge between the officers and the empire's political elite, especially those who had graduated from the law schools. The *legistas*, as people called these lawyers, seemed to epitomize useless culture and electoral corruption, as far as the military was concerned. Legistas were considered responsible for the web of laws and regulations that held the country back.

During good times in the 1850s, the government took some steps toward reforming the army. A law of September 1850 reformed the officer corps and gave people with diplomas from the Military Academy privileges that other officers without diplomas did not get. This was especially true in the technical areas of the officer corps. The Military Academy, which had functioned in Rio de Janeiro since 1810, taught civil engineering combined with a strictly military curriculum. In 1858, the minister of war separated civil engineering from the military program, which was transferred to Praia Vermelha, where it stayed until 1904.

Before the Paraguayan War, there had been some criticism of the imperial government among the officers. Their criticism was aimed at specific matters affecting military life, such as criteria for promotions and the right to marry without getting permission from the minister of war. Other, more general complaints had to do with the quality of life in Brazil. The younger officers were in favor of education, industry, railway construction, and an end to slavery.

Once the Military Academy was reorganized and the war was over, as a guild the army became strong. When they participated in politics, many officers began to express themselves as military men rather than as military men who were also politicians. The most notable examples of differences in two generations of officers are Caxias and Floriano Peixoto. Caxias was beyond a doubt a highly prestigious figure in the army. He was also one of the leaders of the Conservative Party and, even before the Paraguayan War, he was about to become the president of the Council of Ministers. On the other hand, Peixoto, in spite of his connections with the inner circle of the Liberal Party, which had helped him in his career, talked like an officer and a citizen. His ties were, in essence, with the military.

The Praia Vermelha Military School, originally meant to be a place for military studies, in practice ended up as a center for the study of mathematics, philosophy, and letters. It was there that the army's opposition to the government began to focus on the monarchy. The idea of a Brazilian republic was gaining ground. In this process, positivism exerted more and more influence, especially after 1872, when Benjamin Constant became a teacher at the Military Academy.

Auguste Comte's positivism had ample influence in Latin America, in countries such as Mexico, Chile, Argentina, and Brazil. It seemed to offer an orderly, scientific solution for the political and social impasses that oligarchical liberalism had brought about. Its reverence for technical innovations and industry attracted the emerging elites, who criticized the formalism typical of the law school graduates.

In the Brazilian case, positivism brought with it a formula for conservative modernization based on action from the state and on the neutralization of traditional politicians – all of which was tremendously appealing in military circles. However, the military was rarely orthodox in how it accepted positivistic principles. As a rule, army officers took whatever suited their view. Brazil's republican governments became defenders of strong, interventionistic executives who could bring the country up to date. Or, on the other hand, they favored military dictatorships.

One of the empire's most important measures during the 1880s (besides the abolition of slavery) was the approval of an electoral reform – the Saraiva Law of January 1881. This reform established direct suffrage for legislative elections. There would be no more distinction between voters and electors. It kept the minimum income requirement and the economic census, and it added, beginning in 1882, a literary census – that is, only literates could vote. The right to vote was extended to non-Catholics, naturalized Brazilians, and freed slaves.

The Saraiva Law had been planned as a means of making elections honest and of broadening the citizenry. It was first applied successfully in the 1881 elections and results (in certain areas) became less one-sided. The Conservative Party, even though it was in the minority, seated 47 vocal deputies – an impressive feat. In later years, however, the old vices, fraud and voter intimidation, returned. The hope of attaining an "electoral truth," which the empire's city dwellers and men of letters wanted, was snuffed out.

Beginning in 1883, various misunderstandings arose among the government, deputies, and army officers. One of the most notable rifts occurred when in 1884 Lieutenant Colonel Sena Madureira, a prestigious officer and friend of the emperor, invited one of the raftsmen who had participated in the struggle for the abolition of slavery in Ceará to visit his school in Rio de Janeiro. Sena Madureira was transferred to Rio Grande do Sul. In the republican newspaper *A Federação*, he published an article about the episode, in which Ceará raftsmen refused to transport slaves.

Similar to Sena Madureira's, other cases created polemics in the newspapers. The minister of war then signed an order prohibiting military men from discussing political or military matters in the press.

The officers stationed in Rio Grande do Sul called a mass meeting in Porto Alegre and protested the minister's prohibition. Deodoro da Fonseca, the provincial president, refused to discipline the officers and was called to Rio de Janeiro. Finally, a compromise which favored the officers was devised. The prohibition was revoked and the cabinet was censured by Congress.

At this time, June 1887, officers had founded the Clube Militar as a permanent association to defend their rights. Deodoro da Fonseca was elected president. The same month the club was founded, Deodoro requested that the minister of war no longer oblige the army to hunt down runaway slaves. And indeed, the army ceased to do so, even though the minister did not grant Deodoro's request.

Military dissatisfaction and republican propaganda were on the rise when, in June 1889, the emperor invited a Liberal, the Viscount of Ouro Preto, to form a new cabinet. Ouro Preto proposed a series of reforms, but he ruffled feathers when he named a personal enemy of Deodoro's as president of Rio Grande do Sul.

Since 1887 there had been contacts between some Paulista and Gaúcho (Rio Grande do Sul) republican leaders and military men aiming to bring down the monarchy. On 11 November 1889, prestigious civilians and military men such as Ruy Barbosa, Benjamin Constant, Aristides Lobo, and Quintino Bocaiuva met with Marshal Deodoro da Fonseca to urge him to head a movement against the monarchy. A series of rumors spread by younger officers spoke of Deodoro's impending arrest, of a reduction in the number of permanent officers, and even of abolishing the army. These rumors led Deodoro to agree to lead and, at least, to oust Ouro Preto.

During the early morning hours of 15 November 1889, Deodoro took command and marched his troops to the Ministry of War, where monarchist leaders were meeting. There are several versions of the confusing episode that ensued. It is not known for certain whether on that day Deodoro declared Brazil a republic or whether he simply brought down Ouro Preto. Be that as it may, on the following day the monarchy had fallen. A few days later the royal family went off into exile.

2.9   THE FALL OF THE MONARCHY

The end of the monarchy was the result of a series of factors of differing weight. Two forces, of very different natures, should be pointed out first of all: the army and a vocal sector of the São Paulo coffee bourgeoisie who were members of the Paulista Republican Party. The episode on 15 November came about owing to an almost exclusively military initiative. The army had taken a tiny but decisive step to hasten the fall of the monarchy. On the other hand, the coffee bourgeoisie would furnish a stable social footing for the republic that neither the army nor the inhabitants of the city of Rio could provide on their own.

There are also human factors to take into account. The emperor's diabetes had removed him (an important stabilizing agent) from center stage. With his personal prestige and that which he got from the throne, Pedro II absorbed many of the shocks from the military's complaints. His absence put the army officers face to face with the imperial elite whom the officers were hampering. The elite, on the other hand, would not relinquish their belief in civilian authority; they revealed this by appointing civilians to the Ministry of War during times when prudence would recommend the opposite tack.

The other problem came from the lack of an optimistic prospect for a Third Empire. When Dom Pedro II died, Princess Isabel would assume the throne. Her husband, Count d'Eu, was a Frenchmen whose personality was the subject of much debate.

It was common to assign important roles in the fall of the monarchy to two other factors: the dispute between church and state and Abolition. The first of these in some measure helped wear down the government, but its influence should not be exaggerated. The fall of the monarchy was restricted to a dispute among divergent elites, and the church did not have strong influence among monarchists or republicans. On the contrary, positivists, whether they were orthodox or not, kept their distance from the church.

As far as Abolition is concerned, the initiatives aimed at gradually abolishing slavery caused some (generalized) resentment and alienated the coffee planters in the Paraíba Valley. However, by 1888 they were no longer a force with which the government needed to contend.

2.10 ECONOMY AND DEMOGRAPHY

During this time, the first two general population censuses were carried out, in 1872 and 1890. Notwithstanding their defects, these censuses began to produce more reassuring figures than those that up to then had existed. From an 1819 population of some 4,600,000 (800,000 of whom were Indians), Brazil had grown to 9,900,000 people in 1872 and to 14,300,000 in 1890. According to the data from 1872, Minas Gerais was the most populous province, with approximately 2,100,000 inhabitants. Next came Bahia with 1,380,000. Pernambuco and São Paulo both had around 840,000 people. The most relevant changes were São Paulo province's rise in population and Rio de Janeiro province's fall. It went from second to fifth place.

As for racial makeup, mulattos formed 42 percent of the population, whites 38 percent, and blacks 20 percent. The proportion of whites had grown from 30 percent in 1819 because of immigration. Little more than 300,000, or an average of 10,000 per year, had come to Brazil between 1846 and 1875. Half of those were Portuguese.

The early data on education reveal woeful inadequacy. In 1872, 99.9 percent of all slaves were illiterate. Among the free population, 80 percent could neither read nor write, and 86 percent of free women were also illiterate. Even if one discounts the fact that these percentages take in the entire population, including children under the age of six, they are still very high. It was shown that only 17 percent of the population between the ages of six and 15 attended school, and there were only 12,000 students in secondary schools. Still, there were some 8,000 people with college degrees in Brazil.

There was an abyss between the lettered elite and the great mass of illiterates and people with only rudimentary educations. Schools of surgery and of other branches of medicine opened in Bahia and Rio de Janeiro when Dom João VI came to Brazil. These schools, just like the school of engineering, were originally linked to military institutions. As far as the formation of an elite was concerned, the most important step was the founding of the law schools in São Paulo (1827) and Olinda/Recife (1828). These schools produced graduates who, as magistrates and lawyers, made up the nucleus of the empire's political structure.

Brazil was still an essentially agrarian country. Of people gainfully employed in 1872, 80 percent worked in agriculture, 13 percent performed services, and 7 percent worked in industry. (More than 50 percent of the "service" workers were domestic servants.) Industry was obviously just beginning, and mining was considered to be an industry.

Rio de Janeiro had 522,000 inhabitants in 1890 and was the only great urban center in Brazil. The imperial capital was the center of political life and entertainment. There was much investment in transportation, lighting, and beautification. After Rio came Salvador, Recife, Belém, and only then São Paulo with a modest population of a mere 65,000 people. But the city that was becoming the focal point of the coffee business attracted more and more immigrants and had begun to take off. It grew geometrically at 3 percent per annum between 1872 and 1886, and at an 8 percent rate between 1886 and 1890.

Around 1870, the Center-South's tendency to develop economically and the Northeast's decline were facts of life. In large measure, this came from the different overseas stimuli for agriculture. In the coffee-consuming countries, population and income had increased enormously. The world's greatest consumer, the United States, had trebled its population and its coffee drinking between 1850 and 1900. This fact, along with other circumstances, allowed coffee producers to absorb price fluctuations; that is, since demand was on the rise, planters could withstand periodic losses during the times when coffee prices fell on the international market.

While the main economic activity of the Northeast continued to be relevant, it did not have the same fate as coffee. Once it was replaced by coffee, sugar stayed in second place on the list of Brazil's exports. It was replaced by cotton only from 1861 to 1870.

But sugar did not have an easy time in the international market. It faced two formidable contenders: beet sugar, which during the middle of the 19th century Germans began to produce in large quantities; and Caribbean sugar, where the Cuban product stood out. Contrary to Brazil, Cuba had labor problems. Still, the land's fertility and the available capital, at first Spanish and later North American, gave the island a leadership position, not just in sugar production, but also in modernizing the sugar industry. Another factor to be remembered is Cuba's proximity to consumers. Around 1860, 70 percent of Cuba's sugar mills were steam driven, compared to a mere 2 percent in Pernambuco.

In the Brazilian Northeast, government-sponsored modernization efforts went slowly, and their results were much more limited. It comes as no surprise, then, that around 1875 Brazil's traditional 10 percent share in the world sugar market had fallen to 5 percent.

Since colonial times, cotton had been grown throughout the Northeast, but mainly in Pernambuco, Maranhão, Alagoas, and Paraíba. It was planted by small- and middle-scale farmers, who also grew foodstuffs for their own consumption, and to sell on the local market. From the beginning of the 19th century, American cotton competed with Brazil's and began to displace it in the main importing market – the English textile industry. The American Civil War, from 1861 to 1865, provided a sudden stimulus for Brazilian exports, which during the 1860s made cotton reach the number two position on Brazil's export list. But this was shortlived, and cotton exports soon declined. The later impetus for producing cotton would be linked to the internal market, when the textile industry in Brazil expanded.

In the Amazon region, rubber extraction began to gain importance and attracted the sparse local populace as well as available workers from the Northeast. In 1839, once Charles Goodyear perfected the vulcanization process, the worldwide demand for rubber rose. Thanks to vulcanization, rubber could withstand heat and cold and could now be used in diverse products such as belts, hoses, shoes, and raincoats.

Until 1850, Brazilian rubber exports were insignificant. They grew over the years, and during the 1880s reached third place, producing 8 percent of the export revenue. This was very close to cotton's (10 percent) share. The rubber boom began at this point. Not only did exports increase, but a regional economic pole was created. Up to that point, the rubber business had been in the hands of a small group of Portuguese middlemen and a few foreign exporting concerns. When exports increased, a banking network sprang up, and the number of middlemen and firms specializing in importing consumer goods increased. This stimulated the growth of Belém and Manaus. Only the workers and the rubber gatherers were no better off.

In spite of the United States' being the principal importer of Brazilian coffee, Britain was in first place as far as imports from Brazil were concerned, up to the 1870s. Between 1870 and 1873, Britain bought 40 percent of the total worth of Brazilian exports. The United States was in second place with 29 percent. During these same three years, 53 percent of Brazil's imports came from Britain, and French imports were in a distant second place, at 12 percent.

As had been the case in the colony, not everything produced in Brazil was destined for export. Many areas were engaged in raising cattle and other animals as well as in growing foodstuffs for subsistence and to sell domestically. Two areas stand out in this respect: Minas Gerais and the South, especially Rio Grande do Sul.

Owing to deficient routes of communication, Minas Gerais was divided into very different and loosely integrated regions. The Forest Zone (Zona da Mata) grew coffee and was closely tied to Rio de Janeiro. The São Francisco River valley was a cattle-raising region with greater affinities to Bahia and Pernambuco than to the rest of the province. Southern Minas was linked to São Paulo and the imperial capital.

In spite of the growth of coffee, which was exported from Rio de Janeiro, Minas Gerais was not a predominant part of the export economy. Its economic base consisted of animal husbandry and the growing of crops. Seemingly, the great bulk of its crops (corn, beans, and manioc flour) was consumed internally. Bovines, porcines, and their by-products were the most important items Minas exported to other regions.

Up to Abolition, Minas Gerais was the most populous province of the country, and it had the most slaves. However, slaves made up a greater proportion of Rio de Janeiro's population. The growth of coffee plantations absorbed a large number of slaves, but most slaves lived in areas where no coffee was grown. The state of affairs was similar to that of colonial times; that is, Minas combined slave holding with an economy that serviced the internal market.

In southern Brazil, the internal market was supplied by the traditional cattlemen and by the influx of immigrants. The South attracted immigrants earlier than São Paulo did, and immigration to that region was quite different. While in São Paulo the objective of immigration was to furnish workers for large-scale agriculture, in the South immigration was intended to help colonize the area with small farmers.

Shortly before independence, José Bonifácio and Dom Pedro I, for socioeconomic as well as military reasons, made the first efforts at attracting German settlers to the South, especially to Santa Catarina and Rio Grande do Sul. José Bonifácio hoped to stimulate the formation of a Brazilian rural middle class.

Near Porto Alegre the most successful of all German colonies was founded: São Leopoldo, in 1824. German colonization spread into the northeast part of Santa Catarina, where the colonies of Blumenau, Brusque, and Dona Francisca (today Joinville) were founded. These immigrants specialized in raising pigs, chickens, dairy cows, potatoes, green vegetables, and fruits such as apples – up to then nonexistent in Brazil. They played an important role in the setting up of workshops and in industry. It was at this time, and in modest proportions, that concerns involved in rending, milk products, and meat canning, as well as breweries and manufacturers of other beverages, were set up.

Owing especially to their flow southward, Germans were in second place in immigration for the years 1846 to 1875. Still, they were far behind the Portuguese, who numbered around 152,000 as opposed to the Germans' 39,000. Beginning in 1860, the numbers of Germans began to taper off. There are several reasons for this. Among them was the bad treatment settlers received in Senator Vergueiro's experiment in São Paulo. In November 1859, Russia stopped supporting immigration to Brazil, and this measure was extended throughout the German Empire in 1871. Data referring to Rio Grande do Sul show how different the two periods were: Germans made up around 93 percent of the immigrants arriving between 1824 and 1870. They were only 15 percent of those coming between 1889 and 1914.

After 1870, the imperial government encouraged Italians to come and settle in Rio Grande do Sul. Small farmers mostly from Tyrol, Veneto, and Lombardy set up a series of colonies, with Caxias being the most important. The Italians' economic endeavors were similar to the Germans', but they also specialized in vineyards and wine making. Between 1882 and 1889, of the 41,000 immigrants who entered Rio Grande do Sul, 34,000 of them were Italians.

The only similarity between the immigrants' economy and that of the cattle ranchers was that they both produced items for internal consumption. Otherwise, immigrants and ranchers were entirely different. Immigrants were late arrivals and they organized their assets in a different fashion.

The ranchers were and are still today concentrated in the Campanha Gaúcha area, as well as on Uruguayan territory. They held (and hold) huge tracts of land. Their cattle were raised especially for their hides, which were tanned, and secondarily for their meat. The meat was consumed locally or it was made into jerky at the meat-drying concerns along the coast. Jerky was used to feed poor people and slaves in the Center-South. Ranchers and jerky makers in Rio Grande do Sul produced meat for the internal market. Competition from Argentine and Uruguayan beef, which vied favorably with Brazilian jerky, gave these men perpetual headaches.

The country's tenuous territorial and economic integration, which dated from colonial times, persisted when Brazil became independent, notwithstanding relative advances in transportation. Just as during colonial times, imperial administration was concentrated in the regions near the capital and around some provincial capitals. But in more distant regions it crumbled. Even within specific provinces, there were different, dispersed regions. The republic assumed this regional framework as the basis for its federalistic political organization.

3

The First Republic (1889–1930)

As an episode, the passage from empire to republic was almost a lark. The years after 15 November 1889 made up for that ease, however, for they were years of tremendous uncertainty. The several groups that vied for power had diverse interests and did not agree on how they thought a republic should be run. The political representatives of the ruling class in the important provinces (São Paulo, Minas Gerais, and Rio Grande do Sul) espoused the idea of a federal republic which would assure each region a considerable degree of autonomy.

They differed in other aspects as far as power was concerned. The PRP and the Mineiros supported the liberal model. The republicans in Rio Grande do Sul were positivists. There are no clear reasons why, under the command of Júlio de Castilhos, Rio Grande do Sul became the region most influenced by positivism. Positivism may have been supported by the area's military tradition. Also, in that province, republicans were a minority in search of a doctrine that would bring them together to overcome a traditional political current led by the Liberal Party during the empire.

Another sector to be considered is the military, which had considerable influence during the early days of the republic. Marshal Deodoro da Fonseca became head of the provisional government, and scores of officers were elected to the constitutional congress. But the military was far from homogeneous. There was rivalry between the army and the navy. The army had been the author of the republic, whereas the navy was seen as being linked to the monarchy.

There were also personal and conceptual differences separating Deodoro da Fonseca's supporters from Floriano Peixoto's. Veterans of the Paraguayan War gathered around the old marshal. Many of these officers had not gone to the Escola Militar and were unfamiliar with positivist ideas. They had helped bring down the monarchy "to save the army's honor," but they lacked an elaborate notion of the republic. They believed, simply, that the army should have a more important role than it had had under the empire.

Even though Peixoto was not a positivist and had also participated in the Paraguayan War, the officers supporting him had other characteristics. They were young and had attended the Escola Militar, where they were influenced by positivism. They saw themselves participating in society like soldiers, and like citizens whose mission was to set the country straight. The republic should be orderly and should bring progress, which meant modernizing society by broadening technical know-how, by industrializing, and by expanding communications.

In spite of the deep rivalry between the two groups in the army, they agreed on a fundamental point. They did not express the interests of a social class, as was the case of those who advocated a liberal republic. Both factions were, above all else, mouthpieces for a single institution, the army – which was part of the state apparatus. Owing to the nature of their duties and to the type of culture developed within the army, officers (positivists or otherwise) were opposed to liberalism. As far as they were concerned, the republic should have a strong executive, or it should have a more or less protracted dictatorship. Provincial autonomy was suspect – not just because it served the interests of the large rural landowners, but also because it threatened to fragment the country.

The supporters of liberalism made haste in guaranteeing the calling of a constituent assembly because they feared a prolonged semi-dictatorship under the personal command of Deodoro da Fonseca. The new government had been icily received in Europe, and it was necessary to give the country a constitution to guarantee recognition for the republic and to obtain foreign credits.

The first republican constitution was promulgated in February 1891. It was inspired by the North American model and made Brazil a liberal federative republic. The states, which are what the old provinces have been called since that time, were implicitly authorized to exercise different prerogatives such as the right to seek foreign loans and to set up their own military forces known as the state public forces. These rights were in the interest of the larger states, especially São Paulo's. The possibility of contracting foreign loans would be vital to the Paulista government's carrying out its plan for the valorization of coffee.

A specific and important prerogative for exporter states, and therefore for São Paulo, was the right to charge taxes on their export merchandise. This was the way to guarantee a source of income which would allow them to be autonomous. The states were also given the right to organize their own courts.

The federal government, also known as the Union, was not totally powerless. The ultra-federalist idea supported by positivists from Rio Grande do Sul was attacked both by military men and by Paulistas. The crumbling of central authority was a risk that for several reasons these sectors did not want to run. The Union held onto import taxes; it had the right to create banks that would coin money; and it was in charge of the nation's armed services. It could also intervene in all states to reestablish order, to preserve the federal republic, and for other reasons.

With the constitution came a presidential form of government. What had been the emperor's power became known as executive power, which would be in the hands of the president of the republic. And the president would be elected for a four-year term. As during the empire, the legislative branch was divided into a Chamber of Deputies and a Senate, but senators no longer had lifelong appointments. Deputies would be elected in each state in numbers proportional to populations. Their terms would run for three years. Senators were elected in fixed numbers for nine-year terms. Each state and the Federal District (i.e., the capital) would elect three senators.

Direct and universal suffrage was established, with no financial requirements. Except for illiterates, beggars, and military enlisted men, all Brazilian citizens over the age of 21 were considered voters.

The constitution made no mention of women, but it was implicitly understood that they were prohibited from voting. As a one-time exception, the first president and vice-president would be elected by an indirect vote of the constituent assembly, once it became an ordinary congress.

The constitution guaranteed the rights of liberty, personal safety, and property – both to Brazilians and to foreigners residing in Brazil. It abolished the death penalty, which, let it be said, had rarely been applied during the empire.

Church and state went their separate ways. Brazil no longer had an official religion. Important functions that the church had monopolized were taken over by the state. The republic would only recognize civil marriages, and cemeteries would be run by municipalities. At the cemeteries, ceremonies of any religion could be performed. In 1893, another law rounded out these constitutional precepts by creating a public registry for births and deaths. These measures reflected the republican leaders' lay beliefs, which included the need to smooth over the conflicts between church and state and the need to help integrate the mainly Lutheran German immigrants into the mainstream. Another measure aimed at integrating immigrants was the so-called grand naturalization. This law decreed that all foreigners in Brazil on 15 November 1889 would automatically become Brazilian citizens unless, within six months of the constitution's taking effect, they expressed their wish to retain their original nationalities.

The founding of the Brazilian republic was received with reservations in Britain, but was enthusiastically hailed in Argentina, and it brought Brazil closer to the United States. The change occurred during the course of the First International Congress of the Americas, in Washington, D.C., which the United States had sponsored. The Brazilian representative was replaced by Salvador de Mendonça, a longtime republican whose views were compatible with those of the United States.

The clear shift of Brazil's diplomatic emphasis from London to Washington occurred when Baron Rio Branco entered the Ministry of Foreign Relations. He remained there from 1902 to 1912, while many presidents came and went. Rio Branco's policy did not entail an automatic alignment with the United States; it was, rather, a firm approximation intended to make Brazil the most important country in South America.

The fair relationship between Brazil and Argentina was a thing of the past, and the two countries had begun to compete openly with their armed forces and military equipment. Brazil tried to curry favor with smaller countries such as Uruguay and Paraguay. It also approached Chile to try to limit Argentina's influence. Despite all this, especially during the last few years of his administration, Rio Branco unsuccessfully tried to devise a stable accord among Argentina, Brazil, and Chile.

During the Rio Branco period, Brazil cleared up border disputes with several South American countries, among them Uruguay, Peru, and Colombia. Brazilians and Bolivians met in an armed conflict over Acre, in the Amazon region. It had suddenly become valuable owing to the rubber boom. Acre was considered Bolivian territory, but was largely occupied by Brazilian migrants. A negotiated settlement was ratified in the 1903 Treaty of Petrópolis. Bolivia recognized Brazil's sovereignty in Acre in exchange for 2.5 million pounds sterling.

The first year of the republic was marked by a business fever and by financial speculation, which were consequences of massive money printing and easy credit. In fact, the medium of exchange was incompatible with the new reality of salaried workers and the massive entry of immigrants. Many new firms were founded – some of them were real, others existed only on paper. Speculation was rampant on the stock market, and the cost of living went sharply up. By the beginning of 1891, a crisis had arisen: stock prices fell, and various firms and banking concerns went into receivership. Brazilian currency, relative to the British pound, began to plummet in value. This may have happened because of an ebbing of the flow of British capital into Latin America after the grave 1890 financial crisis in Argentina.

In the midst of this crisis, Congress elected Deodoro da Fonseca president and Floriano Peixoto vice-president. Deodoro collided head-on with Congress when he tried to strengthen his executive power by copying the emperor's erstwhile moderating power. He shut down Congress and promised elections in the future along with a revised constitution in which he sought to fortify the executive branch and reduce states' autonomy. The success of Deodoro's plans depended on the unity of the armed forces, which would not happen. Faced with the reaction of Floriano's supporters and faced with civilian opposition as well as opposition from several sectors of the navy, Deodoro finally resigned on 23 November 1891. Vicepresident Floriano Peixoto then became president.

Floriano's vision of the republic did not identify it with the dominant economic forces. He planned to build a stable, centralized, vaguely nationalistic government whose base would be mainly made up of the army and young people in military and civilian academies. His vision was contrary to the one known as the Rancher's Republic, which would be liberal and decentralized. Holders of this view were suspicious of a stronger army and of the urban protests in Rio de Janeiro.

But, contrary to what one might predict, there was a tactical agreement between the president and the PRP. The reasons behind this accord were the sometimes real and sometimes imaginary risks threatening the republican government. The São Paulo elite saw in Floriano a more secure possibility of keeping the republic alive. Floriano, on the other hand, understood that without the PRP's support he did not have enough political backing to govern.

During the early years of the republic, one of the politically most unstable regions was Rio Grande do Sul. Between the proclamation of the republic and the election of Júlio de Castilhos as state president in November 1893, 17 state governments came and went. On one side of the fray were the historical republicans who adopted positivism. They formed the Partido Republicano Riograndense (PRR). On the other side were the liberals. In March 1892, they founded the Partido Federalista and declared Silveira Martins, a prestigious figure from the imperial Liberal Party, to be their leader.

The Federalists' support came mainly from ranchers in the Campanha Gaúcha region of southern Rio Grande do Sul, along the Uruguayan border. They were the traditional political elite whose roots went back to the empire. The Republicans' base was in the population along the coast and in the mountains, where there were many immigrants. They formed a more recent elite who had burst into politics eager to take command.

A civil war known as the Federalist revolution broke out between the Federalists and the Republicans. It began in February 1893 and only ended two and a half years later, after Prudente de Moraes had been elected president. This was a bloody struggle with thousands of deaths. Many of the combatants did not die in battle; their throats were slit after they were taken prisoner.

From the beginning of the confrontation, Floriano had São Paulo's financial support as well as that of its well-organized state militia. At the same time, military influence in the government was on the decline. Rodrigues Alves ran the Ministry of Finance. He was from a Paulista family in the Paraíba Valley and had been a member of the imperial elite, but had gone over to the republic. The presidents of the Chamber of Deputies and the Senate were both PRP members.

The tactical accord between São Paulo's political elite and the president ended when Peixoto's successor was to be chosen. With few bases of support, which included the noisy but ineffectual ultra-nationalists, or *Jacobinos* as they were called, Floriano did not have the power to name a candidate to succeed him. A Paulista by the name of Prudente de Moraes won out and was elected on 1 March 1894. The marshal showed his displeasure by not appearing at the inauguration. According to the news of the day, he stayed in his humble home and tended his rose garden.

Once Prudente de Moraes took office, no more army men became president except for Marshal Hermes da Fonseca, who was elected for the term running from 1910 to 1914. In addition, political activity on the part of the military largely declined. The Clube Militar, which coordinated political activity, was shut down between 1896 and 1901.

During Prudente de Moraes's administration the already existing opposition between the political elite of the major states and Jacobine republicanism became acute. Concentrated in Rio de Janeiro, the Jacobinos were made up of contingents from the lower middle class, workers, and military personnel who had been affected by rising costs and lower standards of living. Their motives were not merely material. They believed in a strong republic which could counter monarchistic threats. These threats, as far as they were concerned, lurked in every corner. They also assumed the old patriotic anti-Portuguese tradition. The "Portuguees," who controlled commerce in Rio de Janeiro, were the target of violent attacks. The Jacobinos supported Floriano and made him their standard banner after he died in June 1895.

An event that took place far from Rio de Janeiro, but which affected the republic's policies, marked Prudente de Moraes's government. In the northern backlands of Bahia, on an abandoned ranch, a settlement known as Canudos was formed in 1893. Its leader was Antônio Vicente Mendes Maciel, better known as Antônio Conseiheiro. He had been born in Ceará and was the son of a merchant who intended to have him become a priest. After some financial problems and domestic difficulties, Conseiheiro worked as a teacher, traveling salesman, and at various other professions. He finally became a *beato*, a sort of half priest, half leader.

He led a nomadic life in the backlands, where he brought people together to build and repair churches, to raise walls around cemeteries, and to follow the ascetic life. He later settled in Canudos and attracted folk from the backlands. Canudos's population reached somewhere between 20,000 and 30,000 inhabitants.

Conselheiro's preaching competed with that of the local churches. An apparently trivial incident concerning the cutting of some timber caused the governor of Bahia to decide to teach those "fanatics" a lesson. Surprisingly, the Bahian expedition against Canudos was defeated. The governor then appealed for federal troops. The defeat of two more expeditions supplied with artillery pieces and machine guns, and the death of one expedition's commander, occasioned a wave of protest and violence in Rio de Janeiro.

In an episode linked to life in the backlands and to the mental outlook of its inhabitants, the Jacobinos saw the hidden finger of monarchist politicians. This fantasy was abetted by the fact that Conseiheiro preached for the return of the monarchy. For him, republics were inventions of atheists and Masons. Proof of this was the introduction of civil marriage ceremonies and a supposed interdiction of the Jesuits.

After a fight lasting a month and a half, a well-equipped expedition made up of 8,000 men under the command of General Artur Oscar razed the village in 1897. The defenders of Canudos died in battle or were taken prisoner and had their throats slit. Conselheiro himself died from disease some days before the end.

According to the positivist officers and the republican politicians, this had been a struggle between civilization and barbarism. In truth, there was barbarism on both sides, especially among those educated men who had been incapable of even trying to understand the people of the backland.

The liberal, oligarchical republic was firmly ensconced when Prudente de Moraes was followed by another Paulista, Campos Sales (1898–1902). The Jacobine movement crumbled after a few of its members were found to be involved in an attempt to assassinate Prudente de Moraes. The majority of the military went back to the barracks.

The political elite of the major states had triumphed, with São Paulo at the head. It was still necessary, however, to create a means for the oligarchical republic to establish a stable political system. The large role of the state gave occasion to power struggles among rival groups. The federal government would intervene in local disputes invoking its controversial powers laid out in the constitution. This made the control of power uncertain in some states. It also made a lasting agreement between the Union and the states less likely. Add to this the fact that the executive branch was having a hard time maintaining satisfactory control of the legislature – which was, of course, contrary to the constitution, which stated that "the branches [of government] are in harmony and independent of one another."

Based on these matters, Campos Sales devised an arrangement known as the governors' policy. Using wily alchemy on the internal regulations of the Chamber of Deputies, he assured that each state's parliamentary representation would be connected to the dominant group in the region. At the same time he guaranteed that the Chamber of Deputies would be more subservient to the executive branch. The intent of the governors' policy was to do away with factional disputes within the states and at the same time strengthen the executive branch, which Campos Sales considered power *par excellence*. The governor's policy was only partly successful.

On the financial plane, the situation, which from the time of the monarchy had been grave, became dramatically so. The republican government had inherited a foreign debt from the empire. This debt on a yearly basis consumed a large part of the foreign exchange that reached Brazil. The situation grew worse as the 1890s wore on and the public debt rose. Many expenditures were related to the cost of military operations during that uncertain period. Appeals for foreign credit were frequently made, and the national debt rose some 30 percent between 1890 and 1897, which created even more debts to foreign banks.

On the other hand, the spread of coffee plantations at the beginning of the decade made for tremendous harvests in 1896 and 1897. The increased supply of coffee on the international market brought about a sharp decline in price and a reduction in the amount of foreign exchange coming to Brazil. At the end of his administration, when it was clear that Brazil could no longer service its debt, Prudente de Moraes began to negotiate with the international creditors. The government had reached some understanding with the London and River Plate Bank, while Campos Sales, as president-elect, went to London to deal with the House of Rothschild. The Rothschild family had been Brazil's financial agent in Europe since independence.

Finally, during the Campos Sales administration, a funding loan which imposed many demands on Brazil was arranged in June 1898. It offered a scheme for debt relief and for guaranteeing interest payments as well as the payment of all previous loans. For this Brazil took out another loan. As a guarantee, Brazil gave its creditors all the income from customs in Rio de Janeiro. It was prohibited from contracting new loans until June 1901. Brazil also committed itself to carrying out a harsh program of deflation. It would have to burn part of the paper money in circulation. This is how the country avoided bankruptcy. But, in the years to come, it would pay a heavy price for these measures and others that followed it during Campos Sales's presidency. Together they occasioned a decline in economic activity and broke banks and other business concerns.

3.2 OLIGARCHIES AND COLONELS

The republic made state autonomy real and allowed each region to pursue its interests fully. This can be seen in the political arena, where each state formed its own republican party. Attempts at organizing national republican parties were transitory, or they failed. Controlled by a tiny elite, the republican parties determined the fate of national politics and settled matters pursuant to choosing candidates for the nation's presidency.

But what did the different state oligarchies stand for? To mention only the most expressive examples, what did it mean to speak in the name of São Paulo, Rio Grande do Sul, or Minas Gerais?

If there was a common trait in the way these oligarchies monopolized political power, there were also differences in their relationships with society. In São Paulo, the oligarchy was closest to the ruling interests, to the coffee economy, and, as time passed, also to industry. This is not to say that the elite was a mere agent of these groups. The Paulista oligarchy managed to organize the state efficiently, keeping in mind the broadest interests of the ruling class.

The Mineiro and the Gaúcho (Rio Grande do Sul) oligarchies controlled the PRM and the PRR respectively and enjoyed considerable autonomy in their relations with society. The PRR prevailed as a mighty political machine inspired by an authoritarian version of positivism. It arbitrated between the ranchers' interests and those of the rising immigrants. The Mineiro oligarchy never acted as a mere "hit man" for coffee growers or cattle ranchers. While it had to take these social groups into account, it was in essence a professional political machine which to a great extent created its own source of power by appointing civil servants, legalizing claims to land, and deciding how much to invest in education, transportation, and so on.

At first glance, it might seem that the oligarchies' power could be broken by the votes of the electorate at large. However, one was not obliged to vote, and as a rule the common people saw politics as a game for "higher-ups" or as an exchange of favors. Their lack of interest increased when, during presidential elections, state parties got together to support a single candidate or when opposition candidates had no chance of winning. The percentage of voters oscillated between a minimum of 1.4 percent of the total population of the country when Afonso Pena was elected in 1906 to a maximum of 5.7 percent when Júlio Prestes was elected in 1930.

It is also worth pointing out that election returns did not reflect reality. Voting was not secret, so most voters were subject to pressure from political chieftains, whom they also tried to please. Electoral fraud was normal practice: records were falsified, dead people and foreigners voted, and so on. These abuses were not new, however. They had been inherited from the monarchy.

In spite of everything, comparatively speaking, more voters turned out than during the empire. When one compares the 1886 elections for the last imperial parliament with the first presidential election (1898) in which voters from every state participated, voter participation rose by 400 percent. On top of this, not all presidential elections in the republic were mere ratifications of a particular candidate. There were contested candidacies in the 1910, 1922, and 1930 elections, when, respectively, Hermes da Fonseca, Artur Bernardes, and Júlio Prestes were elected.

It is common to think of the First Republic as the "Colonels' Republic." This expression refers to the colonels of the old National Guard. They were mainly rural landowners with a local power base. *Coronelismo* was a variant of a more widespread sociopolitical relationship – patronage, which existed both rurally and in the cities. This relationship sprang from social inequality, from the impossibility of citizens' exercising their rights, from the precarious or nonexistent status of state welfare systems, and from the lack of a career civil service. All of these lacks date back to colonial times, but the republic created conditions which allowed local political bosses to accumulate greater sums of power. This permitted more tax moneys to go to municipalities and to mayoral elections.

During elections, "colonels" controlled voters in their area of influence. People voted for the colonels' candidates in exchange for favors as varied as a pair of shoes, a bed in the hospital, or a teaching job. But the colonels did not dominate the political scene in the First Republic. Other groups representing different urban interests played significant roles in politics. On top of this, and in spite of their importance in maintaining the oligarchical system, the colonels depended on other entities for their power. Among these entities, the governments in the larger states stood out. And governments were more than a gathering of colonels. The colonels furnished votes for the political bosses of their states, but they depended on those bosses for many of the benefits voters expected, especially when the benefits were collective.

Coronelismo had different traits according to the sociopolitical reality of each region in the country. An extreme example of the colonels' power can be found in the Northeast backlands along the São Francisco River, where virtual nations controlled by colonels appeared with their own armies. On the other hand, in the more important states, colonels depended on more encompassing structures. That is, they depended on the state political machine and on the Republican Party.

3.3   RELATIONS BETWEEN THE STATES AND THE UNION

The First Republic is often referred to as the period of *café com leite*. The phrase, "coffee and milk," is a metaphor for an alliance between São Paulo (coffee) and Minas Gerais (milk), which ran national politics. The truth is a little less black and white. To understand the politics of the time, one should closely examine the relationship between the Union and at least three states: São Paulo, Minas Gerais, and Rio Grande do Sul – all of which are quite different.

Without intending to undo the federal government, São Paulo was intent on insuring its autonomy, which was safeguarded by the income from an expanding economy and by a powerful military. But the Paulistas could not be so fortunate as to depend only on themselves. To dwell on the most relevant example, it was the Union's responsibility to determine monetary policy and exchange rates, both of which affected the country's financial future and influenced the coffee business.

In the federal sphere, Paulista politicians concentrated on these matters and on initiatives to obtain government support for their coffee valorization plans. Thus, even though São Paulo's economy may have diversified during the First Republic, its political elite acted mainly in the interest of the coffee bourgeoisie. Of course many politicians were also members of that group.

The policy of coffee valorization is one of the clearest examples of São Paulo's role in the federation and of the relations among the different states. Beginning in the 1890s, coffee production in São Paulo grew enormously and created problems as far as earnings were concerned. These problems came from two basic sources. The tremendous supply of coffee made its price go down on the international market. Beginning with the Campos Sales administration, the rise in value of Brazilian currency did not compensate for lower coffee prices. Even less Brazilian money came into the planters' hands.

To protect the coffee business, in the beginning of the 20th century various plans for governmental intervention in the coffee market were devised in São Paulo. An agreement was reached in February of 1906. It is known as the Convênio de Taubaté (Taubaté Agreement) because it was signed in the city of Taubaté. Representatives of the states of Rio de Janeiro, Minas Gerais, and São Paulo signed it.

Its two fundamental points were negotiation of a loan of 15,000,000 pounds sterling to back the state, which would intervene in the coffee market by buying coffee at a price suitable to the coffee growers; and establishment of a means for fixing the exchange rate and not allowing it to rise. The government was to use the loan to buy up abundant harvests. It would stockpile coffee, then sell it on the international market at an opportune moment. The plan was based on the correct notion of alternating good and bad harvests and on the expectation that government purchases would reduce the supply of coffee and make its price rise.

The federal government's opposition to the plan and the reservations of the other states that signed the agreement forced São Paulo to act on its own. It joined forces with a group of United States importers led by Hermann Sielcken. Backing from that group and bank loans made it possible to get coffee off the market. However, it was impossible to operate on those bases for very long without obtaining greater, long-term backing.

During the second half of 1908, President Afonso Pena got Congress to authorize the government to guarantee a loan of up to the 15,000,000 pounds São Paulo wanted. From that point on, São Paulo State could carry out its valorization scheme, with the operation being controlled by international bankers. The first results could be felt in 1909. The international price of coffee began to rise. Thanks to the reduction in supply owing to stockpiling and to smaller coffee harvests, prices stayed high until 1912. In June 1913 the loan was paid off.

There were two other valorization operations under the Union's aegis. In 1924, President Artur Bernardes, out of concern for the federal budget, chose not to support coffee, and the state of São Paulo took over coffee's defense permanently.

This brief account illustrates the kind of relations that existed between São Paulo and the Union. Paulistas had the means to secure their autonomy and, up to a certain point, the means to carry out their economic plans even without support from the federal government. But the Union's exchange policy had unfavorable repercussions on the Paulista coffee business when it took measures to raise the exchange rate. In addition, a guarantee from the federal government was essential, or at least it helped, in obtaining foreign loans.

The position of Mineiro politicians was different. They represented a state economy that was fragmented among coffee, cattle, and, up to a point, industry. None of these sectors ruled supreme. On top of this, Minas Gerais did not have São Paulo's economic potential, so it depended on the Union's generosity.

These circumstances caused the Mineiro political elite to distance themselves from specific coffee or milk interests. They sought power like professional politicians and exerted their influence in the Chamber of Deputies, where they sat 37 members as opposed to the Paulistas' 22. This proportion had been established by the 1890 census. After the 1920 census, which demonstrated São Paulo's tremendous growth in population, Paulistas unsuccessfully tried to revise the formula for proportional representation.

Minas's politicians controlled access to many jobs in the federal government and were successful in one of their primary objectives. They had railways built in Minas Gerais, and these railways benefited the general interests of the state. During the 1920s, almost 40 percent of all new federal railways were built in Minas. At the same time, the Mineiros sought protection for their products which were locally consumed, and, according to the circumstances, they supported coffee valorization.

The presence of Gaúchos in national politics was singularly linked to military presence. This closeness does not mean that the PRR and the military were synonymous. Between 1894 and 1910, both Gaúchos and high-ranking military men were virtually excluded from the federal administration. They showed up once more when Marshal Hermes da Fonseca was elected president.

There are several reasons for this affinity. From imperial times, most military men were from Rio Grande do Sul. During the First Republic, Gaúchos made up between one-fourth and one-third of all career servicemen. The Third Military Region, which was created in 1919, became a causeway to the high echelons of the administration, since several of its commandants were appointed to positions in the Ministry of War. The military's importance lured Gaúchos of a particular social stratum to become career officers. And during the First Republic, most ministers of war and most presidents of the Clube Militar were Gaúchos.

On the other hand, intermittent armed struggles in that region favored contact between army officers and politicians. Many officers' connections with the PRR date from the Federalist revolution.

Certain ideological traits and political peculiarities also brought them together. Positivism, which had spread throughout the army, was their main ideological link. In addition, the economic and financial policies Gaúcho Republicans supported tended to coincide with those of the military. The PRR was in favor of a conservative spending policy on the part of the federal government; it also favored price stability. Inflation would create problems for the jerky market. Since it was mainly consumed by the lower classes in the Northeast and in the Federal District, any loss of their buying power lowered the demand for jerky. This perspective, in spite of different motivations, created a bridge toward the military, which looked favorably on any financial policy that would be conservative.

A block of the northeastern oligarchy could have been influential in national politics. However, a coalition of northeastern states could not be established easily, because of conflicting interests. Since resources from export tariffs obtained in each state were scarce, states competed with one another for governmental favors. They were also involved in interminable disputes concerning the right to charge interstate tariffs on goods going from one state to another.

The union between Paulista and Mineiro oligarchies was fundamental in the political history of the First Republic. In this union, one or the other faction prevailed. As time went by, arguments broke out and at the end the two sides were at odds.

In spite of military influence on the federal level, São Paulo took the lead during the early years of the republic. Paulistas attained their objectives in the Constituent Assembly with support from Minas. They also set the stage for civilian presidents. Between 1894 and 1902, three Paulistas were elected president one right after the other: Prudente de Moraes, Campos Sales, and Rodrigues Alves. This would never be repeated. São Paulo's preponderance during those years cannot be explained only by its economic importance. That state's elite abandoned its old internal differences and closed ranks around the PRP.

The situation was different in Minas Gerais. There, group differences only died down once the Partido Republicano Mineiro was founded for the second time, in 1897. After that, Mineiro presence in national politics steadily increased.

An accord between São Paulo and Minas lasted from the Campos Sales administration up to 1909. During that year, the two states quarreled, which facilitated a provisional return of the military to the national political scene and the permanent return of Rio Grande do Sul.

The presidential campaign of 1909–1910 was the first real electoral contest in the republic. Marshal Hermes da Fonseca, Deodoro da Fonseca's nephew, was the candidate supported by Rio Grande do Sul, Minas, and the military. São Paulo, allied with Bahia in the opposition, supported Ruy Barbosa. Barbosa tried to attract votes from the urban middle class by supporting the principles of democracy and the secret ballot. His campaign had overtones of a reaction against the army's participation in politics. He attacked military leaders, and, instead of the army, he held up public state power as the example to follow. Even though Barbosa's most important political support at that time came from the Paulista oligarchy, his campaign appeared to be the intelligentsia's struggle for personal freedom, culture, and liberal traditions, and against an unlettered, oligarchical, and authoritarian nation. Hermes's victory produced massive disillusion among the tiny intellectual elite.

Rio Grande do Sul's star began to show signs of life when particular understandings gave rise to Afonso Pena's 1906 candidacy. Beginning with Hermes da Fonseca's administration, that star began to shine as one of the third magnitude in the "coffee and milk" constellation. This led São Paulo and Minas to avoid further dissension. In the Minas Gerais city of Ouro Fino, an unwritten pact was concluded in which Mineiros and Paulistas agreed to try to take turns holding the nation's presidency. Even though it failed to call the shots in presidential successions, the Gaucho oligarchy rose in stature after 1910. Its presence could always be felt in federal ministries. On the other hand, São Paulo's oligarchy tended to solidify its position at home.

Finally, President Washington Luis's failure to obey the rules of the game in 1929 became a central factor in the 1930 political rupture. Instead of a Mineiro, he named the Paulista Júlio Prestes as his successor.

Analysis of the accords among different oligarchies indicates that the federal government was more than a mere coffee planters' club. Central power emerged as a proponent of national integration, which, albeit fragile, was far from nonexistent. Its duties included guaranteeing a modicum of internal stability, reconciling diverse interests, attracting foreign investments, and servicing the national debt.

But the coffee business was central to the period's economy. During the entire First Republic, coffee was far and away the leader in Brazilian exports. It averaged around 60 percent of all export revenue. At the end of the period, an average of 72.5 percent of Brazil's export revenue came from coffee. Growth and employment in the most developed part of the country depended on coffee. Coffee also provided the greater part of foreign exchange needed for imports and to service foreign commitments, especially the foreign debt.

When it formulated its policies, the federal government could not ignore the coffee sector, no matter where the president himself came from. But the most significant aspect of this relationship can be found in the fact that leaders supposedly linked to coffee interests did not always support those interests. Curiously, three Paulista presidents – Campos Sales, Rodrigues Alves, and Washington Luis – upset the coffee sector or clashed with it. This apparently strange behavior is owed to the fact that presidents had to attend to what they understood to be the country's overall interests. These interests were served by stabilizing finances and by reaching agreements with foreign creditors, notably the Rothschilds.

3.4 SOCIOECONOMIC CHANGES

Beginning in the last decades of the 19th century, massive immigration was one of the most important factors influencing socioeconomic change in Brazil. Brazil was one of the countries receiving millions of Europeans and Asians who came to the Americas in search of opportunities for work and social betterment. Alongside Brazil, one finds, among other countries, the United States, Argentina, and Canada.

Around 3,800,000 foreigners came to Brazil between 1827 and 1930. The period from 1887 to 1914 brought the highest number of immigrants, approximately 2,740,000, or 72 percent of the total. These figures can be explained by the strong demand during those years for a work force on coffee plantations, among other factors. The First World War greatly reduced the flow of immigrants. After the end of the war, there was another wave of immigration which lasted until 1930.

Beginning in 1930, the world financial crisis of 1929 and political changes in Brazil and Europe effectively stemmed the flow of immigrant laborers. The Japanese were the only exception: if one compares immigration on the basis of decades, between 1931 and 1940 more Japanese came to Brazil than at any other time.

The Center-South, South, and East absorbed masses of immigrants. In 1920, 93.4 percent of the foreign-born population lived in these regions. São Paulo alone received the majority (54 percent) of immigrants. Immigrants' preference for São Paulo can be explained by the subsidies the state provided for passage and lodging and by the abundant work opportunities in its expanding economy.

For the period from 1887 to 1930, Italians made up the largest contingent, with 35.5 percent of all immigrants. They were followed by Portuguese (29 percent) and Spaniards (14.6 percent). Relatively small groups (in global terms) were qualitatively important. The most expressive case is that of the Japanese, who came mainly to the state of São Paulo. In 1920, 87.3 percent of Brazil's Japanese immigrants lived in that state.

The first wave of Japanese arrived in Santos in 1908. They were on their way to the coffee plantations. In spite of the difficulty of keeping the Japanese on the plantations, the state government continued, for several years, up to 1925, to subsidize Japanese immigration. During the First World War, when the flow of Europeans ebbed, people feared there would be "insufficient hands for farming." Beginning in 1925, the Japanese government began to finance immigrants' voyages to Brazil. By this time, the Japanese were no longer sent to coffee plantations. They stayed in the rural areas longer than any other ethnic group, but they stayed as small landowners and played a major role in diversifying São Paulo's agriculture.

Other important minority groups included Syrians and Lebanese as well as Jews, all of whom shared similar characteristics. These groups right from their arrival stayed in the cities, unlike the Japanese, Italians, and Spaniards. They were also spontaneous, nonsubsidized immigrants, since government aid was only given to people who would work on the plantations.

The Italians came mainly to São Paulo and to Rio Grande do Sul. In 1920, 71.4 percent of all Italians in Brazil lived in the state of São Paulo and made up 9 percent of its entire population. Their place of origin changed over the years. Until the turn of the century, northern Italians were the rule. Southern Italians, mainly from Calabria and Naples, began to arrive in greater numbers beginning in the 20th century.

Italians were the most important group joining the labor force for coffee farming. Between 1887 and 1900, 73 percent of the immigrants entering the state were Italian, though not all of them went into agriculture. Among other indicators, these immigrants' poverty is revealed by the fact that the subsidies the government offered constituted a strong attraction. Problems in this scheme had a direct impact on the flow of immigrants.

The shoddy way in which recent arrivals were received made the Italian government take measures against recruiting immigrants. This was provisionally enacted between March 1889 and July 1891. In March 1902, in a measure known as the Prinetti Decree (Prinetti was the Italian minister of foreign relations), Italy outlawed subsidized immigration to Brazil. From then on, anyone who wanted to go to Brazil could do so freely, but without subsidized passages

and other enticements. The decree was the result of growing complaints from Italians living in Brazil. They appealed to their consuls
concerning the precarious conditions in which they lived, which
were made worse by the coffee crisis. It may also be the case that
improvements in the socioeconomic conditions in Italy stemmed the
flow of immigration.

Italian immigrants never stopped coming to Brazil. However, the
Prinetti Decree, the coffee crisis, and the situation in Italy itself all
worked to stem it. If one studies the arrivals and departures of
immigrants through the port of Santos, without considering their
nationality, one will see that for several years the number of those
leaving was greater than the number of those arriving. During the
middle of the coffee crisis, in 1900, around 21,000 migrants came in,
whereas 22,000 left. Right after the Prinetti Decree, in 1903, 16,500
migrants entered Brazil, whereas 36,400 left. In the following year,
too, more left than came.

During the period from 1901 to 1930, the lands of origin of São
Paulo's immigrants became much more balanced. The proportion
of Italians fell to 26 percent, followed by Portuguese (23 percent)
and Spaniards (22 percent).

Portuguese immigration was clearly concentrated in the Federal
District and in São Paulo. The nation's capital received the major
Portuguese contingent, even when one compares their influx to that
of entire states. One characteristic of Portuguese immigration was
its greater concentration in the cities. In 1920, there were 65,000
Portuguese in São Paulo, which represented 11 percent of the total
population. Their numbers rose to 172,000 in Rio de Janeiro, where
they made up 15 percent of the population. These data do not mean
that no Portuguese went to work on coffee plantations or worked in
other forms of agriculture. But they are best known for their roles in
small- and large-scale business, as well as in industry, especially in
Rio de Janeiro.

The greatest influx of Spaniards occurred between 1887 and
1914. But there was a difference. While Italians greatly outnumbered Spaniards from 1887 to 1903, they were outnumbered by
Spaniards from 1906 to 1920. After the Japanese, the Spaniards
were next in line among those with the greatest proportions of

immigrants in São Paulo. Thus, in 1920, 78 percent of the Spaniards lived in that state. In some ways, Spanish immigration shared traits with Japanese immigration. Few Spanish or Japanese immigrants, for example, were single men; most men from both groups came to Brazil bringing their wives and children. Spaniards also resembled the Japanese because they spent more time engaged in agriculture and because they preferred the small cities of the interior to living in the city of São Paulo.

There is no doubting immigrants' upward mobility in the cities. Their success in business and industry in states such as São Paulo, Rio Grande do Sul, Paraná, and Santa Catarina is ample testimony. During the early years of massive immigration to São Paulo, immigrants were subjected to harsh living conditions – that was how all workers were treated in Brazil. Brazilians tended to regard workers as little more than slaves. This situation is borne out by the huge numbers of returnees, by the complaints to the consuls, and by the measures taken by the Italian government.

As time passed, many immigrants attained high positions in society. A few of them became large landowners. Most of them became small and middle property owners who cleared the way for their descendants to become central figures in Paulista agriculture and industry.

The 1934 agricultural census in São Paulo revealed that 30.2 percent of the land was in the hands of foreigners: 12.2 percent belonged to Italians; 5.2 percent to Spaniards; 5.1 percent to Japanese; 4.3 percent to Portuguese; and 3.4 percent to people of other nationalities. These numbers express only one facet of the immigrants' rise, since landowners who descended from earlier immigrants were naturally considered Brazilian citizens.

From the last few decades of the 19th century up to 1930, Brazil was still a predominantly agricultural country. According to the 1920 census, of 9,100,000 working people, 6,300,000 (69.7 percent) were engaged in agriculture, 1,200,000 (13.8 percent) in industry, and 1,500,000 (16.5 percent) in services.

The heading "services" includes low-productivity urban occupations such as paid domestic servant. The most revealing datum is the increase in the number of people employed in industry, which, in the 1872 census, was no more than 7 percent of the working population. It should be remembered, however, that many "industries" were little more than small workshops.

Agricultural exports were not absolutely predominant during the First Republic. Not only did agricultural production for internal consumption have significant impact on the economy, but also industry began, more and more, to hold its own. The state of São Paulo was at the forefront of the process of capitalistic development, which was characterized by agricultural diversification, urbanization, and industrial growth. Coffee was still the economy's linchpin and the initial foundation for this process. An important factor in assuring coffee production can be found in the formula devised to solve the labor supply problem and to stabilize labor relations. The first part of the problem was solved by immigration, the second by *colonato*.

Colonato was what replaced the partnership experiment, which had failed. The *colonos*, that is, the immigrant families, were responsible for taking care of coffee groves and for bringing in the harvest. They were paid twice a year, once for taking care of so many thousand coffee plants and once for the harvest. The harvest payment varied according to how much coffee had been harvested. The plantation owner supplied a dwelling and gave the families small plots of land to grow their own food. Colonato was different from partnership because, among their differences, profits from the sale of coffee were not shared. It was also not a pure form of salaried labor since there were other sorts of payment.

In the case of new plantations which were the object of the so-called formation contracts (*contratos de formação*), colonos planted the coffee and took care of the plants for a period of four to six years, since coffee plants normally begin to produce during their fourth year. The "formers," or people working under these contracts, for all intents and purposes received no salaries. They could, however, grow foodstuffs between the rows of coffee plants. Since colonos preferred this type of relationship with their bosses, one infers that the foodstuffs produced were not just for their consumption, but they were also sold in the local markets.

Colonato stabilized labor relations, but it did not eliminate problems between colonos and plantation owners. There was constant friction between the two groups, as well as strikes. On top of this, colonos were not slaves and had extensive horizontal mobility. They could leave one plantation for another. Or they could go to the cities in search of greater opportunity. But as a whole, on the one hand the supply of immigrant labor and on the other the earning possibilities made available by colonato were sufficient to guarantee coffee production and relative stability of labor relations in the coffee business.

At the same time that coffee production was on the rise, agricultural diversification linked to immigrants' rise in status came about in São Paulo. The production of rice, beans, and corn expanded to meet rising demands in the growing cities. At the beginning of the 20th century, São Paulo imported some of these products from other states, especially rice from Rio Grande do Sul. Around the time of the First World War, São Paulo had become self-sufficient in these items, and had begun to export them. Comparing averages for the years from 1901 to 1906 with those from 1925 to 1930, one sees that rice production grew almost sevenfold, bean production trebled, and corn doubled.

Cotton had also become important. Around 1919, São Paulo became Brazil's greatest cotton producer, with approximately one-third of the total production. Thus raw material for its textile industry was guaranteed. In addition, the combined planting of coffee and cotton, with greater emphasis on coffee, turned out to be providential for the planters. When a frost in 1918 devastated the coffee plantations, many planters were saved from ruin by cotton.

All the cities grew, but the most spectacular jump in population occurred in São Paulo, the state capital. The main reason for this rapid growth can be found in the influx of spontaneous immigrants and of other immigrants who abandoned agricultural pursuits. The city was an open field for artisans, street commerce, cottage industry, builders who called themselves "Italian master craftsmen" (*mestres italianos*), and professionals. To work in the early factories and to work as a household servant were more shaky undertakings. As the link between the coffee plantations and the port of Santos and as the state capital, the city of São Paulo was also the main outlet for imported goods. The head offices of the major banks as well as the principal bureaucratic jobs were all found in São Paulo.

After 1886, São Paulo began to grow at a rapid pace. Its growth took off between 1890 and 1900, when the city's population rose from 64,000 inhabitants to 239,000. That represents a 273 percent rise in ten years, and an annual compound growth rate of 14 percent. In 1890, São Paulo was the fifth largest Brazilian city after Rio de Janeiro, Salvador, Recife, and Belém. By the turn of the century it was in second place, although it was still far behind Rio with its 688,000 inhabitants. When compared to Rio de Janeiro, São Paulo was still just the capital of an important province.

Industrial growth should be seen in a wider geographic perspective which takes in several regions, especially Rio de Janeiro and São Paulo.

The few factories that appeared in Brazil during the middle of the 19th century were designed to produce low-quality cotton cloth for poor people and slaves. Bahia was the initial textile center and was home to five of Brazil's nine textile factories in 1866. By 1885, industrial production had moved to the Center-South. If one considers the number of industrial units, Minas Gerais had taken first place, but the most important factories were in the Federal District. Putting aside the sugar industry, in around 1889 57 percent of Brazil's industrial capital was invested in the Federal District. Several factors contributed to the creation of factories around the nation's capital. Among these were the concentration of capital, a reasonably large consumer market, and steam power, which had replaced water power in the older factories.

While it had begun in the 1870s, São Paulo's industrial growth dates from the period after Abolition. It sprang from two related sources: from the coffee business and from immigration. The latter source was not restricted to São Paulo. It occurred in other regions where immigrants settled, notably in Rio Grande do Sul.

There are several reasons why the coffee business set down the foundation for the first appearance of industry. To begin with, when they supported the use of currency and the growth of incomes, coffeemen created a market for manufactured goods. Then, when they supported investments in railways, they widened and integrated that market. Thirdly, when they developed export and import commerce, they created a distribution system for manufactured goods. Next, when they promoted immigration, they guaranteed a supply of labor. Finally, coffee exports provided the financial resources to import industrial machinery.

Immigrants were present at both ends of industry: as owners and as workers. In addition, many were specialized technicians. The story of foreign workers is part of that immigrant saga in which many people came to "do America" but had their dreams shattered in the new land. They played a fundamental role in São Paulo's manufacturing industry around the capital. In 1893, 70 percent of industrial workers were foreigners. The numbers of immigrant industrial workers in Rio were less dramatic, but, even so, in 1890 they made up 39 percent of that labor force.

The way immigrants became industrialists varied. Some began with almost nothing, but, in Rio Grande do Sul and São Paulo, they took advantage of the opportunities available in those early stages of Brazil's capitalist development. Others, working as importers, caught the scent of industrial opportunity. As importers, they had an advantage in making contacts for importing machinery, and they also knew where to find the most lucrative sources of investment in Brazil. São Paulo's two major Italian industrialists began as importers.

Looking at the value of industrial production, one sees that in 1907 the Federal District was ahead of all the states with 33 percent of the total. It was followed by São Paulo with 17 percent and Rio Grande do Sul with 15 percent. In 1920, the state of São Paulo had reached first place with 32 percent of all production. The Federal District had fallen to 21 percent, and Rio Grande do Sul was in third place with 11 percent. These data compare states' production with that of a city. If one compares only cities, data are imprecise, but the city of São Paulo began to outstrip Rio de Janeiro sometime between 1920 and 1938.

Industry during those years was largely oriented toward textiles and, in second place, toward the production of food and drink, as well as of clothes. The textile industry, especially that sector producing cotton cloth, was truly industrial, if one considers the amount of capital invested in it and the number of workers it employed. Several factories had over 1,000 workers. By the time of the First

World War, 80 percent of the cloth consumed in Brazil was made locally, which suggests that its quality had improved. Notwithstanding this relative advance in industrial production, an industrial base was sorely lacking. No one produced cement, iron, steel, machinery, or equipment. This meant that industry depended largely on imports.

The First World War is commonly mentioned as a period of incentive for Brazilian industry since competition from imported products had been interrupted. But the 1920s were as important as the European war because at that time attempts began to be made to expand industry. With incentives from the government, two important concerns appeared. In Minas Gerais, the Siderúgica Belgo-Mineira (Belgium-Minas Gerais Steel Plant) began operations in 1924. In São Paulo, the Portland Cement Company began production in 1926. At the same time, after having stayed in business and accumulated profits during the war, small repair shops slowly turned into manufacturers of machinery and equipment.

Was the state instrumental or detrimental to industrial growth? Its main concern was export agriculture rather than industry, but one cannot say that the government took an anti-industrial stance.

Brazil's long-term financial patterns were plagued by falling exchange rates which had contradictory effects as far as industry is concerned. Devaluation made imported consumer goods more expensive, and thus less competitive. At the same time, it made the importation of machines needed by industry more expensive. The government at times protected imports of machinery by reducing the duty paid on them at customs. In some cases, the state granted loans and tax exemptions to encourage setting up basic industries. In sum, if the state was not industry's enemy, it was far from being a deliberate promoter of industrial development.

During the course of the First Republic, Rio Grande do Sul was characterized by diversification of its economic activity, which concentrated on local and national consumption. The leaders in this movement were the immigrants who had become small-scale property owners in the highlands and from there spread their interests into other regions. In the agricultural sector, they stood out as producers of rice, corn, beans, and tobacco – in that order of importance.

Just as in other parts of the country, as far as amounts of capital being invested are concerned, the textile industry led the way, followed by beverage manufacturers, especially wineries. Wine was produced in Rio Grande do Sul since colonial times, but its production gathered momentum once German and Italian immigrants had arrived.

The advent of cold storage plants supplanted the precarious means used to preserve meat and allowed it to be stockpiled. By 1917, the American firms Armour and Wilson had established branches in Rio Grande do Sul. An attempt by local cattlemen to set up a cold storage plant failed for lack of funds. The firm was sold in 1921 to a concern known as Frigorífico Anglo.

All these initiatives occurred at a time of relative decline in the cattle business. Demand for jerky and especially for leather had declined. In 1890, these products accounted for 55 percent of the state's exports. In 1927, they made up 24 percent, with leather having fallen from 37 percent to around 7 percent of the total export revenue. In 1927, lard was in first place with 20 percent, followed by jerky at 18 percent and by rice at 13 percent.

Whereas both São Paulo and Rio Grande do Sul had diversified their economies, São Paulo's activities were concentrated on export agriculture, and Rio Grande do Sul's developed to supply the domestic market.

Amazônia lived in an ephemeral dream world thanks to the wealth from rubber. Its production had been picking up beforehand, but in 1880 it took off. Rubber production was stimulated even more by an 1890s phenomenon that can only be called bicycle-mania, and later by the increasing appeal of the automobile beginning at the turn of the century.

During its heyday, rubber easily reached second place among Brazil's export products. Its high point came between 1898 and 1910. During this time, it brought in 26 percent of Brazil's export revenues, and was second only to coffee, which brought in 53 percent. It was far ahead of what was in third place – leather, which garnered only 4 percent.

The rubber boom was responsible for significant migration into Amazônia. Some 110,000 people may have come into the region. They came mainly from Ceará, a state regularly afflicted by droughts.

The rubber economy occasioned the growth of urban centers and improvements in living conditions for at least part of the population in Belém and Manaus. Between 1890 and 1900, Belém's population almost doubled, going from 50,000 to 96,000 people. The region's two major cities took electric streetcar lines, telephone service, running water, and electric street lighting for granted. In other cities these were still luxuries.

These changes, however, did nothing to modify the wretched lives of the rubber gatherers working in the forests. They also failed to lead to diversification of economic activity, which might sustain growth in the event of a crisis in the rubber industry.

And the crisis was devastating when it came, in 1910. Its main symptom was a sharp drop in price. The reason for it was international competition. Brazil's native rubber had always suffered from competition from rubber coming from Central America and Africa, even though this product was inferior to Brazil's. Plantations built mainly by the British and Dutch in their Asian colonies changed everything. This was high-quality, low-cost rubber planted on large tracts of land. At the same time, it was becoming more and more expensive to extract rubber from the far reaches of Amazônia.

In 1910, Asian rubber made up a little more than 13 percent of the world's production. In 1912 it had risen to 28 percent, and by 1915 it had reached 68 percent. Attempts at planting rubber trees in the Amazon region went nowhere. Plants were often attacked by diseases. One good example is Henry Ford's project, known as Fordlândia. By the end of the 1920s it was an enormous failure.

Throughout the First Republic, there were some significant changes in Brazil's international relations, economically and financially speaking. The majority of loans and investments continued to come from Great Britain. The United States kept its position as the main market for Brazil's most important export product, coffee. However, as the years went by, Brazil tended to deal more and more with the United States. This was clearly the case in the 1920s. Since the First World War, the value of imports from the United States surpassed that of imports from Britain.

In 1928, Brazil was the Latin American country with the greatest foreign debt. It constituted 44 percent of the total Latin American debt, and was followed by Argentina's, 27 percent, then by Chile's 12 percent. It is estimated that in 1923, 22 percent of Brazil's export revenues were used to service this debt. The debt had been incurred to cover various needs: to keep the government working, to finance the building of infrastructure (ports and railways), to support the coffee business, or, simply, to pay the existing debt.

During the last decades of the empire, foreign investments went mainly to railways. During the republic, railway investments tended to become secondary. They were overtaken by investments in insurance companies, steamship lines, banks, and electric companies.

Basic services in the major cities were in the hands of foreign companies. The most notable case was "Light" – a Canadian concern by the name of the São Paulo Tramways, Light and Power Company, Ltd., founded in Toronto in 1899. Its first base of operation was São Paulo. In 1905 it had set up shop in Rio. Light unseated a local streetcar company in São Paulo and also took over the supply and control of electricity. The rise of industry in the city was closely associated with Light's investments in infrastructure.

As far as the export economy was concerned, there were few foreign investments in production. But foreign investments were present in various ways: they financed products' commercialization; and they controlled part of the railway system – and practically all exporting, overseas transport, and product insurance.

There are no good data on foreign firms' profits. Seemingly, the biggest winners were the banks, which counted on the instability of Brazilian currency and on recessions. The biggest British bank, the London and Brazilian Bank, had more assets than the Banco do Brasil. In 1929, foreign banking concerns were responsible for half of all Brazilian transactions.

Foreign investors tended to control their spheres of influence and to dislodge national capital. Their advantage lay in the size of their investments. They hired powerful lawyers and they looked down their noses at Brazilians, whom they considered backward. Their methods were not, however, different from those of the local elite. At any rate, foreign capital played an important part in the creation of a basic service and transportation structure which contributed to Brazil's modernization.

3.5 SOCIAL MOVEMENTS

Throughout the First Republic, workers' social movements surfaced both rurally and in the cities. In rural environments, these movements can be divided into three large groups: (1) those combining religion with social need; (2) those combining religion with demands for social justice; and (3) those with no religious content but which sought social justice.

Canudos is an example of the first group. An example of the second group of social movements occurred in an area known as Contestado or "the Contested Region." It was called that because it was on the border of the states of Paraná and Santa Catarina, and both states claimed it.

A 1911 movement in that region was not concerned with that dispute, however. It arose among the followers of a particular *coronel* or "rural boss" who was considered to be a friend of the poor. They united with people of different backgrounds who had been affected by changes taking place in that area. These changes included rural workers' being driven off their land by a railway and a logging firm. Workers let off by the railway once their contract expired also joined the movement.

The rebels gathered around a man known only as José Maria, who became a martyr after he was killed in one of the early clashes with the state militia. They set up several camps and organized them on the basis of equality and brotherhood for all members. While they waited for José Maria's resurrection, they demanded land. They were attacked by the state militia and the army, who finished them off in 1915.

The third type of rural social movement can be clearly seen in the strikes for better salaries and working conditions on São Paulo's coffee plantations. There were hundreds of local strikes which left behind scant records. The most important one occurred in the Ribeirão Preto area during the 1913 harvest. It involved thousands of colonos. Strikers wanting changes in their work contracts brought the major plantations to a standstill. The police intervened, as did the Italian consul, who tried to work as an arbitrator. In the end the strikers lost.

The growth of cities and their diversification were the minimum requirements for building a workers' movement. Cities brought factories and services together, as well as hundreds of workers sharing the same conditions. But, in the cities, freedom of movement was considerably greater, and ideas spread more freely notwithstanding differences in workers' ethnic origins.

Even so, urban working-class movements during the First Republic were limited and only rarely successful. The reasons for this lie in the relative unimportance of industry in Brazil's economy and workers' relative lack of clout. Strikes only had significant repercussions when they were general strikes or when they targeted key sectors of the agricultural export business such as ports and railways. Likewise, the oligarchical political game could be played without any need to please the nascent mass of workers. Workers were divided along ethnic lines and were little inclined to organize, since joining a union put them on industry's blacklist. On top of this, many immigrants had not given up the idea of "doing America" and going back to Europe.

When, at the end of the 19th century, the first workers' parties appeared in Rio de Janeiro, they were characterized by vague notions of socialism and pragmatic syndicalism. They tended to seek short-term goals such as increases in salaries, limits on hours worked per day, or issues of health. Or they sought middle-range goals such as recognition of unions by employers and by the state.

Conversely, in São Paulo, anarchism was predominant – that is, a particular version thereof: anarcho-syndicalism. In practice, keeping in mind the distance between their program and Brazil's social reality, anarchists, despite their revolutionary ideological stance, were moved to concentrate their efforts on the same demands their adversaries sought. This did not stop the two sides from fighting one another, which weakened the already fragile workers' movement.

The ideological and methodological differences between the workers' movements in Rio de Janeiro and in São Paulo are due to a whole set of factors connected to the nature of the two cities and to the makeup of their working classes.

At the end of the 19th century, the nation's capital had a social structure that was much more complex than São Paulo's. In Rio, people less dependent on agriculture rubbed shoulders with one another: middle-class bureaucrats and professionals, career military men, students at the Escola Militar, and university students. The presence of young military men and the reduced dependency of the middle class on agriculture favored, up to a point, cross-class collaboration. Until 1917, protest movements in Rio were broadly based rather than being specifically working-class movements. Besides Jacobinism, another example was the Vaccine Revolt of 1904, during the Rodrigues Alves government. People protested being inoculated against yellow fever.

As for the working class, one should remember that it consisted largely of service employees working on railways, ships, and docks. They were to some extent taken into account by the government. In Rio there were more native-born workers who had assimilated their bosses' and the government's traditional, paternalistic attitude toward workers.

In spite of its growth, São Paulo's social structure was less diversified. The middle class was centered around the coffee bourgeoisie, and there were no restless military men who might join forces with the underdogs. The greater concentration of foreign workers with no roots in the new land favored the spread of anarchism. The bosses and the government, especially the latter, were the Other, the Enemy.

From the beginning of the First Republic, attempts were made to organize and mobilize workers. There were unions, strikes, and workers' parties (albeit with few workers) which quickly disappeared. With the founding of the Brazilian Workers' Confederation in 1906, anarchists went so far as to organize the working class nationally. But the movement was spotty and rarely made the elite take notice or worry. Rights were obtained by pressuring employers, but these rights were not enacted into law. Once pressure abated, those rights were lost.

This framework was broken between 1917 and 1920 when a cycle of large-scale strikes began in Brazil's major cities, especially in Rio and São Paulo. Two factors were at the root of this cycle. Inflation had spiraled owing to upheavals caused by the First World

War and by speculation in foodstuffs. And in Europe there was a revolutionary wave beginning with the February 1917 revolution followed by the October Revolution in Czarist Russia. The workers' movement began to worry people and to appear on the front pages of newspapers.

Brazilian workers did not intend to transform society; they wanted better living conditions and minimal rights. This is not to say that some had not been swayed to follow the dream of creating an egalitarian society. Of the three general strikes during that period, the strike of June and July 1917 in São Paulo has persisted in Brazil's historical memory. Indeed, it persisted to such a point that scholars tended to concentrate on it and to overlook the broader picture regarding worker mobilization.

The wave of strikes died down after 1920, perhaps owing to the difficulty of succeeding, or because of repression. Repressive measures were aimed mainly at foreign working-class leaders who were important organizers. Many of them were expelled from the country.

It would be an exaggeration to say that before the wave of strikes between 1917 and 1920, the government had been entirely uninterested in regulating labor relations and unionization. However, it was only during that period that the government began to consider labor legislation with any consistency. The principal proposals were made in the national Congress. They were gathered in a projected labor code which envisaged an eight-hour work day, limits on women's and children's labor, and maternity leaves. The bill was fiercely attacked by industrialists and by the majority of congressmen. The only part that survived was a law regulating compensation for work-related accidents, which passed in 1919.

During the 1920s, as the workers' movement died down, there were clear indications that the state intended to intervene in labor relations through legislative concessions providing minimal rights for workers. Two laws were especially important. One 1925 law gave workers two-week vacations. The other regulated child labor. Still, to be implemented the 1925 law required a bylaw, and up to 1930 it did not apply to industry, owing to pressure from industrialists.

At the beginning of the 1920s, a crisis arose within the anarchist movement. The scanty gains from its strikes, notwithstanding their momentum, cleared the way for doubting anarchist notions. At the same time, on the international front, news reached Brazil of the break between anarchists and Russia's triumphant Communists. The October Revolution of 1917 seemed to announce the "dawn of a new era," and opposition leftists were apparently "going against the flow of history." Thus, in March 1922, the Communist Party of Brazil was born. Its founders came mainly from the anarchist movement. Its origin is exceptional in Latin America, where practically all Communist parties came from divisions in socialist parties. The PCB (Partido Comunista do Brasil) has been outlawed for most of its history. Until 1930, it was made up mainly of workers, and its membership never exceeded 1,000 people. It was subordinate to the strategy of the Third International, with headquarters in Moscow, which urged colonial and semi-colonial countries to engage in bourgeois democratic revolutions as a first step in the socialist revolution.

3.6   THE POLITICAL PROCESS DURING THE 1920S

After the First World War, the urban middle class was more visible on the political scene. Generally speaking, this segment of society tended to support people and movements that raised the banner of authentic liberalism capable of putting constitutional norms and laws into practice – and capable of transforming the oligarchical republic into a liberal one. This meant, among other things, clean elections and respect for individual rights. In these circles, people spoke of social reform, but they put their greatest hopes in education, the secret ballot, and the creation of the "Justiça Eleitoral," a branch of the judiciary destined to prevent election fraud.

One clear indication of the urban population's greater political participation was the 1919 election. Ruy Barbosa, who had been defeated in 1910 and 1914, presented his candidacy in opposition to Epitácio Pessoa as a sort of protest. Even though he had no support from any political machine, he garnered around one-third of all votes and won in the Federal District.

The adjustments and havoc among competing oligarchies in presidential successions took on new dimensions. One good example is the dispute over who would succeed President Epitácio Pessoa. Early in 1921, the São Paulo–Minas Gerais league proposed the governor of Minas, Artur Bernardes, as its candidate. Rio Grande do Sul, under the leadership of Borges de Medeiros, rose up against this candidate. He denounced the coffee and milk political cabal and considered it a means of guaranteeing resources for coffee protection schemes at a time when the country needed a more even-handed financial policy. He and his followers also feared that a constitutional amendment would be passed to restrict states' autonomy. (It actually was passed under Bernardes in 1926.) Other states joined Rio Grande do Sul and formed the "Republican Reaction," which put forth Nilo Peçanha, a politician from Rio de Janeiro. He was of plebeian origin and a supporter of *Florianismo*.

It was during the campaigns that the military's dissatisfaction surfaced. The army's impression that Bernardes was anti-military was underlined when, in October 1921, a bogus letter was published in the *Correio da Manhã*, a Rio de Janeiro newspaper. Supposedly two letters had been sent by Bernardes to a politician in Minas Gerais. These letters seriously offended the military and added fuel to their fire. Their objective of making the military even more opposed to Bernardes had been reached when, just before the elections of 1 March 1922, two individuals acknowledged their authorship of the "documents."

The situation got even more complicated in June 1922. Bernardes had won, but he had still not been inaugurated, and that would not happen until 15 November. The Clube Militar protested against the government's use of army troops to intervene in Pernambuco's internal politics. In response, the government shut down the Clube. It justified its action by citing a law against anti-social organizations.

These events precipitated the lieutenants' movement, so named because its leadership was made up of middle-echelon army officers – first lieutenants and captains. The first act of rebellion was a revolt at Fort Copacabana, in Rio de Janeiro, on 5 July 1922. The climate of real or imagined offenses to the army and the repression of the Clube Militar made these young "lieutenants" rebel in a protest aimed at "rescuing the army's honor." This revolt did not spread to other units. After firing a few cannon shots, the rebels were bombarded in reprisal and were surrounded. On the following day, hundreds of them surrendered, following an appeal from the government. A group had decided to resist, however. The fort was once more bombarded by sea and by air. Seventeen military men along with a civilian volunteer decided to take on the government's forces on Copacabana Beach. When shots were fired 16 of them died. Lieutenants Siqueira Campos and Eduardo Gomes were wounded. The "Copacabana 18" (*os 18 do Forte*) started *tenentismo*, or the legend of the lieutenants.

In 1924, the so-called "second Fifth of July" occurred in São Paulo. That date was chosen to honor the movement two years earlier in Rio; the locale because of São Paulo's importance among the states. The 1924 revolution was better prepared and was intended to bring down the Bernardes government. During the 1920s, Artur Bernardes bore the brunt of the "lieutenants'" hatred for the ruling oligarchy. The movement's formal leadership was in the hands of retired General Isidoro Dias Lopes, an officer from Rio Grande do Sul who had joined the Federalists during the time of Floriano Peixoto. Among the more active officers, one finds the Távora brothers (Juarez and Joaquim), Eduardo Gomes, Estillac Leal, João Cabanas, and Miguel Costa. Miguel Costa's presence brought in support from part of the state militia because he was a prestigious officer in the Força Pública (State Militia) of São Paulo.

Once the movement had begun, with the taking of a few headquarters, a battle for São Paulo itself got underway. The rebels took control of the city. The presence of the "lieutenants" in São Paulo's capital lasted until 27 July. On that day, they left the capital heading west through the São Paulo countryside. The column set up headquarters in western Paraná, in a hamlet close to the outlet of the Iguaçu River. There these troops from São Paulo expected to meet and join another column coming from Rio Grande do Sul.

In Rio Grande do Sul, a *tenentista* revolt had begun in October 1924. Lieutenant João Alberto and Captain Luis Carlos Prestes took command. The revolt had counted on support from anti-PRR factions in Rio Grande do Sul. This combination would mix lieutenantism with state politics. After several skirmishes, the Gaúchos set off toward Paraná to join forces with the Paulistas. They met in April 1925 and decided to journey through Brazil and spread the word urging people to rise up against the oligarchies. They also wanted to draw the government's fire so that more revolts could take place in the cities.

Thus was born the Miguel Costa–Luis Carlos Prestes Column, better known as the Prestes Column. This force accomplished a tremendous feat, marching some 24,000 kilometers through Brazil's backlands. In February and March 1927, those remaining in the column considered the movement over and retreated into Bolivia and Paraguay. There were never more than 1,500 people in the column, and its numbers varied, with people joining and leaving along the way. By never staying very long in any one place, the Prestes Column avoided clashes with sizable military forces. Popular support was at best an illusion. The column's likelihood of success was practically nil. Still, it did have a symbolic effect on sectors of the urban population that were dissatisfied with the ruling elite. Whatever the outcome, in their eyes, those heroes taking all sorts of risks to save the nation demonstrated that there was a chance of changing Brazil's destiny.

Lieutenantism was largely an army movement. From the navy, the only incident involving middle-echelon officers that attracted attention was the November 1924 mutiny on the dreadnought *São Paulo*. It was led by Lieutenant Hercolino Cascardo. After trading shots with the forts in Guanabara Bay, the *São Paulo* headed for the open sea. It came to port in Montevideo, where the mutineers sought exile.

The actors in the major naval mutiny during the First Republic were almost all blacks and mulattos recruited from the poorest social classes. This was the so-called Switch Mutiny or Revolta da Chibata, which began on 22. November 1910. The mutineers did not want to bring down the government; they simply wanted to put an end to the poor treatment and the harsh physical punishment inflicted on them.

The movement began almost simultaneously on different warships anchored in Guanabara Bay. Several officers were taken by surprise and murdered. One of the main instigators was Seaman João Cândido. Under the threat of an entire squadron in mutiny, Congress decreed an amnesty if the rebels turned themselves in to the authorities. They agreed to do away with the switch as an official means of punishment in the navy.

The mutineers accepted the conditions and the movement was over. It was followed by a revolt in the Marine Corps and intense repression which included João Cândido and the other leaders of the Revolta da Chibata. The *Satélite*, a "death ship," set out from Rio de Janeiro and headed for Amazônia with navy rebels, thieves, pimps, and prostitutes on board. Many died or were shot along the way. The members of the November (Chibata) Revolt were brought to trial and accused of involvement in the Marines' revolt. They were finally acquitted, but they spent 18 months in prison, incommunicado and being tortured.

What was the meaning of lieutenantism? What were its objectives? To answer these questions, one must look at what was going on within the army and within society at large.

Military officers' education had changed considerably since the early days of the republic. The Escola Militar at Praia Vermelha had been closed definitively in 1904, after its final revolt. From then until 1911, the only military school the government allowed was the Escola de Guerra or "School of War" in Porto Alegre. In 1911, the Realengo Military School was founded in Rio de Janeiro. What was taught in Realengo was very different from the curriculum at Praia Vermelha. After 1911 instruction there focused on military knowledge, having abandoned the old school's diversity, which it owed to the influence of positivism. The school's purpose was no longer to graduate citizen soldiers with one foot in the army and another in civilian society and politics. Instead, the school's task was to graduate professional soldiers.

Soldiers' training improved when, between 1906 and 1910, three classes were sent to Germany. Hermes da Fonseca attended that country's massive military maneuvers in 1910 and returned as a great admirer of German military organization. Ten years later the army was renovated further when a mission came from France. Germany had lost the war, and it was inevitable that Brazil should seek a different model.

In spite of their greater professionalism, army officers could not help having ideas about society and about the existing power structure. During Marshal Hermes's administration, a group of civilians and military men had formed a sort of pressure group around the president. They were called "Salvationists" because their intent was to safeguard republican institutions. What exactly was their program for "salvation"? They intended to reduce the oligarchies' powers wherever this seemed easiest and wherever social inequality was most striking. The "lieutenants" can be seen as heirs of the Salvationists who lived at a time when problems had worsened in and outside the army.

As far as the army was concerned, one of the principal sources of bitterness for the middle echelons was career rigidity. It was hard to attain the highest ranks because positions rarely opened. Officers also criticized their superiors' behavior and accused them of conniving with corrupt administrations. Thus, the lieutenants not only wanted to purify society, but they also wanted to purify the institution to which they belonged.

During the 1920s, military rebels had no clear proposal for political reform. They wanted to establish a central authority in the country to educate the citizens and to pursue a vaguely nationalistic policy. They believed it was necessary to rebuild the state in order to rebuild the nation. They maintained that one of the great drawbacks of the oligarchical system was that it broke Brazil into pieces and made it into "20 fiefs" whose lords were chosen by the dominant politicians.

While they did not go so far as to concoct an anti-liberal program, the lieutenants did not believe that "true liberalism" was the country's road to recovery. They imposed restrictions on direct elections and universal suffrage, and they believed in an authoritarian route for reforming state and society.

Scholars often claim that lieutenantism was a middle-class movement. While the lieutenants could count on widespread sympathy from that sector of society during the 1920s, to reduce their movement to a middle-class manifestation would be to simplify it too much. As far as their social origins were concerned, the majority of the lieutenants came from military backgrounds or from impoverished branches of elite families in the Northeast. Very few of them were recruited from the urban population of Rio de Janeiro or São Paulo. Above all else, it should be remembered that the lieutenants were really lieutenants, that is, army officers. Their world view was primarily shaped by their socialization within the armed forces. And that world view was peculiarly theirs, just as their complaints were specific complaints against the institution of which they were members.

Aside from a few points of support, the lieutenants ended up taking on the government practically alone. They could not rally the army to join their cause. Until 1930, no sizable sector of the civilian elite attempted a maneuver as radical as theirs. And the lieutenants' radicalism did not come so much from the content of their actions as it did from their method – armed confrontation.

President Artur Bernardes (1922–1926), from Minas Gerais, ran the country during a difficult period. He had to declare states of siege repeatedly. He was extremely unpopular in the urban areas, especially in Rio de Janeiro, and, given the times, Bernardes instituted an extremely harsh, repressive regime. Popular dissatisfaction was rooted in a complicated financial state of affairs. Epitácio Pessoa's massive printing of money between 1921 and 1923 (to "valorize" coffee for the third time) was responsible for inflation and for falling exchange rates.

During the Bernardes administration, something important came to pass as far as coffee policy was concerned. Among the president's main concerns was how to pay the foreign debt. Payments would begin once more in 1927, and this time Brazil would pay both the interest and installments on the principal. A British financial commission led by Lord Montagu came to Brazil toward the end of 1924 and surveyed the country's condition. In its report to the administration, it pointed out the very serious risks being run in the printing of paper money and in the support of coffee prices. Obviously, Brazil's international creditors feared the country could not meet its commitments.

In this context, the federal government was not exactly favorably disposed to support coffee. At the same time, criticism from the coffee sector was growing because of the industry's apparent state of abandonment. The way out was to transfer coffee support from the Union to the state of São Paulo, which supported coffee up to 1930. Permanent support of coffee created a turnabout in coffee policy. Beginning at that time, the government no longer opened its umbrella to protect the coffee industry during times of crisis; it opened the umbrella permanently. The government of São Paulo assumed the responsibility of controlling the shipping of coffee to the port of Santos and of purchasing coffee whenever it seemed necessary. If the state's action did not end coffee crises once and for all, it has softened them considerably. Bernardes left office peacefully. The rotation between São Paulo and Minas was made once more with the election of Washington Luis, who was, however, known as a "Paulista from Macaé" because he had been born in the city of Macaé, in the state of Rio de Janeiro. The new president's great dream was to stabilize Brazil's currency. His ultimate goal was to make all the paper money in circulation convertible.

During the 1920s, politics in Rio Grande do Sul and in São Paulo took different routes. While Rio Grande's elite tended to join forces after their great armed confrontation, in São Paulo the PRP's monopoly was broken. After the civil war in Rio Grande do Sul, an ex-minister of finance from Washington Luis's administration was elected governor in 1927. This ex-minister's name was Getúlio Vargas. Vargas had engineered a definitive accord between the PRR (Partido Republicano Riograndense) and the opposition, which ushered Gaúchos into federal politics. Their presence became stronger, as events during 1929 and 1930 would show.

In São Paulo, social diversification, among other factors, made it impossible to accommodate all political currents and interests (many of which were personal) within the PRP. Dissension within the PRP was no novelty, but its impact had been minimal up to the 1920s. Then, in 1926, the Partido Democrático (PD) arrived on the scene with a liberal program. Its main objective was political reform through secret, obligatory voting; minority representation; independence of the three branches of government; and judicial power to oversee elections.

At least until 1930, the PD leadership consisted mainly of prestigious professionals and young men who were sons of coffee planters. *Conselheiro* Antônio Prado was chosen to head the PD. Prado was a respected representative of the wealthy São Paulo bourgeoisie and an old adversary of the PRP's policies. The PD attracted a few immigrants, but the stories in its paper, *O Diário Nacional*, indicate that its base was the traditional middle class. Immigrants, especially the "industrial plutocrats," were the target of violent criticism. The PD differed from the PRP because of its liberalism, which the party in power had repudiated in practice. It was also different because of the relative youth of its members. It awakened enthusiasm in a sizable part of the middle class to which the PRP's favors did not extend. The PD aspired to create opportunities in society and in public administration. Still, it did not take the shape of a modern party which controlled the bigger cities, whereas the archaic PRP did control the countryside. The PD did have some rural strongholds where it used the same *coronelista* tactics as its adversaries.

Contrary to what happened in Rio Grande do Sul, on the level of national politics, this party division made Paulista presence problematic.

3.7   THE 1930 REVOLUTION

In the beginning of 1929, after Washington Luis's relatively calm administration, a great schism came about between the São Paulo and Mineiro elites. This schism would bring the First Republic to an end.

Their misunderstanding began when, surprisingly, Washington Luis insisted on nominating a Paulista to succeed him. As if that were not enough, he nominated the governor of São Paulo, Júlio Prestes. Washington Luis's move pushed Mineiros and Gaúchos into the same camp and to a certain extent re-created the alliances of the 1909–1910 campaign.

Halfway through 1929, after various meetings, Minas and Rio Grande, as the opposition, nominated Getúlio Vargas as their presidential candidate with João Pessoa as his vice-presidential running mate. João Pessoa was the governor of Paraíba and a nephew of Epitácio Pessoa. The opposition formed the Aliança Liberal (Liberal Alliance), in whose name the campaign would be directed. Vargas received the support of the PD in São Paulo, while in Minas a splinter group from the PRM supported Júlio Prestes.

The Liberal Alliance's program reflected the aspirations of the regional ruling classes not connected to the coffee nucleus. Its objective was to make the middle class sensitive to the issues at hand. It supported the need to give incentives to national production in general and not just to coffee interests. In the name of financial orthodoxy, it opposed schemes to valorize coffee, and, in this point, its policy was no different from Washington Luis's. It proposed a few measures for the protection of workers. Its major thrust was in defense of individual freedom, amnesty (this was a gesture toward the lieutenants), and political reform, which would guarantee what they called electoral truth.

Vargas was reticent and for a time sought an agreement with the president. However, in spite of his reticence, the campaign gained momentum. The liberal caravans were staffed by younger party members and traveled through the main cities of the Northeast. Vargas was received enthusiastically in rallies held in Rio and São Paulo. In the middle of the electoral campaign, in October 1929, the world's financial markets collapsed, which caught the coffee planters in a complicated situation. Permanent support of coffee had created the expectation of sure profits, guaranteed by the state. Many people took out high-interest loans to plant coffee. The crash brought about an abrupt fall in international coffee prices. Since coffee consumption fell, it became impossible to make up for its fall in price by increasing sales. Planters who had gone into debt counting on future profits found themselves up a blind alley.

The coffee industry and the federal government failed to see eye-to-eye. Coffee growers asked Washington Luis to address the crisis by offering renewed backing and by calling for a moratorium on their debts. The president refused. He was concerned with support-ing the plan for devising a stable exchange rate, but the plan also fell through. A wave of unrest rose in São Paulo. No break occurred between the coffee sector and the federal government, however. The electoral gains from the crisis were scanty. Even though the PD was part of the Liberal Alliance, there was no reason to believe that the opposition's victory would occasion paying greater attention to coffee interests.

Júlio Prestes won the election on 1 March 1930. The Liberal Alliance verbally condemned the reigning political resources, but it also used them. Electoral machines produced votes in every state, including Rio Grande do Sul, where Vargas appears to have won by 298,627 votes to 982.

The election returns were not well received by younger mem-bers of the opposition, who were ready to follow the lead the lieutenants had blazed almost single-handedly. Even though it had been defeated, the lieutenants' movement continued to be an important factor because of its members' military experience and their prestige within the army itself. An alliance between younger politicians and military rebels could now be made. And this is, in fact, exactly what happened, notwithstanding restrictions on either side.

The only important exception was Luis Carlos Prestes. In May of 1930, the most prestigious lieutenant sent out a manifesto in which he declared himself to be a socialist revolutionary and in which he condemned support for dissident oligarchies. As far as Prestes was concerned, the opposing sides were merely a plaything within the greater struggle between British and American imperialism, which sought to control Latin America.

Prestes had been influenced by Communists after a meeting between him and Astrogildo Pereira, one of the founders of the PCB. The meeting took place while Prestes was exiled in Bolivia. Prestes continued to be influenced through his reading and his contact with Argentine and Uruguayan Communist leaders, but did not join the PCB immediately. With a small group of people, he formed the Liga de Ação Revolucionária (League of Revolutionary Action). For several years, the PCB condemned what it called "Prestes's Cult of Personality," but finally, in 1934, an order came from Moscow guaranteeing Prestes's membership in the party.

Midway through 1930, the revolutionary conspiracy was on a bad footing, but an unexpected event revived it. On 26 July, João Pessoa was assassinated in a Recife pastry shop by one of his political adversaries – João Dantas. This crime was motivated by private and public reasons. At the time, only public reasons made the headlines because the private ones would sully the image of João Pessoa as a revolutionary martyr. João Pessoa's death was felt throughout the country and was exploited politically. His body was brought to Rio de Janeiro, where his burial attracted throngs of people. The opposition had been given a tremendous lift. From that time on, developing a revolutionary program became much easier.

Important gains were made within the army itself. Indeed, the movement's command post was given to a man considered typical of the responsible sectors of the armed forces. This man was then Lieutenant Colonel Góes Monteiro. He was born in Alagoas, but his military career was linked to Rio Grande do Sul. Since 1906, when he was a student at the Escola Militar, Góes was familiar with Vargas and other Gaúcho politicians with whom he had collaborated during Rio Grande do Sul's internal disputes. During the 1920s, Góes Monteiro had not rebelled. Quite to the contrary, he had fought the Prestes Column in the states of the Northeast.

The revolution began in Minas Gerais and Rio Grande do Sul on 3 October 1930. In São Paulo, the PD was for all intents and purposes on the sideline of the revolutionary plan, and there was no revolutionary uprising in that state. In Minas there was some resistance. In the Northeast the movement was unleashed before dawn on 4 October. It was under the command of Juarez Távora. Paraíba was the center of operations. To guarantee the revolution's success in Pernambuco, Távora counted on support from the people of Recife, who occupied federal buildings and an arsenal. Local railway workers on the Great Western went out on strike.

The Northeast quickly fell to the revolutionaries, so attention was focused on military contingents which, once they controlled the South, were preparing to invade the state of São Paulo. However, before the decisive confrontation, on 24 October, members of the military high command, in the name of the army and the navy, deposed the president in Rio de Janeiro and set up a provisionary governing junta.

The junta tried to stay in power, but it retreated in the face of popular demonstrations and pressure from soldiers coming from the South. Getúlio Vargas went by train to São Paulo, from where he continued toward Rio. His arrival was preceded by 3,000 soldiers from Rio Grande do Sul. The man who would emphasize national unity once he led the nation made a point of displaying his regionality when he reached Rio. He got off the train wearing a military uniform and a wide-brimmed pampa hat. The symbolism of regional victory was complete when the Gaúchos tied their horses around an obelisk that existed at that time along Rio Branco Avenue, in downtown Rio. Vargas became president on 3 November 1930. This brought the First Republic to an end and inaugurated a new era which, at that time, was still poorly defined.

Brazil's revolutionary movement of the 1930s is part of a framework of general instability brought about by the worldwide crisis of 1929. This situation permeated Latin America. There were 11 revolutionary episodes between 1930 and 1932. General Uriburu's September 1930 military coup in Argentina set the example for Brazil. It was hailed, among the opposition, as a model to emulate.

The 1930 revolution was not carried out by representatives of some supposedly new social class, be it the middle class or the industrial bourgeoisie. The middle class supported the Liberal Alliance, but it was too diverse and too dependent on agrarian forces for a political plan of action to be formed in its name.

As far as industrialists are concerned, one should remember that during the First Republic they acted much more as members of a regional bloc, which included agrarian and commercial groups, than as a specific social class with national dimensions. In São Paulo, for example, it is true that over the years differences began to emerge between the industrial bourgeoisie and the agrarian sector. This became obvious with the founding of the Centro das Indústrias do Estado de São Paulo in 1928. But these differences did not go so deep that they broke the agreement with the ruling class, which favored São Paulo's interests. The great industrialists counted on the support of the PRP, which represented them. Also, they had no reason to sympathize with the opposition since they were targets of the opposition's criticism. That is why it is hardly surprising that industrial associations had openly supported Júlio Prestes's candidacy.

In Rio, industrialists belonged to the Centro Industrial do Brasil (CIB). During the final years of the 1920s, people representing the industrial bourgeoisie could be found in government posts. In 1929, during the economic crisis, the great textile magnate Manoel Guilherme da Silveira was elected president of the Banco do Brasil.

When the 1930 revolution began, the CIB expressed its support for Washington Luis and deemed the insurrection an "event most prejudicial to the country's economic state." Immediately after the revolutionaries' victory, Rio de Janeiro's industrialists tried to approach the government. But this does not suggest that Getúlio Vargas was favored by the captains of industry. What it shows is the belief that before or after 1930, contact with the state was a decisive factor in strengthening the industrial bourgeoisie.

The victors of 1930 were a heterogeneous lot, both socially and politically. They had united against a common adversary, but with different outlooks. The old oligarchs, as typical representatives of the regional ruling class, only wanted greater attention paid to their areas. They wanted more personal power, with minimal changes. The younger civilian sectors were bent on reforming the political system, and, temporarily, they joined forces with the lieutenants. They were known as the "civilian lieutenants." The lieutenants supported centralization of power and some social reforms. They were seen as a threat by the upper echelons of the armed forces. The PD sought to control the state government in São Paulo and supported the adoption of the principles of liberalism, which members thought would guarantee their dominance.

Beginning in 1930, an exchange of elites took place. The traditional oligarchies fell from power. Their place was taken by military men, technocrats, young politicians, and, a little later, by industrialists.

Early on the new government tried to centralize and control both the economic and financial decisions and those pertaining to politics. It began to arbitrate among the different interests vying with one another. Power of the oligarchic type based on the strength of particular states lost ground. However, oligarchies did not disappear, nor did the pattern of patronage. Power now emanated from the center to the periphery rather from the periphery to the center.

A new type of state was born after 1930. It differed from the oligarchical state not only owing to its centralization and its greater degree of autonomy, but also because of other factors: (1) economic policy slowly turned toward the promotion of industrialization; (2) social policy tended to provide some sort of protection for urban workers, who were soon gathered into a working-class alliance supported by the state; (3) the armed forces, in particular the army, were given a central role in support of the creation of an industrial base and in maintaining internal order.

Vargas's state promoted national capitalism from two bases of support: the state apparatus, which counted on the armed forces and society, and an alliance between the industrial bourgeoisie and the urban working class. This was how the industrial bourgeoisie advanced and gained a voice and some power within the government. It was not because of some purported action during the 1930 revolution. The plan for industrialization came more from the government's technocrats than it did from the industrialists.

These transformations did not happen from one day to the next, nor were they part of a unified plan of the revolutionary government. They were carried out over the years, and emphasized different aspects of this program at different times. Thus, an overall view of the Vargas government has only become clear with the passage of time.

4

The Vargas State (1930–1945)

Having risen to power in October 1930, Getúlio Vargas remained there for 15 years: as head of the provisional government, as a president elected by indirect votes, and as dictator. He would be reelected president in 1950 by a popular vote, but he would not complete his mandate because he committed suicide in 1954.

The most weighty figure in Brazil's 20th-century political history came from a family of ranchers in São Borja, located in the Campanha region of Rio Grande do Sul. His father was a local PRR leader and became involved in their struggles with the Federalists. Vargas worked under the wing of Borges de Medeiros, and his career was, up to 1930, typical of the PRR. He was a district attorney, a deputy in the state legislature, the leader of the Gaúcho contingent in the federal Chamber of Deputies, Washington Luis's minister of finance, and governor of the state of Rio Grande do Sul. In 1930, Vargas leaped into the nation's presidency and began a government very different from Brazil's oligarchical administrations.

At the beginning of the 1930s, the provisional government tried, amid all the uncertainty, to consolidate its power. The worldwide crash was responsible for the lack of markets for agricultural products, for planters' financial ruin, and for unemployment in the big cities. Financial difficulties grew. Foreign revenues from exports declined and convertible money went out of circulation.

On the political plane, the victorious state oligarchies sought to rebuild the state according to the old patterns. The lieutenants were opposed to this idea and supported Vargas in his attempt to strengthen power at the center. At the same time, however, the lieutenants were an unruly force that threatened the army's internal hierarchy.

One important base of support for the government came from the Catholic church. Collaboration between church and state was nothing new. It dated from the 1920s, beginning especially with Artur Bernardes's administration. The relationship was now much closer. A symbolic mark of their collaboration was the unveiling of the statue of Christ the Redeemer on Corcovado Mountain in Rio de Janeiro. The ceremony took place on 12 October 1931, the day Columbus discovered America. Overlooking all of Rio de Janeiro, Vargas and his ministers stood on the statue's narrow platform. Cardinal Leme consecrated the nation to "the most holy heart of Jesus, whom it recognized as its King and Lord." The church obtained support for the new government from the bulk of Brazil's Catholics. The government, for its part, took special measures in the church's favor. A decree in April 1931 stands out. It permitted religion to be taught in public schools.

The provisional government's centralizing measures appeared early on. In November 1930, Vargas assumed both executive and legislative power when he dissolved Congress and state and municipal legislatures. All the old governors, with the exception of the newly elected governor of Minas Gerais, were dismissed and replaced by federal *interventores* or governors appointed by the central government. In August 1931, the so-called Código dos Interventores (Interventors' Code) established norms for the subordination of interventors or appointed governors to the central government. It also limited states' autonomy. They could no longer contract foreign loans without authorization from the central government. They could not spend more than 10 percent of their normal budget on their military police. And they could not supply their state police with artillery, airplanes, or firearms in excess of what the army possessed.

Centralization was extended to the economic sphere. The Vargas government did not and could not abandon the coffee sector. It tried, however, to concentrate coffee policy in its hands, and this occurred in 1933, when the Departamento Nacional do Café (DNC) was created.

But coffee's basic problem would not go away. What to do with the present and future stocks of coffee that found no outlet on the international market? This question was answered in July 1931. The government would buy the coffee with the money it received from export taxes and from exchange taxes (*confisco cambial*), that is, from a percentage of the export receipts. It would then destroy a part of the harvested coffee. This was an attempt to reduce the supply of coffee and to maintain its price. This option was similar to the elimination of grapes in Argentina and the killing of flocks of sheep in Australia. Although it was changed from time to time, the Brazilian scheme lasted many years. The government only stopped destroying coffee in 1944. During those 13 years, 78,200,000 sacks of coffee beans were destroyed – an amount equal to the world's coffee consumption for three years.

The nation's financial situation became untenable halfway through 1931. In September, payments on the country's foreign debt were suspended, and the Banco do Brasil once more received the sole right to exchange currency. The latter measure had been decreed during the Washington Luis administration and then revoked by the revolutionary government.

One of the more coherent aspects of the Vargas administration was its labor policy. Between 1930 and 1945, it passed through several stages, but from the beginning it appeared innovative as far as what preceded it was concerned. Its main objectives were to repress efforts of the urban working class to organize outside the aegis of the state and to incorporate the working class into the government's array of supporters.

Concerning the first objective, repressive measures were aimed at leftist parties and organizations, especially the PCB. Immediately after 1930 these attacks became even more systematic than those of the First Republic.

As for the second objective, the sporadic attention given to problems of the working class during the 1920s gave way to a specific governmental policy. It was announced in November 1930, when the Ministry of Labor, Industry, and Commerce was created.

The announcement was followed by laws to protect workers and to allow the state to bring unions into line. Bureaus such as the Juntas de Conciliação e Julgamento (Bureaus of Reconciliation and Arbitration) were created to mediate conflicts between workers and bosses.

Unions were brought into line by a decree in March 1931 which regulated workers' and owners' associations (workers were its primary focus). Unions were defined as departments of consultation which worked hand in hand with the bureaucracy. The principle of exclusive jurisdiction for each trade union was adopted. The state would recognize only one union for each category of worker, and unionization would not be obligatory. The government secured control over the unions by determining that members of the Ministry of Labor would attend union meetings. A union's legality depended on ministerial recognition, which could be revoked whenever it was shown that a particular union failed to obey a series of norms. This decree was in force until July 1934, when it was replaced. The main change consisted of the adoption of a principle of plurality. But union plurality never existed in practice, although this principle was only struck from the laws in 1939.

Although at the beginning industrialist and merchant associations fought these government initiatives, especially those that gave workers some rights, they ended up accepting this labor legislation.

Labor organizations under leftist control attempted to oppose being co-opted by the state. Their attempts failed, however. In addition to pressure from the government, the rank and file in these organizations supported the legislation. Several benefits, such as vacations and the possibility of bringing suit in the Bureaus of Reconciliation and Arbitration, depended on membership in a union recognized by the government. By the end of 1933, the old autonomous unions had given way and, for better or for worse, had come in line with the new laws.

The 1930 victors early on attended to the problem of education. Their main objective was to create a wider, better-trained elite. Attempts at educational reform had begun during the 1920s. They were carried out on the state level, which was consistent with the image of a federal republic. Beginning in 1930, measures intended to create a system of schools and to support education took a different direction and emanated from the center toward the periphery. Education was also brought into line with the leaders' centralizing vision. The first manifestation of educational centralization was the creation of the Ministry of Education and Health, in November 1930.

As in other areas, the Vargas administration's educational initiatives were based on authoritarianism. The state tried to organize a school system from top to bottom without huge mobilizations within society and without supporting, in a consistent fashion, a totalitarian education that would include all aspects of the cultural universe.

Even during the period of the Estado Novo dictatorship, Brazilian education was imbued with a mixture of hierarchical values and Catholic conservatism. It never became an instrument of fascist indoctrination. Educational policy remained essentially in the hands of young politicians from Minas Gerais. They had begun their careers under their old state oligarchy, but set out in new directions after 1930. This was the case of Francisco Campos, the minister of education between November 1930 and September 1932. Gustavo Capanema followed him and remained minister of education from 1932 to 1945 – a long tenure. Between 1930 and 1932, Francisco Campos worked hard as minister of education and attended mainly to secondary and university education.

As far as higher education was concerned, the government attempted to create conditions favorable to real universities dedicated to teaching and research. With secondary education, the top priority was to make it take root. Up to then, in the great bulk of the country, secondary education was little more than preparation for entrance into institutes of higher learning. The Campos Reform established a sequenced curriculum once and for all. There would be two educational cycles, obligatory attendance, and a high school diploma would be needed to enter a university.

The main measures for the creation of universities were enacted in the Federal District and São Paulo; in the latter case there was no federal participation. Thus, in 1934 the University of São Paulo was created and, in 1935, the University of the Federal District.

4.2 THE POLITICAL PROCESS

There are two important and interrelated points which define the political process between 1930 and 1934: the issue of lieutenantism and the struggle between centralized power and regional groups.

With the victory of the 1930 revolution, the lieutenants became part of the government and formulated a clear-cut program. They proposed paying more uniform attention to the needs of various parts of the country; they also proposed some economic plans, installation of basic industry (especially iron), and a nationalization program that included mines, transportation, communications, and coastal navigation. To carry out these reforms, the lieutenants would have to rely on a stable, centralized federal government. They clearly disassociated themselves from liberal points of view and supported the prolongation of Vargas's dictatorship as well as a constitution that would establish class as well as individual representation. In the latter case, each state would have an equal number of representatives.

In two very different regions, the Northeast and São Paulo, Vargas tried to use the lieutenants as an instrument in the fight against local oligarchies. The Northeast was the lieutenants' favorite field of operations. Many of them came from this region, which was marked by extreme poverty and where the ruling classes flagrantly acted in a violent fashion. Several interventors sent to northeastern states were military men. In November 1930, the government created a regional police administration for the North, to be led by Juarez Távora. The lieutenants' movement tried to introduce specific improvements and to respond to some cries for justice from the people. They had taken up the "Salvationist" tradition in a different context. Juracy Magalhães, the interventor in Bahia, appointed commissions to develop agriculture. He sought to increase public health services, and he issued a decree for the compulsory reduction of all rents. Távora intended to expropriate the holdings of the oligarchs who had been strongly committed to the First Republic.

Meanwhile, without the wherewithal or the intention to bring about great transformations, the lieutenants finally lined up with sectors of the traditional regional ruling class. Measures intended to lower rents and to expropriate personal wealth were blocked by the federal government and then abandoned. The lieutenants' action in the Northeast, notwithstanding its circumscribed nature, provoked attacks from the dominant groups in the more developed parts of Brazil. Távora was nicknamed the Viceroy of the North and was violently attacked when he tried to create a block of small states.

In São Paulo, the federal government's lack of control helped set the stage for a civil war. By not paying heed to the PD's ambitions, Vargas marginalized the Paulista elite and appointed Lieutenant João Alberto interventor in that state. This interventor could not withstand the pressure from São Paulo and from the government itself, so he resigned in July 1931. Three other interventors succeeded him between then and the middle of 1932. This shows how serious the so-called São Paulo Case had become.

In command of the state, or based on their influence, the lieutenants sought a base of support for their initiatives. Their targets included marginal associations of the coffee industry and workers' unions. In the latter case, Miguel Costa stood out. He was the secretary of security and commander of the state militia. People said that Costa was a Communist at heart who put Communists in jail. Costa, the old leader of the Prestes Column, supported a resurgence of unions such as the Centro de Estivadores de Santos (Santos Stevedore Center). Its directorship was run under Costa's influence.

The lieutenants were opposed by the great majority of São Paulo's population, who assumed the liberal ideology of the local elite. And the elite wanted a constitution for the new government based on the principles of liberal democracy. As a transition measure, they demanded that a local civilian be named interventor. The cause of constitutionality and autonomy rallied vast sectors of the population and brought the PRP and the PD together. They formed the Frente Unica Paulista (the São Paulo United Front) in February 1932. That very month the provisional government began to respond to the anti-dictatorial pressure coming not only from São Paulo but also from Rio Grande do Sul and Minas Gerais. It passed the Electoral Code, which contained some important innovations. It made voting mandatory, secret, and universal. For the first time in Brazil's history, women could vote. Rio Grande do Norte's 1927 electoral law giving women the vote had blazed the trail, but was restricted to that state.

Election to the legislative branch of government would be proportional, which would guarantee minority representation. While professional representation was based on corporate and fascist ideas, its objective was more immediate. The 40-member professional caucus – bigger than the contingent from Minas Gerais – would be easily managed by the government. It would also provide a counterweight to be used against the larger states, especially São Paulo and Rio Grande do Sul, which at that time were the major nuclei of opposition.

Finally, the Electoral Code was instrumental in stabilizing the electoral process and at least in reducing fraud in elections. It created the organization known as Justiça Eleitoral (Electoral Justice), which was in charge of organizing and watching over elections and of judging appeals.

In March 1932, Vargas seemed to take another step in his attempts at pacifying São Paulo. He nominated a local civilian interventor – Pedro de Toledo. Toledo was, however, hardly a prestigious person in São Paulo. Doubts persisted concerning the call for elections and control of the lieutenants. The government was being severely criticized for having delayed the punishment of a group of lieutenants who, in Rio de Janeiro, had looted the *Diário Carioca* right after the Electoral Code had been promulgated.

The United Front in Rio Grande do Sul, which had been formed out of local parties, broke with Vargas. This development induced the conspiratory groups in São Paulo, most of which were linked to the PD, to step up their preparation for a revolution, which finally began on 9 July 1932. The revolutionaries' plan was to deal a death blow to the capital, Rio de Janeiro, and put the federal government in a situation where it would have to negotiate or capitulate. But the plan failed. While the "Paulista War" created considerable sympathy among Rio's middle class, it was confined militarily to São Paulo, where the navy blockaded the port of Santos. In truth, despite their differences with the central government, the regional elites in Rio Grande do Sul and Minas Gerais were not ready to run the risk of taking on a government they had put in power less than two years earlier. São Paulo was, for all intents and purposes, on its own. To combat federal forces, all it had was its state militia and intense popular support.

The 1932 movement brought together different sectors of society – people from the coffee industry, the middle class, and industrialists. Only organized labor, which had carried out important strikes during the first half of 1932, stayed on the sidelines. The struggle for constitutionality, the issues of autonomy, and São Paulo's supremacy over other states galvanized a good part of the local population. A very effective image of the time depicted São Paulo as a locomotive pulling 20 empty cars – the other 20 states in the federation. For the first time ever, there was large-scale use of the radio to announce rallies and to direct volunteers to the battle line. Answering calls in the campaign for "gold to help São Paulo," many people donated jewels and other family possessions.

The revolutionaries tried to make up for their notoriously deficient arms and ammunition by using the resources in São Paulo's industrial park. They sent envoys to the United States to buy arms and aircraft. But the federal government's superiority was evident. In spite of the unevenness between the two sides, the struggle went on for almost three months, ending with São Paulo's surrender in October 1932.

The São Paulo War was on the one hand inspired by the past. On the other hand, it looked toward the future. The issue of constitutionality brought together both those who hoped to return to the oligarchical form of power as well as those who intended to set up a liberal democracy in Brazil. And the movement had important consequences. Even though it had won, the government more clearly saw that it could not ignore São Paulo's elite. The losers, likewise, finally understood that they would have to give in to the central government. In August 1933, Vargas finally nominated a local civilian interventor. This man, Armando de Salles Oliveira, fit the bill – he was associated with the PD. In August of that same year, the decree known as Economic Readjustment was issued. It reduced the debts of planters hurt by the crash. And São Paulo's political elite became more cautious from that point on.

During 1933, lieutenantism began to come apart as a movement. It had not been able to turn the state into its party; it had failed, or was cut off, in its attempts to secure popular support; and it had lost its influence in the army and was now perceived to threaten the hierarchy.

Between 1932 and 1933, several lieutenant interventors in the Northeast left their posts. The Third of October Club, the lieutenants' main center of organization, was on its way to becoming a "doctrinaire organization, free from demagoguery," as General Góes Monteiro said with satisfaction. Some of the lieutenants joined the Vargas government, while others filled the ranks of leftist and rightist parties.

The provisional government decided to take measures designed to clear the way toward legalization of the new situation. In May 1933, it held elections for the National Constituent Assembly. The electoral campaign revealed an increase in popular participation and in party organization. Many parties, with widely different tendencies, appeared in all the states. Some of them had popular support, others were mere façades. With the exception of the Communists, who were illegal, and the right-wing Ação Integralista party, there were no national parties.

The elections demonstrated the strength of the local elites. In Rio Grande do Sul, most successful candidates were in Flores da Cunha's party. In Minas Gerais, followers of the old governor Olegário Maciel won. In São Paulo the United Front won an overwhelming victory. The lieutenants, on the other hand, obtained meager results.

After months of debates, the Constituent Assembly approved the constitution on 14 July 1934. It was similar to the 1891 constitution in that it reestablished the federal republic, but it also presented several new features which reflected changes in the country. It was modeled on Germany's Weimar constitution.

Three statutes that did not appear in earlier constitutions dealt with economic and social matters – with family, education and culture, and national security. The first proviso was nationalistic. It set the stage for the progressive nationalization of mines, mineral deposits, and waterfalls – all of which were considered fundamental or essential for Brazil's economy and military defense. Provisos of a social nature guaranteed the plurality and autonomy of trade unions and made pronouncements on labor legislation. This legislation prohibited different pay for the same work – be it for reasons of age, sex, nationality, or marital status. It called for a minimum wage, rules for children's and women's labor, weekly days off, paid vacations, and compensation for unjust firing.

In the statute dealing with the family, education, and culture, the constitution established the principle of free primary schools and compulsory attendance. Classes in religion would be elective in the public schools and would be open to all religions rather than just to Catholicism.

For the first time, the issue of national security appeared. All matters referring to national security would be examined by the Conselho Superior de Segurança Nacional (High Council on National Security), which was headed by the president and staffed by ministers and the chiefs of the general staff of the army and navy. Military service was made obligatory. This had been the case in the First Republic, but it had rarely been put into practice.

On 15 July 1934, by an indirect vote of the Constitutional Assembly, Getúlio Vargas was elected president, and his term would run until 3 May 1938. From that point on, presidents would be elected directly. It seemed that finally the country would be democratically run. However, in a little more than three years after the constitution's approval, a coup d'état frustrated any hope of democracy. This denouement was brought about by groups within the government, especially army men, by vacillations among the liberals, and by the Left's irresponsibility.

Beginning at the end of the First World War, totalitarian and authoritarian ideas and movements had gained ground in Europe. In 1922 Mussolini came to power in Italy. Stalin was in the midst of constructing his absolutist regime in the Soviet Union. And in 1933 the Nazis triumphed in Germany. The worldwide depression helped discredit liberal democracy, which, economically speaking, was associated with capitalism. Capitalism, having promised equal opportunity and abundance, had entered a black hole from which it seemed helpless to emerge. Instead of a better life, it had engendered poverty, unemployment, and despair. Liberal democracy, with its parties and its apparently futile political struggles which divided national polities, was seen by totalitarian ideologues as a form of government that would never solve the crisis at hand. Capitalism and liberal democracies seemed to be things of the past.

In Brazil, a few small fascist organizations appeared during the 1920s. A more weighty movement came forth during the 1930s. In October 1932 Plínio Salgado and other intellectuals founded Ação Integralista Brasileira or AIB (the Brazilian Integralist Movement) in São Paulo. Integralism was defined as nationalist in doctrine, and it was more cultural than economic in its content. Without a doubt, however, it did attack finance capitalism, and it was in favor of state control of the economy. But its major emphasis could be found in advocating a national consciousness of a spiritual nature based on unifying principles: "God, Fatherland, and Family" was the movement's motto.

As far as relations between society and state were concerned, Integralism was against political pluralism and the representation of citizens as individuals. The Integralist state would consist of the head of state presiding over specific bureaus representing all professions and cultural entities.

The AIB identified liberalism, socialism, and international finance capitalism (putatively controlled by Jews) as its enemies. It was very effective in using rituals and symbols such as the cult of personality (which it associated with the head of state), initiation ceremonies, and green-shirt parades in which armbands bearing a sigma (Σ) were worn.

AIB national and regional directors were recruited mainly from urban, middle-class professionals, and, to a lesser extent, from the military. Integralism attracted a considerable number of people. Moderate estimates set its membership between 100,000 and 200,000 individuals during the AIB's heyday (around the end of 1937). This is not a small number, when one remembers how low the degree of political participation was in Brazil during that time.

Integralists and Communists were locked in a death struggle with one another during the 1930s. Both movements had, nonetheless, points in common. Both criticized liberal states; both wanted a single political party; and both devised a cult of personality around their leaders. It was not by chance that certain militants shifted from one group to the other.

The war between the two groups was not the product of a misunderstanding, however. In reality, both groups appealed to different sentiments. The Integralists based their movement on conservative themes: family, national tradition, the Catholic church. The Communists spoke of revolutionary concepts and programs: the class struggle, criticism of religion and prejudice, agrarian reform, and national emancipation – to be obtained by countering imperialism. These different views of human relations were more than enough to produce antagonism between the two movements. On top of this, they also represented the struggle between their European models: fascism on one side and Soviet Communism on the other.

Without the same panache but with greater efficiency, the authoritarian current gained strength in Brazil during the 1930s. Authoritarianism was and is a trait of Brazil's political culture. The difficulty in organizing along class lines, of forming representative associations and parties, has always made authoritarian solutions attractive – not just among the conservatives, but also among liberals and leftists. The Left tended to associate liberalism with oligarchical domination. Once that was established, they did not hold formal democracy in high regard. Liberals helped justify that interpretation. They were afraid of social reform, so they accepted or even advocated suspension of the democratic game every time it seemed to be threatened by subversive forces.

The authoritarian current took on, with all its consequences, the point of view known as "conservative modernization." That is, authoritarians believed that in a loosely knit country such as Brazil, the state had the responsibility to organize the nation and to promote an orderly economic development and general well-being. In the course of events, the authoritarian state would put an end to social conflict, partisan politics, and excess freedom of expression – all of which only weakened the country.

There were traits common to the authoritarian current and to totalitarian Integralism, but they were not the same. Integralism sought its objectives through a party that would mobilize the disgruntled masses and storm the state. The authoritarian current put its money not on the party but on the state. It did not believe in large-scale social mobilizations; it believed in the clairvoyance of a few men. The fascist party would push the state crisis to its limit. Authoritarian statism would support the state. The authoritarians could be found within the state itself; their greatest influence was in the high command of the armed forces.

The years between 1930 and 1945 were characterized by a strengthening of the armed forces, especially the army. They were strengthened in their number of careerists, by rearmament, and by the placement of military men in prestigious positions. Comparatively speaking, the state militias lost ground. However, the army did not come forth as a cohesive force during the first few months after the 1930 revolution. Not only was lieutenantism problematic, but also problematic was the fact that many members of the high echelons were still on active duty and were sympathetic to the old republic. The military chief of the revolution was a mere lieutenant colonel. It was necessary to give him three promotions in a little more than a year's time for him reach the rank of general. The 1932 revolution helped purge the army. During that year, 48 officers were exiled – among them seven generals. At the end of 1933, 36 of the 40 generals on active duty had been promoted to that rank by the new government.

The purge and promotions resulted in the formation of a group that was loyal to Vargas. Of this group, two figures stand out: Góes Monteiro and Eurico Gaspar Dutra. Góes Monteiro formulated the army's policy and Dutra carried it out. They monopolized the two main military offices after 1937: Góes was head of the general staff from 1937 to 1943; Dutra was minister of war from 1937 to 1945. In 1945, Dutra stepped down to run for president and was replaced by Góes Monteiro. Góes had also headed the Ministry of War in 1934 and 1935. The loyalty of this new group of officers who ran the army during the Vargas government never faltered – even though the group had been scratched in a couple of episodes.

Workers' strikes and middle-class unrest characterized 1934. A series of strikes occurred in Rio de Janeiro, São Paulo, and Rio Grande do Norte. Particularly noticeable were the shutdowns in the service sector: transportation, communications, and banks. Campaigns against fascism gained momentum and culminated in a violent clash in October 1934 between anti-fascists and Integralists in São Paulo.

The government reacted by proposing, early in 1935, a Law of National Security (LNS) which Congress (including liberal members) approved. This law forbade activities such as strikes by civil servants, inciting animosity within the armed forces, kindling class hatred, subversive propaganda, and organizing associations or parties intending to subvert political or social order by means not permitted by the law.

On the other hand, Communists and their leftist lieutenant sympathizers formed an organization known as the Aliança Nacional Libertadora (National Liberation Alliance) or ANL. It was made public in Rio de Janeiro on 30 March 1935. On that occasion, a young law student by the name of Carlos Lacerda read the organization's manifesto and nominated Luis Carlos Prestes as its honorary president. Prestes was elected by acclaim. Navy Captain Hercolino Cascardo, who in 1924 had led the revolt on the ironclad *São Paulo*, was the titular head of the ANL.

The ANL's program was nationalistic. Not one of its five points was directed specifically to workers' problems. These points were: total suspension of payment on Brazil's foreign debt; nationalization of foreign business; agrarian reform; guarantees of individual rights; and the forming of a government in which "anybody according to their abilities" could participate.

The ANL's creation was in line with the new orientation assumed by Brazil's Communist Party. This orientation had emanated from the Comintern, where Communists had resolved to support antifascist popular fronts throughout the world. The ANL was an example of a popular front suited to the characteristics of the so-called semi-colonial world. They brought together different sectors of society that were ready to take on fascism and imperialism.

At the same time, the ANL's creation was made easier by the transformation that occurred within the Communist Party, once Prestes had been admitted, in August 1934. The party was no longer a small group directed essentially at the working class. It had become a stronger entity both in numerical terms and in its more heterogeneous makeup. Military men who were followers of Prestes as well as people from the middle class joined the PCB. National issues rather than those dealing specifically with the working class took center stage, and this shift coincided with directives from the Comintern.

In a few short months, the ANL acquired a large membership. Conservative estimates suggest that by July 1935 it had between 70,000 and 100,000 members. Its leaders vacillated between attempting to consolidate class alliances and starting an insurrection by which they would come to power. At least rhetorically, the second alternative was favored. In 1935, in commemoration of the Fifth of July, Carlos Lacerda read a manifesto from Prestes, who was in Brazil clandestinely and who called for the overthrow of the "hateful Vargas government" as well as for a takeover by a democratic, national, revolutionary government.

The government, which had been actively repressing the ANL's activities, now had an excellent reason to shut it down. And it did that by decree on 11 July. After that, when many people were imprisoned, the Communist Party began preparations for an insurrection, which resulted in an attempted military coup in November 1935.

As an event, the 1935 uprising was a failure which evokes the lieutenants' revolts of the 1920s. It began on 23 November in Rio Grande do Norte, just before a coordinated movement was to take place in Rio de Janeiro. For four days a junta was in control of Natal (the capital of Rio Grande do Norte) before being defeated. Rebellions followed in Recife and in Rio, where the uprising was greater and the confrontation between rebels and loyalist troops left several people dead before the fight was over.

Especially since the strategy of popular fronts had been established beforehand, what could have induced the PCB, with its decisive support from the Comintern, to undertake the adventure of November 1935? Everything seems to suggest that the attempted coup was the swan song of old-line party politics. The effort was given extra strength by figments of Brazilian Communists' imagination. They had reported that there was a pre-revolutionary climate in the country. The lieutenants' methods also influenced this decision.

The 1935 episode had serious consequences, since it opened the way for far-reaching repressive measures and for an escalation of authoritarianism. The specter of international Communism assumed enormous proportions, especially because the Comintern had sent some foreign cadres to Brazil to help prepare the insurrection. Among them were the German Harry Berger, whose real name was Arthur Ernst Ewert, and the Argentine Rodolfo Ghioldi.

During 1936, Congress approved all the exceptional measures the executive branch had asked for to repress the Communist Party in particular and the Left in general. In March 1936, police invaded

Congress and arrested five parliamentarians who had supported the ANL, or had merely expressed their sympathy for that organization. Congress accepted the justification for these arrests and authorized a trial of the prisoners.

At the same time, specific bureaus for repression were created. In January 1936, the minister of justice announced the formation of the Comissão Nacional de Repressão ao Comunismo (National Commission for Stopping Communism). It was to investigate civil servants' and other people's participation in acts or crimes against political or social institutions. One exceptional tribunal, the Tribunal de Segurança Nacional (National Security Tribunal), began to function in October 1936. In the beginning, the TSN was only to investigate people involved in the 1935 uprising, but it became a permanent fixture which persisted throughout the course of the Estado Novo.

Toward the end of 1936 and during the early months of 1937, presidential candidates began to emerge and outline their programs for the elections to be held in January 1938. The Partido Constitucionalista (Constitutionalist Party), which consisted of the PD and a few minor parties, supported Armando de Salles Oliveira.

The government's candidate was José Américo de Almeida, a Northeastern politician who had been minister of transportation and public works during Vargas's presidency. Finally, Plínio Salgado was the Integralists' candidate for president. The government's candidate had the support of most of the states in the Northeast, Minas Gerais, and the pro-Vargas sectors of São Paulo and Rio Grande do Sul.

The opening of political debates caused the repressive measures to be loosened. By order of the minister of justice, around 300 people were let out of prison in June 1937. A request to prolong the state of war was denied by Congress. Meanwhile, Vargas and the people close to him were not about to let go of power, especially because they trusted none of the three candidates. José Américo de Almeida's campaign was leaning more and more toward populism, and the candidate introduced himself as "the people's candidate" and a denouncer of imperialist exploitation. An observer close to governmental circles went so far as to say that social issues were at the center of the presidential campaign, and Brazil was running the risk of becoming another Spain – to be torn apart by a civil war.

All through 1937, the government intervened in different states and in the Federal District to nip any possible regional difficulties in the bud. There was, however, no compelling reason to merit staging a coup. A reason appeared in the form of the "Cohen Plan," whose true history is in many ways obscure. In September 1937, an Integralist officer, Captain Olímpio Mourão Filho, was caught (or let himself be caught) at the Ministry of War typing a plan for a Communist uprising. The author of that document was purportedly someone named Cohen – an obviously Jewish name which might also have been some sort of variation on Bela Kuhn, the Hungarian Communist leader. The "plan" was evidently a fantasy that was to be published in an AIB bulletin. It described what a Communist insurrection would be like and how the Integralists would react to it. The uprising would cause massacres, rape and pillage, violation of people's homes, and the burning of churches.

The fictitious piece of literature was passed from the Integralists to the army high command. On 30 September, it was broadcast on an official government radio program, and parts of it were printed in newspapers. The effects of divulging the Cohen Plan were immediate. In a majority vote, Congress quickly approved a motion to declare a state of war and to suspend constitutional guarantees for 90 days. The commandant of the Third Military Region declared Rio Grande do Sul's Military Brigade federalized. With no way to fight back, Flores da Cunha abandoned his post and fled to Uruguay.

At the end of October, Deputy Negrão de Lima visited the northern states so as to guarantee their governors' support for a coup. Almost everyone agreed. Only in early November did the opposition mobilize. Armando de Salles issued a manifesto to military leaders in which he asked them to thwart the coup. This gesture only hurried it along. Alleging that the manifesto was being circulated through the barracks, Vargas and the military high command resolved to strike in advance of the designated date – 15 November.

4.3   THE ESTADO NOVO

On 10 November 1937, military police surrounded Congress and barred congressmen from entering. Minister of War Dutra had been against using the army in this mission. That night Vargas announced the beginning of a new political phase and the enactment of a constitutional charter written by Francisco Campos. This was the beginning of the Estado Novo (New State) dictatorship.

This regime was set up in the authoritarian mold, and without a need for massive mobilizations. Social mobilization had decreased and the Communists had been beaten and could not fight back. The ruling class accepted the coup as an inevitability and, indeed, as a blessing. The disbanded Congress gave in and, after several of their fellow congressmen had gone to jail, some 80 congressmen went, on 13 November, to Vargas in a show of support.

The Integralists were still active. They had supported the coup and expected to see Plínio Salgado appointed to the Ministry of Education, an important step in his climb to power. Vargas dashed these hopes. In May 1938 a group of Integralists attacked the presidential palace in an attempt to depose him. The attackers were surrounded and in a clash with the palace guard several of them were killed, apparently by rifle fire within the palace gardens.

The Estado Novo was not a radical break from the past. Many of its institutions and practices had been taking shape between 1930 and 1937. But, beginning in November 1937, they fit together and became coherent within the new regime. The centralizing tendency, which had been revealed during the first months after the 1930 revolution, was now complete. States were governed by interventors named by the central government and chosen according to different criteria. Vargas's relatives in the military were sometimes appointed interventors. In general, however, someone within the local oligarchy was contemplated as interventor in the larger states.

The state's centralization does not mean that state and society became separate spheres. Representation of different social interests changed shape but did not disappear. Until November 1937, these interests were represented in Congress and through some official governmental offices. Under the Estado Novo, congressional representation disappeared, making representation within the various governmental bureaus more important.

Socioeconomically speaking, the Estado Novo reflected an alliance between the civilian and military bureaucracy and the industrial bourgeoisie. Their immediate common objective was to promote Brazil's industrialization without causing large social upheavals. The civilian bureaucracy supported the industrialization program because it considered industrialization the road to true national independence. The military supported it because they believed that the creation of an industrial base would strengthen the economy, which they considered an important component of national security. And the industrialists also supported it because they convinced themselves that industrial incentives depended to a certain extent on active state intervention. The union of the industrial bourgeoisie with the Vargas government occurred mainly after 1933, with the defeat of the São Paulo revolution. The alliance of these specific sectors should not suggest they were of a mind. Contrary to the government's technocrats, industrialists were less radical in their support of state intervention and in the state's restrictions to foreign capital. They mainly wanted measures to be taken regarding foreign exchange and tariffs on imports, which would protect local industry.

The Vargas government's increasing interest in promoting industrialization after 1937 was evident in the field of education. While Minister Capanema had supported a reform of secondary education, the bulk of his attention was spent on setting up vocational education in order to train a work force suitable for industry.

In running the state, Vargas's personal power was the deciding factor in resolving fundamental issues. Trust between the president and his ministers was increased. Between March 1938, when Osvaldo Aranha entered the Ministry of Foreign Affairs, and June 1941, there was not a single change in the ministry. Thanks to the general staff and the Council of National Security (CSN), the armed forces' influence was felt in the many different technical bureaus that proliferated during the Estado Novo. The CSN's power to examine all matters pertaining to national security was broadly defined – to the extent that the Council played an important part in economic decisions.

While many of their recommendations were not heeded, the armed forces were responsible for the creation of the state steel industry. The government approved the military's plans to buy weapons, including artillery produced by the Krupp firm in Germany, warships from Great Britain and Italy, infantry weapons from Czechoslovakia, and aircraft from the United States.

Even though the armed forces' formal and informal power was extensive, it was not absolute. The military neither wanted nor was able to stand in for the civilian elites.

Cohesion within the armed forces came from their agreement about a general objective – the country's modernization through authoritarian rule. But the military's positions regarding relations with the great powers, or regarding economic development with greater or lesser autonomy, varied from group to group or from person to person.

Thus the president was able to manipulate the army and its ambitions and bring it into line with the government's wider interests. He could also take on the military high command if necessary. When, right after the 1937 coup, Vargas decided to halt servicing the national debt, he rallied the military and phrased his decision in the following terms: Brazil could either pay the national debt or it could modernize the armed forces and the transportation system. Years later, in early 1942, the president's decision to support the United States after the Japanese attacked Pearl Harbor caused Generals Góes Monteiro and Dutra to express their reservations. Both tendered their resignations, which the president rejected. According to U.S. Undersecretary of State Sumner Welles, Vargas went so far as to tell the two generals that he relied on the people to contain subversive activities and did not need the armed forces.

The Estado Novo's economic and financial policy did change relative to that of the previous period (1930–1937). During those years, there was no clear policy designed to foment the industrial sector. The government kept its balance while dealing with different interests, which included agrarian interests, and it was also quite sensitive to external pressures. Beginning in November 1937, the state, with greater resolve, undertook a policy of replacing imports with domestic products, and of establishing an industrial foundation. The supporters of this approach were reinforced both by the crisis-level problems related to Brazil's balance of payments (which had been pressing since 1930) and by the increasing risk of a world war. A world war was likely to and did in fact create great restrictions on imports.

Until 1942, the policy of replacing imports was carried out without an overall plan. Each sector was considered a case unto itself. In

August 1942, with Brazil's entry into the war, the government began to run the economy in order proceed with the conflict. It created the department known as Coordenação de Mobilização Econômica (Coordination of Economic Mobilization), headed by the former lieutenant, João Alberto.

The motivations behind industrialization have often been associated with nationalism, but Vargas avoided rallying the nation in a nationalistic crusade. The 1937 charter restricted the exploitation of minerals and waterfalls to Brazilians. It determined that the legal system would regulate their progressive nationalization, as it would those industries considered essential to economic or military defense. It also established that only banks and insurance companies whose shareholders were Brazilian could operate within Brazil. It gave foreign companies a grace period to be set by law during which time they could become Brazilian firms.

These guidelines were subject to several decree-laws which reflected pressure from different groups and the absence of a strict policy line on the part of the government. The electric energy firms had been left intact, and in October 1941 Vargas refused to accept a proposal that by August 1946 all banks and insurance companies should be owned by Brazilians. Even the state's solution for the steel industry was not produced by a clash but by an agreement with the American government.

Steel and petroleum are particularly significant cases if one is to understand the state's investment policy for basic industry. Both steel and petroleum were treated differently by the government. The founding of the iron industry occurred during the Estado Novo. Concerning petroleum, its story is protracted, and its denouement came during the second Vargas presidency.

Plans for the organization and construction of the steel mill at Volta Redonda, in Rio de Janeiro State, were concluded in July 1940. It was financed by American credits which came from the Export-Import Bank, as well as by funds from the Brazilian government. It was controlled by the Companhia Siderúrgica Nacional (National Steel Company), itself a mixed-economy firm which was organized in January 1941. This solution was not the product of any clear decision on the part of the government (i.e., the Estado Novo), nor was there any consensus on the matter within the government. The different groups only agreed to increase and diversify steel production. The expansion of transportation services and the creation of heavy industry depended on solving this problem. On top of this, steel imports represented an increasingly heavy weight on Brazil's ever-unfavorable balance of payments.

Private groups and Vargas himself were inclined to accept some sort of partnership with foreign capital, be it American or German. The greatest pressure for putting industry beyond foreign control came from the armed forces. However, the military had no means of immediately imposing the solution that was finally reached. On the contrary, during 1939 negotiations between the Brazilian government and the United States Steel Corporation dominated the scene. A plan was drawn up in which a steel industry would be set up with the participation of the American firm, private groups, and the Brazilian government. But the American company withdrew its membership, in spite of Vargas's and the State Department's conciliatory efforts. From that point on, the state option prevailed.

In contrast to steel, the development of a petroleum industry was not a pressing concern during the 1930s. Petroleum imports only began to increase after the Second World War. For a long time, they did not cause major upsets in Brazil's balance of payments. Until the middle of 1939, when oil was discovered in the state of Bahia, Brazil's petroleum industry had been limited to refineries. Even after its discovery, production was insignificant, and into the 1950s doubts persisted concerning petroleum reserves. This is why differences of opinion concerning an oil policy were greater than they had been for steel, and the army itself was more divided on this issue. Still, the army was the source of the main initiatives concerning petroleum.

Beginning in 1935, some industrialists began to be interested in setting up oil refineries. Their interest caused Standard Oil (in 1936), Texaco, Atlantic Refining Company, and Anglo-Mexican (all in 1938) to offer to set up huge refineries in Brazil. Discussions began concerning the possible options, and the government's interventionist policy was established in a decree-law of April 1938 which nationalized the refining of foreign or Brazilian oil. Nationalization meant that the capital, the board of directors, and the management of these companies should be in Brazilian hands. This was not a state monopoly, however. The decree also created the Conselho Nacional do Petróleo (National Council of Petroleum), or CNP, which would be made up of people appointed by the president. These appointees represented the different ministries and interest groups. Between 1938 and the middle of 1943, the CNP was dominated by army contingents that favored wider state control. This was under the leadership of General Horta Barbosa, himself a military engineer. Horta's attempts to build huge state refineries failed, and the CNP was blocked by interest groups, ministers, and by Vargas.

American policy toward petroleum was different from that toward steel. In the case of oil, it supported the interests of the large corporations that had traditionally controlled the field. Pressured from several sides, Horta Barbosa resigned halfway through 1943, when the period of domination by private interests began.

Actually, the Estado Novo's accomplishments in the petroleum sector were minimal. Still, they were important in two respects. First, even though it got no alternative response to its proposals, the CNP's policies blocked initiatives from the large foreign firms. Second, General Horta Barbosa's action established a precedent and reference point for those groups which, during the 1950s, pressed for a policy similar to his. And this policy came out the winner when Petrobrás, the state firm, was founded in October 1953.

In the financial field, the Estado Novo tried to keep itself within conservative bounds, which were embodied in Minister of Finance Souza Costa, whom Vargas kept in office during almost the entire period. Necessity caused a few drastic, albeit exceptional, measures to be taken. To tackle the crisis in Brazil's balance of payments, Vargas, right after the coup, suspended service on the foreign debt. He decreed a monopoly on the sale of foreign currency, and he imposed a tax on all currency exchange transactions. Control of foreign commerce was permanent; but in dealing with the foreign debt, an agreement was reached with Brazil's creditors, and payments started again in 1940. This happened in spite of resistance from the military, who believed that servicing the debt would reduce public investments.

The Estado Novo's labor policy had two facets: it offered workers specific gains; and it turned Getúlio Vargas into a symbolic figure – the workers' guardian. Concerning material initiatives, the government systematized and furthered practices that dated back to the early 1930s. This legislation had been inspired by the Carta del Lavoro (Labor Charter), which was the order of the day in fascist Italy. The 1937 charter once more adopted the principle of trade union unity, which in practice had never been abandoned. Strikes and lockouts were prohibited. In August 1939, a decree-law established guidelines for union organization and for making unions even more dependent on the state. The already existent vertical organization of unions was also strengthened by the creation of regional federations as well as national confederations.

In July 1940, the *imposto sindical*, a union tax, was established. It was a basic instrument for financing the union and for subordinating it to the state. The tax took the form of an obligatory yearly contribution amounting to one day's pay. It was to be paid by all employees, whether or not they were members of unions. The Banco do Brasil would have to collect the funds, 60 percent of which were given to the union, 15 percent to the federation, 5 percent to the confederation, and 20 percent to the union's social fund (Fundo Social Sindical). The Fundo Social Sindical was frequently used as a secret "slush fund" for financing ministries and, later on, electoral campaigns.

The union tax supported the *pelego* or union boss. A *pelego* is a sheepskin or cloth placed on a saddle to cushion the jolts on the rider's body. The word metaphorically came to mean a union boss who, as the union's director, acted more in his own interest and in the state's interest than on behalf of the workers. The notion of union bosses' working as mollifiers was accurate because they absorbed the friction. Their job was relatively easy since they were not required to bring huge masses of workers into the union. The tax guaranteed that the union would survive and made the number of union workers of secondary importance as far as bosses were concerned.

To resolve labor matters, the government in May 1939 set up a bureau knowm as Justiça do Trabalho (Labor Court), which had its origins in the Bureaus of Reconciliation and Arbitration. Systematization and broadening of labor legislation came about with the Consolidação das Leis do Trabalho (Consolidation of Labor Laws), or CLT, in June 1943.

In the field of salary policies, the Estado Novo ushered in an important innovation. In May 1940, it established a minimum wage which was intended to satisfy workers' basic needs. In the beginning, the minimum wage fulfilled this objective. As time went by, it lost ground and lagged far behind its original purpose.

The construction of Vargas's image as the workers' guardian took shape in a gamut of ceremonies and thanks to intensive use of the communications industry. The ceremonies included May Day celebrations, which, beginning in 1939, took place in soccer stadiums. In these meetings, which brought together masses of workers and people in general, Vargas began his speeches with the exhortation "Workers of Brazil." He routinely announced some hoped-for measure of social importance. He also used the radio as a means of bringing workers and the government together. The minister of labor made weekly speeches on the radio. In his speeches, he gave the background for specific social laws, he presented case studies, and he sometimes addressed specific audiences, such as retirees, women, parents of child laborers, migrant workers.

With this and other ploys, the image of Getúlio Vargas was assembled. He was Brazilians' (especially workers') manager and guide. He was a friend and father modeled after the pater familias in the societal sphere. Guide and father handed out benefits to his people and in exchange he had the right to expect loyalty and support. The benefits were not a fantasy. But the real political dividends came from social factors and from the efficacy of the image of Getúlio Vargas, which acquired form and content during the Estado Novo.

The 1937 regime did not just address workers to build its image. Quite to the contrary, it tried to influence public opinion on its behalf. It censured criticism and independent sources of information and worked out its own version of the historical phase the country was going through. The Vargas government's attention to these matters dates from the early days, when, in 1931, the Departamento Oficial de Publicidade (Official Department of Publicity) was founded. In 1934, within the Ministry of Justice, the Departamento de Propaganda e Difusão Cultural (Department of Propaganda and Cultural Dissemination) was founded. It operated until December 1939, when the Estado Novo set up a real propaganda ministry – the Departamento de Imprensa e Propaganda (Department of Press and Propaganda), or DIP. It was directly under the president. The DIP had extensive functions. It supervised movies, radio, theater, the press, and literature of a "social or political" nature. It produced the government's official radio program. It prohibited the entry into Brazil of "publications that might harm Brazilian interests." It collaborated with foreign journalists to avoid the publication of "information that might harm the country's credit and culture." The DIP was responsible for the daily broadcast of the *Hora do Brasil*, a radio program that for years would be a propaganda instrument and a herald of the government's operations.

The Estado Novo persecuted, arrested, tortured, and forced politicians and intellectuals into exile – especially leftists and some liberals. However, its persecution was not indiscriminate. Leaders understood the importance of having learned people at their service. Catholics, Integralists, authoritarians, and leftists in disguise took the jobs and the benefits the regime offered.

In the many manifestations directed at the public at large, or in the pages of publications such as *Cultura Política*, which were sent out to a more restricted public, the Estado Novo attempted to transmit its version of the country's history. Within the realm of the most recent events, it presented itself as the logical consequence of the 1930 revolution. It made a radical cut between old, ununited Brazil, which was dominated by large estates (*latifúndios*) and by oligarchies, and a new Brazil born of the revolution. The Estado Novo claimed to have achieved its revolutionary objectives. It maintained it had promoted nationwide integration by searching for new roots and formed a united country not torn asunder by partisan politics, and it claimed to have fostered Brazil's entry into modern times.

Public service during the First Republic was run by political patronage. Notwithstanding a few rare exceptions, there was no open competition for jobs, and specialized sectors were restricted to a tiny elite. The Estado Novo sought to reform Brazil's public service and to turn it into an agent of modernization. It tried to create a bureaucratic elite which identified with the administration's principles and was unencumbered by partisan politics. Through its single-minded devotion to national interests, that elite was supposed to foster criteria based on efficiency, economy, and rationality.

The main institution responsible for public service reform was the DASP, Departamento Administrativo do Serviço Público (Administrative Department of Public Service). It was created in 1938 as an office linked to the presidency. As far as the recruitment of personnel was concerned, token efforts were made to establish a career track in which merit was the basic qualification for entry. This criterion opened the possibility for middle-class professionals to follow a civil service career, but in practice there were many restrictions. The legislation itself, along with reality, was hardly conducive to the formation of a huge bureaucratic stratum subject to formal rules of entry with promotion based on merit. In the bureaucracy's high command, most policy continued to be made according to Vargas's preferences or those of his ministers in the so-called positions of trust, which the president could vacate at any moment. These jobs depended on their occupants' having at least minimal qualifications, but they were not necessarily filled by people from the pool of career civil servants.

Brazil's foreign policy can be better understood by considering the period from 1930 to 1945 as a whole. Its alignments and realignments derived from Brazil's interactions with the great powers, and the Estado Novo was just one of the elements in this equation.

The 1929 crash accelerated the decline of British hegemony and the rise of that of the United States. This was especially the case once President Roosevelt's measures to combat the depression began to show their effects. At the same time, in 1933, another competitor had arrived on the international scene – Nazi Germany. In this situation, Brazil's government took a pragmatic stance and attempted to take advantage of the rivarly among the great powers and trade with whoever might offer the best deals.

The period from 1934 to 1940 was characterized by Germany's greater participation in Brazilian foreign trade. Germany was the main buyer of Brazilian cotton and its second biggest coffee customer. In the import sector German influence grew most notably. In 1929, around 13 percent of Brazil's imports came from Germany, while 30 percent came from the United States. In 1938, the Germans had managed to exceed the Americans slightly; their exports to Brazil amounted to 25 percent of Brazil's imports, whereas the U.S. exports made up 24 percent. Also during 1938, 34 percent of

Brazil's exports went to the United States, and 19 percent went to Germany.

Transactions with Germany were welcomed not only by certain exporting concerns, but also by people who believed Brazil needed to industrialize and modernize. Germans had always beckoned to Brazil and offered the possibility of breaking away from Brazil's traditional commercial connections with the great powers. Germans offered material for railways, and they offered machinery.

On the other hand, some factors affected trade with Germany in a negative fashion. The Reich always insisted on doing business with nonconvertible money. They paid with the so-called compensation marks in an attempt to turn deals with Brazil into bilateral agreements which would shut out other competitors. German representatives tried to control their commerce with other countries by imposing quotas, the price of products, and the exchange rate for their compensation marks.

In the face of Germany's gains, the United States adopted a policy combining pressure and caution. American economic concerns (investors, bankers, and importers) wanted the government to retaliate. Roosevelt preferred to avoid drastic measures that might move Brazil to become a German ally or to assume a radical nationalist stance.

In government circles and in the economic sphere, a clear choice emerged: Brazil could move closer to the United States or to Germany. Osvaldo Aranha, the ambassador in Washington beginning in 1934, and Valentim Bouças, IBM's representative in Brazil, were in the American camp. Members of the military high command such as Dutra and Góes Monteiro revealed their sympathy for Germany.

After the 1937 coup, which was enthusiastically hailed in Germany and Italy, Brazil's pragmatic line remained unchanged. The military pressured on behalf of Germany, and in 1938 they negotiated a tremendous contract with Krupp for supplying artillery. But shortly before this, Vargas had shown his preference for retaining the essence of Brazil's foreign policy by nominating Osvaldo Aranha minister of foreign affairs.

Paradoxically, in spite of a modicum of ideological affinity, which could have facilitated an approximation between Brazil and

Germany, relations between these countries were set back in 1938. During this year, the Vargas administration eliminated Integralism from the political scene. At the same time that it distanced itself from native fascism, the Estado Novo was attacking Nazi groups in the South. A German agent, the leader of the Nazi party in Rio Grande do Sul, was arrested. The German ambassador was declared persona non grata and forced to leave the country. Later the conflict was smoothed over, but its marks remained.

The outbreak of the Second World War was more important than the establishment of the Estado Novo in determining Brazil's foreign policy. Britain's blockade weakened German commerce in Latin America, but Britain was in no shape to take advantage of the vacuum it had created. The United States appeared with greater strength owing to this.

Well before the war began, Roosevelt was convinced that there would be a world war which would involve the United States. This belief caused American strategists to increase what they felt were the United States' security perimeters. These included South America and especially the part of northeast Brazil that protrudes farthest into the Atlantic Ocean. The Americans also began a political and ideological offensive by sponsoring, among other initiatives, the Pan-American Conferences, which would have the common objective of defending the Americas under the command of the United States – regardless of the forms of government specific countries might have.

On the economic plane, the Americans tried to establish an extremely conservative policy. They were mainly interested in strategic materials such as rubber, iron ore, magnesium, and so forth. And they tried to control the purchase of these items.

Brazilians responded to these initiatives by drawing closer and closer to the Colossus of the North. They tried to take advantage of the new situation. The United States' entry into the war in December 1941 forced Brazil to decide. Vargas began to speak Pan-Americanist language more clearly, while at the same time he reiterated that the condition for Brazil's support was for the United States to help Brazil economically and militarily.

By the end of 1941, without waiting for authorization from the Brazilian government, American troops had set up bases in the

Northeast. In January 1942, notwithstanding Góes Monteiro's and Dutra's reservations, Brazil broke off relations with the Axis. In May, Brazil signed a secret political and military treaty with the United States.

Meanwhile, the Americans put off shipments of military equipment because they considered a good part of Brazil's officers to be Axis sympathizers. Brazil's indecision came to an end when, between 5 and 17 August 1942, five Brazilian merchant marine ships were sunk by German U-boats. Pressured by huge public demonstrations, Brazil entered the war in August.

Brazil's alignment with the anti-fascist forces was complete on 30 June 1944, when an expeditionary force, the FEB (Força Expedicionária Brasileira), was sent to fight in Europe. The FEB was not imposed on Brazil by the Allies. Indeed, it was a decision made by the Brazilian government, which had had to overcome American restrictions and the outright opposition of the British. Some leaders in both of those countries thought it would be difficult to include Brazilian troops in the war effort successfully. More than 20,000 Brazilian men fought in Italy up to the end of the war in that country, on 2 May 1945 – a few days before the European conflict was entirely over. A total of 454 Brazilians died in combat. The return of the FEB *pracinhas* (recruits) to Brazil beginning in May 1945 triggered great public enthusiasm and helped step up the pressure for Brazil's democratization.

4.4 THE END OF THE ESTADO NOVO

The Estado Novo was set up as an authoritarian, modernizing state and designed to last for many years. However, its lifespan was a short one, less than eight years. The regime's problems came more from Brazil's entry into the sphere of international relations than they did from Brazil's internal conditions. Its presence on the international scene set opposition forces in motion and cleared the way for differences of opinion within the government.

After Brazil's entry into the war, individuals in the opposition began to exploit the contradiction between the country's support of democracies and Vargas's dictatorship. Within the government itself, at least one figure showed himself frankly in favor of a shift to democracy – Osvaldo Aranha, the minister of foreign relations and Vargas's close friend.

A more serious event was General Góes Monteiro's gradual withdrawal from the Estado Novo. The general had been one of the Estado Novo's theoreticians and military backers, but had become convinced that the regime could not survive the new era. In Montevideo, Góes Monteiro abandoned his post as the Brazilian ambassador to the Emergency Committee for the Political Defense of Latin America. He returned to Brazil and joined the Ministry of War in 1945, more to direct Vargas's departure than to try to keep him in power.

Around 1943, university students had begun to mobilize against the Vargas dictatorship. They founded the União Nacional dos Estudantes (National Student Union) or UNE and set up offices in different states. In São Paulo, law students had a long tradition of protests, but were never part of the UNE. In a December 1943 demonstration, students, with their mouths gagged to symbolize the lack of freedom of speech, paraded arm in arm. The demonstration was violently broken up by the police. Two people died and more than 20 were wounded – all of which triggered a wave of indignation.

The government tried to cope with pressures coming from different sectors and used the war to justify prolonging the dictatorship. Simultaneously, it promised to hold elections once the war was over. A maneuver of the liberal opposition toward the end of 1944 brought about a change in attitude when they nominated air corps Brigadier-Major Eduardo Gomes as their candidate for president. Gomes was not just anybody. He was a career officer linked to lieutenantism and the legendary revolt at Fort Copacabana. The press, in the meantime, increasingly flouted censorship.

Given this state of affairs, in February 1945, Vargas attached the so-called Ato Adicional (Additional Act) to the 1937 charter. Among other things, the Ato announced a period of 90 days during which time a date for general elections would be designated. Exactly 90 days later, the new electoral code was decreed to regulate voter registration and the elections themselves. It established 2 December 1945 for the election of the president and a constituent assembly. State elections would be held on 6 May 1946. At this juncture,

Vargas declared that he would not run for president. To run against Eduardo Gomes, Minister of War General Dutra was nominated by the government itself.

During the decisive year of 1945, the three principal parties of the next two decades came forth. The old liberal opposition, the heirs to the state democratic parties and foes of the Estado Novo, formed the União Democrática Nacional (National Democratic Union) or UDN. In the beginning, the UDN took in the small group of democratic socialists and a few Communists.

Owing to the initiatives of bureaucrats, appointed governors in different states, and Vargas himself, in June 1945 the Partido Social Democrático (Social Democratic Party) or PSD was formed within the state political machine. In September of the same year, the Partido Trabalhista Brasileiro (Brazilian Labor Party) or PTB was formed. It was also inspired by Vargas, the Ministry of Labor, and the union bureaucracy. Its objective was to bring the working masses together under the Vargas banner. The UDN rallied around Eduardo Gomes as their presidential candidate. The PSD supported Dutra. The Brazilian Labor Party came onto the political stage with no important names on its slate and, it appeared, with no presidential candidate.

The opposition was not pleased with the idea of a transition process toward democracy headed by the chief of an authoritarian government. Vargas, however, behaved in a manner that surprised the conservative liberal opposition as well as the high-ranking military officers. Having perceived a lack of support for his government among the military high command, Vargas sought wider support among the urban masses, as well as support from the Ministry of Labor, from union bosses (pelegos), and from Communists.

The PCB's (Brazilian Communist Party) support of Vargas can be explained largely by directives coming from Moscow. Moscow ordered Communist parties throughout the world to support their countries' governments, whether they were dictatorships or democracies, as long as they were part of the anti-fascist front. Brazil not only entered the war against the Axis, but also in April 1945 it established diplomatic relations with the Soviet Union for the first time in its history. As a consequence of a decree of amnesty, Prestes was let out of jail after relations with the USSR were established.

He confirmed what (under his influence) the party had decided – in the name of "historical necessity" the PCB would lend a hand to yesterday's enemy.

Worker strikes, which had been repressed during the Estado Novo, began to reappear in 1945. Workers mobilized thanks to a gradual restoration of democratic freedoms. They were suffering because inflation had worsened during the last years of the war. During 1945, the Communists tried to check these mobilizations. They believed that the time was not right for strikes, which would encumber the government; it was, rather, a time for "belt-tightening."

Halfway through 1945, an initiative coming from workers' circles linked to Vargas and supported by the Communists changed the direction of presidential succession. This was the "we want" (*queremista*) campaign. It was given this name because its objective could be expressed with the slogan: "We want Getúlio." Queremistas went into the streets supporting the election of a constituent assembly with Vargas in power. Only after this would direct presidential elections be held, and Vargas should be a candidate.

The campaign's effect on the liberal opposition and within the military was profoundly negative. It seemed clear that Vargas intended to stay in power as dictator or president-elect, and in the process he would do away with the other two candidates in the running. As the dispute continued, tempers flared when, on 29 September, Ambassador Adolph Berle, Jr., of the United States expressed his confidence that elections would be held on 2 December 1945. Queremistas denounced American meddling in Brazilian affairs and, predictably, described the election as a reactionary maneuver.

Meanwhile, events in neighboring Argentina had repercussions in Brazil. Since the revolution of June 1943, the influence of Colonel Juan Domingo Perón had been growing in that country. Peronism and Getulism were similar in several points. In the economic sphere, both sought to create a state-supported national capitalism. Politically, both sought to reduce class rivalry by calling the working masses and their country's middle class to work together on behalf of the state. Thus the state would embody the entire nation's aspirations, rather than just the particular interests of this or that social class.

This was how Latin American populism came about – with different roots and nuances from country to country. In Argentina, whose social structure was much more clearly defined than Brazil's, Peronism was moved to support syndicalism much more thoroughly. At the same time, it attempted to break away from the rural ruling class. In the Brazilian case, the symbolic appeals and the economic concessions to the mass of workers operated as a sort of soothing tonic, at least during the first Vargas government. This government's support of the industrial bourgeoisie would not result in an open clash with the rural ruling class.

During 1945, while Vargas was attempting to keep his balance and run the state by trying his hand at populist politics, Perón was taking his first steps on the way to the presidency. In October, a military plot took him out of the vice-presidency and put him in prison. An enormous popular uprising with support from sectors of the army got him out of jail in a week's time. The road was clear for a Peronist electoral victory in February 1946.

The events that favored Perón moved Vargas's enemies (with whom the American government sympathized) to hasten his fall. Neither Getúlio Vargas of the last few months nor Perón were trusted in the United States, but the Americans did not burn all their bridges to Perón.

Vargas's fall from power was not, however, a foreign conspiracy; it came, instead, as the result of an intricate political maneuver. A specific event set the process in motion. On 25 October, Vargas made the wrong move when he removed João Alberto from the strategic post of chief of police for the Federal District. This gambit was all the worse because João Alberto's substitute was the president's truculent brother, Benjamim Vargas. When this happened, General Góes Monteiro, from the Ministry of War, mobilized the troops in the Federal District. Dutra, to no avail, suggested a compromise, and asked Vargas to rescind his brother's nomination. This request was denied. In the end, Getúlio Vargas was ousted dispassionately. He was forced to resign and left power making a public declaration claiming to agree to leave. He did not have to be exiled, but was able to retire to São Borja, his place of birth.

The transition between the two governments was brought about by the military. Indeed, an important figure in the 1930 revolution, which brought Vargas to power, was General Góes Monteiro, who played the decisive part in Vargas's removal, 15 years later. These and other circumstances made the transition to democracy a change of direction rather than a break with the past. In this change, many things remained the same.

4.5   THE SOCIOECONOMIC SITUATION

Between 1920 and 1940, Brazil's population went from 30,600,000 to 41,110,000 people. In both years, the numbers of males and females were almost equal. The population was young. People under the age of 20 made up 54 percent of the population in 1920 and 1940.

Looking at the different regions in 1940, the North contained only 3.5 percent of the population; the Northeast 32.1 percent; the East (Minas Gerais and Espírito Santo) 18.1 percent; the Center-South 26.2 percent; and the South (Santa Catarina and Rio Grande do Sul) 10.9 percent.

One important change was the decreased significance of foreign immigration and the rising volume of internal migration. Events after 1929 were especially important in establishing this pattern. The worldwide depression and a proviso in the 1934 constitution which established immigration quotas worked hand in hand to reduce the flow from abroad, except for the flow of Japanese, as has already been mentioned.

Internal migration had different meanings according to specific regions. The North had a high index of negative migration. During the rubber crisis, some 14 percent of its population left. This shift was, in large part, a return of Northeasterners to their birthplaces. Contrariwise, as a whole the South and Center-South had an 11.7 percent growth owing to (internal) migration.

It is important to remember that up to 1940 migrants to southern Brazil came mainly from Minas Gerais and not from the Northeast. The nucleus of greatest attraction was the Federal District. Migration to São Paulo only became relevant beginning in 1933, and this was brought about by an industrial upswing and the restrictions on foreign immigration.

Economic historians often take the year 1930 as the starting point for the process of replacing imported manufactured goods with those made in Brazil. This is a bit of an exaggeration, since the process had begun decades earlier. There is no doubt, however, that the difficulty of importing goods beginning with the 1929 crash, the existence of an industrial foundation, and idle capacity (especially in the textile sector) contributed to the replacement process.

If one compares the value of agricultural production with that of industrial production, the rise of industry becomes obvious. In 1920, agriculture was responsible for 79 percent of the gross national product, while industry accounted for 21 percent. In 1940 these percentages were 57 and 43 respectively, which indicates yearly indices of industrial growth that were much higher than those for agriculture.

The period beginning in 1929–1930 is extremely relevant, both from the agricultural and the industrial points of view. During those years, the coffee crisis began, and the role of coffee in export agriculture began to decline. Cotton production increased, and cotton was both sent abroad and used in the Brazilian textile industry. Between 1929 and 1940, Brazil's share of the world's territory dedicated to cotton planting increased from 2 percent to 8.7 percent. During the years from 1925 to 1929, coffee's share in the total worth of Brazilian exports was 71.1 percent; cotton's was only 2.1 percent. Between 1935 and 1939, coffee's share fell to 41.7 percent and cotton's rose to 18.6 percent.

A significant datum indicates the growing importance of activities linked to the internal market. There was a sizable increase in the relative importance of agricultural production for this market. Rice, beans, meat, sugar, manioc, corn, and wheat accounted for 48.3 percent of farm revenues between 1939 and 1943. Between 1925 and 1929, they made up no more than 36 percent of that revenue.

The yearly rates of industrial growth are good indicators of the industrialization process after 1930. There was considerable growth between 1933 and 1939, whereas its momentum decreased between 1939 and 1945. This means that Brazilian industry quickly recovered from the depression years that began in 1929, and this in spite of there being no consistent pro-industry policy in the government.

The failure to modernize industrial equipment and the disturbances in international trade owing to the Second World War together contributed to the lower rates of growth between 1939 and 1943. From the qualitative point of view however, this was an important period because it sustained the industrialization process and set the stage for industry's postwar expansion. Governmental investments in infrastructure helped eliminate or attenuate serious slowdowns. In the basic industry sector, in which private capital showed little interest during the 1930s, the role of the state in some cases (Volta Redonda and the Rio Doce Valley Company) was decisive.

The importance of different branches of industry gradually changed between 1919 and 1939. Basic industries – metallurgy, mechanics, electric equipment, and material for transportation – practically doubled their share in the total value of industrial production. The traditional industries (mainly textile, clothing and footwear, food, beverage, tobacco, and furniture) had their relative share reduced, from 72 percent of the total industrial revenue in 1919 to 60 percent in 1939. The growth of chemical and pharmaceutical industries was phenomenal: its share trebled between 1919 and 1939.

In education, between 1920 and 1940 there was some decline in the percentage of illiterates in the Brazilian population, although it was still quite high. Among people over the age of 15, the rate of illiteracy fell from 69.9 percent in 1920 to 56.2 percent in 1940.

The data indicate that the effort to expand the school system produced improvements over the very low rates of school attendance in 1920. It is estimated that in 1920 the number of boys and girls between the ages of 5 and 19 attending primary or middle schools was around 9 percent. In 1940 the number was up to 21 percent. Concerning higher education, there was a 60 percent increase in the total number of university students between 1929 and 1939 – an increase from 13,200 to 21,200.

5

The Democratic Experiment
(1945–1964)

5.1 THE ELECTIONS AND THE NEW CONSTITUTION

After Vargas's fall, the armed forces and the liberal opposition, in agreement with the two presidential candidates, decided to turn power over, temporarily, to the Federal Supreme Court. The timetable setting elections for 2 December was maintained.

Judging by the size of crowds at rallies, it seemed that Brigadier Eduardo Gomes's candidacy was forging ahead, while Dutra's was marking time. Gomes's campaign rallied sectors of the urban middle class in the larger cities. They united under the banner of democracy and economic liberalism. Dutra excited no one, and people went so far as to propose replacing him with a candidate with greater electoral appeal. Almost on the eve of the election, Vargas finally came out in favor of Dutra. Even so, he added that he would be on the side of the people against the president if the president did not fulfill his campaign promises.

The 1945 elections aroused great interest among Brazilians. After years of dictatorship, the Electoral Justice was not accustomed to gathering and tallying votes. The people waited patiently in long lines to vote. In the last direct presidential elections, in March 1930, 1,900,000 people had voted, or 5.7 percent of the total population. In December 1945, 6,200,000 people voted – 13.4 percent of the population.

At a time when there were no pre-election polls, the opposition was surprised by Dutra's clear victory. Based on the votes for the candidates, and excluding voided ballots as well as those left blank, Dutra won with 55 percent of all votes over Gomes's 35 percent.

This outcome showed the strength of the PSD electoral machine devised by the appointed governors, and it demonstrated Vargas's prestige among workers. In addition, it showed how the great bulk of the nation repudiated the anti-Vargas movement, which was linked to the interests of the wealthy. Dutra's victory can be explained by these factors; it was not so much a victory of back-wardness over modernity or of the countryside over the city. Dutra won soundly in the three largest states: Minas Gerais, Rio Grande do Sul, and São Paulo. Gomes did best in the Northeast, where he lost by a small number of votes.

The PCB's voting was especially significant, now that the party was legal. With an unknown candidate, the PCB garnered 10 percent of all presidential votes, and it had significant support in the big cities. Internally, Communists benefited from Luis Carlos Prestes's prestige; the Soviet Union's prestige helped them from abroad.

Vargas was one of the big winners in the 1945 elections, and not just because of his role in Dutra's victory. Because of the way the electoral laws had been written, Vargas was elected deputy and senator in several states, and he chose to serve as a senator from Rio Grande do Sul.

Legislative elections were held for the Chamber of Deputies and the Senate. Both houses would meet jointly as a constitutional congress until a constitution was approved. After that, they would separate and work like any other congress. Voting clearly showed how the Estado Novo political machine, whose original purpose had been to support the dictatorship, was also very efficient in capturing votes under a democratic government. For a considerable part of the electorate, personal patronage was much more important than a choice between backers and opposers of the Estado Novo. This choice had no meaning in voters' daily lives and was too abstract for an electorate with only a rudimentary education. The PSD won an absolute majority of seats in both the Chamber of Deputies and in the Senate, and was followed by the UDN.

At the end of January 1946, Dutra was inaugurated and work began on the constitution. In September, the new constitution was ratified. It was different from the 1937 charter because it had been cast in the liberal democratic mold. In some points, however, it opened the way for a continuation of the corporate state.

Brazil was defined as a federal republic, with a presidential form of government. Executive power would be exercised by a president elected by a direct, secret vote for a period of five years. On the other hand, professional representation was eliminated. It had been instituted in the 1934 constitution and bore the mark of the fascist, corporate state.

In the chapter on citizenship, the right and obligation to vote were conferred on literate Brazilians of both sexes, 18 years of age or older. At least on the level of political rights, equality was established between men and women. The 1934 constitution had made voting obligatory only for those women who were paid civil servants.

In its economic section, the constitution's chapter on social and economic order established criteria for using mineral resources and electric energy. In the part on society, it enumerated the minimum benefits that the law could provide, and they were very similar to those provided in the 1934 constitution.

The chapter on the family gave rise to long and heated debates between those in favor and those against divorce. Pressure from the Catholic church and the most conservative congressmen carried the day. The constitution claimed marriage bound the family together, and that knot could not be untied.

In the part of the constitution dealing with workers' organizations, the constituent assembly revealed its affinity with the Estado Novo. The union tax, the main support for union bosses, was not revoked. The right to strike was recognized in principle, but other legislation nullified it. The law defined which activities would be "essential," and where strikes would not be permitted – this included almost every field of endeavor. Cesarino Júnior, a professor of labor law, has observed that if this decree had been obeyed, the only legal strikes would have been at perfume shops.

Under Dutra's government, the Communist Party began to be repressed. Repression derived from the influence of conservatism, from the growth of the party itself, and from the changing relations among the great powers. The PCB was, in 1946, the fourth largest party in the country. In 1946, it was estimated to have between 180,000 and 200,000 members.

On the other hand, the brotherly rejoicing among the winners in the struggle against National Socialism and fascism was soon over. China and Greece became battlefields of civil war. The United States' hegemony and the European balance of power were threatened by direct or indirect Soviet occupation of the countries in eastern Europe. These moves seemed to confirm pessimists' suspicions concerning Stalin's intentions. To sum it up, the hopes for world peace were sapped by the cold war.

In May 1947, based on accusations presented by two obscure deputies, the Federal Supreme Court decided to outlaw the Communist Party. This resolution was disputed, and was passed by a single vote. On the same day the Communist Party was shut down, the Ministry of Labor ordered intervention in 14 unions and closed the headquarters of a union controlled by the Communists. More repressive action followed during the coming months, to the extent that more than 200 unions were under intervention during Dutra's last year in office. While Communist influence in many unions was real, it was evident that in the name of fighting Communism, the government attempted to break the back of workers' organizations that were against the government's policies.

In January 1948, the measures that forced the PCB underground were in place. A law approved by the nation's Congress ousted deputies, senators, and city councilmen elected as Communists.

From the point of view of economic policy, the Dutra administration began following a liberal model. State intervention was condemned, and Estado Novo controls were abandoned one by one. People believed that Brazil's development and the end of inflation, which had begun in the last years of the war, depended on open markets in general and, mainly, on the unrestricted importation of goods. Brazil's financial situation was favorable since the country had accumulated foreign funds from its exports during the war. In spite of this, liberal policy ended in failure. A wave of all kinds of imports, which was facilitated by a favorable exchange rate, for all intents and purposes wiped out Brazil's reserves and had no positive effect.

In response, during June 1947 the government changed its orientation and established a system of import licenses. In practice, licensing criteria favored the importation of essential items such as equipment, machinery, and fuel. It restricted the importation of consumer goods. Taking into consideration that Brazilian money had a favorable rate of exchange vis-à-vis the U.S. dollar, exports suffered, whereas production for the internal market was stimulated.

This new economic policy came about mainly as a reaction to the problems connected to Brazil's balance of payments and its inflation, but it ended up helping industry. During the final years of the Dutra administration, economic growth was obvious. Beginning in 1947, growth began to be more accurately measured in the yearly tallying of the Gross Domestic Product (GDP). Taking 1947 as a baseline, the GDP grew an average of 8 percent per year between 1948 and 1950.

On the other hand, repression of the union movement allowed real salaries to go down. The rise in the cost of living is estimated to have been 15 percent in São Paulo and 23 percent in Rio de Janeiro, whereas the average salary increased by 10.5 percent in São Paulo and 12 percent in Rio.

Maneuvers related to presidential succession began before Dutra was halfway through his term of office. Vargas was one pole of attraction. He rarely attended Senate meetings, but he took a few strategic trips to different states, and he received gestures of allegiance (*beija-mão*) from politicians who came to São Borja. His strategy was clear: he wanted guaranteed loyalty from the head men in the PSD's rural political machine, and he wanted to build a solid base of support.

In São Paulo, a new force appeared with which Vargas would have to contend. In the 1947 state elections, Ademar de Barros, with the Communists' support, was elected governor. He had begun his career in the PRP; he had been an appointed governor in São Paulo during the Estado Novo; and he was able to adapt to the new times, in which political success depended on getting votes from a huge electorate.

Ademar de Barros set up a party machine, the Partido Social Progressista (Progressive Social Party) or PSP. This party's raison d'être was Barros himself. Without developing anything resembling an ideologically consistent program, Barros propagated an image of administrative ability with no political morals. He was hated by the members of the UDN, who harped on the theme of morality in public affairs, but he attracted people from the working class and sectors of the lower and middle bourgeoisie in both the capital and in São Paulo's rural areas.

At the beginning of the 1950s, Barros did not have the backing to run for president, but he could make his support work for one of the candidates. When he came out in favor of Vargas, whose campaign was underway, he broadened the Vargas current with an important base of support in São Paulo, and this base was spreading into the Federal District.

Dutra refused to support Vargas's candidacy because Vargas would not follow Dutra's line of government. He twisted the arm of the PSD and got it to nominate a presidential candidate – the almost unknown lawyer-politician from Minas Gerais, Christiano Machado. In fact, the majority of the PSD chiefs abandoned Machado. The UDN once more nominated Brigadier Eduardo Gomes, who no longer had the appeal he did in 1945. He was supported by the old Integralists, and was so insensitive to the times that he argued for revoking the minimum wage law.

Vargas based his campaign on supporting industrialization and on the need to widen labor legislation. His speeches changed according to where he gave them. In Rio de Janeiro, where Communist influence was real, he went so far as to claim that if he were elected, the people would come to power; they, along with Getúlio, would climb the stairs of the presidential palace. In addition to his support from the PTB and the PSP, Vargas had the open or veiled support from part of the PSD and even from the UDN.

Still, the division between the PSD and the PTB made it impossible for Vargas to get the percentage of votes Dutra got in 1945. Even so, in the election held on 3 October 1950, he won a huge victory. He received 48.7 percent of all the votes, while Brigadier Gomes got no more than 29.7 percent, and Christiano Machado 21.7 percent.

5.2 THE RETURN OF VARGAS

Vargas was inaugurated on 31 January 1951. The UDN had attempted to invalidate the election, claiming that a candidate could only win with an absolute majority of votes. This requirement was not part of the current legislation, and by behaving in this fashion, liberals exposed their own contradictions. While in principle they supported democratic legality, in the important elections they were not able to attract votes from the bulk of the population. So they ended up challenging election returns with dubious arguments, or, more and more, they appealed for intervention by the armed forces.

Vargas began his administration trying to play the same role he had played earlier, but in a democratic government; that is, he wanted to arbitrate among the different social forces. He tried to curry favor with the UDN and chose very conservative ministers, predominantly from the PSD. Meanwhile, for the strategic post of minister of war, he nominated Estillac Leal, an old lieutenant, president of the Clube Militar, with links to the nationalistic faction in the army.

Within the armed services, an ideological split had formed between nationalists and their adversaries, scornfully known as the *entreguistas* or "capitulaters." This split was based both on matters of internal political economy and on Brazil's position in the international community.

The nationalists supported development based on industrialization. They emphasized the need to create an autonomous economic system independent of international capitalism. To do this, the state needed to play the important role of economic regulator and investor in strategic areas: petroleum, iron metallurgy, transportation, and communications. Nationalists were suspicious of foreign capital, but they did not rule it out. Their suspicions had sprung from economic concerns, or because they believed that the investment of foreign capital in strategic areas would put national sovereignty at risk.

The nationalists' adversaries supported minor economic intervention from the state; they did not give industrialization the same high priority; and they maintained that Brazil's development depended on a controlled opening to foreign capital. They also stuck to the position of fighting inflation by limiting the printing of money and limiting government spending.

Within the sphere of foreign relations, the nationalists were in favor of a distancing from or even opposition to the United States. The other side believed Brazil needed to line up with the United States unconditionally in the worldwide struggle against

Communism. At that time, international tension was high, and the war had started in Korea. One clear sign that the military faction in favor of lining up with the United States was becoming the majority among army officers was the victory of the nationalists' enemies, whose candidate assumed the directorship of the Clube Militar in May 1952.

At the beginning of the 1950s, the government enacted several measures destined to promote economic development, with emphasis on industrialization. Provisions were made for public investment in transportation and energy. These provisions were based on the opening of a foreign line of credit worth U.S. $500,000,000. The government attempted to increase the supply of energy for the Northeast, and the problem of the nation's coal supply was taken into account. There was a partial reoutfitting of the merchant marine and of docking facilities. In 1952, the Banco Nacional de Desenvolvimento Econômico (National Bank of Economic Development) or BNDE was formed; its purpose was to accelerate the process of industrial diversification.

At the same time that it was trying to galvanize the economy, the Vargas administration had to face a problem laden with social repercussions – inflation was on the rise. In 1947, inflation coming from the last years of the war had lost its momentum. But it sped up once more. It had gone from 2.7 percent in 1947 to an annual rate of 13.8 percent between 1948 and 1953, and during 1953 it reached 20.8 percent.

Vargas was obliged to sail in a sea of contradictory currents. On the one hand, he had to attend to the demands of workers suffering from the high cost of living. On the other, he had to take unpopular measures aimed at controlling inflation. Between June and July 1953, he replaced his ministers. As minister of labor he named a young rancher and politician from Rio Grande do Sul – João Goulart, better known as Jango. Jango had begun his political ascent in the town of São Borja, thanks to his family's connection with the Vargas family. He had joined forces with the PTB unions and appeared as someone capable of containing the growing Communist influence among union workers. In spite of the role he might have played, Jango was turned into a hateful figure by the UDN, whose influence among the middle class was considerable.

Anti-Vargas military men had the same opinion of Jango. Within both circles, he was seen as a supporter of a republic dominated by trade unions, and as Peronism personified.

Vargas nominated his old collaborator Osvaldo Aranha minister of finance. Aranha had stood out in this post during the early 1930s. The new minister's program was known as the Aranha plan. Its goal was to control the expansion of credit and the exchange rate in foreign transactions. In the latter aspect, it merely continued what had begun in January 1953. These measures allowed the exchange rate to fluctuate according to the goods being exported or imported. Great flexibility in the exchange rate was supposed to restore the ability of exports to compete internationally and to favor the importation of goods considered vital for the nation's economic development.

In October 1953, the so-called *confisco cambial* was established. This measure set a lower exchange rate for dollars received by coffee exporters when they converted their dollars into cruzeiros – Brazilian currency at that time.

Thanks to confisco cambial, the government was able to divert revenue from coffee exports into other sectors of the economy, especially into industry. This occasioned repeated objections from the coffee sector, which tried to hold protest marches of a political nature. The army stopped these marches before they began. (During the Kubitschek government [1956–1960], these marches were known as production marches.) It would, however, be an exaggeration to say that the Vargas administration simply abandoned coffee growers. Even though it had bad results, the government managed to keep coffee prices high abroad, which irritated the United States. A commission from the United States Senate actually investigated the "exorbitant prices" paid for Brazilian coffee.

Beginning in 1953, American policy vis-à-vis Third World countries changed direction. President Truman (1945–1953) had forced these countries to take sides regarding Communism, especially after the beginning of the Korean War. However, the United States went on helping those countries included in the American orbit. In 1953 former general Dwight Eisenhower became president and named George Humphrey secretary of the treasury and John Foster Dulles secretary of state. In addition to turning anti-Communism into a true crusade, the United States government adopted a stern attitude concerning the financial problems of developing countries. The prevailing opinion favored stopping state aid to these countries and replacing it with private investments. Brazil's possibility of obtaining public credits for building its infrastructure and covering its balance of payment deficits shrank perceptibly.

From the beginning of his administration, when he attempted to gather all the conservative forces around him, Vargas had not forgotten one of his main bases of support, urban workers. In a rally held on May Day 1951, he took a step toward establishing stronger ties with the working class. He did not restrict himself to generalities. Rather, he asked organized labor to help him in his struggle against "speculators and profiteers." At the same time he eliminated the so-called *atestado de ideologia* or "loyalty oath" sworn to democratic principles required of union members. With these declarations, he facilitated the return of Communists and other people who had been shut out during the Dutra administration.

But the government would not be able to control the working world entirely. The liberalization of the union movement and the problems stemming from the rising cost of living gave rise to a series of strikes during 1953. Especially important were the general strike in São Paulo during March and the seamen's strike in Rio de Janeiro, Santos, and Belém during June. Each strike meant something different.

While it began in the textile sector, the São Paulo strike eventually included 300,000 workers – cabinetmakers, carpenters, workers in footwear factories, typesetters, and glazers joined. Its main demand was a 60 percent raise in wages, but it also challenged the laws restricting the right to strike. Punctuated by clashes with the police, the strike went on for 24 days. It finally ended with separate agreements reached in each sector. This massive strike, known as the *greve dos 300,000*, signaled a defeat for Vargas's policy in São Paulo. The president held on to some of his personal power, but the PTB and the government's union bosses had been left behind in this movement. Communists at that time solidly opposed Vargas and accused him of being an "imperialist lackey." They played the major role in the strike.

The seamen's strike involved nearly 100,000 workers. The unions involved in the strike asked for a raise in salary, improved working conditions, and the removal of the board of directors of the Federação dos Marítimos (Seamen's Federation), which they accused of working closely with the Ministry of Labor. This last demand met the objectives of Vargas's ministerial reform head on.

João Goulart was appointed head of the ministry while the strike was in progress, and he worked efficiently as an intermediary. Since this was a strike within a government-run sector of the economy which was subject to state economic regulation, Goulart was able to attend to the majority of the strikers' demands. At the same time, he forced the resignation of the directors of the Seamen's Federation, which opened the road for another group, closer both to the workers and to Goulart himself.

During March 1953, coinciding with the "greve dos 300,000" in São Paulo, there was, also in São Paulo, a political event that at the time was considered important, but its real impact could only be understood after several years had gone by. A city councilman and ex-high school teacher was elected mayor of the state capital. As the candidate of the Partido Democrata Cristão (Christian Democratic Party) and the minuscule Partido Socialista Brasileiro (Brazilian Socialist Party), Jânio Quadros defeated other, supposedly stronger parties' candidates. His success was based on a populist campaign known as the *tostão contra o milhão*, "the dime against a million," which rallied under the banner of fighting corruption. Quadros understood that this theme would have huge political returns if he broke his ties with the UDN elite and expressed himself using compelling images. The broom was the best of his symbols. The desire to innovate and defeat party machines and the belief in the magical powers of a man fighting corruption unified different sectors of society, from the working masses to the middle class, who rallied around Quadros.

While this was happening, on the federal scene, Goulart was the focus of attacks from the anti-Vargas civilian and military factions. His name was linked to putative plans for a unionized republic and, soon thereafter, to a possible 100 percent increase in the minimum wage. Among the government's civilian adversaries were most of the UDN members, members of smaller parties, and a good portion of the press. Owing to his radicalism and his verbal prowess, the ex-Communist Carlos Lacerda stood out among these adversaries. As the years passed by, Lacerda had not just broken away from his old comrades, he had become one of their most dedicated adversaries. Populism and Communism were his favorite targets. From his newspaper the *Tribuna da Imprensa*, Lacerda began a violent campaign against Vargas and called for his resignation. Vargas's resignation should be coupled with a state of emergency decree. During the state of emergency, democratic institutions would be reformed so as to stop what Lacerda considered to be their perversion by populist politicians.

Among the military's governmental opponents, one could find anti-Communist officers, anti-populists, a few people belonging to the UDN, and others who were anti-politician in general. The best known among these people were generals such as Cordeiro de Farias, Juarez Távora, and Brigadier Eduardo Gomes. After them, the strength of younger members of the officer corps could be seen. The degree of turmoil within the military can be measured by the issuing of the so-called Colonels' Memorandum in February 1954. A total of 42 colonels and 39 lieutenant colonels signed the document which protested what they considered to be the material and moral deterioration of army standards. This manifesto also criticized raising the minimum wage to heights incompatible with the country's reality.

5.3   VARGAS'S FALL

In February 1954, Vargas once more changed his cabinet. Goulart was replaced by a lackluster individual in the Ministry of Labor – after he had proposed a 100 percent raise in the minimum wage. The image he left behind was that of a man who was ousted because he wanted to benefit workers. Hoping to calm the armed forces, Vargas named General Zenóbio da Costa minister of war. Costa was a man Vargas trusted – as well as a known anti-Communist.

In spite of all these maneuvers, the president opted more and more for a line of argumentation and for actions that would clash with the interests of conservative sectors of society. He adopted a nationalistic line in the economic sphere and blamed foreign capital for Brazil's balance of payment problems. When American and Canadian electric energy firms were reluctant to make new investments, Vargas reacted, in April 1954, with a bill creating a state firm for this area – Eletrobrás.

That same month a former minister of foreign relations, João Neves da Fontoura, gave an interview in which he provided a sharper focus for the opposition's criticism. Neves accused the president and Goulart of having signed a secret agreement with Chile and Argentina. The object of this agreement was to bar American presence from the so-called Southern Cone of Latin America. This supposed alliance, especially with Perón's Argentina, sounded like one more step toward the installation of a republic dominated by trade unions.

Within the realm of labor relations, Vargas's announcement of a 100 percent increase of the minimum wage on May Day provoked a storm of protests.

In spite of all the pressure and, by that time, the total lack of a solid base of support for his government, Vargas was still in power. The opposition needed an event so traumatic that it would cause the armed forces to break the law and depose the president. This event would be offered by men in Vargas's circle of intimates. These men had become convinced that for Vargas to remain in power it was necessary to get Lacerda off the political stage. According to what came to light later on, people close to Vargas suggested to Gregório Fortunato, the chief of the presidential guard at the Palácio do Catete (the presidential palace), that he should teach Lacerda a lesson. As Vargas's faithful servant for over 30 years, Fortunato arranged for the assassination of the best-known person in the opposition.

If this criminal plot was conceived under an evil star, it was more ill-stared in its execution. In the early morning of 5 August 1954, a gunman tried to shoot Lacerda as he approached his apartment building in Rio de Janeiro. He managed to kill Lacerda's companion, air force Major Rubens Vaz. Lacerda was slightly wounded. Now Vargas was charged with a criminal act, an act that elicited widespread indignation. His enemy now had higher cards to play against him. And the air force was in a state of rebellion.

Police investigations of the crime as well as the air force's investigation started to reveal the darker side of the Vargas administration. Still, it was impossible to link the president directly to what even Vargas called the "sea of mud" around him.

The movement for Vargas's resignation took on huge dimensions. Vargas fought back, insisting that he represented the principle of constitutional legality. On 23 August, it was clear that the government had lost the support of the armed forces. A manifesto to the nation, which was signed by 27 army generals, was published on that day and demanded the president's resignation. Among the signers, one finds not only Vargas's known adversaries, but also generals, such as Henrique Lott, who were far removed from Vargas's systematic opposition. A little more than a year later, Lott would become the mouthpiece of legality.

As the opposition closed ranks around him, Vargas responded with one last and tragic act. On the morning of 24 August, he committed suicide in his chambers at the Palácio do Catete by shooting himself in the heart. Vargas's suicide was an expression of his personal despair, but it was also deeply meaningful politically. The act itself was so dramatically charged that it electrified the nation's masses. In addition, the president left behind a dramatic message to Brazilians – the so-called *carta-testamento*, a suicide letter. In it Vargas presented himself as victim and at the same time accuser of his unpopular enemies. He claimed that international groups allied with his Brazilian enemies were responsible for the country's impasse.

Vargas's suicide had an immediate effect. Masses of people poured into the streets in all the big cities. They struck at obvious targets of their hate: opposition newspapers and the United States embassy in Rio de Janeiro. In all these manifestations, the Communists were present. After having spent the duration of his administration opposing it and finally calling for Vargas's resignation, the Communists turned completely around from one day to the next. From then on, they abandoned their radical stance, which had often helped their greatest enemies. In its stead, more and more they supported nationalistic populism.

Owing to the army high command's preference for a legal solution to the crisis, as well as to the impact of the show of force in the streets, no coup occurred. Vice-President Café Filho became president. He formed a cabinet with a UDN majority and assured the country that there would be a presidential election in October 1955.

The first party to nominate a presidential candidate was the PSD, which in February announced Juscelino Kubitschek's candidacy. Kubitschek had begun his career within the PSD in Minas Gerais and had been elected governor. He was well rooted in one of Vargas's sources of power, and he would be likely, as indeed happened, to get the support of the PTB. The PSD-PTB alliance, which had given Dutra his extraordinary victory, was restored. In May, Ademar de Barros decided to run, even though he had been defeated by Quadros in the São Paulo gubernatorial race in October 1954.

A month later, the UDN nominated another military candidate. It could no longer support Brigadier Gomes, who had been exhausted by two defeats. Another old member of the lieutenants' movement, General Juarez Távora, would be the party's candidate.

In his campaign, Kubitschek drove home the need to proceed down the road of economic development with the help of public and private capital. Távora campaigned for morality in politics. At the same time, he came out against excessive state intervention in the economy, which was leading the country into a quagmire that threatened its progress.

There was no lack of dirty tricks during this campaign. In September 1955, Kubitschek's and his running mate Goulart's enemies had a letter published in various newspapers. This letter, known as the Brandi letter, was supposed to have been sent to Goulart in 1953, when he was Vargas's minister of labor. It was from the Argentine congressman Antonio Jesús Brandi and referred to Goulart's and Perón's agreement to set off an armed movement in Brazil which would bring about a government run by trade unions. An investigation carried out by the army right after the elections proved that the letter was the product of Argentine forgers who had sold it to Goulart's enemies.

On 3 October 1955, the ballots gave the victory to Kubitschek, albeit by a narrow margin. He received 36 percent of the votes, while Távora garnered 30 percent, Barros 26 percent, and Plínio Salgado, who ran for the old Integralists, 8 percent. At that time, one could vote for presidential and vice-presidential candidates on different party slates. Goulart was elected vice-president, with a vote count slightly higher than Kubitschek's. Goulart's success showed how the PTB was gaining ground.

After Kubitschek's and Goulart's victory, a campaign was begun against their taking office. In early November 1955, Café Filho suffered a heart attack which obliged him to relinquish power temporarily. The president of the Chamber of Deputies, Carlos Luz, took his place. Luz was accused of openly favoring those supporting a military coup. This accusation occasioned the military's intervention to guarantee rather than prevent Kubitschek's taking office.

The lead character in the events of 11 November 1955 was General Lott, who mobilized soldiers in Rio de Janeiro. The troops took over government buildings, radio stations, and newspapers. Army commandos sided with Lott, while the navy and air force ministers denounced his action as "illegal and subversive." Army units surrounded navy and air force bases, precluding any confrontation among the armed forces. Ousted from the presidency, Carlos Luz, along with his ministers and other political figures including Carlos Lacerda, took refuge on the cruiser *Tamandaré*, from where they unsuccessfully attempted to organize a resistance movement.

Rapidly – it was still 11 November – Congress met to take stock of the situation. Overriding the votes of the UDN, the parliamentarians judged Carlos Luz out of office, and the presidency was passed on to Senate President Nereu Ramos, as the constitution stipulated. Ten days later, Café Filho, apparently recovered from his heart attack, tried to regain the presidency. He too was considered out of office by Congress, and Nereu Ramos was confirmed as chief of state. Soon thereafter, responding to a request from military ministers, Congress declared a state of siege for 30 days, which it extended for another 30 days. This series of exceptional measures guaranteed Kubitschek's and Goulart's inauguration on 31 January 1956.

5.4 FROM NATIONALISM TO DEVELOPMENTISM

In comparison with the Vargas administration and the months following the president's suicide, the JK (Juscelino Kubitschek) years can be considered politically stable. Indeed, they were optimistic years soothed by high rates of economic growth and by the dream come true in Brasília. The official motto "50 years in five" resounded widely throughout the nation.

The high command of the armed forces, especially the army, was in favor of backing democratic governments. There were, however, limits imposed by the need to preserve internal order and continue the war on Communism. Vargas only ran afoul of this military majority when he wandered into the terrain of aggressive nationalism or when he appealed to workers' organizations.

There were sectors of the military that did not follow the majority line. On one side were the nationalist officers. Some of them were Communist sympathizers and preferred a radical nationalism to counter what they called Yankee imperialism. On another side were the "purifiers of democracy," who were convinced that only with a coup, after which institutions would be renovated, would it be possible to check the encroachment of trade unions and Communism.

Not all of those in favor of a coup were *entreguistas*. Some of them melded the idea of a coup with a desire to favor national interests. Some of the air force officers who rebelled in January 1956 denounced supposed understandings between the government and international financial concerns. These "understandings" entailed handing over Brazilian petroleum and selling strategic minerals. They also denounced Communist infiltration in military command posts.

When the JK administration got underway, the military high command calmed down. Those in favor of a coup had played a high card in Vargas's resignation and in their attempt to stop Kubitschek from taking office. But they had lost. Kubitschek began his administration underlining the need for "development and order" – standard objectives compatible with those of the armed forces. As far as updating military equipment was concerned, the president tried to attend to specific demands from the armed forces. He also tried, as much as possible, to keep the union movement under control. In addition, the tendency to appoint military men to strategic governmental posts was accentuated. In Petrobrás as well as in the Conselho Nacional do Petróleo (National Petroleum Council), the important positions were controlled by the armed forces.

One of the chief backers of military support for the JK administration was General Lott, who was minister of war during almost all of Kubitschek's presidential term. While Lott had not been a great leader in the army itself, he had two important credentials: his service record was impeccable, and he did not belong to a political party. The latter factor made his job of smoothing over divisions among the armed forces much easier.

In partisan politics, the agreement between the PSD and the PTB guaranteed congressional support for the government's major projects. The parties had taken shape over the last ten years. They were still vehicles for personal disputes and a way of accommodating rival groups in search of privileges. But at the same time, each party had come to represent more generalized aspirations and interests.

In spite of their differences, a common trait united the PSD and the PTB, and that trait was Getulism. There was, however, a PSD Getulism and a PTB Getulism. The PSD variety was made up of some sectors of the rural elite; of government bureaucrats who had come to power under the Estado Novo; and of the industrial and commercial bourgeoisie who had benefited from development and business opportunities made possible by inflation. The PTB variety of Getulism included the union bureaucracy and the Ministry of Labor, which controlled unions' internal hierarchies and important areas such as Social Security (Previdência Social). It also included part of the industrial bourgeoisie that was more inclined toward nationalism, as well as the majority of urban union workers.

For this bipartisan alliance to go on working, it was necessary that neither party become radically entrenched. On the one hand, the PSD could not become so conservative that it would clash with the union bureaucracy and the demands of workers. On the other hand, the PTB could not go too far with its demands or with its encroaching on the most sought-after government posts; nor could it turn nationalism into a banner of social agitation.

During his administration, Kubitschek was able to keep both parties in line. The principle of development and order satisfied the PSD. On the social plane, Kubitschek did not oppose the union bureaucracy, and he tried to limit strikes. Thus, he did not hobble the PTB or Goulart, but one cannot say that he followed the PTB line.

Kubitschek's economic policy was defined in his *Programa de Metas* (Program of Goals), which consisted of 31 objectives spread over six large areas: energy, transportation, foodstuffs, basic industry, education, and the construction of Brasília (which was known as the synthesis goal).

In an attempt to go around bureaucratic routines, the Kubitschek administration created bureaus parallel to those already in existence, and it created new departments. Alongside the useless and corrupt Departamento de Obras Contra as Secas (Anti-Drought Department) or DNOCS appeared, surrounded by dreams that never came true, SUDENE, the Superintendência do Desenvolvimento do Nordeste (Superintendency of Development for the Northeast), which was set up to foster plans for industrial development of the Northeast. To undertake the construction of Brasília, NOVACAP (Nova Capital) was formed.

The JK administration promoted widespread state intervention in infrastructure and in supplying direct aid to industry. But it also openly sought to attract foreign capital, offering it special incentives as well. Nationalist ideology lost ground to development. The government permitted widespread use of a piece of legislation passed during Café Filho's administration. This law allowed firms to import foreign equipment without putting foreign funds in escrow to pay for such imports. To take advantage of this benefit, all a firm needed was to own the equipment elsewhere and to transfer it to Brazil, or to have the resources to pay for it. Foreign concerns could easily fulfill these requirements and found themselves in a favorable position for transferring equipment from their headquarters and incorporating it into their Brazilian assets. Legislation favored foreign investment in areas the government considered priorities: automotive industry, air transport, railways, electricity, and steel.

Kubitschek's Program of Goals produced impressive results, especially in the industrial sector. Between 1955 and 1961 revenue from industrial production, in inflation-adjusted terms, increased by 80 percent. Steel production increased 100 percent, the production of machinery 125 percent, electricity and communications 380 percent, and transportation material 600 percent. Between 1957 and

1961, Brazil's GDP grew at a yearly rate of 7 percent, which corresponded to a per capita rate of almost 4 percent. Considering the 1950s as a whole, the GDP per capita growth in Brazil was approximately three times that of the rest of Latin America.

Although in earlier times there had been a small number of assembly plants and auto parts factories in Brazil, the Kubitschek administration has been associated with the creation of Brazil's automotive industry. The government provided incentives for private (including foreign) capital to invest in automobile and truck manufacture. Foreign companies came to Brazil both because of the advantages they were given and because of Brazil's market potential.

Great multinational corporations such as Willys Overland, Ford, Volkswagen, and General Motors changed the face of the land around the towns of Santo André, São Bernardo, and São Caetano when they set up shop in that (ABC) area of greater São Paulo. Among its other effects, the automotive industry concentrated, for Brazil, unforeseen numbers of workers in a single area. In 1960, the last year of the Kubitschek administration, the four firms mentioned above produced 78 percent of the 133,000 vehicles made in Brazil, which satisfied the demand at the time. Foreign firms continued to expand, while the Fábrica Nacional de Motores (National Motor Factory) became less and less important and was finally bought out by Alfa Romeo in 1968. During that year, Volkswagen, Ford, and General Motors produced 90 percent of all vehicles made in Brazil.

From a numerical and organizational point of view, the installation of an automotive industry was an undeniable success. However, this industry was destined to create a "civilization of cars," to the detriment of mass public transportation. Beginning in 1960, the tendency to manufacture cars increased, and by 1968 58 percent of the vehicles produced in Brazil were cars. Since railways were for all intents and purposes abandoned, Brazil became more and more dependent on extending and preserving its highways and on the use of petroleum derivatives in transportation.

In Brazilians' memories, Kubitschek's five-year administration is thought of as a period of optimism associated with tremendous accomplishments, the greatest of which was the building of Brasília. At the time, the founding of a new capital divided opinion and was considered a punishment by government employees in Rio, who would have to move to the country's central highland. The idea of Brasília was not new. Indeed, the nation's first republican constitution in 1891 gave Congress the power to "change the nation's capital." Kubitschek, however, was the one who got the project underway enthusiastically, mobilizing resources and workers, largely migrants from the Northeast. In the vanguard of planning Brasília were the architect Oscar Niemeyer and urban planner Lúcio Costa, two men of international renown.

The bill for Brasília's construction was sent by the president to Congress and passed in September 1956, over strong opposition by the UDN. The UDN maintained that the project was mere demagoguery and would create more inflation as well as isolate the seat of government. As work went on, UDN Deputy Carlos Lacerda headed a call for forming a parliamentary committee to investigate irregularities in construction contracts, which got nowhere. Finally, on the symbolic date of 21 April 1960, Kubitschek solemnly inaugurated the new capital.

During JK's administration, unionism underwent changes that would come to light clearly during the early 1960s, under Goulart. Union leadership of different persuasions began to understand how the tight, official union structure hobbled the workers' movement, which was spreading. Thus, alternative associations were created and worked outside the official structure. These organizations included the Pacto de Unidade Intersindical (Pact for Interunion Unity) or PUI, created in 1955 in São Paulo, and the Pacto de União e Ação (Pact for Unity and Action) or PUA, set up in Rio de Janeiro. Contrary to the PUI, the PUA worked in the public sector or with public utilities controlled by state firms as well as with public service concessionaires. It prepared the way for the formation of the Comando Geral dos Trabalhadores (Workers' General Staff) or CGT, which would play an important part in the strikes during the Goulart administration.

Concerning unions' spheres of influence, the creation of the PUA accentuated a tendency that was already extant years before. The public sector and public utilities were being targeted more and more. In addition, in the market sector, the relative influence of organized labor was greater in the traditional but declining industries. One case in point was the textile industry.

During this time, Brazilian unions found making headway difficult in one conspicuous area – the automotive industry. There are two factors which explain this difficulty. First, it can be explained by the union movement's (and especially the Communists') traditional rootedness in firms linked to the state. Second, unions were at sea when it came to the new types of labor relations fostered by multinational companies.

At the same time that they set up alternative organizations, union leaders tried to politicize their unions. This meant that they supported nationalistic trends and proposals for basic social reform, which included agrarian reform.

Not everything was rosy during the Kubitschek period. The greatest problems could be found in those areas where foreign trade and government finance were enmeshed. Government spending on the industrialization program and on the building of Brasília coupled with a serious decline in the cruzeiro's exchange rate created growing deficits in the federal budget. The deficit went from 1 percent of the GDP in 1954 and 1955 to 2 percent in 1956 and to 4 percent in 1957. This trend was accompanied by inflation, which, except for 1957, increased and reached its highest level under Kubitschek in 1959 – 39.5 percent.

There were several reasons for the rise in inflation. Among the main ones were the government's expenditures on the construction of Brasília and on increases in salary for selected government workers, which Congress approved. The falling rate of exchange was also a factor, as were coffee purchases with money printed to support declining coffee prices and the easy terms of credit available to the private sector.

In June 1958, Minister of Finance José Maria Alkmin resigned. He had become worn out trying to deal with these problems. Kubitschek named an engineer, Lucas Lopes, to replace Alkmin. Lopes had been the first president of the National Development Bank in the JK government. Roberto Campos succeeded him. Together they worked out a plan to stabilize Brazil's economy by trying to reconcile efforts at fighting inflation and reducing the national debt with the objectives of the Program of Goals.

Their plan did not call for tremendous sacrifices, but even so it occasioned strong, contrary reactions. In the first place, while each sector of society might have expected some other group to take a loss, no social group was willing to lose the slightest amount whatsoever in the interest of stability. Second, inflation was a good deal for many social sectors. Inflation made it possible for industry and business to make extraordinary amounts of money in price readjustments and in speculating with stocks of merchandise. On top of this, since debts were not subject to *correção monetária*, or readjustment for inflation, inflation made taking out loans extremely attractive, especially for people who took them out from state banks and other financial organizations.

Within organized labor, resistance came from two main sources. The stabilization program was associated with suspected "deals with imperialism," which caused the PTB and the Left to shudder. At the same time, any plan of that nature would, at the beginning, entail additional sacrifices. Union leaders and workers under their influence feared that wage earners would be obliged to make these sacrifices, while other members of society would refuse to make them. Wage earners would be caught in the worst of all worlds: ongoing or exacerbated inflation and greater reductions in real wages.

Attempts at withholding credit from industry were protested in São Paulo, with support from the president of the Banco do Brasil. Coffee growers organized a "production march" in October 1958 to protest "confisco cambial" and new government policies that limited purchases of stockpiled coffee.

Whenever it had to deal with Brazil's foreign accounts, the stabilization program could only work under the guidance of the International Monetary Fund. Brazil consulted that international organization in various circumstances, including when it was expecting a $300,000,000 loan from the United States. Contrary to what the plan's detractors said, the IMF was not behind it. The IMF expressed reservations concerning Brazil's slow approach to curtailing inflation, and it criticized the government's expenditures to subsidize the importation of wheat and petroleum.

Indecision in the relations between Brazil and the IMF lasted almost a year, but ended in June 1959. By that time, Kubitschek was at the end of his mandate and had turned his eyes toward his successor. Nationalists and Communists attacked the president for his willingness to "sell out national sovereignty to international bankers and the IMF." Only the UDN favored deals with the IMF, but even if Kubitschek had taken their route, he could not have relied on political support from the opposition.

These circumstances led to the government's break with the IMF, which was tantamount to abandoning the plan for stabilization once and for all. In August 1959, Lucas Lopes and Roberto Campos resigned. Their resignations created a wave of support for Kubitschek. As one might expect, the PTB applauded their leaving. Communists were present at a demonstration held on the grounds of the presidential palace in support of the president. Luis Carlos Prestes had come out of hiding in 1958 and was among the demonstrators. The Communist Party, in spite of still being formally illegal, was finding ways to express itself. But support came from other quarters besides the PTB and the Left. Kubitschek's break with the IMF was supported by the São Paulo Industrial Federation (Federação das Indústrias do Estado de São Paulo) and by the military high command.

However, this enthusiasm did not extend to the great mass of people, as the presidential election on 3 October 1960 would show. It was 1959 and candidates had already entered the race. After having been elected governor of São Paulo, Jânio Quadros was nominated in April by a small party. He was supported by Lacerda. Ademar de Barros had been buoyed by the votes he had won in 1955 and came out as the PSP candidate. The PSD and PTB once more united and nominated General Lott, with Goulart as their vice-presidential candidate.

The UDN was undecided between nominating its own candidate and supporting Quadros, who was running on his own ticket, criticizing government corruption and financial chaos. With no specific program and scorning political parties, Quadros attracted supporters with his folksy, threatening image as a man who promised to punish unmercifully anyone benefiting from dirty deals or from any type of corruption. He was far from being the sort of well-mannered type the UDN favored, but at the same time and in his own way he appropriated a good bit of the UDN's line.

Indeed, apparently he was offering the UDN a wonderful opportunity to come to power, albeit using an unknown shortcut. At the November 1959 UDN convention, support for Quadros carried the day.

From the early days of the campaign, Quadros's lead had been obvious. He rallied the hopes of the anti-Vargas elite; of the middle class hurt by the high cost of living and wanting morality in politics. He also rallied the hopes of the great bulk of the working class. Lott was a disastrous candidate. He had played an important role in the tiny power circles, where he personified a guarantee of democratic continuity. In a wider forum, his weaknesses became obvious. He was a bad public speaker and sounded artificial when he mouthed the Vargas line. He displeased the PSD when he came out in favor of allowing illiterates to vote. He displeased the PTB and, mainly, the Left, when he criticized Cuba and Communism.

Over the four presidential elections since 1945, the electorate had grown considerably thanks to the growth of cities and owing to citizens' greater interest in political participation. In 1945 5,900,000 people voted; in 1950 7,900,000; in 1955 8,600,000. In 1960, the last direct presidential election the country would experience until 1989, 11,700,000 people voted.

Quadros won the October elections with 48 percent of those 11,700,000 votes. Lott received 28 percent, and Barros 23 percent. Still, this win did not exceed, percentagewise, Dutra's 1945 share of the electorate. Notwithstanding Lott's resounding defeat, Goulart was elected vice-president.

For the first time ever, as an embodiment of hope for the future, a president was inaugurated in Brasília. With Quadros's resignation, less than seven months after his inauguration, these hopes would be dashed, and the country would be plunged into a grave political crisis.

Quadros began his administration in an embarrassing way. He spent a disproportionate amount of time on matters unworthy of his position – matters such as outlawing bikinis and cock fights as well as the perfume atomizer (which people used during Carnival to spray one another with perfume-scented ether). In the more serious spheres, he coupled measures the Left wanted with those the Right wanted and ended up alienating both sides.

His foreign policy rankled conservatives, especially the majority of the UDN. It was during Quadros's administration that the United States government established the Alliance for Progress. This was a reform plan which contained a promise to send 20 billion dollars to Latin America over a ten-year period. The Alliance was approved in a meeting of American countries held in Punta del Este, Uruguay. The Cuban delegation, headed by Ernesto "Che" Guevara, did not sign the Punta del Este Charter. On his way back to Cuba, Guevara stopped in Brasília. During this stopover, he received a significant medal from Quadros – the Cruzeiro do Sul Order. With that gesture, the new president had no intention of showing support for Communism. It was intended to show the public at large that Quadros had opted for an independent foreign policy in which Brazil would take a route different from that offered by either of the two opposing power blocks.

In the financial domain, Quadros announced a plan to take on the problems inherited from the Kubitschek government. In his inauguration speech, he had dwelled on the country's difficulties. He chose an orthodox stabilization plan which involved a weighty devaluation of the cruzeiro, and containment both of public spending and of the printing of money. Subsidies for importing wheat and petroleum were reduced, which caused the price of fuel and bread to double.

These measures were well received by Brazil's creditors and by the IMF. The Club of the Hague, which was made up of European as well as American creditors, rescheduled Brazil's debt in 1961. More loans were obtained in the United States, with the support of President Kennedy. Quadros was seen as a way to stop the largest Latin American country from slipping off the road of instability into Communism. In August 1961, Quadros had begun to loosen the reigns on financial restraint, but he never actually carried out a change in policy. During that month, in a single act, he ended his administration.

Quadros had been governing the country without a base of political support. The PSD and the PTB dominated Congress. Lacerda had joined the opposition and was criticizing Quadros with the same vehemence with which he had supported him. The UDN had several reasons to complain. Quadros had been acting for all intents and purposes without consulting the UDN leadership in Congress.

On top of this, his independent foreign policy and his sympathy for agrarian reform worried the party.

On the night of 24 August 1961, Lacerda, who had been elected governor of Guanabara, made a speech on the radio. In that speech he denounced an attempted coup by Quadros, which had allegedly been set up by Minister of Justice Oscar Pedroso Horta. Oddly enough, Lacerda claimed he had been invited to join. Pedroso Horta denied the accusation. On the following day, Quadros resigned and conveyed his decision to the nation's Congress.

His resignation has never been satisfactorily explained. Even Quadros has refused to offer a clear version of what went on. He has always alluded to "terrible forces" that led him to resign. The most likely explanation of his resignation combines Quadros's unstable personality with a political long shot. According to this theory, Quadros expected his theatrical gesture would get him more power to govern and would, to an extent, cut him free from Congress and the parties. He considered himself absolutely essential to those parties during his presidential campaign, and he considered himself indispensable as president of Brazil. He believed the conservatives and the military would never turn the country over to João Goulart.

Quadros quickly left Brasília and surfaced at a military base in São Paulo. There he received an appeal to reconsider from some state governors. But, beyond this, there was no other significant effort to get Quadros back in office. Every group had reasons to complain about him and had begun to find their footing in the new situation. Since resignations are merely communicated and not voted on, Congress simply acknowledged Quadros's resignation and set off the struggle for power.

Constitutionally, there was no doubt about Quadros's successor – he would be Vice-President João Goulart. However, his swearing in was checked by actions from the armed forces, who considered Goulart the embodiment of trade unionism in government and the opening through which Communists would come to power. By chance, but highly symbolically, Goulart at this time was outside the country – visiting Communist China.

While the president of the Chamber of Deputies provisionally assumed the office, Quadros's military ministers blocked Goulart's return to Brazil for reasons of national security. Those in favor of blocking his return did not, however, have the full support of the armed forces' high command. In Rio Grande do Sul, the commandant of the Third Army declared his support for Goulart, and this started what has been called the Legality Battle. The main character in this movement was the governor of Rio Grande do Sul, Leonel Brizola, Goulart's brother-in-law. Brizola helped organize military resistance forces and sponsored huge popular demonstrations in Porto Alegre. When the minister of the navy announced the dispatch of a naval force southward, Brizola threatened to block the entrance to Porto Alegre's harbor by sinking several ships.

Finally, Congress adopted a compromise solution. The system changed from being presidential to parliamentary, and Goulart took office with diminished power on 7 September 1961. Used as a mere expedient to resolve a crisis, parliamentarianism could not and did not last very long.

From the beginning of Goulart's administration, it was clear that social movements were on the rise and new actors were on the scene. Forgotten rural sectors (virtual orphans of populist politics) began to mobilize. The backdrop for their mobilization can be found in the great structural changes that had come about in Brazil between 1950 and 1964. They were the products of urban growth and rapid industrialization. These changes had increased the demand for agricultural products as well as for livestock, and these demands had changed land-holding and land-utilization practices. Land began to produce more income than it had in the past, and owners tried to evict longtime squatters or to make their working conditions worse. This brought about massive discontent among the rural population. In addition, migration had brought country and city closer together, which made people aware of how oppressed country folk were.

The period's most important rural movement was that of the peasant leagues, whose ostensible leader was a man from the urban middle class – a lawyer and politician from Pernambuco, Francisco Julião. Julião supported these leagues, which were different from unions, and tried to organize the peasants. He believed that it would be easier to attract peasants into a significant social movement than to appeal to salaried workers.

Peasant leagues had begun to appear around the end of 1955. Their purposes, among others, were to keep peasants from being thrown off their land; to keep the price of renting land down; and to fight the practice known as *cambão*, whereby the tenant farmer (in southern Brazil a *colono*, in the Northeast a *morador* or "resident") had to work for free, one day a week, for the owner.

Julião tried to give these leagues a centralized organization. He established league headquarters in state capitals or in the more important cities of specific regions. He justified this strategy by claiming that in large cities there were classes and groups on the peasants' side: workers, students, revolutionary intellectuals, and the petit bourgeois. And also in these cities the courts were less reactionary. Leagues appeared in several parts of the country, especially in the Northeast, in states like Pernambuco and Paraíba.

In November 1961, the First National Congress of Agricultural Workers was held in Belo Horizonte. At this meeting several different orientations for organizing the rural masses were proposed. The meeting was planned by Julião together with other league members, and by Communist leaders whose major support came from salaried rural workers from São Paulo and Paraná. In Belo Horizonte, these two currents became divided. While the leaders of the leagues maintained that the top priority should be the expropriation of land without prior indemnity, Communists preferred to concentrate on promoting rural unionization and the extension of labor legislation to the rural worker.

An important gain was made in the legislative sphere in March 1963. Goulart sanctioned a law which set up the Rural Workers' Statutes. This law instituted official status for rural workers; it regulated how long a day's work would be; it required that workers be paid the minimum wage; and it set out rights such as a weekly day off and paid vacations.

During the Goulart administration, mobilization in other sectors of society had also begun. Students in the União Nacional de Estudantes (National Student Union) or UNE radicalized their program for social transformation and began to take a direct part in politics.

There were also important changes in the behavior of the Catholic church. Beginning in the 1950s, many of its members began to worry, especially about the lower stratum of society, which made up the church's social foundation. Its monolithic anti-Communism began to give way to a more balanced attitude. Communism would still be fought, but church members acknowledged that the evils of capitalism had brought on the revolt and that was why Communism was spreading.

The church was internally divided among several different stances. On the right there were a few ultraconservative bishops; on the left the Juventude Universitária Católica (Catholic University Youth) or JUC, which argued for rapprochements with the political Left. Affected by the radicalizing climate of the student movement, JUC began to assume socialist stances which brought it into direct conflict with the church hierarchy. Ação Popular (Popular Action) or AP sprang from JUC in 1962. It had revolutionary objectives and was not connected to the hierarchy. AP actively participated in the political struggles of the time and was harshly repressed after the military came to power, in 1964.

The Catholic church supported rural unionization in the Northeast, while at the same time it opposed peasant leagues head-on. The papal encyclical "Mater et Magistra" by Pope John XXIII, published in May 1961, was the first to deal explicitly with Third World problems and was an important incentive for reform-minded Catholics.

João Goulart's swearing-in as president signaled the return of populist politics at a time when mobilizations and social pressures were considerably greater than they had been during the Vargas period. Government ideologues and union leaders tried to strengthen the populist scheme, which they tried to base on the state (including nationalistic officers in the armed forces and the intellectuals who determined policies), organized labor, and the nation's middle class. The state would be the focal point in this alliance, whose ideology would be nationalistic and would include sociopolitical reforms known as *reformas de base* or "basic reforms."

These reforms covered a wide range of measures. On the social level, agrarian reform had the goal of ending conflicts over land tenure and guaranteeing access to land for millions of rural workers. To this end, a constitutional change was proposed to eliminate a proviso which allowed land to be expropriated for reasons of need, public use, or social interest – but only if the owners were paid in advance for the land.

Alongside agrarian reform, urban reform was also mentioned. Its main objective was to create conditions under which tenants could become owners of the houses they rented.

In the sphere of political rights, the need to extend the right to vote to two different sectors of society was supported: illiterates and armed service enlisted men (e.g., those in the army with the rank of sergeant and below). This would be a way of widening support for a populist government, since the great disenfranchised masses and the lower ranks of the military would supposedly support such a government.

In addition, basic reforms contained nationalist measures and allowed for greater state intervention in economic matters. These measures provided for the nationalization of public service concessionaires, meat-packing plants, and the pharmaceutical industry. They would also strictly regulate companies sending profits abroad, and they extended the monopoly of the Petrobrás.

These basic reforms were not intended to make Brazil a socialist state. Rather, they were an attempt at modernizing Brazilian capitalism and at reducing its deep social inequalities through state action. These reforms entailed great changes which the dominant classes vehemently opposed. The government and middle-class intellectuals who supported basic reforms believed they could count on support from the middle class at large in their battle against imperialism and in favor of agrarian reform. From this point of view, foreign investors were considered disloyal competitors with Brazilian capitalists. Agrarian reform would bring about rural Brazilians' integration into the market economy and create more demand for industrial products. In fact, Brazil's middle class preferred another route and distanced itself more and more from the government because of the restive air in society and the uncertain investment climate.

Union leadership remained faithful to the populist framework. These leaders were mainly *trabalhistas*, that is, members of the PTB, and Communists who worked closely with the state without being as servile as the old pelegos or union bosses had been. The tactic of creating parallel organizations was continued and eventually produced the CGT (Workers' General Staff) in 1962. In these circumstances, unions made their demands more and more political. Demands pertaining specifically to workers were not forgotten, but they were considered less important.

Three factors should be pointed out regarding strike movements: (1) the number of strikes had increased greatly; (2) work stoppages tended to occur mainly in the public sector; and (3) strikes became more important in parts of Brazil other than São Paulo. Whereas in 1958 31 strikes had been registered, there were 172 in 1963. No less than 80 percent of the work stoppages in 1958 had been in the private sector; in 1963 58 percent of all strikes were in the public sector.

The propagation of strikes is an indicator of increasing social mobilization. The shift from the private to the public sector is linked to the political nature of several strikes which were sponsored by the government to impose the acceptance of specific measures believed to be in the government's interest.

Concerning the spread of strikes, it should be remembered, first of all, that private enterprise and especially multinational corporations were concentrated in São Paulo. It was more difficult for unions to get a toehold in this area, where company boards of directors had to be concerned with profits and had no intention of incorporating the working class into their political designs.

Nationalism had scant repercussion in São Paulo, since using it to unions' advantage was problematic in that state. There is also the fact that while the federal government was open to union leaders, São Paulo's governor, Ademar de Barros, harshly repressed strikes.

All this created an illusion that would have dire consequences for union leadership. Their proximity to power, their escalation of strikes, and their ubiquitous rallies made leaders euphoric at the same time that these factors hid the union movement's weak points. Their weak points, which in retrospect one can clearly see, resided in two interrelated facts. First, there was a proportional decline of the workers' movement in São Paulo, which was the most dynamic sector of the economy. And second, the movement depended far too much on the state. When Goulart's government fell, it would drag the populist union movement down with it.

In the domain of politics, as social mobilization increased, different groups' growing ideological identities became clearer. In several cases, these identities dated from the Kubitschek period and transcended party lines. Thanks to the illegality of the Communist Party, the PTB had grown and garnered many of the votes that would have gone to the Communists. The PTB also benefited from industrial growth because it was, in essence, an urban party. It also profited from a state of affairs favorable to nationalism and social change.

If there was no intraparty homogeneity, party divisions were exacerbated during the Goulart administration. And they bespoke ideological differences much more than they did disputes over personalities. To different extents, tendencies within specific parties pointed toward the advancement of nationalistic and left-leaning patterns. Within the PTB, the "compact group" was formed. It maintained an aggressive, nationalistic stance and supported concrete measures for social reform. In the UDN, a *bossa nova* contingent was formed which favored basic reforms and the government's financial plans.

However, the bulk of the UDN sympathized with Goulart's enemies in the military, and several UDN members formed the ultraconservative Ação Democrática Parlamentar (Parliamentary Democratic Action Group). These conservative circles were behind the coup d'état that would bring to an end the democratic government instituted in 1945.

The PSD watershed had occurred even earlier with the formation of the Ala Moça (Youth Wing) in 1955, during the Kubitschek campaign. The Ala Moça cautiously took on the PSD old guard and adopted a nationalistic outlook. It fell apart when Lott was defeated in 1960, but its members were instrumental in setting up the Frente Parlamentar Nacionalista (Nationalist Parliamentary Front).

There was also a rupture on the Left which derived mainly from events in the Soviet Union, where Stalinism had entered a crisis owing to the dissemination of the Khrushchev report. One sector of the Brazilian Communist Party opposed the liberation measures promoted within the party. They also opposed the line that advocated open collaboration with the Goulart administration. From this internal dissidence, the Partido Comunista do Brasil (Communist

Party of Brazil) or PC do B was born. It sought its supposedly authentic Marxist-Leninist inspiration first in China and later on in Albania. The name Partido Comunista do Brasil was the original name of the PCB which, in the wave of nationalism during 1961, started to call itself the Partido Comunista Brasileiro (Brazilian Communist Party).

While this realignment was taking place in civilian society, a vision of international relations was gaining momentum in sectors of the armed forces. This vision was formed by people mindful of guerrilla warfare. The notion of guerrilla warfare had been formulated in the context of the cold war, but it became much clearer after Fidel Castro came to power in Cuba. For specific sectors of the armed forces, the victory of the Cuban revolution was proof positive of the implantation of a revolutionary war in the underdeveloped world. This war ran parallel to the confrontation of the two great power blocks.

The objective of this revolutionary war was the spread of Communism. It involved all levels of society, and as instruments it used everything from indoctrination and psychological warfare to armed struggle. For these reasons, it was necessary to counter it with a force of equal strength. In this context, the armed forces acquired a permanent, active role. Their goal was to defeat the enemy and guarantee national security and development. This is how the doctrine of national security came about.

Under foreign influence, this doctrine was elaborated within the confines of the Escola Superior de Guerra (Higher War College) or ESG, which had been founded in August 1949 with help from French and American advisors. The United States mission stayed in Brazil from 1948 to 1960. Among Brazilians, the main technician and organizer was General Golbery do Couto e Silva. Courses at the ESG were open not only to military men, but also to civilians. Civilian participation was important for the establishment of a union between civilians and military men who identified with the reigning vision at the ESG.

The defining lines of a government believed to be capable of halting subversion and guaranteeing a specific type of economic development emerged from the ESG and entities such as the Instituto de Pesquisas e Estudos Sociais (Research and Social Studies Institute) or IPES and the Instituto Brasileiro de Ação Democrática (Brazilian Institute for Democratic Action) or IBAD, which was financed by the U.S. CIA. As the Goulart administration grew more and more radical and unstable, the associated members of the ESG, the IPES, and the IBAD became convinced that only an armed movement would put an end to populist anarchy and stop the spread of Communism.

Goulart had begun to govern with his power restrained by the parliamentary system. His first cabinet was headed by Tancredo Neves, a politician who had been Vargas's minister of justice in 1954. The president pursued a moderate line early on – in an attempt to demonstrate his adherence to democratic principles and his rejection of Communism. During a trip to the United States, he addressed a joint session of Congress and obtained resources to help northeast Brazil.

Then the matter of presidential powers appeared on the docket. The act that established a parliamentary government called for a plebiscite in 1965 in which Brazilians would definitively decide which system of government they would have. In Goulart's circles, a campaign began to move the plebiscite up.

The presidential form of government was almost certain to win. In the context in which it had come about, the parliamentary option had been devised to limit Goulart's power. On top of this, people were convinced that a president with greater power could stabilize the country and bring about the basic reforms. The majority of the military high command was also in favor of a stronger executive.

Tancredo Neves resigned his post as prime minister in June 1962. He, along with several other ministers, had to leave the cabinet so as to run in that year's October elections for the Chamber of Deputies and state governments. In addition, even Neves did not believe in parliamentary government. To succeed Neves, Goulart nominated San Thiago Dantas. As foreign minister in the cabinet led by Neves, San Thiago Dantas had defended Brazil's neutrality in the Cuban case and incurred the wrath of the Right. The Chamber of Deputies rejected this nomination and proposed Senate President Auro de Moura Andrade.

The period's first political strike was called in opposition to Moura Andrade, a conservative. Announced on 5 July by a nationalist cabinet as a 24-hour general strike, work stoppage was not complete. It mainly affected state firms or firms under state control. Longshoremen shut down almost all Brazilian ports. In several places, strikers were supported by the army. In Rio de Janeiro, the First Army protected workers from Governor Lacerda's threats of repression. Finally, Congress approved a little-known member of Rio Grande do Sul's PSD as cabinet head. This man, Brochado da Rocha, had the job of proposing and obtaining an early plebiscite from Congress. It was set for January 1963.

Before the plebiscite, the October 1962 elections for state governments and Congress demonstrated that centrist and rightist forces carried considerable weight throughout the country. It is true that they benefited from resources furnished by IBAD and similar organizations, but the government also employed its machinery. In São Paulo, Barros defeated Quadros by a narrow margin. In Rio Grande do Sul, Ildo Meneghetti, supported by the UDN and the PSD, beat Brizola's candidate. Nationalists and leftists could celebrate the victory of Miguel Arraes in Pernambuco as well as Brizola's extraordinary success in Rio de Janeiro. As a candidate to the Chamber of Deputies, Brizola garnered the highest number of votes any candidate had ever received in legislative elections up to then – 269,000 votes.

In January 1963, around 9,500,000 of a total of 12,300,000 voters voted "no" on parliamentary government. This brought back the presidential system, with Goulart heading the government.

The cabinet he chose was indicative of his strategy. He sought to take on economic and financial problems seriously, by engaging members of the so-called Positive Left, including San Thiago Dantas in the Ministry of Finance and Celso Furtado as minister of planning. At the same time, he tried to reinforce bases of support for his government – what at that time were called the "Union Apparatus" and the "Military Apparatus." For labor minister, Almino Afonso was chosen. He was well received by the left wing of the PTB and by the Communists. In the Ministry of War, General Amaury Kruel, a moderate, was kept on – he had been minister under the parliamentary government. But nationalist officers such as Osvino Alves, commander of the First Army, in Rio de Janeiro, and

Jair Dantas Ribeiro, commander of the Third Army, in Rio Grande do Sul, apparently strengthened the Military Apparatus.

The financial situation continued to worsen. Inflation was on the rise. Its annual index went from 26.3 percent in 1960 to 33.35 percent in 1961 and to 54.8 percent in 1962. To handle this and other problems, Celso Furtado set out his Three Year Plan, which sought to combine economic growth and social reform with fighting inflation. The plan depended on the collaboration of those sectors that had a voice in society. That collaboration once more failed to materialize. People benefiting from inflation had no interest in these measures' success. Goulart's enemies longed for his government's ruin and the coup. The workers' movement refused to accept wage restrictions. And the Left saw the finger of imperialism everywhere. During San Thiago Dantas's trip to Washington in March 1963, foreign creditors appeared reticent, and Dantas's trip counted for little.

Halfway through 1963 it was clear that the plan had failed. The crowning blow was a 70 percent increase in government workers' wages in the midst of 25 percent inflation for the first five months of that year. In addition, the economy as a whole was on the decline. The GDP had grown by 5.3 percent in 1962, but it only grew by 1.5 percent in 1963.

At this juncture, Goulart reshuffled his cabinet. San Thiago Dantas, who had carried out the plan, left the government – he had cancer of the lung. Almino Afonso left the Labor Ministry. General Dantas Ribeiro became minister of war. To show that he did not intend to take a radical course in financial policy, Goulart nominated a conservative as finance minister. He was an ex-governor of São Paulo by the name of Carvalho Pinto.

Also midway through 1963, positions became more radical. In the countryside, rural landowners who viewed agrarian reform as a catastrophe began to arm themselves. On the other hand, the league movement, rural unionization, and the invasion of private land gained momentum. When, in October 1963, Congress rejected a constitutional amendment which authorized expropriation of land without prior payment, a forceful takeover seemed to be the only way left for the redistribution of land.

With Brizola at its head, the left wing of the PTB complained about Goulart's vacillation in the area of social reform and relations with imperialism. Before 1963 was over, Brizola began to organize groups throughout the country to come together to resist coup attempts and to foster measures such as the convocation of a constituent assembly and a moratorium on Brazil's foreign debt.

Within the military, the anti-Goulart conspiracy grew. It was reinforced by supporters of "defensive intervention" against the government's excesses. General Humberto de Alencar Castelo Branco, himself the chief of the general staff, was one of these supporters. A noncommissioned officers' rebellion in the air force and navy during September 1963, in Brasília, helped turn that group of army officers into conspirators. The revolt had been in protest of a Federal Supreme Court decision which confirmed the disenfranchisement of the sergeants. The rebels went so far as to occupy government buildings. They controlled communications and took several officers prisoner before they were defeated.

The tragedy of the last few months of the Goulart administration can be captured in the fact that a democratic solution to the conflicts was discarded as impossible or objectionable by all political actors. The Right had won the moderate conservatives over to its thesis: that a revolution was necessary to purify democracy, to end the class struggle, to topple the unions, and to avoid the dangers of Communism.

Goulart opted for a route that required the adoption of special measures. In October 1963, inspired by the Military Apparatus and justifying his action by the need to contain rural agitation and reestablish order, he asked Congress to declare a 30-day state of siege. His proposal was rejected. It had been received poorly, by both the Right and the Left, and it increased suspicion concerning the government's intentions.

The Left saw "formal democracy" as a mere tool to aid the privileged. How could the Left accept the difficult game of protests and counterprotests, given that there was a world to be won by implementing the basic reforms, "within the law or by force"?

At the start of 1964, on the advice of his inner circle, Goulart chose a course that would prove disastrous. With support from the

Military and Union Apparatuses, the president expected to circumnavigate Congress and enact basic reforms by decree. As a show of governmental strength, he would gather huge masses of people for a series of demonstrations in which he would announce specific reforms. The first great rally was held on 13 March in Rio de Janeiro. Nearly 150,000 people met under the protection of troops from the First Army to listen to Goulart and Brizola, who, by the way, were no longer getting along.

The red banners advocating legalization of the Communist Party and the placards demanding agrarian reform were shown on television and elicited shudders among conservatives. On this occasion, Goulart signed two decrees. The first one was more symbolic than anything else: it expropriated oil refineries still not under the control of Petrobrás. The second one, known as the SUPRA (Superintendência da Reforma Agrária or "Superintendency of Agrarian Reform") decree, declared that underused property was subject to expropriation, and it specified the location and the size of properties that would be affected by this measure.

The president also revealed that urban reform was underway; this scared the daylights out of the middle class, who feared losing their buildings to their tenants. He also announced proposals to be sent to Congress for changing taxes and for giving the vote to illiterates and enlisted men in the armed forces.

Goulart's first reform demonstration was, in reality, the beginning of the end of his administration. The *Marcha da Família com Deus pela Liberdade* (The Godly Families' March for Liberty) was a storm sign. It was organized in São Paulo by associations of Catholic women linked to the conservative wing of the church. On 19 March, nearly 500,000 people paraded through the streets of São Paulo. They showed that those in favor of a coup could count on significant social support.

A serious military event helped create an even more favorable climate for the conspirators. The Sailors' Association (Associação dos Marinheiros) had stood out in the struggle for sailors' rights and for better pay. Their most important leader was Corporal Anselmo, who later would become (or by that time already was, according to some) an informant for CENIMAR, the Centro de Informaçoes da Marinha (Center for Naval Intelligence).

On 24 March, Minister Sílvio Mota ordered the arrest of the Sailors' Association's directors, whom he accused of subverting authority. On the following day, some 2,000 recruits from the navy and the marine corps gathered at the metal workers' union. The directors for whom an order of arrest had been issued were there. The purpose of the meeting was to celebrate the second anniversary of the Sailors' Association founding and to advance more demands. Minister Sílvio Mota surrounded the locale with a group of marines and asked for help from the First Army. The affair ended with a negotiated settlement.

Under pressure and feeling that he had lost face, the minister of the navy resigned. To replace him, Goulart nominated retired Admiral Paulo Rodrigues, who had been chosen with the support of the CGT. The new minister tried to calm tempers by announcing that the rebels would not be punished. What he did was throw more wood on the fire. The Clube Militar and a group of high-ranking naval officers denounced this act as support for challenging the military hierarchy.

When Goulart made one last dangerous gesture by going to address an assembly of sergeants in Rio de Janeiro, the coup was already afoot. It had been set off by General Olímpio Mourão Filho, who, back in 1937, had been involved in shady dealings concerning the Cohen Plan. On 31 March, Mourão mobilized troops in Minas Gerais under his command and headed for Rio de Janeiro.

The battle lines were drawn with unexpected rapidity. In Rio, Lacerda had garrisoned himself inside the Palácio do Governo and waited for the marines to attack, which they never did. On 1 April, Goulart took a plane to Brasília, avoiding any action that might result in bloodshed. Troops from the Second Army under the command of General Amaury Kruel left São Paulo for Rio de Janeiro, where they joined forces with the First Army.

On the night of 1 April, after Goulart had left Brasília for Porto Alegre, the president of the Senate declared the office of president vacant. According to the constitutional chain of command, Chamber of Deputies President Ranieri Mazzilli took over. But by this time power was out of civilian hands – the military was in command.

Brizola tried to repeat his 1961 feat and mobilize troops and civilians in Rio Grande do Sul, but he could not. By the end of April, he had sought exile in Uruguay, along with Goulart.

That was the end of the democratic experiment. For the first time in Brazilian history, the military had come to power and intended to stay there. It began to set up an authoritarian regime. The Goulart administration, apparently based on powerful forces, had crumbled.

To understand the government's demise, it is necessary to consider several factors, and to give weight to the situation within Brazil. It is true that the United States government supported the coup and knew about it beforehand. It even dispatched a naval task force to support the revolutionary movement in the event of a prolonged struggle. But that measure was not necessary, given the ease with which the military came to power.

João Goulart and his advisers had a mistaken vision of Brazil's politics. They took what was going on around them for what was happening in society. They also believed that to a large extent the army supported the reforms the government proposed, because, thanks to its history and the origins of its members, the army expressed the people's will. Officials acknowledged the existence of coup plotters, but they considered them to be a minority under the control of the Military Apparatus and checked by the actions of enlisted men.

It is true that over the years the majority of the officer corps had preferred not to upset constitutional government. But for the military, there were more important principles: maintaining social order, respect for hierarchy, controlling Communism. When these principles had been violated, order turned into disorder, and disorder justified intervention.

Goulart's loss of legitimacy, the subsequent breach of discipline, and the rapprochement between military enlisted men and organized labor finally led armed forces moderates to join the conspirators in a shift that resembled what was happening in civilian society. As far as the so-called Union Apparatus was concerned, it could mobilize sectors of the working class, especially state employees, but, beyond this, it could not do much. The great mass of salaried workers, battered by inflation, for all intents and purposes ignored the CGT's call for a general strike. At any rate, workers' mobilization could not get very far unless the armed forces were to divide, and that did not happen.

Thus, while social movements had gained significant ground in Brazil, Goulart was left dangling in air. Around him, the only ones who remained were the minister of war, who had lost his command; union leaders who were targeted for repression and who had scant following; and personal friends who had been responsible for fomenting an illusion.

6

The Military Government and the Transition to Democracy (1964–1984)

The movement of 31 March 1964 had been undertaken purportedly to free the country from corruption and Communism and to restore democracy. The new government began to change the country's institutions by invoking what it called *Atos Institucionais* (Institutional Acts) or AIs. The acts were justified as a consequence "of exercising constituent power, which is inherent in all revolutions."

The first AI was decreed on 9 April 1964 by the commanders of the army, navy, and air force. Formally, it preserved, with several modifications, the 1946 constitution. Congress would also continue to meet. The second proviso would be one of the military regime's characteristics. Whereas the real power had been placed in another sphere, and the basic principles of democracy had been violated, the military government almost never showed itself to be unequivocally authoritarian. Except for short periods of time, Congress continued to meet, and measures that interfered with people's rights were considered temporary. Even the first AI was set to expire on 31 January 1966.

Several measures in AI-1 were intended to strengthen executive power and reduce the domain of Congress. The president was authorized to send bills to Congress. The Chamber of Deputies had 30 days to consider them, as did the Senate. If either house took longer, the bills were considered to be approved. Since it was easy to stall votes in Congress, and since Congress managed to drag out its deliberations, approval of executive bills through "elapse of time on debate" (*decurso de prazo*) became common. The president was also the only one empowered with proposing bills that would create or increase public spending.

Parliamentary immunity was suspended, and the Revolutionary Supreme Command was authorized to cancel mandates and to suspend politicians' political rights for a period of ten years. The seniority rights and employment guarantees which other public employees enjoyed were suspended for six months in order to facilitate civil service purges.

The act also created the foundations for setting up *Inquéritos Policial-Militares* (Police and Military Investigations) or IPMs to deal with people responsible for "crimes against the state or its patrimony, as well as for crimes of a social or political nature, and for acts of revolutionary war."

Based on these exceptional powers, the regime's enemies began to be persecuted, arrested, and tortured. But the system was not yet entirely closed. In court, people still had the right of habeas corpus, and the press was still relatively untrammeled. Largely because of the Rio de Janeiro newspaper *Correio da Manhã* and its reports of torture, President Castelo Branco ordered an investigation presided over by the then president of the Casa Militar (Military House), General Ernesto Geisel. His investigation was shelved "owing to insufficient evidence," but at any rate, for some time, torture stopped being a systematic practice.

Students who had stood out politically during the Goulart period were especially targeted for repression. Immediately, on 1 April, the headquarters of the UNE were invaded and burned in Rio de Janeiro. After being officially dissolved, the UNE continued to operate clandestinely. The universities themselves were another special target. The University of Brasília, which had been created with the purpose of renewing Brazilian university life, was considered subversive by the military and was invaded one day after the coup.

But the most violent repression occurred in the countryside, especially in the Northeast, where people involved with peasant leagues were singled out. In cities, many unions and worker federations were taken over, and their leaders were jailed. As a rule, these takeovers were aimed at the stronger unions, including 70 percent of organizations with over 5,000 members.

In 1964, 49 judges were purged. Fifty congressmen had their mandates canceled. Of the 40 deputies who lost their mandates on the first go-round, the PTB was in the lead with 18. Not a single member of the UDN was ousted from Congress.

Conservative estimates indicate that more than 1,400 people were dismissed from the civil service and around 1,200 from the armed forces. People who had shown themselves to be nationalistic and leftists were especially targeted. Some governors were removed from office. Among the better-known figures whose mandates were canceled or who lost their political rights, in addition to Goulart and Brizola obviously, were Quadros and Kubitschek, who at that time was a senator from the state of Goiás. In Kubitschek's case, the government clearly intended to eliminate a prestigious civilian candidate from future presidential elections.

Everything said up to this point is inadequate in its portrayal of the climate of fear and betrayal that gradually overtook the country. In June 1964, the military regime took an important step toward controlling the citizenry by creating the Serviço Nacional de Informações (National Information Bureau) or SNI. It was the brainchild of its first director – General Golbery do Couto e Silva. The SNI's explicit objective was to "collect and analyze data pertaining to national security, counterintelligence, and information on matters of internal subversion." In practice, the SNI became a center of power almost as important as the president. It was entirely on its own in the "struggle against the internal enemy." Later on, in an attempt to justify his actions, General Golbery went so far as to claim that he had unwittingly created a monster.

AI-1 had provided for the election of a president by an indirect vote in Congress. On 15 April 1964, General Humberto de Alencar Castelo Branco was elected president. His term of office would last until 31 January 1966. The men who had taken power were largely individuals with strong connections to the ESG or Higher War College. The president himself had been one of its directors. Politically, Castelo Branco's backers had the goal of instituting a "restricted democracy" once they carried out the surgery called for in AI-1. Economically, they sought to reform Brazilian capitalism, to modernize it both as an end in itself and as a way of containing the Communist menace. To reach these objectives, they needed to take on the chaotic economic and financial situation coming from the last few months of the Goulart administration; they needed to control the urban and rural working masses; and they needed to promote reform within the governmental apparatus.

To pursue the first of these goals the Programa de Ação Econômica do Governo (Government Economic Action Program) or PAEG was founded. It was under the aegis of Minister of Planning Roberto Campos and Minister of Finance Octávio Gouveia de Bulhões. The PAEG tried to reduce the public sector deficit, to restrict private credit, and to shrink salaries. It sought to control states' expenditures by proposing a law that prohibited them from contracting debts without federal authorization. Equilibrium in the nation's finances was obtained by improving circumstances in public firms, by cutting subsidies for basic products such as wheat and petroleum, and by increasing tax collection. The first two measures had an immediate impact on the cost of living since it was necessary to raise rates for utilities like electricity and telephone service. And the price of gasoline and bread had also to be raised.

The increase in tax collection was obtained by better use of the state machine, which up to then had been notoriously deficient. The introduction of *correção monetária* (adjustment for inflation) in the payment of back taxes helped, at least in part. Being in debt to the state was no longer the good deal it had been. Salary readjustment formulas were set below the rate of inflation. This was accompanied by anti-strike legislation and measures which facilitated laying off workers, to the advantage of business.

The strike law approved by Congress in June 1964 created bureaucratic demands that made legal work stoppages practically impossible. It is, however, well to remember that in almost 20 years of democratic government, Congress had not approved a single law embodying the constitutional precept of the right to strike. However, in practice, the right to strike was freely exercised during the later years of that period.

The government ended one of the most highly regarded rights of urban salaried workers – lifelong employment after ten years' service, guaranteed by the Consolidação das Leis do Trabalho

(Consolidated Labor Laws) or CLT. The government's substitute appeared in September 1966, when it created a compensatory mechanism, the Fundo de Garantia por Tempo de Serviço (Service Time Guarantee Fund).

As far as rural Brazil was concerned, the Castelo Branco government's repressive policy against so-called agitators was accompanied by measures intended to get solutions underway for the problem of land tenure. In November 1964, Congress approved the Estatuto de Terra (Land Statute), whose purpose was to get agrarian reform underway and to promote an agricultural policy. But this law, just like other instruments that came later, was little more than words on paper.

One of the important central changes of Ministers Campos and Bulhões was enacted in the area of foreign commerce. They broke away from the then popular idea of "strangling of exports," that is, from the idea that Brazil's exports should be limited because they were not viable internationally. Campos and Bulhões felt that Brazil's potential had been underestimated. So they undertook a campaign for exports – not only to exploit the country's enormous natural resources and to market agricultural produce, but also to promote manufactured goods abroad. They expected foreign capital to come in, especially into the export sector. To encourage its flow, in August 1964 a new law was approved (thanks to Congress's inaction). It regulated foreign investment and the sending of profits abroad. The government revoked a restrictive law that in 1962 had occasioned protests from Americans and from foreign investors in general.

The PAEG accomplished its objectives. The cut in spending combined with increased tax collection reduced the yearly public deficit from 4.2 percent of the GDP in 1963 to 3.2 percent in 1964 and to 1.6 percent in 1965. The high rate of inflation in 1964 tended to decrease gradually and the GDP once more began to grow in 1966.

Why was the PAEG successful while other plans were not? Campos and Bulhões had adequately diagnosed the situation, but that is not the whole explanation. An authoritarian regime made the government's action easier. In order to work, any stabilization plan depended on sacrifices from society. Given the characteristics of Brazilian society and the narrow vision of the political actors, this

was hard to bring about in democratic circumstances. The authoritarian government allowed Campos and Bulhões to take measures
that entailed forced sacrifices, especially for the working class, which
could not fight back. The critical problem of Brazil's foreign debt
could be provisionally solved thanks to a green light from the IMF
and massive aid from the United States through the Alliance for
Progress.

Internationally, the Castelo Branco government clearly got in line
with American policy. During the civil war that broke out in the
Dominican Republic in the early months of 1965, the United States
intervened in the conflict and sent 42,000 marines to that island.
Along with Honduras and Paraguay, Brazil also agreed to send
troops, as part of the "Inter-American Peace Force."

In October 1965, direct elections were held in 11 states. By this
time, most of the enthusiasm for the revolution had died down. It
was hard to go on kidding oneself with the propaganda concerning
the end of corruption, and the pockets of the middle class were
empty.

In spite of armed forces hard-liners' vetoes of certain candidates,
the opposition won in important states such as Guanabara and
Minas Gerais. The election returns startled the military. The hard-
line groups opposed to Castelo Branco considered the election to
be proof that the government was very soft on its enemies. They
advocated an authoritarian regime with strict military control of
the decision-making process so they could carry on the fight against
Communism and corruption.

Under pressure from these sectors, only 24 days after the state
elections, Castelo Branco decreed Institutional Act number two in
October 1965. AI-2 established once and for all that the president
and vice-president would be elected within Congress and by an
absolute majority – in a public, roll-call vote. AI-2 strengthened the
president's powers even more by establishing that he could issue
decree-laws dealing with matters of national security. The government began to legislate on important matters through decree-
laws, and it extended the concept of national security to fit its
needs.

Another important measure contained in AI-2 was the extinction
of all political parties. The military held the multiparty system partly

responsible for the political crises. Thus the parties created at the close of the Estado Novo came to an end. For better or for worse, these parties had represented different currents of public opinion.

Legislation on political parties mandated, in practice, the formation of only two parties: the Aliança Renovadora Nacional (National Alliance for Renewal) or ARENA, which was the government party; and the Movimento Democrático Brasileiro (Brazilian Democratic Movement) or MDB for the entire opposition. The majority of the politicians who joined ARENA had belonged to the UDN, and an almost equal number came from the PSD. The MDB was formed by people from the PTB and, to a lesser extent, from the PSD.

The Castelo Branco government completed its tinkering with Brazil's institutions and had Congress approve a new constitution in January 1967. With more mandates canceled, Congress was shut down for a month during October 1966. It met once more in an extraordinary session to approve the new constitution. The 1967 constitution incorporated the legislation which had broadened executive powers, especially those pertaining to national security. It did not, however, contain special provisions for canceling mandates and depriving people of their political rights.

Castelo Branco's supporters were not able to name his successor. General Arthur da Costa e Silva was elected president and Pedro Aleixo, from the UDN, was elected vice-president. They took office in March 1967.

In spite of having been Castelo Branco's minister of war, Costa e Silva was an outsider to the group. The "Old Uncle," as he was called by the 1964 conspirators, had had a solid military career which included months of training in the United States and the command of the Fourth Army during the tense years of 1961 and 1962. His style, however, did not jibe with that of the more intellectual Castelo Branco. He was not interested in difficult texts on military strategy; instead he preferred lighter reading and horse races. More significant than these differences in personality was the fact that the hard-liners and authoritarian nationalists in the armed forces put their hopes on Costa e Silva. They were unhappy with Castelo Branco's policy of rapprochement with the United States and the incentives given to foreign capital.

However, Costa e Silva, once in power, did not become a mere tool of the hard-liners. He took societal pressures into account, he built bridges with the opposition, and he listened to the voice of discord. At the same time, he began an offensive in the labor sector and encouraged the organization of unions and the formation of union leaderships that he could trust. Events would cause this policy of restricted liberalization to stumble, however.

6.2 POLITICAL CLOSURE AND ARMED STRUGGLE

Starting in 1966, once the first impact of repression had passed, the opposition began to gather strength. Many members of the church hierarchy openly challenged the government. Especially noticeable was Dom Hélder Câmara, archbishop of Olinda and Recife, in the Northeast. Students also began to mobilize through the UNE. In the political scenario, Lacerda had been cast aside. He approached his traditional enemies, Goulart and Kubitschek, to form the Frente Ampla (Wide Front). When they met in Montevideo, the front's leaders chose to fight for Brazil's redemocratization and for workers' rights.

In 1968, a highly charged year for the entire world, mobilizations in Brazil stepped up. The catalyst for street demonstrations was the death of a student who was killed by the Military Police during a small demonstration in Rio de Janeiro, in March. Thousands of people attended his funeral. Public indignation grew with the outbreak of further violence. These events created the conditions for a wider mobilization which took in students, representative sectors of the church, and the Rio de Janeiro middle class. The high point of these converging forces dedicated to struggle for democracy was the so-called Passeata dos 100,000 (Protest March of the Hundred Thousand) in June 1968.

At the same time, there were two aggressive, but very different, worker strikes: in Contagem, near Belo Horizonte, and in Osasco, in the greater São Paulo area. While the strike in Contagem was up to a certain point spontaneous, the one in Osasco (July 1968) was the result of the combined efforts of workers and students. It began with their occupation of a large firm. This show of strength, in which a strike was used to prove a point to the government, came out badly. The minister of labor intervened in the metal workers' union and a heavily armed military contingent violently routed the strikers. The Osasco strike suffered from the influence of leftist groups who believed that only an armed struggle would bring down the military government. These groups were influenced to a large degree by the Cuban revolution and by the appearance of guerrilla rebels in several Latin American countries: Guatemala, Colombia, Venezuela, and Peru.

In Brazil, the long-standing leftist organization, the PCB, was opposed to armed struggle. In 1967, a group headed by the veteran Communist Carlos Marighela broke with the party and formed the Aliança de Libertação Nacional (Alliance for National Liberation) or ALN. The AP had already chosen armed struggle and new groups began to appear, among them the Vanguarda Popular Revolucionária (People's Revolutionary Vanguard) or VPR, which contained a large contingent of leftist military men.

Groups dedicated to armed struggle first began to act in 1968. A bomb was planted in the American consulate in São Paulo. "Expropriations," that is, robberies to gather funds, also began to occur. All these facts were sufficient to reinforce hard-liners in their conviction that the revolution was being lost, and it was necessary to create new means of doing away with subversives. The pretext for ending restricted liberalization was a seemingly innocuous act, a speech given in Congress by Deputy Márcio Moreira Alves. It was considered offensive to the armed forces.

The text of the speech, which was unknown to the public at large, was circulated through the armed forces. Once an air of indignation was created, government ministers from the military demanded that the Supreme Court allow Moreira Alves to be charged with offending the armed forces' dignity. It was up to the Congress to permit the process to begin. In an unexpected decision, Congress refused to suspend Moreira Alves's parliamentary immunity. Less than 24 hours later, on 13 December 1968, Costa e Silva announced AI-5, which closed Congress.

AI-5 was the tool of a revolution within a revolution, or of a counterrevolution within a counterrevolution. Contrary to the earlier acts, this one had no date of expiration. The president regained his power to shut Congress down, which he had lost in the 1967 constitution. AI-5 reestablished presidential power to cancel mandates and to suspend political rights, as well as to dismiss or to retire public servants. With AI-5, the military nucleus of power became concentrated in the so-called information community, that is, among those people in command of intelligence and repression. Another cycle of canceled mandates began, along with more losses of political rights and public service purges – including many university professors. Censorship of the media was put into practice. And torture became an integral part of the government's methods.

One of AI-5's many tragic effects was that it strengthened the theses of groups dedicated to armed struggle. The military government appeared incapable of giving in to social pressure and of reforming itself. To the contrary, it began to act more and more like a brutal dictatorship. Starting in 1969, armed encounters multiplied.

In August 1969, Costa e Silva suffered a stroke which left him paralyzed. The military ministers decided to replace him – in violation of the constitution, which stipulated that the vice-president, Pedro Aleixo, should succeed him.

Radical leftists began to kidnap members of the foreign diplomatic corps in order to exchange them for Brazilian political prisoners. The incident with the greatest impact was the kidnapping of the United States ambassador in Rio de Janeiro. In exchange for freeing Ambassador Burke Elbrick, the kidnappers obtained the release of 15 political prisoners who were sent to Mexico.

The ruling junta created a banishment penalty. Any Brazilian who "might become inconvenient, prejudicial, or dangerous to National Security" would be expelled from the country. The first to be banished were the prisoners exchanged for the American ambassador. The death penalty was established for cases of "subversive warfare," but was never formally applied. There were, instead, summary executions, or people died during torture. These cases were passed off as the result of clashes between subversives and the forces of order or as mysterious disappearances.

Up to 1969, the Centro de Informações da Marinha (Naval Intelligence Center) or CENIMAR was the organization most blatantly involved in torture. In 1969, Operação Bandeirantes or OBAN appeared in São Paulo. It was connected to the Second Army, whose radius of action was the Rio–São Paulo axis. OBAN gave way to the Destacamento de Operações e Informações de Defesa Interna (Operations and Intelligence Detachment for Internal Defense) or DOI-CODI. DOI-CODI became the military regime's principal torture center and had offices in several states.

While the country was enduring one of its most murky political periods, the government was successful in the economic arena. Campos and Bulhões had stabilized finances during a relatively short recession. After this, Finance Minister Delfim Neto tried to stimulate economic growth by expanding credit. At the same time, he set up price controls to keep down inflation, which, having leveled off at 25.4 percent in 1968, began to decline. There was a vigorous industrial recovery in 1968 headed by the automotive, chemical, and electrical industries. Construction in the private sector grew considerably owing to funds supplied by the Banco Nacional de Habitação (National Bank for Housing) or BNH. In 1968 and 1969, the economy grew at an impressive pace. The GDP increased by 11.2 percent in 1968 and by 10 percent the following year. This corresponds to per capita increases of 8.1 percent and 6.8 percent respectively. The "economic miracle" was underway.

Halfway through October 1969, Costa e Silva was still alive, but had no possibility of recovering. The junta's solution was to declare vacant the posts of president and vice-president and to schedule an election for these positions. The election would be held in Congress on 25 October. The high command of the armed forces chose General Emílio Garrastazu Médici as president and Minister of the Navy Augusto Rademaker as vice-president.

Médici was from Rio Grande do Sul, just like Costa e Silva. He was of Italian background on his father's side, while his mother was a Basque. During the 1950s, he had been chief of Costa e Silva's general staff when the latter was commandant of the Third Military Region. They became close friends. He supported the movement in 1964, and, after Goulart's fall, Médici was named military attaché in Washington. When Costa e Silva became president, Médici was appointed chief of the National Intelligence Bureau (SNI).

Médici was a name unknown to most of the public. On top of this, he did not take pleasure in power. He delegated running the government to his ministers. This brought about a paradoxical situation in which presidential command was divided while his government was the most repressive in Brazilian history.

The armed urban groups, which at the beginning had created the impression of destabilizing the regime with their spectacular deeds, began to decline and for all intents and purposes disappeared. This denouement was the result, in part, of the efficacy of repression. It swept up activists involved in the armed struggle and their sympathizers, who were mainly young professionals. The other factor was the groups' isolation from the majority of the population, whose interest in their action was minimal or nonexistent. The radical Left had been totally mistaken when it thought it could turn Brazil into another Vietnam.

There was one last focus of rural guerrilla warfare, begun by the PC do B (Communist Party of Brazil) in the Araguaia River basin next to Marabá, in the western part of Pará State. During 1971 and 1972, the guerrillas, some 70 in all, made connections with local peasants and taught them methods of cultivation and health care. The army discovered this focus in 1972, but repression there was not as efficient as it had been in dealing with urban guerrillas. It was only in 1975, after the region was turned into a national security zone, that the army was able to capture or finish off this group. None of this was made known to the public at large since dissemination of news about the matter was prohibited. At best, scattered rumors circulated concerning guerrilla action in the Araguaia region.

On the other hand, the legal opposition reached its nadir during the Médici administration. This was the result of favorable economic conditions, repression, and, to a lesser extent, a campaign for casting blank ballots. During the 1970 congressional elections, when two-thirds of the senators were reelected, ARENA won by a landslide.

The Médici administration did not stop at repression. During those years of economic prosperity, it clearly distinguished between a significant social minority that was against the regime and the great bulk of the population whose daily life was acceptable. The government directed its repressive measures at the first group, whereas its propaganda was designed at least to neutralize the second group.

After 1964, Brazil's telecommunications improved tremendously. Easy personal credit made it possible for more and more people to own television sets. In 1960, only 9.5 percent of urban residences had televisions. In 1970, this proportion had risen to 40 percent. During this time, thanks to the benefits it received from the government, TV Globo expanded and became the national network and controlled the medium. It also became the government's mouthpiece – a propaganda channel the likes of which had never existed in Brazil. The campaign promoting "Brazil – a Great Power" caught the nation's imagination. During this period, many older, middle-class Brazilians bemoaned the fact that they would not live until the millennium, when Brazil would be on an equal footing with Japan.

The so-called miracle extended from 1969 to 1973. It combined extraordinary economic growth with relatively low rates of inflation. The GDP grew at a yearly average of 11.2 percent during the period and reached its apex in 1973, with a 13 percent increase. Average yearly inflation did not go beyond 18 percent.

There was an earthly explanation for the miracle. Led by Delfim Neto, the technicians who had planned it took advantage, in the first place, of a worldwide economic situation characterized by an ample availability of funds. The more advanced developing countries took advantage of the new opportunities to take out foreign loans. These countries' (nonproducers of petroleum) total foreign debt increased from under 40 billion dollars in 1967 to 97 billion in 1972 and to 375 billion in 1980. Together with the loans, foreign investment in Brazil also grew. In 1973, 4.3 billion dollars flowed in. That was almost twice the amount for 1971 and over three times the amount for 1970.

One of the most important areas of foreign investment was the automotive industry, which led industrial growth with yearly increases of over 30 percent. Widened consumer credit and new production norms, which made it possible to manufacture medium-sized cars, brought in tremendous investments from General Motors, Ford, and Chrysler.

Foreign trade expanded greatly. Increased importation of certain goods was necessary to sustain economic growth. Exports diversified. The concession of favorable terms of credit, exemptions from or reductions in export tariffs, and other measures designed to subsidize exports were some of the government's incentives for exporting manufactured goods.

The effort to diversify, to make Brazil less dependent on a single product, paid off. Between 1947 and 1964, coffee accounted for 57 percent of Brazil's export revenue. Between 1965 and 1971, it fell to 37 percent, and between 1972 and 1975 it sank to 15 percent. In addition, Brazil's ability to collect taxes and tariffs increased, which helped reduce the public debt and checked inflation.

But the miracle had its weak points and its negative side. Its main point of vulnerability was its excessive dependence on the financial system and on international commerce. They created the easy terms for foreign loans, for the investment of foreign capital, and for the expansion of exports. Economic growth made Brazil more and more dependent on certain imported products, the most important of them being petroleum.

The negative aspects of the miracle were mainly of a social nature. Delfim Neto's economic policy favored the accumulation of capital, as has been indicated. It also created anticipatory rates of salary increases while it underestimated the rate of inflation. From the point of view of personal consumption, industrial expansion, especially the automobile industry's expansion, favored high- and medium-income classes and pinched unskilled workers' wages.

This produced an accentuated concentration of income, a long-standing feature of Brazilian society. If the minimum wage of January 1959 had been 100, that wage would have fallen to 39 in January 1973. This datum is especially significant if one considers that in 1972 52 percent of the working population was making less than one minimum wage, and 22 percent was making between one and two minimum wages. The social impact of income discrepancies was, however, attenuated. The growth in job opportunities allowed many more people within a single family to work.

Another negative but lasting offshoot of the miracle was the imbalance between economic growth and the decline or even abandonment of state-sponsored social programs. Brazil became notorious worldwide for its high industrial potential coupled with low standards of health, education, and housing – factors which measure a nation's quality of life.

"Savage capitalism" characterized the miracle and the years to come. Its massive projects had no regard for nature or for local inhabitants. The word "ecology" had scarcely been added to dictionaries, and industrial and automobile pollution was thought of as a blessing. During the Médici administration, the Trans-Amazonia Highway exemplified this spirit. It was constructed to guarantee Brazilian control of the region, whose loss was a specter that eternally haunted the military. It was also a means of settling Northeastern workers in farming villages. After wreaking considerable havoc and fattening certain firms, the endeavor was abandoned as a fiasco.

As was the case with Castelo Branco, Médici was not able to name his successor. Halfway through 1973, the armed forces nominated General Ernesto Geisel. Geisel was born in Rio Grande do Sul, the son of a German Lutheran who had come to Brazil in 1890. Alongside his career in the army, the general had occupied administrative posts, the most important of which was that of president of Petrobrás. He also had his sights trained on politics. He collaborated with the Dutra administration and helped to formulate the compromise that brought João Goulart to power in 1961. His connections to Castelo Branco and his followers were notorious. And he was a member of the permanent corps of the Escola Superior de Guerra (ESG) and chief of Castelo Branco's Casa Militar. In his capacity as chief, he was instrumental in keeping the hard-liners in check.

Within the military, Geisel was not chosen because he favored liberalization. He was chosen because of his ability to lead and because of his administrative skills. Also influential in this choice was the fact that his brother, Orlando Geisel, was minister of the army. In opposition to Geisel, the MDB nominated Ulysses Guimarães as its symbolic candidate. He would attack indirect elections, the suppression of freedom, and the income inequities produced by the economic model of the time.

A 1967 constitutional amendment changed how the president was to be chosen. This amendment set up an electoral college made up of members of Congress and delegates from the states' legislative assemblies. Geisel was the first president chosen by the Electoral College. He was elected in January 1974 and took office on 15 March.

6.3   THE PROCESSES OF POLITICAL LIBERALIZATION

The Geisel administration has been associated with the beginning of political liberalization, which the president defined as slow, gradual, and secure. This program of liberalization was first referred to as "distension." It was, in practice, a difficult process with timid advances and retreats. There were several reasons for this. On the one hand, Geisel was under pressure from the hardliners, who held onto most of their strength. On the other hand, he too wanted to control liberalization or *abertura* (opening), as it is called in Portuguese. Geisel wanted it to lead to a then-undefined conservative democracy in which the opposition would not come to power too quickly. Thus, abertura was slow, gradual, and insecure, since hardliners threatened reaction constantly and all the way to and through the Figueiredo government (1979–1985).

The distension strategy was conceived by the president and General Golbery, the head of Geisel's civilian cabinet. Why did Geisel and Golbery decide to support liberalization? Could their decision have been the fruit of pressure from the opposition? Without doubt, by 1973 the opposition had begun to show clear signs of life on its own. The rift between the Catholic church and the state had been very taxing on the government. Geisel's transition team tried to build bridges to the church based on a specific point of understanding – the struggle against torture.

However, the opposition and the church were not the most sensitive indicators of the need to loosen up. The main indicator could be found in the relations between the armed forces and power itself, which had been taken over by the organizations of repression. The armed forces hierarchy reacted negatively to this state of affairs. The military's function and its basic principles had been distorted, which had jeopardized the integrity of the armed forces. To preserve the hierarchy, it had become necessary to neutralize the hard line, to tone down repression, and, in an orderly fashion, to support "the return of the military to its barracks."

The government began to wage a backstage war against the hard line. At the same time, it allowed the November 1974 legislative elections to be held in an atmosphere of relative liberty, granting parties access to radio and television. ARENA was expected to win with ease, but the election returns surprised the government when they indicated a considerable MDB gain, especially in the larger cities and the more developed states. During 1975, Geisel combined liberalizing measures with repressive ones. He suspended censorship of newspapers, and he authorized a strong crackdown on the PCB, which was blamed for the MDB's victory.

A public confrontation between the administration and the hard line finally occurred in São Paulo. While guerrilla warfare had been eliminated, military hard-liners continued to see subversives everywhere. Torture was still going on and was even increased as people "disappeared." In October 1975, during a wave of repression, a newspaperman by the name of Vladimir Herzog, one of the editors of the state television channel, was told to present himself to the DOI-CODI in São Paulo. He was suspected of having ties with the PCB. Herzog showed up at the DOI-CODI, but did not come out alive. His death was presented as a suicide by hanging – a crude cover-up for torture followed by death.

Herzog's death produced a massive public outcry in São Paulo, especially among middle-class professionals and the Catholic church. The church and the Ordem dos Advogados do Brasil (Brazilian Bar Association) or OAB mobilized and denounced the systematic use of torture and assassination cover-ups.

A few months later, in January 1976, a metal worker by the name of Manoel Fiel Filho died in circumstances reminiscent of Herzog's. Once again, the official version was suicide by hanging. President Geisel decided to act. An unofficial repressive organ had been set up in São Paulo with the blessing, or at least compliance, of the commandant of the Second Army. Geisel replaced him with a general he trusted completely. This man had a different orientation and began to build bridges to society. While violence did not come to an end in São Paulo, torture ceased in the branches of DOI-CODI.

After the November 1974 election, political campaigns began to worry the administration. Municipal elections were scheduled for November 1976, and the possibility that ARENA might be defeated was real.

Months before, in July 1976, an amendment to electoral legislation barred candidates' access to radio and television. This law was proposed by the minister of justice and was known as the Falcão

Law. In principle, it would handicap both ARENA and the MDB, but the opposition (MDB) was the big loser because it lost its best opportunity to make its ideas known. Even so, the MDB won mayoral elections as well as majorities in the city councils of 59 of the 100 largest cities in Brazil.

Geisel tightened his siege when, in April 1977, after recessing Congress, he introduced a series of measures known as the April Package. The April Package included the creation of "bionic senators," whose purpose was to keep the MDB from having a majority in the Senate. Bionic senators were elected, or better yet "manufactured," in the indirect elections of an electoral college. Simultaneously, in 1978, the administration called for meetings with opposition leaders and the church. Their purpose was to advance the process of restoring public freedom. Beginning in 1979, AI-5 was no longer in effect, and individual freedom and Congress's independence were restored.

The MDB did well in the legislative elections of 1978. The party had become the political channel for public dissatisfaction; it included every political persuasion, from liberals to socialists. The electoral campaigns of 1978 had support from militants belonging to different sectors of civilian society: students, union members, lawyers, and members of the Catholic church's base communities. These groups set up a bridge between the MDB and the population at large, which attenuated the serious inconvenience of lacking free access to radio and television.

The MDB garnered 57 percent of the valid senatorial votes, but did not gain a majority in the upper house. This is because senatorial representation is by state, and not proportional. In addition, the bionic senators were still there. ARENA held the majority in the Chamber of Deputies with 231 seats as opposed to the MDB's 189. Most of the MDB's votes were cast in the more developed states and in the larger cities. Its share of the votes in São Paulo was 83 percent, in Rio de Janeiro State 63 percent, and in Rio Grande do Sul, 62 percent. Still, the administration held onto its majorities in Congress.

In October 1973, during the Médici administration, the first international oil crisis occurred. It was a consequence of the so-called Yom Kippur war against Israel, which the Arab states had started.

This crisis deeply affected Brazil, which imported more than 80 percent of the oil it used. But in March 1974 when General Geisel was sworn in, there was still some of the miracle-related euphoria in the air. Economic policy was put into the hands of Mário Henrique Simonsen and João Paulo dos Reis Veloso. Simonsen replaced Delfim Neto in the Ministry of Finance, whereas Reis Veloso was a holdover from the Médici administration.

The new administration began the Second National Development Plan (PND II). The first plan, intended to stabilize finances and fight inflation, had been formulated by the Médici government in 1967. The second plan sought to complete the process that had been set up years before to phase out imports. It was no longer a matter of replacing the importation of consumer goods. The goal now was to enter the terrain of basic input (oil, steel, aluminum, fertilizers, etc.) as well as to enter the terrain of the capital goods industry.

The second plan's concern with the problem of energy was obvious – it proposed further oil exploration, a nuclear program, partial replacement of gasoline by alcohol, and the construction of hydroelectric plants. The most important hydroelectric plant was Itaipu, on the Paraná River, between Brazil and Paraguay. This was a joint endeavor between Brazil and Paraguay. Itaipu, which began to operate in 1984, is the largest hydroelectric plant in the world.

Instead of slowing down the economy, in 1974 the government had opted for growth. This decision was based as much on economic criteria as it was on political factors. The insistence on growth showed how strongly Brazil's ruling sectors believed that the country was destined to grow. This belief was not merely a product of the miracle years; it began back in the 1950s. On the other hand, the distension policy was not conducive to a government-induced recession that would weigh most heavily on the wage-earning masses. If the opposition had grown during relatively good economic times, what would happen if there were a recession?

The second plan for national development tried to encourage private industry to invest in the production of capital goods. All BNDE (National Development Bank) incentives and credits were aimed at capital goods. However, this new policy put state economic firms at center stage. The gigantic investments by Eletrobrás, Petrobrás,

Embratel (telecommunications), and other public enterprises were, strictly speaking, the mainspring of the operation.

Many businessmen, especially those from São Paulo, had reservations about where this new economic policy was headed. And their doubts gave rise to a campaign against excessive state intervention. A dominant sector of civilian society was attempting to intervene in the political scene, which up to then had been the jurisdiction of technocrats and the military.

There is considerable controversy among economists concerning the consequences of the second development plan. At one extreme, there are people who see the plan as an untimely attempt at accelerated growth which only put off economic adjustment and exacerbated the problem of foreign debt. At the other extreme, people believe that the plan was a veritable about-face in Brazil's industrialization, and that it made a qualitative leap toward replacing imports.

Using hindsight, one can see that the plan suffered from setbacks caused by the worldwide recession and from the rise in interest rates – in addition to a basic flaw. The plan adopted a pattern of industrialization that was being abandoned in the more advanced countries of the industrialized world because of its negative aspects. Industries such as steel, aluminum, and chlorine consume great quantities of energy and create tremendous pollution. Notwithstanding all these reservations, it is important to point out that beginning with PND II some important gains were made in replacing imports – especially imported oil.

A problem that had existed from the time of the miracle was that accelerated economic growth used idle plant capacity as an important brake wheel. To go on growing, greater investment would be necessary, which would require more and greater foreign resources, since the internal money supply was insufficient. These outside resources could be found. They came into Brazil mostly in the form of loans. This, however, increased Brazil's public and private foreign debt. At the end of 1978, Brazil was 43.5 billion dollars in debt, which was more than twice the national debt of 1975.

On top of this, interest payments on the debt weighed more heavily on the balance of payments, since most of the loans had been taken out with floating interest rates. And rising interest rates were a sign of the times, so Brazil was left to cope with heavier and heavier burdens incurred to service its debt. The international rise in interest rates was the result of an American policy. The United States was trying to lessen its balance of payments deficit by attracting capital from other countries.

It cannot be said that the funds acquired through loans were thrown out the window or were used only to fatten a few middlemen. All this happened, but employment of these funds in expensive, poorly administered projects of only long-term or dubious gain was an even greater problem.

In raw numbers, the Geisel period produced satisfactory results. Between 1974 and 1978, the GDP grew at an average annual rate of 6.7 percent, or at a per capita rate of 4.2 percent. Inflation was pegged at an average annual rate of 37.9 percent during the same period. The situation was dangerous, however. This relatively moderate inflation was artificial, because goods produced by state enterprises were sold below cost, which put these firms farther and farther into the red. The foreign debt went on growing, and there was no way of servicing it other than by taking out more loans. Another problem loomed on the horizon: Brazil's internal debt had become unwieldy. The mechanism known as *correção monetária* (readjustment for inflation) and the high interest rates compromised the national budget. Salary readjustment, which only occurred once a year, exacerbated wage-earners' dissatisfaction.

The military government kept union leaders linked to populism under its thumb, but it did not dismantle unions. In the countryside, the Confederação Nacional dos Trabalhadores Agrícolas (National Confederation of Farm Workers) or CONTAG had, by 1968, begun to act independently and encouraged the formation of rural federations and unions throughout Brazil. The number of rural unions had been 625 in 1968. It grew to 1,154 in 1972, to 1,745 in 1976, and to 2,144 in 1980. The tremendous increase in unionized rural workers after 1973, from a little more than 2.9 million to more than 5.1 million in 1979, was brought about through the administration of social programs by the unions.

Under the influence of the church and its Comissão Pastoral da Terra (Pastoral Land Commission), militant groups began to appear. Thus in the countryside a curious situation arose: the government assistance policy helped give rise to an active social movement. The old alternatives of a struggle for land or for extending workers' rights to agricultural workers had divided the rural movement before 1964. These issues now divided it even more. Depending on the particular scenario, unions emphasized one or the other of these alternatives. The struggle for land continued and even strengthened. At the same time, events such as the cane workers' strike in Pernambuco, which began in 1979, alerted people to the new state of affairs in the rural world.

On the other hand, white collar unions sprang up. These included not just traditionally organized workers such as bank employees and teachers, but also doctors and public health workers. Unionization in these professions was linked to a change in their nature: arenas formally dominated by independent professionals were ceding ground to physicians who worked for salaries.

During the Geisel administration, the workers' movement resurfaced with greater momentum and with different features. Unionism was now relatively independent of the state. It often began at the workplace, and workers themselves organized and broadened their shop committees. The most combative labor organizations were no longer involved with the public sector, but with the automotive industry. The huge concentration of workers in a small number of firms and their density in the "ABC" area around São Paulo were of capital importance in the organization of the new workers' movement. In São Bernardo during 1978, there were around 125,000 workers employed in the manufacture of machinery, and most of them were auto workers. Of those workers, 67.2 percent were employed by companies with over 1,000 workers. During 1976, in the city of São Paulo there were 421,000 in the same branch of industry, but only 20.8 percent of them were employed by firms with over 1,000 workers.

While these conditions are necessary, they are not sufficient to explain the appearance of this new type of unionism. This union movement had been fostered by organizers whose leadership was often linked to the church. The unions' lawyers also played an important role. Even though liberalization had taken a long time in reaching the sphere of collective rights of workers, it did facilitate the workers' movement's emergence.

In August 1977, the government admitted that it had manipulated the officially accepted rates of inflation for 1973 and 1974. Since the official inflation rates determined the rates for salary increases, it was acknowledged that wage-earners' buying power had actually gone down by 31.4 percent during that time. The metalworkers' union in São Bernardo undertook a campaign to bring salaries up to date, and this opened the way to the great strikes of 1978 and 1979, in which millions of workers took part. Union president Luíz Inácio (Lula) da Silva showed himself to be in command both in the daily goings-on of the union and in the huge assemblies that met in São Bernardo. The metalworkers were at the head of a movement that included workers from other sectors. In 1979, nearly 3.2 million Brazilian workers went out on strike. There were 27 work stoppages by metalworkers – 958,000 people all told. At the same time, there were 20 teachers' strikes in which 766,000 workers left their posts. The object of these strikes included a wide range of demands: wage increases, guaranteed work, recognition of factory committees organized by workers, and democratic freedoms.

The spread of strikes in 1979 showed that conservatives were wrong-headed. They believed that São Bernardo was somehow a world apart from the rest of Brazil. But what was happening in São Bernardo had repercussions elsewhere. There is, however, no doubt that ABC unionism sprang forth and grew with features peculiar to itself. Its most important characteristics included greater independence from the state and an increased level of union membership. Around 1978, 43 percent of all workers belonged to a union, and their leadership was free from the influence of the traditional Left, that is, free from the PCB.

General Geisel was able to name his successor – General João Batista Figueiredo, who on 14 October 1978 defeated the MDB candidate in a vote of the Electoral College. Before this, General Figueiredo's nomination had survived another serious test of strength. Minister of the Army Sílvio Frota had declared his own candidacy within the military. He had also sounded Congress out. Frota was the mouthpiece for the hard-liners. He unleashed an offensive in which he accused the government of being soft on subversives. Geisel fired him and halted his campaign.

General Figueiredo had been chief of the military cabinet during the Médici administration and was head of the National Intelligence Bureau (SNI) under Geisel. He seemed cut out to continue in the slow process of liberalization. At the same time, he could neutralize the hard line. At any rate, this was but one of the paradoxes in Brazil's liberalization process – the man chosen to carry it out had been the head of a repressive branch of the government.

The Figueiredo administration combined two traits that many considered incompatible. Political liberalization went forward at the same time that the economic situation worsened. The new president, General Figueiredo, was sworn in during March 1979. He kept Simonsen at the economic helm, as minister of planning. After a stint as ambassador to France, Delfim Neto was appointed minister of agriculture. He did not fit in.

Simonsen's attempt at imposing a tight money policy was attacked from various quarters. Among the attackers, Brazilian businessmen stood out. They benefited from rising inflation. Many people in the government itself also attacked this policy because they wanted money to spend and to be able to show their constituents what they had built. In August 1979, Simonsen left the Ministry of Planning and Delfim Neto, still prestigious owing to the miracle, took his place. The situation had, however, changed, both internally and internationally. The second petroleum crisis, with its rise in the price of oil, worsened Brazil's balance of payments. Internationally, interest rates continued to rise, further complicating everything. It was harder and harder to obtain more loans and terms of payment tightened even more. The sought-after period of economic growth coupled with control of inflation was soon over. Under pressure from foreign creditors, by the end of 1980 Delfim Neto opted for a policy of tight money. Printing more money was severely limited; state corporations' investments were cut back; internal interest rates went up; and private investment also fell off.

The 1981–1983 recession had dire consequences. For the first time since 1947, when the indicators of the GDP were first established, the gross industrial product for 1981 fell by 3.1 percent. For the three years of the recession, the GDP fell at an average annual rate of 1.6 percent. The hardest-hit sectors were those producing durable consumer goods and capital goods. These industries were concentrated in the more urban parts of Brazil so unemployment in these areas became a serious problem.

In spite of all these sacrifices, inflation did not abate appreciably. Having hit a high of 110.2 percent in 1980, inflation fell to 95.2 percent in 1981 and went back up to 99.75 percent in 1982. During those years, "stagflation," a combination of economic stagnation and inflation, was the order of the day.

The Brazilian government was technically insolvent, but it pounded its chest when, in August 1982, Mexico declared bankruptcy and asked for help from the IMF. Government officials said, with an air of superiority, that Brazil is no Mexico. In actuality, Mexico's moratorium on its debt service effectively buried the already scant possibility of getting more foreign loans. And finally, once its dollar reserves were exhausted, Brazil had to ask the IMF for help in February 1983. In exchange for modest financial aid and a chance to restore its international credibility, Brazil accepted the prescription from the IMF, which consisted mainly of efforts to put the country's foreign accounts in order by continuing to service its foreign debt. Internally, it called for cuts in spending and an even greater shrinkage of salaries.

This was followed by a series of disagreements between Brazil and the IMF. In Brazil, there was pressure against restrictive measures and against payment of the foreign debt. The IMF became upset because Brazilians did not live up to their part of the bargain. Given that state of affairs, international creditors did not renew the terms for servicing the Brazilian debt, nor did they offer more favorable interest rates, as they had done for Mexico.

In spite of everything, efforts toward putting the foreign debt in order began to pay off. Starting in 1984, Brazil's economy improved, thanks mainly to a rise in exports of, especially, manufactured goods. The fall in the price of oil made that product's share less weighty among Brazil's imports. In addition, imports of both oil and other products declined thanks to the second national development plan. But inflation kept on rising and reached 223 percent in 1984.

At the beginning of 1985, when Figueiredo left office, the country's financial situation had been remedied temporarily, and the economy began to grow. But the balance for those years is extremely negative. Inflation had gone up from 40.8 percent in 1978 to 223.8 percent in 1984. During the same period, the foreign debt had risen from U.S. $43.5 billion to U.S. $91 billion.

Figueiredo continued with the liberalization process begun under the Geisel administration. General Golbery and Minister of Justice Petrônio Portela Filho were in charge of specific initiatives. In August 1979, Figueiredo snatched away one of the opposition's main banners – the struggle for amnesty. However, the amnesty law approved by Congress was restricted, and it made an important concession to the hard-liners concerning those responsible for torture. At any rate, the law allowed political exiles to return and was a significant step in the direction of individual freedom.

The liberalization process continued to be hampered by the hard line. A series of criminal acts culminated in an attempt to set off bombs at a convention center in Rio de Janeiro. They were to explode during a music festival attended by thousands of young people. One of the bombs did not make it to the center. It went off inside an automobile with two soldiers inside. One of them died on the spot and the other was seriously wounded. The government conducted an investigation which ended up supporting an absurd rendition of the facts and acquitting those responsible for the bombs. Golbery's resignation as head of the Casa Civil, a strategic post in the government, in August 1981 was most assuredly related to his refusal to manipulate the incident.

The electoral legislation passed in 1965 had turned into a trap for those in power. More and more, elections were becoming plebiscites in which people voted for or against the government. The nay votes that went to the MDB were cast by people with many different ideologies and reflected all types of discontent. In an attempt at weakening the opposition, in December 1979 the government got Congress to ratify a new law for setting up political parties. It abolished the MDB and ARENA and obliged new organizations being set up to contain the word *partido* (political party) in their name.

ARENA had a bad reputation, so it tried to perform some window-dressing and became the Partido Democrático Social (Social Democratic Party) or PDS. The MDB leadership was able simply to add the required word to its title, and it became the Partido do Movimento Democrático Brasileiro or PMDB. But the days of a united opposition had passed. Its different factions had united in the face of an all-powerful common enemy. As the authoritarian regime grew more liberal, ideological and personal differences began to emerge with the opposition. The Partido dos Trabalhadores (Workers' Party) or PT sprang forth from a coalition of rural and urban union members, factions within the Catholic church, and the professional middle class. The PT sought to represent the interest of the wide body of wage-earners in Brazil. Its basic program advocated fundamental rights for individuals and social transformations that would lead to socialism. It took a tack that was contrary to the PCB's and against any cult of the Soviet Union. Indeed, it avoided making compromising statements about the nature of its brand of socialism. The party was noncommittal on this issue because there were opposing currents within it. At one extreme, its members supported social democracy; on the other, they advocated a dictatorship of the proletariat. Concerning unions, the party established intimate ties with the labor movement in the ABC triangle around São Paulo. That specific movement was one of the most important factions in the PT, and union leader Luíz Inácio da Silva, or Lula, as he is known, became prominent.

Brizola did not join the PMDB. He ran for office on his own, trying to capitalize on the prestige of the old PTB, which had disappeared during the military government. A court decision deprived him of using the initials PTB, however. So he founded the Partido Democrático Trabalhista (Democratic Labor Party) or PDT.

Lines were also drawn among the unions. In August 1981, the first Conferência Nacional da Classe Trabalhadora (National Conference of the Working Class) or CONCLAT was held and brought together the various currents of Brazilian unionism. Two main factions emerged there. One of them, which was closely allied to the PT, opted for an aggressive line of demands and considered workers' mobilization more important than the meandering path of liberalization. Its mainspring was ABC unionism.

The other faction wanted to restrict union action to struggles that would not put the liberalization process in jeopardy. It had no clear ideological definition, but supported the importance of workers' making immediate, concrete gains. This side included important unions such as the São Paulo Metalworkers, who were controlled by politically less defined unionists and by members of Brazil's two Communist parties.

In 1983, the labor movement identified with the PT founded the Central Unica de Trabalhadores (Workers Unified Center) or CUT with no representation from the so-called moderates. In March 1986, the moderates formed the Central Geral dos Trabalhadores (Workers General Center) or CGT. Thus, two union movements were set up in Brazil. They had opposite outlooks and, over the years, would clash head-on with one another.

Figueiredo stuck to the electoral calendar, which called for elections in November 1982. In spite of the existing restrictions on speech, which included the still valid Falcão Law, there was ample debate during the electoral campaign. In November 1982, more than 48 million Brazilians went to the polls to vote for everything from city councilmen to state governors. For the first time since 1965, governors were being elected by direct ballot.

Congressional elections gave the PDS victories in both the Chamber of Deputies and the Senate. In gubernatorial elections, opposition parties made impressive gains, but the PDS won in most states. The opposition won in São Paulo, Minas Gerais, and Rio de Janeiro. In Rio de Janeiro State, notwithstanding an attempt at electoral fraud, Brizola was elected governor, and this showed that his prestige from the 1960s had not vanished.

During 1983, one of the PT's priorities was to start a drive for direct presidential elections. For the first time, PT leadership was willing to join forces with other parties to attain this objective. After several demonstrations, in January 1984 a huge rally of some 200,000 people was held in São Paulo. From then on, the movement in support of direct elections transcended party organizations and became, for all intents and purposes, a nationwide movement. With an enthusiasm rarely seen in Brazil, millions of people filled the streets of São Paulo and Rio de Janeiro. The campaign known as "Direct Elections Now" showed both the strength of popular sentiment and the difficulty parties had in representing the population effectively. Brazilians put all their hopes on direct elections.

They expected that authentic representation would solve many of their problems: insufficient salaries, personal safety, inflation. But to solve these problems, more was needed than a mere direct presidential election.

And of course there was quite a distance between street demonstrations and a PDS congressional majority. Direct elections depended on a constitutional amendment approved by a two-thirds majority in Congress. With Brazilians' hopes high, the amendment went to the floor in Congress. In Brasília, Figueiredo declared a state of emergency. While the amendment was approved, it did not get sufficient votes to become law.

The rejection of this amendment for direct presidential elections created a good deal of frustration among the people. The battle for presidential succession remained confined to the Electoral College. Three figures were likely PDS candidates: Vice-President Aureliano Chaves, Minister of the Interior Mário Andreazza (also an army colonel), and Paulo Maluf. Maluf had been mayor of São Paulo. He was elected state governor by indirect ballot. He was also elected to the Chamber of Deputies with a landslide vote.

By 1984, the choice of a government candidate did not have to be approved by the military; however, the military still weighed in on any decision. Maluf waged a vigorous campaign among the delegates to the PDS convention and managed to be nominated. In August 1984 he beat out Mário Andreazza. His victory brought about the final split in the PDS forces supporting other candidates. By July, Aureliano Chaves had abandoned his campaign and went to work organizing party dissidents. This led to a new party, the Partido da Frente Liberal (Liberal Front Party) or PFL.

The Liberal Front approached the PMDB, which had nominated Tancredo Neves as its presidential candidate. The two parties signed an accord and, in opposition to Maluf, formed the Aliança Democrática (Democratic Alliance). Tancredo Neves was their candidate for president, and José Sarney for vice-president. The PMDB was considerably skeptical about Sarney because up to then he had been one of the chief figures in the PDS. He had been the PDS president, and as a PDS candidate he was elected senator. His name had little or nothing to do with the democratization banner that the PMDB had raised. But the Liberal Front demanded Sarney and the PMDB relented. No one could have imagined, back then, the far-reaching consequences of that decision.

In spite of being a candidate in an indirect election, Tancredo appeared on television and at rallies. This strengthened his prestige and increased popular support of his candidacy. In an attempt at wining over members of the Electoral College one by one, Maluf tried to utilize his techniques of personal seduction. This time his strategy failed. On 15 January 1985, Neves and Sarney won a clear victory in the Electoral College. By negotiating a difficult trail and using a system imposed by an authoritarian regime, the opposition had come into office.

What were the main traits of the government set up in Brazil after 31 March 1964?

For the first time ever, the armed forces directly took power and ran the government. However, the military rarely acted as a block in the political arena. While there were points of contact, the military was divided into different currents: supporters of Castelo Branco, hard-liners, and nationalists. The power of each one of these groups varied just as appeals to broad sectors of the armed forces varied. Middle-echelon officers were sometimes petitioned in attempts to impose certain candidates or to legitimize specific orientations.

The regime set up in 1964 was not a personal dictatorship. It can be likened to a partnership in which one of the military chiefs, a four-star general, would be chosen to govern for a set period. Change of command was actually accomplished within the military itself, with greater or lesser input from the troops according to the particular case and the final decision of the military high command. In appearances, and according to law, Congress chose the president the ARENA party had nominated. But, setting aside opposition votes, Congress merely solemnized an order from higher up.

The military did not govern alone, and often they did not closely control the civilians with whom they shared power. The government that began in 1964 gave considerable leeway and visibility to individuals involved in formulating economic policy. Delfim Neto and Mario Henrique Simonsen are two cases in point. It also favored certain sectors of the state bureaucracy – especially the directors of state companies. State firms were not run entirely by the military, however. It was possible to see these firms as partnerships between the state's technocrats and the military, which had the final say.

The regime had authoritarian characteristics, but was different from fascism. No effort was made to organize massive governmental support. No attempt was made to build a single party to run the state, nor to devise an ideology that might win over the educated members of society. Quite to the contrary, leftist ideology continued to dominate thought at the universities and among Brazil's intellectuals in general.

The differences between the representative government of 1945 to 1964 and the military government are clear. Professional politicians were no longer in charge, nor was Congress an important decision-making body. The military high command, the bureaus of information and repression, and the state technocrats ran the show.

Populism stopped being used as a means for attaining power. The groups who had had a voice before (the working class, students, and peasants) were all weakened. However, unions were not destroyed, even though many of their leaders were persecuted. The union tax went on being collected, and it guaranteed unions' survival and, as time passed, allowed unions to grow.

The regime was not just a mere instrument of the ruling class, although the latter benefited from the government's policies in different degrees and in different sectors. But for many years the military had nothing to do with carrying out economic policy, which was determined by the powerful ministers of finance and planning, as well as by the state bureaucracy.

In economic policy, some things did not change after 1964. The state continued to play an important role in economic activity and in running the economy. There were variations according to specific administrations. Geisel's government played a greater role in the economy than Castelo Branco's did. But if all did not change, some things did. The model outlined during the Kubitschek administration took on greater dimensions. Foreign loans and incentives for bringing in foreign capital became essential elements for financing and promoting economic development. This favored large firms – multinational and Brazilian, public and private. This was one way the military government made a clear break from the Goulart government, which was built on a populist foundation and included a failed attempt at having Brazil's bourgeoisie support economic development independently.

With Neves's election, the transition to a democratic government was not yet complete; it would still be subjected to a few setbacks. The new president's inauguration, set for 15 March 1985, did not take place. After a trip abroad, Neves was hastily admitted to a hospital in Brasília, where he underwent a controversial operation. There were friends and politicians present in the operating room. This was the first of many operations. While this was going on, Sarney climbed the ramp at the Palácio do Planalto and was inaugurated in the president-elect's stead. Everyone thought this state of affairs would be temporary.

But after this, Neves continued to decline. He was flown to São Paulo and underwent a whole series of operations. The country lived from newsbreak to newsbreak, some of which sustained a false optimism. Neves died on a symbolic date: 21 April, the anniversary of the death of Tiradentes. Throngs poured into the streets to accompany his body, which was sent from São Paulo to Brasília and to Belo Horizonte before reaching his birthplace, where it was buried. These demonstrations had been triggered in part by the commotion coming from a president's death; they were exacerbated by the painful circumstances in which Neves died. But people also felt the country had lost an important political figure at a crucial juncture. Such a belief was not unfounded. Neves had rare qualities in the world of politics: he was honest, balanced, and his positions were coherent. These virtues overrode ideological preferences on the right and on the left.

To make matters worse, Neves's substitute was a johnny-come-lately in the opposition, and he had no authority within the Democratic Alliance. Sarney began to govern under the towering shadow of Neves. He appointed the ministers Neves had selected. Politically speaking, attention was fixed on two points: on revoking the "authoritarian debris," as the military regime's laws restricting democracy were called; and on electing a constituent assembly which would write another constitution. Sarney respected individuals' rights, but he did not sever all his ties with the past. The SNI went on operating and went on receiving substantial monies.

In May 1985, legislation once more provided for direct presidential elections; it gave illiterates the vote; and it legalized all political parties. Both the PCB and the PC do B became legal. They also became minority parties because of the crisis in Stalinism and because of the increasing prestige of the PT in leftist circles. Elections for the national constitutional assembly were set for November 1986. The deputies and senators elected would be given the task of writing another constitution. On that day, there would also be state elections.

When Sarney took office in 1985, the economic outlook was less bleak than it had been previously. The great economic push coming from Brazil's exports had brought growth. The decline of imports and rising exports had produced a trade surplus of U.S. $13 billion. This surplus allowed the interest on Brazil's debt to be paid. In addition, at the end of 1984, the country had accumulated reserves of U.S. $9 billion. Thus there was some room to negotiate with foreign creditors, and the government could avoid the discomfort felt whenever the IMF withdrew its support. It could, in fact, deal directly with private creditors and banks. But the problem of the foreign debt would not go away, nor would inflation, which reached 233.8 percent in 1984 and 235.5 percent in 1985.

Minister of Finance Francisco Dornelles (one of Neves's nephews) prescribed an orthodox remedy to fight inflation, but anti-austerity pressures concerning public spending and struggles for key government positions led to Dornelles's dismissal at the end of August 1985. His successor was the president of the National Development Bank, Dilson Funaro. A businessman from São Paulo and ex-secretary of the treasury for São Paulo, Funaro had connections with economists at universities, and he had little sympathy for fighting inflation with recessions. When Funaro and Minister of Planning João Sayad took control of the economy, the Sarney administration was in serious trouble. Party disputes were on the rise; there were more and more accusations aimed at Sarney and his special treatment of friends and specific economic groups. To Brazilians, Sarney appeared to stand still – except when it came to helping out particular interest groups.

A group of economists at the Catholic University of Rio de Janeiro had been actively criticizing the thesis that economic restraint and a reduced national debt would necessarily cause inflation to drop. They pointed to the 1981–1983 recession as a case in point – the country had gone backward economically, and at a high social cost, but inflation did not go down significantly. This example contrasted with recessions in the developed world, where, in spite of their drawbacks, recessions were an effective weapon in fighting inflation. Why didn't this happen in Brazil? The principal argument went like this: In an indexed economy such as Brazil's, past inflation was built into future inflation – as "inertial inflation." Inflation operated in a vicious circle and could only be conquered by breaking with the indexation mechanism. And this break could only be made "cold turkey" – correction for inflation (*correção monetária*) should be done away with and a new, strong monetary unit should be devised to replace the flagging cruzeiro. The announcement (with great fanfare) of a cold-turkey break with inflation served the administration's political interests. It needed to regain its prestige.

On 28 February 1986, Sarney unveiled the Cruzado Plan nationally, on radio and television. The cruzeiro would be replaced at a rate of 1,000 to 1 by a new, strong currency, the cruzado. Indexation was abolished. Prices and rates of exchange were frozen for an undetermined period. Rents were frozen for a year. The government tried to avoid aggravating workers and even tried to improve their standard of living. The minimum wage was pegged at its average for the last six months, with an 8 percent bonus. Later readjustments would be automatic whenever inflation reached 20 percent.

Sarney appealed to the masses to collaborate with the government plan and to wage a war of life and death against inflation. From one day to the next, his prestige took off and soared. Price freezing struck a sympathetic chord with Brazilians who could not keep up with the economy's meandering and preferred to believe in their leader's acts of will. Measures taken in the area of wages gave some relief to the poorer sectors of society. An air of unlimited optimism settled over the country. Traffic became impossible, and, in compensation, for the first time, many people drank huge quantities of beer.

After the first blush of optimism, the Cruzado Plan began to falter. It had begun during a time when the economy was expanding, and in many cases it occasioned real salary raises. Because prices were frozen, there was a veritable dash to consume everything from meat and milk to automobiles and trips abroad. Consequently, the freeze began to be violated. Another serious problem was the upsetting of the balance of payments brought about by the demand for imports, a by-product of the artificial strengthening of Brazil's currency.

By November, when elections were being held, the Cruzado Plan had failed. However, the public at large was not yet aware of this. PMDB candidates could still blame the plan's problems on someone else. Once elections were over, the rise in public fees and in indirect taxes (all of which had been put off) caused inflation to explode. The foreign debt crisis caused Brazil to declare a moratorium in February 1987. This was received indifferently, both in Brazil and abroad. The euphoria of the Cruzado Plan was followed by a generalized feeling of disillusion and mistrust, as far as the economy was concerned.

The November 1986 elections showed that the PMDB and the administration still enjoyed tremendous prestige. PMDB candidates were elected governor in every state except Sergipe, and the party garnered an absolute majority in the Chamber of Deputies and in the Senate. At that juncture, people began to say that Brazil was in danger of being "Mexicanized." The PMDB might just become another Partido Revolucionario Institucional (Institutional Revolutionary Party) or PRI, which in Mexico had monopolized power for many years.

The National Constitutional Assembly began to meet on 1 February 1987. The country's attention and hopes were trained on the new constitution. People expected it to settle matters concerning individual freedom and fundamental institutions. They also expected it to solve problems it could never solve.

The constituent assembly worked long and hard. It came to an end formally on 5 October 1988, when the new constitution went into effect. Its text was severely criticized for dealing with subjects that technically speaking have nothing to do with constitutions. These subjects reflected pressure from different sectors of society. In a country whose laws are not good for much of anything, different groups tried to put the greatest possible number of laws into the constitution, believing that somehow this would guarantee their being obeyed.

With all its defects, the 1988 constitution showed how the country had advanced, especially in extending social and political rights to citizens in general and to the so-called minorities, including Indians. At the same time, it created a series of problems. One of the most crucial was how to distribute revenue among the federal government, the states, and the municipalities. An excessively decentralizing proviso has created enormous problems for the federal government and has exacerbated the state crisis. On the other hand, the constitution reflected the country's instability at the time – it was devised not to last long, in its original form. The very definition of the presidential form of government and, even, of the republic itself would be subjected to a plebiscite set for 7 September 1993. On that date, Brazilians were to decide whether they wanted a presidential or a parliamentary form of government, and whether they wanted a republic or a monarchy. In addition, provisions were made for revising the constitution five years after it went into effect.

The 1988 constitution can be seen as the mark that eliminated the final formal vestiges of the authoritarian regime. The democratic *abertura* or "opening" begun by General Geisel in 1974 took more than 13 years to widen into a democracy. Brazil's transition from military government to democracy fits into the wider context of almost every country in South America. Brazil came out ahead, as far as its most important neighbors were concerned. The Argentine dictatorship abruptly fell in 1983, as a consequence of that country's war with Britain over the Falkland Islands. The Pinochet government in Chile came to an end in 1987–1988. Because of the possible occurrence of acute social conflicts in those countries, they appeared to be examples worth avoiding. Both those in the government supporting liberalization and many people in the opposition looked to Spain rather than to Latin America for a model of concerted transition.

However, there were more differences than similarities between the situation in Brazil and the one in Spain. The degree of articulation among social groups in Spain is greater than Brazil's, and this gives people at the head of Spain's groupings greater representative power, which in turn facilitated the grand accord attained in the Moncloa Pact. A similar pact was attempted in Brazil, to no avail. As far as political actors were concerned, there was no one in Brazil to match King Juan Carlos, who, in addition to being king, had had a career in the military. His prestige was such that he could bring different political forces together and direct Spain's transition to democracy.

Why did the Brazilian transition take so long? And what were the consequences of how it was carried out? The "slow, gradual, and secure" transition strategy came from the government itself. Its rhythm and its breadth could only be changed if the opposition forced them to change, or if the authoritarian regime were in such bad shape that it collapsed. Neither alternative happened.

The Brazilian transition had the advantage of not causing great social upheaval. But it also had the disadvantage of not dealing directly with problems that went far beyond granting political rights to the population. It would be wrong to say that these problems were the fruit of the authoritarian regime. Inequality of opportunity, the absence of reliable state institutions that are open to the public, corruption, and political patronage are deeply rooted in Brazil. Certainly these problems would not be fixed from one day to the next, but they could have begun to be faced during this crucial transition.

The fact that almost all political actors seemed to have been in agreement and in favor of democracy facilitated the continuation of practices that are contrary to true democracy. Thus, the end of authoritarianism left the country in what could be called a "democratic situation," rather than in a consolidated democracy. Consolidation was one of the government's and society's tasks for the years after 1988.

The first direct presidential elections since 1960 were held in 1989. The new constitution had stipulated that candidates receiving more than 50 percent of the valid votes could consider themselves elected in the first round. In the event no candidate received an absolute majority of votes, the two with the most votes would face each other in a runoff election.

The latter possibility obtained. Fernando Collor de Mello faced Luiz Inácio da Silva (known as Lula) in the runoff. Lula campaigned on the theme of social inequality and appealed to the organized sectors of the population. Collor's campaign hammered on the need to fight corruption, to modernize, and to reduce government spending.

He constantly criticized the exorbitant salaries of some public servants he called "maharajas." Running virtually as an independent, but with support from the media, especially from the very powerful TV Globo, which reaches almost every corner of Brazil, Collor defeated Lula. He amassed around 36 million votes against Lula's 31 million.

This election demonstrated two important facts. Brazil was becoming a massive democracy with some 100 million voters, around 85 percent of whom showed up at the polls in this and later elections. This high voter turnout was not merely due to the fact that voting is obligatory for Brazilians between the ages of 18 and 70; it was also owed to the tremendous symbolic value voting has for Brazilians. The other significant fact coming from the 1989 election was the amount of votes Lula received. This PT candidate emerged as a popular leader whose prestige outstripped that of his party.

Collor, the winning candidate, was preferred over an openly leftist candidate. In spite of the support he received from the elite, he was, to an extent, a stranger to the political establishment. He was governor of the small northeastern state of Alagoas and one of the owners of a communications firm. He had few connections with financial circles and the industrial complex of central and southern Brazil.

When Collor took office in March 1990, inflation for February had hit 80 percent and threatened to increase. Collor announced a radical economic plan that froze all bank deposits for 18 months. It allowed withdrawals to be made up to approximately U.S. $1,000. The plan also froze prices, cut government spending, and raised some taxes. At the same time, Collor began to take measures toward modernizing the country. He began privatizing state firms; he further opened the country to foreign trade; and he reduced the number of civil servants, but with no criteria for which ones would be let go.

In September 1992, accusations of crippling governmental corruption, some of which even came from the president's brother, caused the Chamber of Deputies to vote for removing Collor from office until the Senate ruled on his impeachment. The debate and vote were broadcast on television, and the entire nation watched.

Young people from the middle class went into the streets demanding Collor's impeachment. All this foretold that Collor would never regain his office. With defeat certain, Collor resigned in December 1992. Even so, the Senate found him guilty of abuse of power, and his political rights were suspended for eight years.

The ouster of a president on grounds of corruption in a country where honesty is not common in public or private affairs can be explained. First, during the investigations Collor behaved in a graceless manner and minimized the risks he was taking. This cost him support in Congress, where he never had the backing of the majority. At the same time, the economic elite, with whom he was never on good terms, distanced themselves from Collor. Second, the unexpected impetus from the middle class youth movement was a gauge of the revulsion felt for the level of corruption to which the country had sunk. Young people influenced Congress and were an important factor in the president's downfall.

Vice-President Itamar Franco became president. This ex-senator from Minas Gerais was an old moderate and foe of the military regime. The main problem facing him was the return of inflation in the aftermath of Collor's measures, which had failed. During the first month of the new administration, January 1993, inflation was edging up to 29 percent. For December of that year, inflation hit 36 percent.

During the first months of 1994, Minister of the Treasury Fernando Henrique Cardoso began to take the preparatory measures of yet another plan to stabilize the economy. With the first initiatives underway, he left the ministry to run for president. Cardoso was a highly respected intellectual who had made a successful transition from academic life into politics. He was still relatively unknown to the public at large when he decided to run as the candidate of an alliance made up of his PSDB (Partido da Social Democracia Brasileira – a splinter group from the PMDB) and the PFL. Cardoso's *Real* Plan went into effect in July 1994 and was clearly different from earlier schemes to harness inflation. Brazilians were not taken by surprise the way they had been with earlier plans. This plan created another currency known as the *real*. This move was facilitated by the foreign debt's having been eased and by the fact that Brazil had accumulated around 40 billion dollars in reserves.

The *real's* relation to the dollar was not fixed. It was allowed to fluctuate, albeit within specific limits. Argentina's example, where parity with the dollar brought on serious problems in currency liquidity, showed Brazil what formula it should not adopt. The stabilization plan did not freeze prices and intended to de-index the economy gradually. The exchange of currencies, from *cruzeiros reais* to *reals** was not merely symbolic. In a few months, all the money in the country was exchanged for *reais*. It was a significant operation, both because of its degree of organization and because of the way in which Brazilians behaved.

In the October 1994 elections, Cardoso was elected president on the first ballot, with around 54 percent of the valid votes. Lula, once more a candidate, came in second. This outcome was the product of several factors, but the *Real* Plan was the decisive one. The opposition, especially the PT, committed a serious error in judgment when it maintained that the *Real* Plan was merely an electioneering "come-on" that, in the short run, would cause a serious recession. While it had been put into effect at a strategic moment to facilitate Cardoso's election, the plan was, nevertheless, more than just a come-on. The bulk of the population did not suffer from the recession's impact. Indeed, it saw its buying power increase, thanks to a noticeable drop in inflation.

6.4   THE GENERAL FRAMEWORK OF THE PERIOD FROM 1950 TO 1980

In total numbers, Brazil's population went from 51.9 million in 1950 to around 146.1 million in 1990. In 40 years it almost trebled.

According to the data gathered in the 1980 census, there was an almost equal number of men and women: 59.1 million men and 59.8 million women. Of these people, whites were in the majority (54.2 percent), with racially mixed people (especially mulattos) next at 38.8 percent, then blacks (6 percent), Asians (0.6 percent), and those who claimed no color (0.4 percent). It may be that the number of whites is too high because some respondents may have been sufficiently prejudiced that they identified themselves as

---

* *Reais* is the plural of *real* in Portuguese. – Trans.

"white" rather than as racially mixed. In essence, the population was relatively young – nearly half (49.6 percent) was under the age of 20. But, as has been the case since 1960, the index of aging increased; that is, the ratio of old people (65 and over) to young people (15 and under) has gone from 6.4 percent in 1960 to 7.5 percent in 1970 and to 10.5 percent in 1980.

The most significant demographic phenomenon was the reduction in the birth rate, especially during the 1970s. During the 1940s, Brazilian women gave birth to an average of 6.3 children. This fell to 5.8 during the 1960s, and during the first half of the 1980s it fell to 3.3. That is, the birth rate was cut almost in half. While birth rates differ according to social class and according to specific regions, it must be noted that the falling birth rate is a nationwide phenomenon. Thus, between 1975 and 1986, the greatest proportional decline in birth rate occurred in the Northeast, where it fell from 6.1 to 5.

It seems that the falling birth rate is the result of campaigns for the use of birth control devices and the sterilization of women. Since abortion is considered a crime except in special cases, it cannot be said whether or not that practice has increased. Be that as it may, the use of birth control devices reflects not only government policy (which the Catholic church has feverishly attacked); it also reflects the desire of women and of couples to limit the size of their families. Standing out among the reasons behind that desire is the awareness of the impossibility of feeding and minimally educating a large number of children.

In spite of the reduced birth rate, the population growth rate remained high, because there was a noticeable decline in the mortality rate. The annual population growth rate at the beginning of the 1980s was 2.3 percent. This was similar to the average of 2.4 percent for less developed countries, but it was almost four times higher than the 0.6 percent average for developed countries. However, since it is not likely that the mortality rate will go much further down, the future reductions in birth rate will likely bring about a great slowdown in population growth.

As far as regional demographics are concerned, great migrations from the Northeast and from Minas Gerais toward the Center-South and the occupation of the agricultural frontier were significant. This frontier was first located in Paraná and then in the Center-West (Goiás and Mato Grosso), then in the Northwest (Rondônia).

The strong movement of Northeasterners toward the Center-South was the result, on the one hand, of industrialization. On the other hand, the dramatic droughts of the Northeast, especially during the 1950s, were also responsible for people's leaving.

Movement toward center-west and northwest Brazil was, during that period, the second great migratory phenomenon. Its original impulse was created by the opportunities directly or indirectly offered by the federal government. The construction of Brasília can be interpreted as a starting point in the "westward march" – itself a longtime aspiration dating from Vargas's Estado Novo. The migratory movement went beyond the country's borders toward Paraguay, where a large number of independent workers known as *brasiguaios* or "Braziguayans" settled down to grow mainly soybeans and coffee.

Demographic movements into empty spaces had an important sociopolitical effect. With its new opportunities, the frontier helped alleviate land-based conflicts in the areas of longer settlement. Without the frontier, conflicts over land would have reached even greater proportions.

The urban population has grown considerably. Using a relatively restricted definition of "city" – a community of over 20,000 people – it can be shown that in 1980 the majority of Brazilians (51.6 percent) could be considered urban. In 1940, only 16 percent of the country lived in cities.

Ever since the 1950s, the transition has been extremely rapid. In comparison, the United States' urban population took 80 years, from 1870 to 1950, to rise from 25 percent to 64 percent of that nation's citizens. Around 1980, the percentage of Americans living in cities was 61 percent, which is not so much greater than the percentage of urbanites in Brazil's population. That is as far as this comparison goes. The distribution of income and the quality of life in cities of the United States and Brazil are very different, a fact that mere numbers tend to obscure.

In 1980, nine state capitals had more than a million inhabitants. The number had climbed to 11 in 1990, with São Paulo out in front followed by Rio de Janeiro, Belo Horizonte, and Porto Alegre. Increased urbanization is the result of several factors. First, beginning in the 1950s, opportunities for employment both in the industrial and especially in the miscellaneous service sector grew. Second, notwithstanding the existence of the agricultural frontier, people were pushed from the country into cities by the expulsion of squatters, the trend toward mechanization, and changes in rural activities which reduced the need for large labor forces.

In spite of the growth of industry over several decades, in 1950 Brazil could still be thought of as a mainly agricultural country. Thirty years later the situation is so different that the definition no longer holds. While 59.9 percent of the gainfully employed population worked in primary activities in 1950, that percentage had fallen to 29.2 percent in 1980. The primary sector's contribution to the GDP was 24 percent in 1950 and only 9.8 percent in 1980.

Another indicator of change can be found in the nature of Brazil's exports. Over the years, raw materials such as coffee and iron ore (but not soybeans) have tended to lose their importance vis-à-vis manufactured products. Beginning in 1978, manufactured goods have produced more revenue than exports of raw materials. Still, many of the manufactured goods that are exported (e.g., orange juice) entail minimal processing in Brazil.

The fact that industry has expanded to a greater extent than agriculture does not mean that agriculture has stagnated. Quite to the contrary, a series of changes has occurred in agricultural production, and these changes have profoundly affected labor relations. After one last spurt of production during the early 1950s, coffee began to lose ground in relation to other export products. Its high point occurred in 1950, when it brought in 63.9 percent of all the export revenue. From that point on, faced with international competition and falling prices, coffee began its decline and by 1980 accounted for only 12.3 percent of Brazil's export revenue.

In Paraná, huge coffee plantations were destroyed and in their place, soy farms sprang up; orange trees replaced coffee groves in São Paulo. Especially after Proalcool (an organization to promote the consumption of alcohol as fuel) was formed, sugar cane planting was expanded in São Paulo and in the Northeast.

While in the cases of both orange and cane farming, independent producers continue to exist, agribusiness has tended to move into both sectors and to handle production and processing of these crops. Given the amount of capital necessary for agribusiness, there has also been a strong tendency toward the creation of oligopolies. One of the main consequences of the replacement of coffee with other crops and the increase in land used for pasture was the drop in the number of workers needed for farming. In addition, scientific farming methods put to use in the interest of greater productivity and greater profits have caused a crisis in the old system that employed tenant farmers in the Center-South and the Northeast. Tenant farmers have disappeared, giving way to people known as *boias frias* or "cold grub."

Boias frias are salaried workers hired to work on farms during specific seasons – during cane cutting or during the orange harvest. Unlike tenant farmers, these workers are only partly integrated into rural life. They live in cities close to the large farms, and agribusiness or independent contractors known as "Cats" in the Center-South recruit them seasonally. The appearance of *favelas* or shantytowns in the smaller cities of the state of São Paulo is largely because of the existence of this unfortunate group of workers. Still, the shantytowns are not as large as those around the capital.

It would be hasty to say that boias frias are rural counterparts of urban workers and that capitalism has come to the backlands. The typical form of modernization on large properties consists of the introduction of machinery and the consequent replacement of a large number of unskilled workers with a small number of semiskilled workers. Time will tell if this process will reduce the importance of or do away entirely with the boias frias.

The rise of wage labor in rural settings has occasioned increasing demands from workers associated with rural labor. For the boias frias, owning their own land has become at best a dream. Through strikes and negotiation, these workers have attempted to secure concrete advantages and the rights to which salaried workers are entitled.

However, the struggle for land has not ended. Indeed, in specific regions it has become more violent and bloody, with landless people or squatters on one side and large landowners on the other. The principal victims in this confrontation have been the leaders of rural unions, who have been targets in assassination attempts in the North and Northeast.

One of the main structural bases in the struggle for land can be found in landowning patterns. In 1980, *minifúndios* or farms less than ten hectares in size made up 50.4 percent of all agricultural enterprises, but they only accounted for 2.5 percent of all the land used for agriculture. On the other extreme, *latifúndios* or farms and ranches of over 10,000 hectares accounted for only 0.1 percent of all establishments, but occupied 16.4 percent of all farmland.

In view of this, agrarian reform movements have not disappeared, they have simply changed their emphasis. Until the mid-1960s, agrarian reform melded social objectives with economic ones. Advocates of agrarian reform supported rural workers' right to property and maintained that the key role of reform would be to increase the supply of foodstuffs and to bring the masses on the fringe into the economy. An increase in the consumer market was seen as absolutely necessary if the industrialization process was to go ahead.

Once the military regime was in place, industrialization grew considerably, with no help from reforms in the agrarian sector. This was not a chance occurrence; it was the result of a choice. The military government discarded the idea of increasing demand by giving greater buying power to the poor. Instead, they elected to support the production of durable goods such as automobiles for middle- and upper-income people.

This choice and the rural transformations have made the economic aspect of agrarian reform relatively secondary nowadays. Policy makers insist that the productivity of new rural undertakings depends on investments and on help from a state that is in a crisis of its own. Thus, more than anything else, agrarian reform has sought social justice for the so-called landless masses.

There are still an enormous number of poor and entirely destitute farmers. In 1975, around 3.64 million farms (i.e., 73 percent of all farms) tilled their land without a plow – machine drawn or otherwise. In 1980, the same proportion of rural families (73 percent) had a per capita income of half or less than half the minimum wage. In the South and Southwest, one sees a very different picture in the profitable family farms involved mainly in growing wheat and soybeans, and to a lesser extent the same situation obtains among the fruit farms of the Northeast.

During the years from 1950 to 1980, Brazil became a semi-industrialized country, and its total industrial output was the highest of all the so-called Third World countries. Brazil's industrial autonomy grew considerably as well. According to data from 1985, 80 percent of the country's need for capital goods (machines and equipment) was produced domestically. In 1981, a recessionary period began and persisted until the end of 1992, notwithstanding a period of recovery between 1984 and 1987. All through the 30 years between 1950 and 1980, traditional sectors of Brazil's economy tended to decline. Nondurable consumer goods such as foods and beverages accounted for less and less of Brazil's industrial production.

On the other hand, some sectors of industry grew, especially those producing durable consumer goods and capital goods. The leading producer of durable goods was the automobile industry, which has accounted for around 10 percent of the GDP. These structural changes in industry have taken place throughout the country, including the Northeast. The traditional industrial leaders of the Northeast produced textiles and foodstuffs. Now the chemical industry is in first place, followed by foodstuffs. Within the processing plants of the agro-industrial complex, both sugar and alcohol stand out, the latter product being closely linked to the automobile industry.

Foreign enterprises are not as important, numerically speaking, as they are when one considers their quality. If one looks at Brazil's 15 largest private businesses, as far as sales during 1991 are concerned, only two of them were Brazilian-owned. Over the years, there has been diversification in the source of foreign investments. United States capital has continued to be in the lead, but its actual share is less.

There has been a high level of complementarity among foreign firms and private Brazilian industry. The most typical case is the auto parts industry, which has developed alongside the automobile manufacturing industry, which is owned by foreign investors. This complementarity is one of the factors which have attenuated a possible conflict between Brazilian interests and foreign ones.

In spite of impressive industrial advances over three decades, the long recession during the 1980s, which affected both industry and the economy as a whole, makes one uncertain of the future. It is hard to be optimistic, as Brazilians once were. The recessionary scenario is (among other reasons) the result of international difficulties, of a crisis in the state itself, and of a crisis in governmental anti-inflation policies, which have failed.

In the field of education, if one considers people age five and older, there has been a rise in the literacy rate between 1950 and 1985. According to data from the 1950 census, 53.9 percent of Brazilian men and 60.6 percent of Brazilian women were illiterate. In the 1980 census, these proportions fell to 34.9 percent and 35.2 percent respectively. By 1987, they had fallen again, to 25.8 percent of the men and 26 percent of the women. The trend toward literacy was boosted considerably by gains women made. And these gains are an indirect indicator of their greater participation in national life.

Considering the school-age population to be people between the ages of five and 24, in 1949 there were 23.8 million school-age people with only 4.8 million attending school – that is, 15.1 percent of that population. According to data from 1987, there were 74.3 million potential students in Brazil; 34.4 million attended school – some 47 percent of the total number.

After the Second World War, Brazil's growth rate in education exceeded those of the more advanced Latin American countries such as Chile, Argentina, and Uruguay. Even so, the results of this expansion were not favorable, qualitatively speaking. The experience of industrialized countries indicates that once a particular educational level becomes saturated, the growth rate of that sector diminishes, and the growth rate of the next highest level accelerates. That is, educational growth begins in primary school and proceeds to the university. This model of growth does not apply to Brazil. During the 1970s, the educational level that grew the most was that of graduate students (31 percent). It was followed by undergraduate students, which grew by 12 percent; then secondary school (11 percent); and, in last place, primary school, which grew at a rate of 1 percent. At the beginning of the 1990s, Brazil was spending around 60 percent of its educational budget on public universities. This distorted form of growth has occurred because political pressure on education comes, mainly, from the educated elite.

But the problems in education are not just those associated with growth rates and distribution of spending. Looking at the more developed parts of Brazil, it appears that over 95 percent of each generation enrolls in first grade. Notwithstanding that apparently positive datum, failure and dropout rates are high. Public school's failure to meet the needs of Brazil's poor and socioeconomic pressure cause poor people to finish only the primary grades – if that.

The relationship between public school and the quality of instruction is another negative point worth remembering. For primary school, some private schools are notably high in quality, which is not the case for public schools. The situation is reversed at the universities, where enrollment is free. The best chance for entering a university comes from a student's having done well in high-quality primary and secondary schools as well as from having gained knowledge through the so-called hidden curriculum one gets at home and from one's social contacts. This is what makes access to prestigious schools in public universities quite difficult for Brazil's poor and lower middle class. These people are the favorite clientele of private institutions of higher education. Save a few exceptions, instruction at these institutions is poor.

The growth of private higher education can be appreciated when one considers that in 1960 44 percent of university students were enrolled in private institutions. That percentage jumped to 50 in 1970 and reached 65 percent in 1980.

These factors and several others, such as the limited availability of scholarships, have produced a school system for the few, and a school system which is, nonetheless, not particularly noteworthy. Education is thus a privilege rather than an important means for offering opportunities to young people of different social classes.

At the same time, other indicators suggest both progress and failure. Average life expectancy, a function of health in general and of access to doctors, grew significantly between 1950 and 1980: it rose from 46 to 60 years. This increase has been nationwide. Taking the southern region as the most positive and the Northeast as the most negative, one sees that in the South one could expect to live to age 53 in 1950. In 1980, life expectancy had risen to 67. In the

Northeast, life expectancy was 38 in 1950 and 51 in 1980. Infant mortality has also gone down. It is measured by the number of newborn children out of 1,000 who die before reaching the age of one. In Brazil as a whole, infant mortality fell from 130 in 1950 to 86 in 1980.

All of this shows that Brazil underwent a great transformation between 1950 and 1980. The country has become more urbanized; it has experienced high rates of economic growth; and there were several advances in the social sphere.

Beginning in 1980, things changed. Growth rates fell and there were several years of negative growth. Recessionary measures exacted a high social price which could be seen in the unemployment rates, and, even so, they did not manage to set the country on a stable course. It is not by chance that the 1980s have been called the lost decade. During those years, wage earners in particular and Brazilians as a whole became poorer. Between 1989 and 1990 wage earners lost an average of 20 percent of their buying power; in September 1990, the minimum wage was around 36 percent less than it had been a year earlier. It is true that this social shock was partially absorbed by an informal market made up mainly of street vendors and workers without established wages. But this was a less than satisfactory solution to the problem.

One of Brazil's most urgent problems is income distribution. According to data from the World Bank, in 1989 Brazil's gross industrial product was U.S. $319.15 billion. Brazil's per capita income of U.S. $2,540 put it among those countries the World Bank counts as having an upper middle income. Brazilian per capita income was higher than all Latin American countries' except Uruguay's.

However, per capita income is derived by merely dividing total income by the number of people in a particular country. It says nothing about the distribution of income among the country's different social groups. When one looks at income distribution, the picture is woeful. According to data from 1993, the ratio of the income going to the richest 10 percent and that going to the poorest 40 percent is 5.8, while in Asia and the rest of Latin America it does not exceed 3. In Africa, only Botswana approaches Brazil's level of income disparity.

There are also gross disparities in income distribution when one looks at variables such as color and gender. Starting in 1970, women began to occupy a larger share of the workplace. During that year, 71.9 percent of all men were part of the *População Economicamente Ativa* (Economically Active Population) or PEA, whereas only 18.2 percent of women were gainfully employed. In 1985, these numbers were 76 percent and 36 percent respectively.

The presence of women in the workplace is the result of several factors, among them huge economic growth (which produced a greater supply of jobs), greater incentives to consume, and increased social inequities. Many women have gone to work outside the home in hopes of supplementing the family income and increasing their families' purchasing power. Brazilian society gradually began to consider women's employment to be normal – at least in certain professions.

Still, sexual discrimination in the workplace has not disappeared. Women have been largely restricted to what is known as "women's work," which, in 1980, accounted for 70 percent of the jobs women held. For less educated women, these jobs are those of domestic servant, laundress, and laborer. Women with middle-level educations work as secretaries, clerks, and nurses. Professions open to women are often given lower salaries and less prestige because they are considered "women's work." But even when one examines men and women performing identical jobs, one finds that women's salaries are lower. Oddly, disparities in income according to gender tend to increase in upper-echelon jobs and in management, where salaries are highest.

As far as life expectancy is concerned, compared with other Latin American countries, Brazil during the 1980s was behind Uruguay, Chile, Argentina, Mexico, and even Paraguay. It was ahead of only Peru and Bolivia. The same relationship obtains for infant mortality, which in 1992 was 63 deaths before age one for every thousand births. Brazil's illiteracy rate is higher than that of all countries surveyed except Bolivia's.

In education, considering the proportions of students enrolled at all three levels, Brazil's percentages were closer to Paraguay and Bolivia than to Mexico's or Chile's. Almost two-thirds of Brazilians over the age of 20 have no more than four years of schooling.

During the last few decades, there has been a significant change in the sphere of religious affiliation. Brazil has always been an overwhelmingly Catholic country. According to data from 1994, Catholics are still the majority and account for some two-thirds of the adult population. However, it is clear that other religions have made gains.

These rising religions or sects are characterized by their appeal to emotion. In their rituals, they use techniques designed to bring about miraculous healings of entire groups, and they practice exorcism. The best example of this tendency is the Pentecostal churches, based on the North American mass gatherings led by the so-called TV evangelists. Ten percent of Brazil's adult population are Pentecostals – that is, some 10,000,000 people recruited from Brazil's poor. And they are different from the mainstream Protestants, who make up 3.3 percent of the population.

Even within the Catholic church, there has been a charismatic movement for renewal based on a similar model current in the United States. In 1994, 3.8 percent of the adult population were charismatics. They represent a reaction against the currents within the Catholic church that participate in the struggle for social reform. Charismatics are markedly conservative and concentrate on themes such as family, proper behavior, and personal faith. But to compete with Pentecostal churches they also seek to extend their appeal by holding mass gatherings.

7

Modernization under Democracy (1985–2010)*

Sergio Fausto

7.1 INTRODUCTION

In the last two decades Brazil has undergone many changes. On the political plane, broadly speaking, the biggest has involved the challenge of finding ways and means of reconciling the aspirations embodied in the 1988 constitution with the demands of integrating the country into the global economy.

At the beginning of the 1980s, Brazil had one of the most closed economies in the capitalist world. This was the result of the industrialization model wrought in the 1950s. The closure was further exacerbated at the beginning of the 1980s, in the wake of the so-called external debt crisis. The need to generate growing trade surpluses led the last military government to devalue the currency and tighten import controls.

The new policy boosted exports and thus resolved the balance-of-payment crisis – but at tremendous economic and social cost. Economic growth practically stood still throughout the 1980s. Under the fiscal effects of the external debt crisis – most Brazilian external debt was public – and the exchange devaluations, inflation accelerated and economic indexing mechanisms began to operate at ever shorter intervals, stimulating of inflation. The attempts to reverse the process by economic measures such as price freezing failed, driving inflation to higher and higher levels. The fear that a new price freeze might be just around the corner provoked preemptive price increases, bringing the country to the edge of hyperinflation.

---

* Translated by Raymond Maddock

Poverty and social inequality grew as a result of this process, because the poorer segments had no protection against the corrosive effects of inflation. The beneficiaries were the banks, big companies – particularly those with large cash surpluses to invest in the financial markets – and the state, because inflation eroded scheduled public budget expenditure while protecting revenues through the indexing of taxes.

Nothing could be more at odds with the social aspirations embedded in the 1988 Constitution than this economic situation. The high, chronic, and growing inflation increased poverty and social inequality and prevented the state from implementing public policies aligned with the provisions of the constitution. In parallel, a number of these provisions, in particular those addressing the economy, did nothing to help the country escape the structural crisis in which it found itself.

While progressive in the social area, the constitution proved anachronistic in economic regulation, reinforcing and extending state monopolies and discrimination against foreign capital. It was also fiscally inconsistent, calling for expenditures without corresponding sources of revenue. In this respect, the greatest burden fell on the federal government, whose revenues decreased, transferred partially or entirely to the states and municipalities, while its obligations grew in the Social Security area, in particular pensions.

Thus Brazil entered the 1990s in a distinctly unfavorable position to resume economic growth and social progress toward the creation of a fairer society.

To the specter of socioeconomic regression was added the looming threat of ungovernability. After the Sarney government and Collor's brief term in office, which ended in his impeachment, the general impression was that the Brazilian political system was utterly incapable of producing a stable, effective government.

There was nothing at that time, therefore, to suggest that, little more than fifteen years later, Brazil would be in the situation in which it found itself in 2010. It has become a more normal country, starting with inflation, which is now around 5 percent per year, close to the level of the more developed economies. The economy is still relatively closed, but Brazil is no longer an autarchy. It has been exposed to international competition and has not succumbed.

Today, Brazil has the most competitive tropical agriculture in the world. It is among the leaders in the production and exportation of a broad range of agricultural products. Brazilian industry has adapted to the open economy. It is proportionally smaller than in the past, but technologically more advanced. New sectors have developed, such as the ethanol industry, which places Brazil in the forefront of global biofuel production. The country's economy is international (foreign capital registered in the central bank was around U.S.$400 million in 1985; currently it exceeds U.S.$400 billion), but large Brazilian groups – new and traditional – have gained strength, to the point where they too have internationalized their operations.

At the same time, the majority of social indicators have improved. The Institute of Applied Economic Research (IPEA) estimates that 40 percent of the Brazilian population was below the poverty line at the beginning of the 1990s, after a decade of rising prices. This dropped below 35 percent after the Real Plan and is currently at around 20 percent. Moreover, social inequality measured by the Gini coefficient has been declining steadily since 1993, a trend that has accelerated in recent years.

It is estimated that between 2003 and 2009 more than 30 million Brazilians rose from low-income groups to medium-income groups. The latter now comprise most of the country's population (almost 100 million people with family incomes between BRL 1,200,00 and BRL 4,800,00).

The gloomy diagnosis of congenital failure in the Brazilian presidential regime has not been confirmed. Over the last 17 years, not a single political crisis has threatened the country's governability. Important reforms in the state and in the country's economy have been undertaken. And it has been possible to address the social conflicts that emerged with force in the 1980s, particularly in the rural area, where there was conflict between landowners and the nascent landless workers' movement.

Here it is not a question of painting a rosy picture. There are limitations in the advances observed, in relation to the dimension of Brazil's challenges as well as in comparison with what other countries have achieved in a similar time span. Brazil still has low rates of saving and investment compared with other so-called emerging countries. Investment rates are low not only in physical capital (machinery, equipment, and infrastructure) but also in human capital. Fundamental education is now effectively universal, but this was accomplished with a delay of decades compared with other countries in the region, not to mention the developed nations. The level of schooling has increased and continues to grow, particularly among young people. But the quality of the education Brazilian students receive is still poor, as shown by their inferior performance in international proficiency tests in mathematics, language, and science, such as the Program for International Student Assessment (PISA). The country in general and the private sector in particular invest little in innovation. There are doubts about the future of industry.

Furthermore, while it is true that democracy has been consolidated in the essential but insufficient aspects of electoral competition and alternation of power, it is no less true that the rule of law has yet to take root in the country and that the political parties and congress inspire ever lower levels of confidence. This is a sign of serious problems with the efficiency and representativeness of the political system. Citizenship in Brazil is still not universal, and thus democracy is not experienced in its more substantive dimension. There is a lack of equality before the law and impunity for those able to contract good lawyers.

The country still has a high level of poverty and great social inequality to overcome. Brazil has one of the worst Gini coefficients on the planet, and some 70 million class D and E Brazilians, the base of the social pyramid, have family incomes lower than twice the statutory minimum salary. While access to consumer goods has expanded, half of Brazilian homes are not connected to sewage networks. In the large cities, violence is endemic. In the last decade, while homicides have decreased significantly in some cities, such as São Paulo, they have soared in many others. The country's homicide rate, at 26 per 100,000 inhabitants, is one of the highest worldwide. And the main victims are poor, young, nonwhite males. One of the vectors of this violence is drugs, with consumption and traffic on the increase nationwide.

In this chapter the reader will encounter as broad a view as possible of the changes that the country has undergone in the twenty-two years from the 1988 Constitution to the end of President Lula's second term in office. The chapter presents a balance of the assets and liabilities the country has at its disposal to tackle the challenges that lie ahead in the foreseeable future.

This chapter is organized chronologically. It covers the end of the José Sarney mandate and the governments of Fernando Collor and Itamar Franco, lasting from 1988 to 1994; Fernando Henrique Cardoso's two terms as President of the Republic (1995–1998 and 1999–2002); and the two presidential terms of Luiz Inácio Lula da Silva (2003–2006 and 2007–2010). Space limitations have forced us to make choices, leaving aside some important subjects or giving them less attention than they might otherwise merit.

7.2 DEMOCRATIZATION AND UNCONTROLLED INFLATION: THE JOSÉ SARNEY GOVERNMENT

The end of the Sarney government was melancholic. The failure of the economic plans and the moratorium on external debt interest payments created great instability, while all sorts of accusations accumulated against the government. Positive elements of his term included respect for the rules of democracy – which, at that stage, was no small achievement – and some decisions in the international sphere. Of these, the most important was the joint initiative with Argentinean president Raul Alfonsín to strengthen political and economic ties between the two countries.

This initiative put an end to the unrelenting tension that had pervaded bilateral relations for decades, if not centuries, and reinforced the recently re-established democratic regimes in the region. It also led to the birth of the Common Market of the South, Mercosur, which was formally constituted in Asuncion, Paraguay in March 1991, with Argentina, Brazil, Paraguay, and Uruguay as members. The strengthening of ties between Brazil and Argentina also resulted in an agreement whereby the two countries committed to relinquishing the military objectives of their nuclear programs.

For the general population, the Sarney years were characterized by economic difficulties and public outcry against privilege, in a climate that favoured the emergence of Fernando Collor de Mello's candidacy in the November 1989 presidential elections. Collor presented himself as a savior, the fearless opponent of corruption and the "maharajahs" – highly paid and over privileged civil servants. This popular image was associated with a program of state and economic reforms influenced by the liberal winds blowing through the world in the second half of the 1980s, particularly after the collapse of real socialism in Eastern Europe, preceding the end of the Soviet Union. These winds were also blowing in Brazil, fanned by the crisis in the country's autarchic government, the most evident symptom of which was uncontrolled inflation.

7.3 POLITICAL CRISIS AND ECONOMIC CHANGE: THE BRIEF TERM OF FERNANDO COLLOR IN OFFICE

The son of an ex-senator, Collor belonged to the oligarchy of one of the poorest and most backward states in the country, Alagoas, of which he had become governor in 1986. He was an outsider in relation to the economic elites of the country's south-central region, although he had been brought up in the city of Rio de Janeiro and his first marriage was to the heiress of one of the largest business groups in the country. In the first round of the election, his main opponents were the political heir to Getúlio Vargas, Leonel Brizola, and Luiz Inácio Lula da Silva, from the Partido dos Trabalhadores (PT) or Workers Party.

Collor did not have the support of the major political party groupings, having constituted an ad hoc party, the ephemeral PRN (National Reconstruction Party). He did however have the sympathy of the Globo TV channel, part of the largest communications conglomerate in the country, which viewed the possibility of Brizola or Lula winning with extreme suspicion. The vice president on his ticket was a politician without national visibility, the senator for Minas Gerais, Itamar Franco.

None of the contenders achieved an absolute majority in the first round, resulting in a runoff ballot between the two candidates with the highest number of votes, Collor and Lula. Exploiting the fear that Lula might adopt radical measures, including the confiscation of bank deposits, Collor won with approximately 43 percent of the votes, against 38 percent for Lula.

As soon as he took office on March 15, 1990, Collor announced a monetary stabilization program that included a drastic financial measure: the freezing of all bank deposits over 50,000 cruzeiros novos. This "confiscation" was the cornerstone of the Collor Plan, launched as extreme therapy to cure an inflation that had reached 80 percent per month and was threatening to increase further. The measure's shock element and reach, caused a trauma among Brazilians that was to last for years. The funds remained frozen for 18 months, depreciating in value during this time. This extreme measure, accompanied by price and salary freezes, cuts in public spending, and tax increases, did not produce the results expected. By the end of 1990, it was evident that inflation was regaining momentum. At the beginning of the following year, the president exchanged his young, heterodox economic team for one following an orthodox line. The adoption of a policy of high interest rates, cuts in expenditures, and the rejection of new "economic shocks" prevented the explosion of prices, but proved incapable of eliminating the inertia of inflation. Inflation stabilized at the very high level of about 20 percent per month.

The Collor government was a blend of political adventures and fundamental ruptures, with a development model that, with certain modifications, had been in place since the 1940s and 1950s. These ruptures included the liberalization of external trade and the privatisation of companies in the industrial sector. In one fell swoop Collor abolished many of the administrative controls on imports and exports and established an external trade liberalization program that reduced the average import tariff from more than 50 percent in 1990 to around 15 percent in 1994. Privatizations, hitherto limited to less important areas, spread to fundamental sectors of Brazilian industry, such as steelmaking and petrochemicals. The law, approved under the Sarney government to protect the computer industry and considered the epitome of autarchic nationalism, was changed, making it possible to import products in these areas.

This reformist facet of the Collor government explains why it attracted names of weight to a number of high-level administrative and even ministerial posts, and aroused enthusiasm among certain sectors of the elite, in spite of the trauma caused by the stabilization plan. The Liberal Front Party (PFL) joined the government in its second year, after the removal of the team responsible for the "confiscation." Soon after, the president sought the support of the Partido da Social Democracia Brasileira (PSDB) or Party of the Brazilian Social Democracy, which was in agreement with the overall lines of the government's external trade liberalization and denationalization programs.

Created in 1988, after a split in the Partido do Movimento Democrático Brasileiro (PMDB) or Party of the Brazilian Democratic Movement, and led by Mario Covas, Fernando Henrique Cardoso, José Serra and Franco Montoro, the PSDB emerged as a center-left party (its main leaders, from the state of São Paulo, had gained prominence in the fight against the dictatorship and a development model that promoted income concentration) representing innovation in the "progressive" camp. Without the PT's roots in the union and social movements, the PSDB appeared as a middle class party, with ample acceptance among more modern elements of the business world.

In mid-1992, allegations emerged about a corruption scheme in the government, supposedly seeking rapid and voracious primacy over already existing schemes. The accusations were made by none other than the president's younger brother, in an interview with one of the county's major magazines. He directly implicated the treasurer of the presidential campaign, Paulo César Farias, and indirectly implicated the president himself, accusing him of being the ultimate beneficiary of the ex-treasurer's actions. After President Collor's fall, Farias was murdered, a crime that was never solved.

A Parliamentary Enquiry Commission (CPI), requested by a PT deputy, started investigations in the Chamber of Deputies, initially with limited repercussions in public opinion or among the majority of politicians. But soon the allegations proved to be founded, and a popular movement emerged, demanding Collor's impeachment. The movement primarily consisted of middle-class youth, known as the "*caras pintadas*," because of the paint they daubed on their faces, in particular the green and yellow of the Brazilian flag. With no alternative, Collor resigned at the end of 1992. Even so, the parliament voted for impeachment, suspending his political rights for eight years.

Although Collor's conduct in office deflated many hopes, the episode of the impeachment did reveal the stability of the country's democratic institutions and the capacity of civil society to exert pressure, even if without the force shown some years before in the campaign for direct presidential elections.

7.4   THE ITAMAR FRANCO GOVERNMENT: FROM POLITICAL CRISIS TO THE REAL PLAN

Once again a vice president was succeeding to the presidency, as had happened after the death of president-elect Tancredo Neves in April 1985. Brazil would now be governed by a provincial individual with an unstable personality and nationalist leanings. His government brought together several parties, with the PMDB and PSDB assuming positions of greater prominence. The PT refused to support it, and was joined in the opposition by the PFL, which had remained with Collor until the end.

Contrary to expectations, the Itamar Franco government did not interrupt the privatization program (the Companhia Siderúrgica Nacional, a symbol of state-driven industrialisation, was privatized in 1993). His government would be marked by the launch of the Real Plan, conducted by the senator Fernando Henrique Cardoso, who assumed the ministry of finance in May that year, after a few months as Itamar Franco's external relations minister.

There was enormous skepticism about the possibility of executing a successful stabilization program in a government that had had three finance ministers in slightly more than six months. The president was providing ample proof of his mercurial personality. To make matters worse, the government did not have a solid majority in the congress. As if that were not enough, the congress was immersed in a crisis of its own after the discovery of a scheme of corruption in the commission responsible for the federal budget.

The lack of confidence was not only internal. The IMF was also skeptical about the chances of stabilizing the Brazilian economy under such circumstances, notwithstanding the successful conclusion of the renegotiation of Brazilian external debt. The renegotiation took more than ten years, with many twists and turns and stops and restarts, and was completed merely months before the launch of the new currency.

In 1993, annual inflation came close to 2,000 percent, accelerating in the second half of the year. There was growing pressure for the finance minister to act. Cardoso, however, refused to adopt new shock tactics. There had been six unsuccessful plans since the Cruzado Plan, an average of almost one a year. Cardoso believed that the only way to reestablish confidence in the government and achieve lasting success in combating inflation was to formulate a stabilization program that would be known to the public in advance and would function more on a voluntary basis rather than compulsory participation.

Cardoso put together a team of economists who had participated in the Cruzado Plan and reflected on the reasons for its failure. André Lara Rezende and Pérsio Arida were the intellectual authors of the Unidade de Referência de Valor (URV or Value Reference Unit). Edmar Bacha thought up the fiscal measures preceding the creation of the URV. Pedro Malan, who had not participated in the Cruzado Plan but had broad experience in multilateral financial organizations and had headed the team negotiating Brazil's external debt, took over the central bank. In addition to forming a team respected both inside and outside the country, Cardoso played a key role in garnering the political support necessary to carry out the Real Plan, not only in congress and society as a whole, but also within the executive branch. A number of key figures in the government would have preferred an alternative along the lines of the original Cruzado Plan.

Launched on February 28, 1994, the URV was the instrument that made it possible to defeat inflation without resorting to salary and price freezes. Salaries and prices were denominated in URVs. The former were converted compulsorily at the average of the four previous months. At the same time, prices were converted into URVs gradually and voluntarily, through negotiation between economic agents, with government mediation when necessary. For four months, the embryonic new currency coexisted with the old one. Prices and salaries were denominated in URVs, but payments were made in cruzeiros, at a conversion rate that varied daily. The former represented a stable reference of value, while the latter eroded daily owing to the effects of inflation.

Thus the ground was prepared for the launch of the new currency without the need for another freeze. This avoided reusing a tool that, having been employed in the previous plans, had lost credibility because of its inefficiency in combating inflation, the disorganization it caused in the economy, and the numerous legal actions against the government that it had inspired.

Before the launch of the URV, the government had managed to approve an emergency fiscal adjustment in congress. Part of this adjustment was the creation of a new tax on financial transactions (IPMF) and of a law that ended the government's obligation to spend 20 percent of revenues on expenditures previously defined in the constitution. This "revenue decoupling" mechanism was called the Emergency Social Fund (FSE) and, like the IPMF, would be extended successively in the years to come, with various changes in name. Cardoso threw all his political weight behind the approval of the FSE, managing to obtain the support of the PFL, then in the opposition. This was to be the beginning of an alliance that would sustain his candidacy for the presidency.

Increasing revenues and partially decoupling them from obligatory expenditures were essential for the government to offset the negative effects of the decrease in inflation on public accounts. This was another of the lessons learned from the failure of the Cruzado Plan. It was a minimal fiscal adjustment, taken as an emergency measure. Tackling the structural causes of the public deficit would be one of the major challenges for Fernando Henrique Cardoso's future government.

Adherence to the URV was widespread. Thus, in May, the government was able to announce that on July 1, the cruzeiro would be exchanged for the real, the new currency, at the cruzeiro/URV conversion rate on that date. The ingenious convergence of prices and salaries to a stable unit of value, which was not the dollar but was linked with the exchange rate, paved the way for an abrupt drop in inflation. The fact that the liberalization of the economy had progressed beforehand was essential for the success of the real. A stabilization program "without shocks and surprises" re-established confidence in the government and produced political dividends for its main proponent.

In the elections on October 3, 1994, Fernando Henrique Cardoso ran for president with Senator Marco Maciel as his vice presidential candidate. This ticket sealed the alliance between the PSDB and the PFL. The PSDB attracted criticisms for this alliance, many from its own party members and sympathizers. This was because the PFL had its origins in the military dictatorship and was seen as representing old practices of oligarchic patronage in politics. However, the position of the party leadership, starting with the presidential candidate, prevailed. For Cardoso, the alliance with the PFL was essential, if not to win the election, then certainly to carry out the structural reforms he intended. The PFL was in favor of a more open economy and lower state participation in the economy.

The PT once again presented Luiz Inácio Lula da Silva as its candidate, his companion on the ticket, Leonel Brizola, being selected from among the left-wing parties. The party opted for absolute opposition to the Real Plan, mobilizing its union movement connections to this end. It denounced the plan as "electoral fraud." This approach took a heavy toll on the PT and its candidate. Leading in the polls until June, Lula was overtaken by Cardoso soon after the launch of the new currency and ended up losing the election in the first round.

With inflation on the decrease and the income of poorer sections of the population on the rise, Cardoso won the election with about 54 percent of the vote. In spite of his initial popularity, Lula got only 27.04 percent. Cardoso's presidency would last two terms – that is, eight consecutive years. In the October 1998 elections, he won by another absolute majority (a little over 53 percent of the valid votes), once again defeating Lula in the first round.

Cardoso called himself "an accidental president" in a book published in English after his two terms in office. In his earlier career there had been no indication that he might become president. Although on his father's side there were links with the state and with politics – his father, General Leônidas Cardoso, had been a federal deputy for the PartidoTtrabalhista Brasileiro and an ardent nationalist – Cardoso had gained distinction initially as a sociologist, with a reputation both inside and outside the country. At the end of the 1960s, he had written a book that was to become a classic, arguing that the entry of the Latin American countries into the international economy would not condemn them to under-development and opposing the interpretation then in vogue among the more orthodox left. In the 1970s, his intellectual production was centered on democracy and the democratization of Brazil, with books and articles published in opposition newspapers.

He entered party politics in 1978, at almost 50 years old of age, to run for the senate. He remained in the senate until achieving the presidency, except for two brief intervals in command of the ministries of external relations and finance during the Itamar Franco government. He also ran for mayor of the city of São Paulo in 1985, but was defeated by the ex-president Jânio Quadros.

A founder of the PSDB, he maintained a distance from the nation-alism and statism guiding many participants in the National Con-stituent Assembly, including members of his own party, at that time the PMDB. The following year, together with José Serra, another leading light in the PSDB, he espoused his thesis that to develop Brazil would require a "shock of capitalism" – a position that would be adopted by Mário Covas, the party's candidate for president in 1989. The "shock of capitalism" included liberalization of the econ-omy, an end to state monopolies, and heightened participation of the private sector in production and infrastructure.

For his critics, this was final proof that Cardoso had betrayed his leftist past. From his standpoint, these changes were essential, given the country's internal stagnation and the transformations taking place in an increasingly globalized world economy. He believed that "economic modernization" and redressing Brazil's immense "social debt" were not incompatible. And putting an end to inflationion was a necessary condition for both of these things.

A key figure in Brazilian political and intellectual debates, Car-doso was nonetheless a politician who had shown little electoral potential in the early 1990s. He himself was considering not stand-ing for re-election to the senate. Thus the title of his autobiography, *The Accidental President of Brazil: A Memoir* (Public Affairs, USA, 2006).

7.5 THE FHC GOVERNMENT: ECONOMIC STABILIZATION AND STRUCTURAL REFORMS

The coalition of parties through which Fernando Henrique Cardoso had been elected was insufficient to give the government the majority it needed to carry out the reform agenda the candidate had put forward in his campaign program. These reforms would require two thirds of the votes in both houses. Thus the PSDB, PFL, and PTB, members of the electoral coalition, were joined by the PMDB and later by the Partido Popular (a small party that, like the PFL, had its origins in Aliança Renovadora Nacional (ARENA, the party grouping that had sustained the military dictatorship).

All the parties in this heterogeneous coalition gained ministries, but most of the top-ranking posts were reserved for the PSDB and in particular for individuals who enjoyed the president's trust. The president sought to insulate the economic area from political pressures. Members of the team who had formulated the Real Plan occupied the main positions in the finance ministry and the central bank, which achieved de facto but not de jure autonomy.

For the ministries of education, health, and pensions and social assistance, accounting for almost the entire social area budget, the president nominated three ministers with technical backgrounds.

Cardoso placed in the telecommunications ministry his friend and fellow party member Sergio Mota, known as "Serjão," a superlative nickname suited to his build and his larger-than-life personality. A ministry to deal with public administration and state reform was created and led by Luiz Carlos Bresser Pereira, who also had a technical background. These nominations indicated which were to be the priority areas in a government that was proposing to execute a wide-reaching reform program.

The agenda was not restricted to changes in the economy. The new government was also proposing to carry out reforms in the social area to realize the rights assured in the "Citizen's Constitution," as Ulysses Guimarães had called it. Thus, in along with the liberal agenda, there was a social democratic agenda.

These agendas were not incompatible, as European countries such as Spain and France had shown since the 1980s. In fact, the liberalism in the new government's program was mild and restricted to the

ways in which the state would participate in the economy, not imply-
ing the reorganisation (or reduction) of the social services provided
by the state, as occurred in Great Britain under Margaret Thatcher's
government. For the new government in Brazil, it would be a question of reducing the amount of direct state intervention in the economy in order to strengthen its capacity for action in the social area.
The greatest divergence within the government was to arise around
the new economic functions of the state, between those favouring
a "developmental" approach, promoting sectors considered strategic for development, and the "liberals," more inclined to policies
that reduced costs and increased overall economic efficiency. The
former were aligned with the thinking of CEPAL (ECLAC to speak-
ers of English – Economic Commission for Latin America and the
Caribbean), with which Cardoso himself had been closely associated
and which was very influential in the region, particularly during the
1960s and 1970s. Without breaking with the CEPAL tradition, the
president had grown progressively closer to the liberal economists
in the Rio de Janeiro Catholic University (PUC-Rio), which from the
1980s was the center of the most innovative thought on Brazilian
inflation and therapies for combating it.

While not incompatible, the liberal and social democratic agendas
were not a perfect fit. The difficulty was real, given that what was
good for the goals of one was not always good for the goals of the
other, at least in the short term. For example, executing the social
democratic agenda while consolidating the country's economic stability would require a great increase in the tax burden, which would
in turn jeopardize private investment. Reconciling these two agendas was not always possible, and this generated tension in the government and in the president's party. In general terms, there was
a degree of political overlap between the "developmentalists" and
the "social democrats."

In addition to the difficulty of reconciling these two agendas,
there was a symbolic difficulty for the government, given that in
the Brazilian political tradition economic liberalism was suspected
of insensitivity to the country's social ills and was associated with
the interests of large foreign business groups. The opposition was
to exploit this ideological element intensely. It made a point of por-
traying Cardoso as president of a "neoliberal" government, hostage

to the economic logic imposed on the country from without by the "Washington Consensus."

Cardoso himself attacked this interpretation, arguing that there was an archaic left and a modern left. For the latter it was neither possible nor desirable to reject the market economy, which had proved its superiority to the socialist economy. Globalization was an inescapable fact; it was a question of globalising or being globalized, and Brazil should be inspired by countries like Spain, which, under the leadership of prime minister Felipe Gonzalez, had integrated its economy with the European and world economies, consolidated democracy, and at the same time, produced a more prosperous and fairer society. The archaic left, according to the president, with the collapse of the revolutionary utopia, was clinging to outdated forms of nationalism and nostalgia for the state as leader of the nation.

For the opposition, Cardoso was surfing the neoliberal wave that had swept the world since the governments of Ronald Reagan in the United States and Margaret Thatcher in Great Britain, reinforced by the fall of the Berlin Wall and the collapse of the Soviet Union. The president had abandoned the left to execute the program of the new Brazilian right, which on the political plane nurtured the time-honored practice of clientelism and viewed the privatizations and the internationalization of the economy as the most promising route to a new round of (socially regressive) capital accumulation.

Bringing the "Vargas Era" to a Close

The presence of several parties in the cabinet did not necessarily make things easier for the government with respect to the congress. The major difficulty for the administration was guaranteeing cohesive support from members of the PMDB, the largest party in the senate and the second largest in the Chamber. In votes on constitutional amendments, an average of the 30 percent of the PMDB party's deputies would vote against the government. The fact that legislative procedure was especially complex in the cases of constitutional amendments also made life difficult for the government. Moreover, the concern about insulating certain areas of the administration from political pressure created tension with the parties.

Although a minority in Congress, the PT and smaller left-wing groupings put up fierce opposition to the government, using every legal instrument at their disposal. The PT also counted on sympathizers in the public prosecution area to press its war of attrition against the government.

The Battle of the Privatizations

In spite of these setbacks, the government had no great difficulty in approving the constitutional amendments and associated laws related to the economy in 1995. These put an end to state monopolies and opened a number of infrastructure areas to private capital in the form of concessions (telecommunications, oil and gas, electrical energy, ports, etc.), as well as eliminating the differences in treatment the constitution gave to locally and foreign owned Brazilian companies.

The relatively straightforward approval of the economic amendments reflected the fact that a relative consensus had formed in public opinion about the need to update the state and the country's economy, in view of what had been happening in the developed world. The amendment that encountered the greatest resistance was the one liberalizing the state monopoly in the oil and gas sector. The oil workers came out on strike in the first months of the government, occupying the Petrobras refineries. The government did not give in, fearing that a victory for the movement would encourage other public sector strikes, with demands for higher salaries and the rejection of reforms. After the strike was declared illegal by the labor courts, the president ordered the army to empty the facilities by force. Given the close relations between the oil workers' union (Federação Nacional dos Petroleiros) and the Central Única dos Trabalhadores (CUT) or United Confederation of Workers (loosely translated), a union confederation associated with the PT, the end of the strike was considered a political victory for the government. To have the petroleum industry amendment approved in the congress, the president had to send a letter to the senators promising not to privatize Petrobras, a move that had not been part of the government's plans, but which was feared by some members of Congress.

With the approval of the constitutional amendments and the corresponding complementary legislation, privatizations of state companies and service concessions were initiated in some areas. Unable to mobilize large numbers of demonstrators in opposition to the privatizations, nationalist and left wing parties and movements embarked on a series of judicial battles to combat the auctions of state companies. In the case of Telebrás, privatized in June 1998, 140 suits seeking to suspend the sale were brought by union organizations linked with the opposition parties. Prior to this, the PT had already filed two suits with the Federal Supreme Court or Supremo Tribunal Federal (STF) claiming that the privatization was unconstitutional. Telebrás was sold for more than BRL 22 billion, 60 percent over the minimum price. Nevertheless, the opposition accused the government of having sold Telebrás for an "appalling sum," questioning the minimum established for the auction.

A similar debate had occurred the year before with the privatization of Companhia Vale do Rio Doce (CVRD), a large state mining operation, one of the icons of Brazilian industrialization from the 1940s on. Opponents of the sale of the company to the private sector ranged from left-wing parties to the CNBB (National Conference of Brazilian Bishops), the top-ranking body of the Catholic Church in Brazil, and included a number of prominent lawyers who sought to impede the process judicially.

Criticism of the sale of CVRD may be summarised in the following argument: much more than a mining operation, the company was a driver of national scientific and economic development, a projection of Brazil's power and potential in the world. As such, it should remain in the hands of the state. For the government, however, national sovereignty was not at stake: mining was no longer a strategic sector and control over the country's mineral resources was assured by legislation, to which the future controllers of CVRD would have to submit, whether they were Brazilian or foreign. Under private control, the argument went, the company would be better able to compete with other global giants and the state would receive more in taxes than it would in dividends were the operation to remain under government control.

CRVD was sold in May 1997 to a consortium led by a Brazilian group, the same one that had acquired control of the Companhia

Siderúrgica Nacional when it was privatized in 1993. The consortium also included the National Bank of Economic and Social Development or Banco Nacional de Desenvolvmento Econômico e Social (BNDES) and state company pension funds which, together with a large private Brazilian financial institution and a Japanese steelmaker, were to assume control of the company some years later. This model of shareholder structure was not restricted to CVRD. In fact, the state company pension funds acquired significant holdings in many privatized companies. Foreign capital accounted for approximately half of the U.S.$87 billion raised from the sale of state companies between 1991 and 2002. Large private Brazilian groups gained strength and sufficient stature to internationalize their operations in the following years.

In light of Vale do Rio Doce's later growth, which by any measure improved extraordinarily after privatization, the debate generated at the time might seem irrational. The same may be said about the struggle over the privatization of the Telebrás system, in view of the undeniable expansion and modernization of telephone service following its transfer to the private sector.

One of the apparent paradoxes of Brazilian politics during the last two decades is the gap between the generally positive results produced by privatization and the mostly negative perception Brazilians have of the process. This may be partly explained by the failed attempt at change in the electricity sector, associated with the energy rationing imposed in 2001. This episode became known as the "FHC blackout" and represented one of the major political setbacks of Cardoso's government.

Another factor was the suspicion, raised by opponents of the privatizations, that the government was favoring private groups. One highly publicized incident was the articulation by the two main leaders of the Telebrás system auctions of a consortium to participate in the auction of a particular area of the country that had thus far attracted the manifest interest of just one group of private companies. Government saw this as a legitimate initiative to foster competition and increase the sales price at the auction. The opposition considered the initiative an illegal maneuver to favor a specific bank, of which one of the formulators of the Real Plan had become a partner upon leaving the central bank. The case threatened to turn into a political scandal when illegal wiretaps surfaced at the end of 1998. In the end, the courts found the parties innocent. The prevailing thesis was that they had sought to up the stakes in the auction of one of the Telebrás companies in order to boost the sale price. Nevertheless, the incident marred the image of the government and the privatization process.

The Battles in the Congress

More difficult than the economic amendments were the amendments related to the reform of Public Administration and Pensions. These were only approved at the end of 1998, after many altercations and under pressure from an international crisis that threatened to sweep away the monetary stability achieved with the real. Tax reform, in spite of general agreement over the need to rationalize the system and lighten the burden on exports and investment, was unable to advance in Congress because of disputes among the federal government, states, and municipalities over the division of the tributary cake.

Another area in which reform proved unviable was the country's labor legislation, which dated back to the *Estado Novo* in the late 1930s. The government wished to allow more room for direct negotiation between employers and employees in order to adapt the overall legislation to specific situations in an economy that was becoming increasingly diversified. A bill was sent to the congress. Although it gave the unions the right of veto over negotiated agreements and ensured the rights established in the constitution, the bill was opposed by the union movement, in particular the CUT, and it did not succeed.

The pension and administrative reforms also drew organized resistance from the unions, in particular those representing civil servants, which had become CUT's main base of support. Along with the organized opposition, there was, on the part of members of parliament, a reluctance to support reforms that could cost them the votes of civil servants and their families, a significant portion of the electorate, in particular in smaller municipalities in the less developed states, which were over-represented in the congress. The population as a whole was wary about changes in the National

Institute of Social Insurance or Instituto Nacional de Seguridade Social (INSS) regime, which governed the pensions of private sector workers. The government advocated the adoption of minimum retirement ages to contain the trend toward growing INSS deficits and to reduce expenditure on the already significant deficits resulting from the special early-retirement privileges granted to civil servants. For the opposition, the government intended to eliminate "acquired rights" and favor financial institutions interested in expanding the private complementary pension market. Together with the privatisations, pension reform was one of the main targets of the opposition to the Cardoso government.

After great difficulty and partial defeats in the congress, the government was able to approve measures that proved important but insufficient to control the growth of public sector pension deficits. The little that was left of the administrative reform after the law's passage through congress was later blocked in the courts through suits brought by the opposition parties and civil service unions. The original proposal was aimed at modifying the organization and management of the public sector, as well as differentiating typical civil service careers from public posts that did not require stability. Only one important provision of the law was to survive, the establishment of a maximum percentage of expenditure on personnel, which was incorporated into the Fiscal Responsibility Law approved in 2000.

Amidst the manoeuvres to approve the public administration and pension reforms, a dispute arose over another constitutional change. The amendment allowing the re-election of mayors, governors, and the president of the republic had been presented by a PFL deputy from Pernambuco, José Mendonça Filho, a member of the government-allied group. The reduction of the presidential term from five to four years had been approved in the constitutional revision at the end of 1993. However, the institution of re-election, due to concern about the candidacy of Lula, at the time the favourite in the polls for the October 1994 elections, had not been examined. The measure was reintroduced on the political agenda at the beginning of 1996.

Cardoso allowed the initiative to gain force. He was facing resistance from congress in approving the reforms and pressure for a parliamentary inquiry into the program to restructure the financial system (this is covered in the next section). He believed that the mere possibility of approval of the re-election amendment would prevent the loss of power all presidents experience to a greater or lesser extent toward the ends of their terms. For Cardoso, keeping the question on the table would enable him to retain control over his support base and to advance his reform agenda. The opposition, on both the right and the left, saw the possibility of re-election as a maneuver to keep the government in power, jeopardising the candidacies of Paulo Maluf and Lula.

The re-election amendment was approved by a large majority in the Chamber at the beginning of 1997 and in the senate six months later. The same year there were press reports about deputies from Acre selling their votes to approve the re-election law in the Chamber. The allegation that the government had sponsored the purchase of deputies from the small state of Acre was not proven. Nonetheless, the "vote-buying scandal," as it was called by the opposition in general and the PT in particular, represented one of main factors of political wear and tear that would mark Cardoso's second term in office.

During this period, Cardoso's reforms lost momentum. In addition to the difficulties of the previous four years, a decisive factor in the government's loss of popularity was the devaluation of the real in January 1999, one month into its new four-year term in office. The PT considered promoting a national campaign demanding the removal of the president. With the slogan "Out FHC," the plan was defeated by only one vote in the party leadership. The PT's allegation was that the new mandate was illegitimate because the president had altered exchange-rate policy just months after his victory. In addition to this allegation, there was growing friction within the government's support base, pitting the leaders of the PFL and the PMDB against each other. In 2001, the PFL left the government base. The combination of events that was to lead to Lula's election in October 2002 was taking shape.

The Winding Road to Stabilization

The Cardoso government began with the expectation that stability would lead to an acceleration in economic growth. This expectation was in large part frustrated. If the reforms passed proved fundamental for fiscal and financial robustness and greater economic efficiency, their effects on economic growth were not so impressive. From 1995 to 2002, GDP grew on average 2.4 percent annually, more than during the long period between the external debt crisis (1982) and the adoption of the Real Plan (1994), but less than was needed to absorb a growing contingent of job seekers into the labor market.

A series of international crises of growing intensity contributed to this poor performance: the Mexican crisis, with its so-called tequila effect in 1995, the Asian crisis in 1997, and the Russian crisis in 1998. All these crises began in determined countries and spread through interrelated global financial markets affecting countries perceived as vulnerable by investors. The effect of the international crises on Brazil grew in intensity, not only because they became increasingly severe, but also because the Brazilian economy had become more vulnerable to external shocks between 1995 and 1998.

The Debate on Political Economy

The appreciation of the real in the first six months of the Real Plan – for a time the Brazilian currency was actually worth more than the dollar – had been useful in reducing inflation. However, from the beginning of the Cardoso government, part of the economic team and the president himself were convinced that the negative consequences of the "excessive" appreciation of the real no longer compensated its immediate benefits. Particularly sensitive to this appreciation in the currency was the trade balance, which had rapidly gone from a surplus to a deficit, indicating a trend toward a progressive deterioration in current account transactions (in addition to the trade balance, current account transactions include services, historically a deficit for Brazil).

An attempt at a rapid correction of the appreciation in the exchange rate was made in March 1995, in order to stimulate exports and put a brake on imports. And it failed. The effects of the Mexican currency sudden devaluation in December 1994 was still being, felt and the new exchange policy announced by the government provoked a mass flight of capital. After staunching this flow, the government implemented a minor devaluation and opted for the gradual devaluation in the exchange rate. The central bank started operating with a system of bands, restricting the interval within which the exchange rate could vary. However, the exchange rate was not fixed. The currency was devalued by about 20 percent over the next four years.

After the failed attempt at a rapid solution to the overvaluation, the question was still a point of contention within the government, at least until mid-1996, when the planning minister José Serra left office to run for mayor of the municipality of São Paulo. Serra was concerned about the damage the "cheap dollar" was doing to industry and exports.

Outside the government, criticism of the exchange policy came mainly from the business community in the state of São Paulo, birthplace of the country's industrialisation in the 1950s. According to critics, this gradual approach was insufficient to resolve the stabilization plan's "original sin." The evolution of the trade balance endorsed this viewpoint. A surplus of U.S.$10.5 billion in 1994 turned into a deficit of U.S.$3.5 billion in 1995, increasing to U.S.$5.6 billion in 1996.

However, the gradual approach defended by the central bank and the ministry of finance, headed by Pedro Malan, prevailed. If on the one hand, the trade balance was negative and the current account deficit was rising, on the other hand foreign investment in production assets was on the increase. This covered the current account deficit with good, quality capital. Where critics of the exchange policy saw a time bomb, its advocates saw a process of absorption of foreign savings that propelled the country's development. Growing imports did not represent a threat, but rather a means of driving the modernization of the production system. Previously complacent in a protected environment, companies now saw themselves forced to compete with imported products in the domestic market. The reduction in import tariffs and the "cheap dollar" enabled them to import new machinery and equipment to function in this new environment. It was the fastest way for the country to overcome the technological backwardness that had grown during decades of a closed economy. The temporary "external imbalance" would be offset by gains in efficiency and productivity for the companies already installed in

Brazil and those about to start operations here, and not by artificial "manipulations" of the exchange rate, as in the past.

Although in general terms the president agreed with this viewpoint, he approved a proposal from his planning minister to the opposite effect. In the first half of 1995, measures were adopted to curb the growth of imports in some sectors, such as vehicles and domestic appliances. At the same time, a special incentive regime was introduced for car manufacturers, aimed at attracting new investment to the sector, a typical industrial policy intervention in a sector deemed strategic because it generated employment and technological advance.

The decision was in conflict with commitments assumed by the country in the World Trade Organisation (WTC), which imposed restrictions on industrial policies to stimulate exports. It also created tensions with Argentina, where an automotive production center was under development in the city of Córdoba.

This was where the difference in vision between the liberals and developmentalists became explicit. With some nuances and exceptions, the difference coincided with the division in opinion over economic policy. The distinction between one group and another was around the role the state should play in promoting economic development. The "developmentalist" group comprised the main members of the PSDB in the higher echelons of the government, starting with José Serra, who led the initiative to adopt a special regime for the automotive sector. Serra was the most prominent heir to CEPAL-inspired thinking within the government.

In general, the developmentalist group agreed with the liberals on defending the privatizations, the liberalization of trade, and stability. They differed by arguing that the state should adopt specific industrial policies for sectors considered strategic for the country. They believed that the decision to produce locally, innovate, and export should not be left exclusively up to business. The state should provide sector incentives to induce companies to make the right decisions from the standpoint of the country's development.

The liberals, on the other hand, were more skeptical about the government's capacity to know what was best for the country's development. They maintained that the best industrial policy

consisted of reducing production and logistics costs for all economic sectors. They also underscored the mistakes of past industrial policies and their costs for society. There were no politicians
among the liberals. This was a group of academically highly qualified economists, educated in major North American universities,
most of whom had participated in previous governments and had
constituted the core of the economic team since the beginning of the
Real Plan. The power they wielded derived from the success of that
plan.

Cardoso's first term in office was marked by his efforts to maintain these two groups in the government and arbitrate the conflicts
between them. Although the developmentalist group influenced several important sector policies, the liberals prevailed in the choices
made in fundamental macroeconomic policy. The president feared
that a change in the strategy of gradually devaluing the exchange
rate could undermine monetary stability, the cornerstone of his presidency and source of social support that would enable him to carry
out the reforms in which he had invested a large part of his political
capital. The economic policy formulated by the central bank and
by the ministry of finance fulfilled the priority objective of ensuring a continual decrease in inflation. This dropped from the level
of 20 percent a year at the end of 1995 to less than 10 percent
a year at the end of 1996. Those who had formulated the policy
believed, however, that this was still high, a position supported by
the president.

For the finance ministry and the central bank, if anything needed
correcting, it was the fiscal policy. With stronger expenditure cuts,
it would be possible to reduce interest rates more rapidly without jeopardising the fight against inflation. Politically, however, the
government was not willing to pay the cost of a fiscal adjustment.
The social democratic component of Cardoso's platform as candidate, and later as president, attributed importance to the social
programs. Furthermore, the realisation of the aspirations set forth
in the 1988 constitution was a generalized demand of Brazilian society. It was within this context that the public sector primary surplus, which had averaged approximately 3 percent of GDP between
1991 and 1994, turned into a small deficit over the next four
years.

The Side Effects of Disinflation

While striving to keep inflation on a downward path, the government had to deal with the side effects of this process. These were felt in the sectors more dependent on high inflation: the public and private banks and the states and municipalities, whose previously buried imbalances had surfaced.

There was an imminent threat of bank failures in the second half of 1995, when two medium- to large-size banks became insolvent. One was controlled by a business group in Bahia with close ties to the powerful senator Antonio Carlos Magalhães, who epitomized the modern version of the old provincial "*cacique*" (political regional/local boss). The other belonged to the family of the banker and ex-governor of Minas Gerais Magalhães Pinto, whose daughter was married to president Cardoso's elder son. This constituted a political as well as a financial problem. To undermine the threat of a systemic crisis that could destabilize the whole economy and trigger a recession, the government decided to develop a program to restructure the financial system.

The PROER program (Stimulus for Restructuring and Reinforcing the National Finance System) achieved its objective of preventing bank failures and their economic consequences. The fiscal cost was low in comparison with programs implemented in other countries to remedy financial systems after serious crises. Over time, there was growing conviction that the program had a lasting effect in reinforcing the country's financial system, as was shown decisively in periods of turbulence in international financial markets in the years to come. However, when it was adopted, PROER became the favored target of the opposition, which used the unpopularity of the banks and bankers to attack the government.

The state-owned banks, in particular those run by provincial governments, were even more problematic than the private ones. Since the 1980s, the central bank had been trying to force them to operate more responsibly. The imbalances in the state banks reflected the budget deficits of their controllers, the state governments, driven mainly by spending on personnel. Previously curbed by the corrosive effect of inflation, these expenditures exploded in 1995. A number of states started to take shorter and shorter term bank loans at high interest rates. If left unchecked, this process would bankrupt the state governments.

This was the context in which the PROES program (Incentive Programme to Decrease State Public Sector Participation in the Financial System) was launched in the first half of 1996. The program led to a drastic decrease in the number of state banks, from more than 30 to just a handful. This attacked the root of the problem of fiscal indiscipline on the part of the states and the resulting instability in the Brazilian financial system.

The proceeds from the sale of their banks helped the state governments to reduce their levels of indebtedness. These, however, were very high and grew even further, due to the interest rates charged by the market. To tackle this problem, in 1997 the federal government developed a plan to assume the debts of the state governments that would agree to long-term fiscal adjustment. The conditions this time were radically different from the state debt rollovers in the 1980s. Now there would be effective sanctions for states that failed to comply with their contractual obligations.

The programs to clean up the financial sector and the state and municipal governments did not produce immediate fiscal results. On the contrary, initially they led to an increase in the federal government's public debt. But their importance was demonstrated soon after, as we shall see in the following section. Furthermore, these programs represented a change in the dynamics of federalism, restoring part of the powers lost to the states and municipalities in the 1988 Constitution.

The End of Gradualism and the Test of Exchange Devaluation

Between mid-1996 and mid-1997, the controversy over economic policy died down in the light of the positive results achieved: after absorbing the effects of the Mexican crisis, which obliged the government to raise interest rates and tighten credit, the economy resumed growth, reaching a rate of almost 4 percent in 1997. Purchasing power increased with the decrease in inflation and interest rates (while still high, interest rates fell steadily from June 1995 to November 1997, as did inflation, which stood at 5 percent at the end of this period). Imports of production inputs and machinery became the larger part of total imports, reflecting the modernization of the means of production. Foreign direct investment also increased, covering an ever larger proportion of the current account deficit, which was growing, but not explosively. And the country was accumulating international reserves.

This situation changed in November 1997, when Brazil felt the effects of the crisis that had begun in Thailand in June and had since swept through various Southeast Asian countries, leaving abrupt currency devaluations and deep recessions in its wake. Like many of these countries, Brazil had a high current account deficit (this was close to 4 percent of GDP, compared with less than 1 percent in 1994). The country came to be seen as the next domino in the chain.

Not only was the international crisis greater than it had been in 1995, but the Brazilian economy was also more fragile, due to the increase in external debt, contracted to cover successive current account deficits, as well as internal debt. The external debt affected mainly businesses, which had contracted dollar-denominated debts encouraged by the prospect of the continuation of the exchange policy. The internal debt directly hit the public sector, whose debt had been growing since the beginning of the Real Plan. An interest rate hike applied by the central bank worked in the short term, interrupting the "speculative attack" against the real, but did not change the overall picture, because the external environment had undergone a radical, long-term alteration.

The period between August 1998 and January 1999, in the middle of the succession process, was to be the epilogue to the economic policy strategy initiated in March 1995. Russia's moratorium on its external debt in August led to a climate of near panic in the financial markets. Different from the previous crises (Mexico and Asia), this time the contagion reached the heart of the system, particularly after a Wall Street investment bank went bankrupt. On the eve of the October 1998 presidential elections, president Fernando Henrique Cardoso, who was seeking re-election, announced to the country that there would be hard times ahead and that a tough fiscal adjustment would be necessary. A three-year fiscal stability program with annual primary surplus (revenues less expenditures before interest payments) targets, sustained by a series of cuts in costs and increases in taxes, was approved in congress. The targets indicated a fiscal effort far greater than the one underway since 1995. The government committed itself to these targets in law. The fiscal stability program included the approval of the reforms initiated during the previous years, such as those to pensions. Only the specter of an imminent crisis perceived as potentially fatal to stability could have convinced the congress to approve such measures. And that was precisely what happened.

Based on this program, the country obtained a loan from the IMF to reinforce its reserves. Carried by the majority feeling that he was better prepared to face the crisis than Lula, Cardoso was re-elected in the first round in October. In his inaugural address on January 1, Fernando Henrique declared that he had been re-elected to overcome the crisis rather than to manage it. However, soon after his inauguration, the attack on the real resumed. With the market forcing the devaluation of the currency, the government was obliged to let the exchange rate float in order to protect the country's rapidly dwindling international reserves and to renegotiate the agreement with the IMF, resulting in an increase in the fiscal adjustment targets. The IMF wanted Brazil to introduce a convertibility regime as had been done in Argentina, an imposition that the government refused.

In the following weeks, Brazil experienced moments of great uncertainty and disruption, with rumours of runs on the banks and fear of inflation spiralling out of control. Depreciation of the exchange rate hit about 100 percent. However, the worst prediction did not materialise in the coming months. Underpinned by a credible fiscal program and bolstered by IMF funds, the central bank, now under the command of Armínio Fraga, used the monetary policy instruments to dampen the exchange depreciation and prevent inflation from getting out of control. At the end of 1999, the exchange rate had devalued by around 40 percent. During the same year, inflation for the consumer was just under 10 percent, higher than the two previous years, when it had approached the 1 percent mark, but lower than the 1995 and 1996 rates, and vastly lower than the annual inflation rates in the period prior to the Real Plan.

By mid-1999 the threat of uncontrolled inflation had abated. The government then set about establishing an inflation-targeting regime. With this, a new anchor for the expected inflation was defined, and the exchange rate was left to float more freely to adjust external accounts. In May 2000, against the vote of the PT, the congress approved the Fiscal Responsibility Law, a law that complemented the constitution. This established wide-ranging rules for fiscal and financial management at the three levels of government. At about the same time, the negotiations involving the fiscal adjustment programs for the states and the main municipalities were concluded. This led to a new economic policy based on three pillars: a floating exchange rate, an inflation target regime, and rules governing fiscal responsibility.

In the second half of 1999, it became clear that the economy was recovering, with growth exceeding 4 percent in 2000. The rate was not sustained in 2001 and 2002 for various reasons. The main reason in 2001 was energy rationing; in 2002 the cause was uncertainty about the future of economic policy due to Lula's leadership in the polls. Nonetheless, the three-pillar policy proved effective, producing concrete results: decreasing inflation within the targets established; a decrease in the current account deficit (reduced to around 1.5 percent of GDP in 2002), and the stabilization of public indebtedness as a proportion of GDP.

Even with inflation under control, the exchange devaluation inevitably had a negative effect on workers' incomes and the level of employment, as we shall see further ahead.

Stabilization and Modernization of the Economy: A Brief Balance

In spite of the crises the country experienced, the Brazilian economy that emerged from this successful exchange rate devaluation showed signs of renewed vitality, although this varied according to the sector and the size of the company.

We were no longer producing "jalopies," as president Collor had referred to the vehicles manufactured in the country before liberalization. New car makers set up in the country. Previously concentrated in São Paulo and Minas Gerais, the automotive industry now spread ouţ through the states of the central-south region, with one manufacturer undertaking a significant investment in Bahia. Installed capacity increased by around 50 percent, and the auto parts supply chain kept apace. This expansion was due in part to the adoption of the automotive regime mentioned previously, bolstered by support from the BNDES to drive the consolidation of a modern auto parts sector in the country. Equally successful is the case of Embraer, a producer of mid-size jets for civil and military use. After being privatized in 1994, the company went on to become the world leader in its sector.

Industry's share in GDP, which had dropped significantly in the previous 15 years, remained practically stable during the Cardoso government. In addition to the robust performance of the mining industry and oil and gas sector, the core steelmaking and mechanical sectors of the transformation industry were preserved. Foods and beverages also prospered in this new environment, whereas labour-intensive sectors such as textiles, furniture, and footwear lost considerable ground.

The area that benefited most from this open, stable environment was agribusiness. During this period, Brazil became the most competitive tropical agricultural producer on the planet. The grain harvest practically doubled, with virtually no increase in planted area. The country also became one of the biggest global producers and exporters of animal protein (beef, poultry, and pork). The improvement in the economic environment strengthened producers who had modernized their operations in previous years under adverse conditions. Agribusiness, a system that incorporates innovation, articulating primary production with processing and a broad range of services, gained significant ground during this period. In subsequent years, agribusiness was to drive surpluses in Brazil's trade balance, in contrast with the trend toward deficits in industry.

As with everything in Brazil, the new rural and industrial scenes were marked by heterogeneity. In industry, a broad range of mid-sized businesses were unable to withstand the pressure of economic liberalization under adverse competitive conditions (high cost of capital, heavy tax load, etc.). Micro and small companies, in spite of special conditions such as a simplified tax regime, found it very difficult to grow. This was reflected in the dynamics of the labor market, as we will see ahead.

7.6 DEMOCRACY AND SOCIAL RIGHTS

Since the approval of the "Citizen's Constitution" in October 1988, the social rights set forth in it had not been reflected in concrete social policies or palpable reforms. With inflation defeated, the conditions were now right for such reforms. It is first necessary to understand the background to this challenge, though.

The constitution established that the provision of free education (basic level) and healthcare were obligations of the state. In the education area, minimum rates were established for the ICMS value added tax, the principal state tribute, but no provisions were created for federal government action. In the health area, there was direct federal participation through a single system, the SUS, created to implement actions at the three levels of government in order to guarantee the provision of full healthcare services for every Brazilian citizen nationwide. To ensure the financing of healthcare, social assistance, and pensions, a social security budget, with its own sources of funding, was established, indicative of the desire to create a social welfare state in Brazil. New rights were also established in the social assistance and pensions areas. For example, the members of the Constitutional Assembly determined that all elderly and disabled people whose income was proven to be insufficient would be entitled to a minimum stipend. However, the sources of funding created to finance social security were insufficient. The blanket was too short to cover growing costs. The most serious case was the healthcare area, where problems in payment to participating hospitals were frequent.

There was no acute crisis in the education area, but the problems were chronic. Brazil continued to exhibit out of school rates for children far above what would seem natural for the country's level of economic development. At the beginning of the 1990s, about 10 percent of children aged 7 to 14 years were not in school; this rate was two to three times higher in the north and northeast of the country, among the poor and among black people. This occurred in spite of the provisions in the constitution.

In a country undergoing democratization, there was political pressure to reduce the gap between rights established by law and their effective realization. There was also pressure to improve the remuneration of the people and institutions involved in executing social policies. In the healthcare area, the federal government felt the demand for greater funding directly. The sector consisted of interest groups, which did not always have the same objectives. For example, there were members of parliament having links with hospitals in the SUS system on one hand, and movements to strengthen basic health assistance led by public health specialists on the other. In education, the pressure was on the states and municipalities, which were responsible for the provision of basic education.

The most important civil service category in terms of numbers and electoral influence, the teachers and other public education professionals, was organized into unions, a right that civil servants had acquired as a result of the 1988 constitution. Strikes among teachers and other groups increased, in movements that combined specific professional claims with more general demands, such as higher funding for public education. The PT and the CUT grew in conjunction with the unionization of the civil service, gaining hegemony in this area.

Inherent to democracy, the politicization of social policy was explosive when it involved agrarian reform, which, at least in theory, had become a priority since the end of the authoritarian regime. President Sarney had created a ministry specifically to deal with this question in 1985, and the members of the Constitutional Assembly had emphasized it in the new charter. This made land ownership conditional on fulfilment of its "social function" and provided for the expropriation of properties considered unproductive, in accordance with criteria established in later legislation.

This was the context in which the Landless Workers Movement or Movimento dos Trabalhadores Sem Terra (MST) grew. The movement had its origins in the south of the country, where the number of small family holdings had been declining, squeezed out by agricultural modernization. From the end of the 1980s, the MST expanded its geographical reach and its activities, typically invasions of land (or "land occupations" in the language adopted by the movement) to force the expropriation process and the settlement of landless workers. Supported by the branch of the Catholic Church linked with Liberation Theology and by the PT, the landless workers garnered sympathy among a broad range of social segments identifying with progressive causes.

In opposition to the growth of the MST, farmers formed the UDR (Rural Democratic Union or União Democrática Ruralista). The UDR accused the landless of not respecting private property. To defend themselves or on the pretext for self-defense, some landholders organized militias. If agrarian reform was advancing slowly, violence in the countryside was increasing rapidly.

This was the situation at the beginning of the Cardoso government: insufficient funding and great pressure for increased social spending, particularly in the health area; a lack of national basic education policies; and intense conflict in the countryside.

A specific tax, the CMPF, a transitory tax on financial transactions, was approved to finance the health area, relieving the sector's financial problems. In addition to greater resources, the SUS improved distribution of funding, ensuring better assistance to poorer segments of the population. Previously, funding had been distributed in accordance with the number of hospital beds, which favoured wealthier regions and jeopardized preventive health measures in poorer areas. With the introduction of the new rule for the distribution of funding, direct health assistance programs for lower-income families grew. The expansion of prevention-oriented direct family assistance programs contributed to a drastic reduction in child mortality, resulting in Brazil attaining its target for this component of the UN Millennium Goals, announced in 2000, ahead of schedule.

At the end of Cardoso's term in office, with José Serra back in the cabinet as minister of health, a constitutional amendment was approved, obliging the federal government, states, and municipalities to invest pre-established percentages of their budgets in healthcare. The same amendment also contained a mechanism assuring a real increase in health spending. Nonetheless, as would become clear in the Lula government, managing and financing the SUS would continue to be an issue of high political and social relevance.

In the education area, policies were created to extend schooling, particularly deficient among the poorer segments of society. Although, unlike the healthcare area, the basic education area did not receive new sources of funding, it did benefit from extraordinary revenues resulting from the cellular telephony auctions, where the president made an exception to the directive that the funds raised from the privatizations would be used to reduce public debt. FUNDEF (Basic Education Maintenance and Teacher Support Fund) was created against the vote of the opposition. This provided funding for municipalities with the highest number of school enrolments and ensured a minimum level of spending per student, with supplements from the federal government when necessary (the cost of this supplement was the object of intense political and judicial dispute). FUNDEF encouraged the municipalities to increase enrolment in basic education and made possible an increase in teachers' salaries in the less developed regions of the country. In parallel, the school allowance (bolsa escola) program was introduced, providing financial assistance for poor families with children aged between 7 and 14 years, on the condition that the children attended school. The sum of these policies enabled the country to reach its target of putting all children in school.

For children in this age group, the problem in education was now no longer one of "quantity." The quality of public education, however, remained lamentable, as was demonstrated by assessment systems introduced by the government. Some assessments actually indicated a decrease in the quality of education as measured by student performance. This was an unintended, possibly inevitable, effect of the incorporation into the school system of students from poorer families with a lower level of education.

In the social assistance area, the Cardoso administration broke with the tradition of clientelism in the LBA (Brazilian Assistance Legion). Created by Getúlio Vargas, the organisation was at the center of a scandal related to the politically oriented distribution of resources during the Collor government. Cardoso extinguished the LBA. In 1996, the congress approved the LOAS (Organic Social Assistance Law). A number of conditioned income transfer programs were also created, including the aforementioned school allowance program, and the maternity allowance, whereby poor families received benefits in return for the fulfilment of certain obligations, such as ensuring that their children attended school and, in the case of mothers-to-be, undergoing prenatal examinations. These programs marked a change in the relationship between the state and the poor, in that the benefit granted was now characterized as a right rather than a favor, eliminating the need for intercession by politicians or their canvassers. Even more potentially innovative, albeit on a small scale, was the creation of the Comunidade Solidária (Solidary Community), led by the anthropologist Ruth Cardoso, Fernando Henrique Cardoso's wife. This program was based on two premises: the Brazilian social challenge was too broad and diversified to be tackled by the government alone; and there are resources, capabilities, and know-how dispersed throughout society that could be mobilized to produce innovative solutions for social problems. Initially, some members of the government saw Comunidade Solidária as ineffective ("sociological masturbation" was how one minister qualified them). Among the opposition, there were doubts about the political neutrality of the program. Ultimately, the program gained legitimacy and recognition because of the results it achieved, but even more important, because of the conceptual innovations it introduced.

Among the social policies, agrarian reform was undoubtedly the most highly charged. Considering the amount of land expropriated or bought to settle landless rural workers, the program was a success. The government streamlined legal procedures for the expropriation of land. More than 450,000 families were settled, a number far greater than the total settled after the promulgation of the 1964 land statute, the legislation through which the first military government had sought to deal with agrarian reform, a question that was the focus of intense political radicalisation between 1961 and the military coup.

The degree of radicalisation in the Cardoso government was lower. But there were frequent and sometimes sharp clashes, involving the government, landowners and their political representatives, and the rural social movements, in particular the Landless Workers Movement (MST), which was associated with the PT. At the beginning of 1996, in Eldorado do Carajás in the south of Pará, a region in which agrarian conflict was particularly violent, landless workers were killed by military police who had been mobilized by the state government to open a highway they had been picketing. The case gained national and international projection. The "Carajás massacre" generated great sympathy for the MST cause, both inside the country and abroad. It provided a graphic condensation of a history of violence and social injustice in the countryside.

As a result, the government saw itself under pressure to accelerate the agrarian reform program. The MST decided to intensify its invasions of rural properties. The government reacted by determining that invaded lands could not be expropriated for the purpose of agrarian reform for at least two years. And participants in the invasions were prohibited from taking part in settlements created by the public authorities. This led the PT and MST to accuse the government of "criminalizing the social movement."

The government's reaction was effective in containing the wave of farm invasions. The MST responded by occupying public buildings in urban areas, leading it to lose the public sympathy and support it had garnered after the "Carajás massacre."

The advance of the agrarian reform program led to the exhaustion of unproductive lands in areas with higher quality soil and more developed infrastructure. Furthermore, over time the difficulty of making the settlements commercially viable and less dependent on public funding became clear.

The bases for funding and the range and diversity of social policies increased under Cardoso. Programs were instituted with the intent of continuing them in the long term. Nevertheless, Cardoso's government was criticized for having done "little in the social area," a perception that was to predominate. This may be partially explained by the fact that, in spite of the improvement in a wide range of indicators, from child mortality to school attendance, privation and social inequality in Brazil were still acute. Another reason for this perception was the government's inadequacy in the battle of political communication, faced with an opposition that was more effective in this area. However, the principle explanation for the perception that little was done in the social area was the increase in unemployment and insecurity about jobs that prevailed in the country's major cities throughout the 1990s.

7.7 (IN)SECURITY AND (UN)EMPLOYMENT: THE CRISIS IN THE METROPOLISES

Between 1994 and 2002, the unemployment rate varied greatly, from a minimum of 4 percent just after the Real Plan to a maximum of 8 percent during the financial crises of 1997 and 1998, ending the period at around 7 percent. These figures represent the country's six main metropolitan regions, where about 40 percent of the labor force lives. Outside the metropolitan regions the picture was slightly better, but not radically different.

The increase in unemployment compared with historical levels was due to a series of factors. It may not be explained by low GDP growth alone. After all, the economy had been growing slowly for a decade. To understand the increase in unemployment it is necessary to consider the structural transformations taking place in the country.

In the first years after trade liberalization, industry adjusted defensively to an environment of weak internal demand along with the prospect of heightened competition from imported products.

With the Real Plan, the macroeconomic environment changed. During the phase of the URV, the erosion of salaries by inflation ceased. With the launch of the new currency, there was an increase in purchasing power among the poorer segments of society, who had been most badly hit by high inflation. The economy started to accelerate rapidly, driven by internal consumption. And unemployment fell to its lowest level in decades. By the end of 1994, it stood at less than 4 percent.

However, the initial pace of growth did not prove sustainable. With consumption outstripping supply, imports soared, favored by the appreciation of the exchange rate. The government was therefore obliged to slow down the rate of growth to keep inflation on a downward path and prevent an "explosion" in imports.

The economic slowdown, from the first half of 1995, was soon reflected in the labor market, particularly in industry. Economic policy was exerting great pressure on a sector that was used to operating with low exchange rates. High interest rates combined with a high exchange rate were not conducive to heavy investment or hiring of workers. With the real, modernization of the country's industrial base intensified. However, it did so at the cost of industry's capacity to generate jobs, at least in the short term.

Protected from foreign competition and less vulnerable to technological transformation, the service sector temporarily offset the reduction in jobs available in the industrial sector. This compensation, however, was only partial, and by the end of 1996 unemployment had risen to 6 percent. This increase was exacerbated toward the end of the decade by the series of financial crises that were to lead to the devaluation of the real in January 1999. The change in the exchange rate produced a positive effect on production, exports, and industrial employment, but this was not sufficient to reverse the deterioration of the job market during the previous years.

To understand the insecurity in relation to employment, it is not sufficient to analyze only the fluctuations in the unemployment rate. Together with the rise in unemployment, there was an increase in informal labor. In 1990, about 40 percent of the labor force was employed informally. Ten years later, this figure had risen to more than 50 percent. In reality, the numbers are a little lower, given that, strangely enough, the statistics included statutory civil servants among the "informal workers." What matters, however, is the trend. And this was clear in the 1990s: there was a reduction in industrial employment, typically supported by work contracts based on Brazil's CLT labour laws, and an increase in "informal" employment, in which labor rights guaranteed by law generally did not exist.

The labor market was also becoming more selective in hiring. In other words, companies were demanding higher levels of schooling from employees, a reaction to the introduction of new technologies and efforts to increase productivity. This led to a significant increase in the level of schooling among those employed and to a longer stay in the school system for young people. On the other hand, it made entry into the labor market and finding a new job more difficult, increasing the number of discouraged unemployed and the average time workers remained unemployed.

It is not surprising then that insecurity related to employment became a major concern and one of the main focuses of opposition criticism. The fact that unemployment and the more precarious nature of employment were felt especially strongly in the metropolitan regions amplified the political effects of the opposition's criticisms, because these are the regions in which visions of the "country's reality" are formed and from which they radiate.

Another source of "metropolitan malaise" was to be found in criminality and the violence associated with it. There was a major increase in violent crime in the 1980s, when the homicide rate practically doubled. But it was in the 1990s that violence assumed first place among the concerns of the Brazilian people (and started to influence the public agenda). This was when the relationship between the increase in violence and the proliferation of organized crime, in the wake of the expansion of drug and arms smuggling, became clear.

In some of the main cities in the country, notably Rio de Janeiro, organized crime or corrupt police forces preempted the power of the state in large areas occupied by low-income populations. Essential for the logistics of drugs distribution, the conquest and maintenance of these territories spurred a race for increasingly heavy armaments. The disputes between criminal factions and occasional incursions by the police into shanty towns in response to public outcries became routine images for Brazilians, akin to those we associate with civil war.

The "spectacle of violence" gained visibility via the media, especially television, and caused nationwide repercussions. With specific characteristics depending on the region, organized crime grew in all the country's major cities. Violence associated with crime became the major cause of death among young men aged 15 to 24, affecting mainly poor residents of the larger urban conurbations who were the victims of confrontations between drug dealers, indiscriminate police actions, or simply extermination.

The state police forces proved incapable of dealing with this upsurge in violence. Moreover, elements within these forces had themselves become involved in drug traffic and other illicit activities.

This situation forced the federal government to act. Although public security was and still is the responsibility of the states, an exception is the functions attributed to the Federal Police, a judicial police force restricted to investigating and fighting federal crimes. Thus, in 2000 – and very late according to critics of the government – a National Security Plan and National Security Fund were created to help the states train and equip their police forces. There was discussion of employing the armed forces in specific situations, but this came up against both legal restrictions and the military authorities' reluctance to get involved in public security, fearing the contamination of the armed forces by the corruption inherent to organized crime.

The National Public Security Plan established a model of federal cooperation on public security, which would be further developed in the Lula government, along with progress toward the definition of specific conditions under which the armed forces might be employed in this area.

The metropolitan crisis that exploded in the 1990s is the result of a long and complex accumulation of problems: the disordered and intense migration from rural areas between 1950 and 1980, causing the cities to swell without a corresponding increase in the necessary urban infrastructure; the "deindustrialisation" of the urban areas after the liberalization of the economy, with a service sector incapable of taking up the slack caused by the migration of manufacturing industries to other regions; and an increase in the consumption of drugs (Brazil was no longer just a way point for drug traffic, having become an important consumer market).

7.8 FOREIGN POLICY: AUTONOMY THROUGH INTEGRATION

Autonomy through integration was the main idea driving Fernando Henrique Cardoso's foreign policy. In the past, the country had preserved relative autonomy in its foreign policy, maintaining a certain distance from the world – an option appropriate for an inward-oriented development model and for avoiding automatic alignment with the United States. But by the mid-1990s the Cold War had ended, and development required growing integration with international trade, capital and technology flows. With democracy and economic stability, Brazil was in a more favorable situation to participate in the global economy and to have a more active voice in international organisations. To this end, the consolidation of Mercosur was considered essential.

From the mid-1980s, Brazil and Argentina had shed their military dictatorships and put behind them long periods of economic instability and decades of mutual mistrust on a strategic level. The closeness between the two main countries in South America intensified with the Cooperation, Integration, and Development Agreement, signed in 1986; the Brazil-Argentina Agreement on the Exclusively Pacific Use of Nuclear Energy, signed in 1991, a first step toward both countries' adherence to the Nuclear Non-Proliferation Treaty some years later; and finally, the Asuncion Treaty, also signed in 1991, whereby Brazil and Argentina agreed to eliminate import tariffs between block members by December 31, 1994. On this date, a custom union between Brazil and two other neighboring states, Uruguay and Paraguay, known as Mercosur, was created. In addition to free internal trade, the block would adopt a common tariff for the diverse items imported from third-party countries by its four members: Brazil, Argentina, Uruguay, and Paraguay.

The ambitions of this customs union were not inconsiderable. In addition to eliminating trade barriers among member countries and adopting a common trade policy toward third-party countries and blocks, the plan was that Mercosur would coordinate its members' macroeconomic and sectoral policies.

Brazil and Argentina constituted the backbone of the block. In the negotiations to establish the common external tariff (CET) rates, the Argentinean government yielded to the Brazilian government: the CET practically mirrored the tariff structure already in place in Brazil, whose economy at that time was much more closed than Argentina's. Allowance was made for a list of exceptions to the CET to accommodate specific situations in each country. But this list was to be reduced over time, until it could be completely eliminated.

Argentina saw Mercosur as a gateway to Brazil's large domestic market. For Brazil, Argentina represented a complement to its domestic market and a space in which Brazilian companies could gain scale and strength in order to compete more effectively on a global level. Between 1991 and 1994, with the progressive reduction in trade tariffs between the member states, transactions of goods and services within Mercosur grew from U.S.$4 billion to U.S.$12 billion, generating optimism about the future of the customs union.

The reality, however, did not fully confirm this initial optimism. The reduction in exceptions to the CET that was proposed did not materialize. Brazil, for example, used the list to promote industrial policies favoring its exclusive interest in the capital goods and telecommunications sectors. Similarly, Argentina was adamant about protecting its sugar sector. The Mercosur institutions did not develop according to plan: commercial disputes continued to be settled on an *ad hoc* basis, in accordance with political interests. The major problem, however, stemmed from the differences between the macroeconomic policies of the two main members.

Between 1995 and 1998, trade within Mercosur grew from U.S.$12 billion to U.S.$20 billion, in an environment of renewed hope for the future of the customs union. The belief was that Mercosur would become a pillar of a future South American common market, reinforced by free trade agreements signed with Chile and Bolivia during this period.

During these years, with the trade balance in its favour, Argentina benefited from transactions with Brazil, obtaining a significant proportion of the dollars it needed to maintain the peso at parity with the U.S. currency, an exchange rate fixed by law. Parity was an essential element of the convertibility regime, adopted with success at the beginning of the decade to defeat the hyperinflation rife in the country.

This situation changed after January 1999, with the devaluation of the real and the resulting inversion of the trade balance, which shifted in Brazil's favor. From this moment on, disputes between the neighbors multiplied, with Argentina putting up barriers to Brazilian imports.

Faced with this new situation, the Brazilian government decided to adopt a posture of "strategic patience." The conviction was that localized and supposedly temporary commercial tensions should not compromise the future of a strategic integration. In the words of the then-minister of external relations Celso Lafer, Mercosur was "not an option, it was destiny."

Mercosur had in its DNA the political component that had led to the closeness between Brazil and Argentina during the Sarney and Alfonsin governments. However, with the consolidation of democracy and the deactivation of the nuclear arms program in both countries, the political component was subordinated to commercial considerations in evaluations of the advantages of the block. In this respect, the period from 1998 to 2002 was discouraging: trade between the member countries dropped by half, barely exceeding U.S.$10 billion at the end of 2002.

With the crisis in Mercosur, in mid-2000 Fernando Henrique Cardoso convened a summit meeting of South American presidents, the first of its kind. The objective of the meeting was to discuss the physical integration of the region, and it was to result in the IIRSA (South American Infrastructure Integration Program). Cardoso sought to open a new action front for regional integration, a theme which would be taken up by his successor. The Brazilian government had reinforced its credentials in the region. An example was the country's mediation of a solution to a border conflict between Peru and Ecuador that had been dragging on since the 19th century, reinforced by a renewed outbreak of armed skirmishes in 1995. At the end of 1998, the countries signed a definitive global peace treaty in Brasilia.

In spite of the obstacles and frustrations, Mercosur did not cause ideological divisions in Brazil. The same may not be said for the Free Trade Area of the Americas (FTAA), a project launched by the U.S. government at the Americas Summit held in Miami in December 1994. From the U.S. standpoint, this was a question of extending the scope of the 1993 free trade agreement with Canada and Mexico, known as NAFTA (North American Free Trade Agreement). In addition to liberalizing trade and services, the United States wished to establish common rules for the protection of investments and intellectual property.

Brazil engaged in the FTAA negotiations, which effectively began in 1998, after the second Americas Summit in Santiago. The previous year, in Belo Horizonte, an FTAA ministerial meeting had determined three premises for negotiation: 1. decisions would be taken by consensus; 2. parts of the agreement were not to be implemented in isolation; and 3. the rules would have to be compatible with those of the sub-regional blocks, including Mercosur. In spite of these premises, opponents saw the FTAA as a United States project to achieve economic domination over the countries in the region. This feeling was shared by the nationalist left in various other countries in the region. A phrase in common use to describe it was: "The FTAA is not integration, it is annexation."

From the standpoint of the Brazilian government, the Free Trade Area of the Americas might or might not be favorable to the country's interests, depending on the outcome of the negotiations. Abandoning the talks, however, was out of the question. The concern was that this might leave the path open for the United States to establish agreements that would harm Brazilian exports to other countries in the region. There was special concern about Argentina, which made no secret of its intention to establish "carnal" relations with the United States, even at the cost of Mercosur, as its foreign minister declared at the time.

As negotiations advanced, Brazil made it clear that it would not join the FTAA unconditionally. The prerequisites were set forth at the third Summit of the Americas in the Canadian city of Quebec in 2001, in a speech made by the president Fernando Henrique: equal access to markets, common standards for the adoption of antidumping measures, and a balance between respect for intellectual property and the technological development needs of countries with a lesser degree of development.

The same year, in Brazil, left wing parties and organisations with ties to social movements, ranging from the National Conference of Bishops, the leading authority of the Catholic Church, to the MST (Landless Workers Movement), started to demand a plebiscite on whether Brazil should join the FTAA or even continue negotiations related to its formation. Predictable in outcome, the plebiscite was held in September 2002, just before the election that would choose Lula as Cardoso's successor. Without any legal effect, it did however mobilize 10 million people, according to the organizers.

Opposition to the FTAA was not limited to Brazil. With the election of Chávez in Venezuela in 1998, the deepening of the crisis in Argentina, which would result in the resignation of Fernando de La Rua at the end of 2001, and the generalized disenchantment with globalization after the 1997–1998 financial crisis, which had started in Asia and spread worldwide, anti-free trade sentiment gained force in the Americas and virtually everywhere else. Even the United States underwent an important change after the September 11 attacks. If under Clinton the priority had been to win markets by integration agreements, with Bush the focus shifted to the war on terrorism. The FTAA negotiations were discontinued definitively in 2005, as we will see in the section on the Lula government's external policy.

While maintaining its games on the Mercosur and FTAA chess boards, Brazil remained active in the multilateral sphere, now within the context of the World Trade Organisation, which had enlarged the scope and replaced the General Agreement on Tariffs and Trade (GATT) in 1994. For Brazil, this multilateral forum occupied a central place in negotiations with the developed countries. The belief was that the presence of many countries and the broad range of possible alliances offered better negotiating conditions than more restricted forums.

The country's main interest lay in reducing barriers to agricultural products, in particular in the highly protected European market. These markets had still not been opened after the Uruguay Round, in spite of the fact that the developing countries had agreed to reduce tariffs in their industrial sectors. Brazil and other countries with significant agricultural exports insisted on correcting this asymmetry. However, little progress was made on this question, with the impasse continuing until today.

Nonetheless, Brazil's participation in the WTO did produce some positive results during this period. In the meeting that launched the so-called Doha Round in 2001, Brazil achieved a significant victory in the decision on the rules regarding property rights for medications essential for public health. The case in point was retroviral medications used in combating AIDS, the cost of which weighed heavily on the Brazilian HIV treatment program.

The political dimension also had some importance in foreign policy in this period. In addition to signing the Nuclear Non-Proliferation Treaty, Brazil joined the missile technology control regime and signed the Comprehensive Test Ban Treaty, as well as the Chemical Weapons Convention. This represented the external reaffirmation of the country's commitment to the peaceful use of nuclear technology, already enshrined in the 1988 constitution.

An international commitment to democracy was set forth in the Ushuaia Protocol, signed in 1998, with the inclusion of a clause to this effect in the Mercosur rules. The same clause would later be included in resolutions passed at the first South American Summit, held in Brasilia in 2000, and incorporated into the FTAA at the third Americas Summit in Quebec in 2001. The defense of democracy had become a requirement for participating in economic and commercial integration agreements.

7.9   DAMNED OR BLESSED LEGACY?

An impartial assessment of the Cardoso's two terms in office could not deny his government at least two merits.

The first was the stabilization of the Brazilian economy after more than a decade of chronic, high, and growing inflation, a process involving the restructuring of the banking system and the reorganization of public finances, the most visible and wide-ranging expression of which was the Fiscal Responsibility Law.

The second undeniable merit of the Cardoso governments was the consolidation of Brazilian democracy. In this respect three facts are particularly noteworthy: state recognition of the crimes committed during the military dictatorship; the creation of the Ministry of Defence, signalling the subordination of the armed forces to civil authority; and the transition of power from the Cardoso government to its successor, providing the new administration with access to the information necessary to govern the state.

It was during the Cardoso government that the closed economy model was abandoned, both practically and conceptually. This involved broad state participation in the production sector and generalized discretionary state intervention in economic activities. The state's capacity to promote and regulate competition was reinforced, especially in the sectors previously submitted to state monopoly.

However, the end of the "Vargas era" was not followed by a minimized state, restricted to regulating economic activity. The Cardoso government opened the oil and gas sector to private capital, but did not privatize Petrobras, which had been created in the second Vargas government. The company was allowed to operate with greater freedom and efficiency, enabling it to grow in the more competitive environment to which it was exposed. Similarly, the Banco Nacional de Desenvolvimento Econômico e Social (BNDES), also created in the second Vargas administration, took on an expanded role in government policy, supporting the restructuring of industrial sectors and the exportation of manufactured goods. The Banco do Brazil was capitalized by the treasury, remaining in the hands of the state and providing lines of finance for exports and agriculture.

Finally, although this is rarely remembered, the Cardoso government saw the institutionalization of a wide and varied range of social policies that went a considerable way toward fulfilling the social rights set forth in the 1988 constitution.

This range of positive changes boosted Brazil's prestige and position in the world.

In spite of these positive changes, in addition to the enormous number of challenges inherent to a developing country, the Cardoso government bequeathed its successor a series of problems that represented limitations to growth.

Between 1995 and 2002, public debt increased from 30 percent to more than 50 percent of GDP. This increase occurred in spite of the elevation of the tax burden from 26 percent to 35 percent of GDP and the use of practically all the funds raised from privatization to pay down public debt. High interest rates and a heavy, cumulative tax load inhibited private investment.

Growing expenditures on interest and social policy precluded the resumption of public investment, which had been falling since the 1980s. Private investment in infrastructure, stimulated by the privatizations, was not enough to offset the dearth of public investment. In the electricity sector, the change in model was only half completed, with the privatization of the distribution companies but not the generating companies, creating an environment of uncertainty that discouraged investment. If and when the economy were to start growing rapidly again, there was a considerable risk of a repetition of the energy rationing experienced in 2001.

In this situation, the country grew little, and economic modernization was accompanied by an increase in unemployment and informality in the labor market.

From the government's perspective, the increase in public debt and the tax load reflected the costs of the successful stabilization of the economy in adverse conditions. It was also a result of commitment to the social area. In fact, a significant portion of the increase in public debt was due to the assumption of state and municipal liabilities, the cleaning up of the financial system, and the recognition of previously unaccounted debts, referred to as "skeletons." Another large part of the increase in the tax load was due to the growth in social expenditures.

For his supporters, Cardoso was leaving his successor a country in a position to accelerate growth without sacrificing stability, as long as the reforms implemented were not reversed and the general lines of the economic policy instituted since the exchange devaluation were preserved.

The point of view of the opposition was radically different. For the PT, Lula would receive a "damned legacy," the result of the previous government's "neoliberal orientation" and "errors" in economic policy. The "neoliberal orientation" had led to the deliberate weakening of the state's capacity to implement development policies and to the irresponsible liberalization of the economy. The root of the "errors" in economic policy was in opening the Brazilian economy to global financial flows. This left the economy vulnerable to the changing humors of the international financial market. The privatizations were part of this logic of subordination to international financial interests at the expense of public assets and the developmentalist state.

From this viewpoint, the Cardoso governments represented a radicalized extension of the Collor administration, because it had the same "neoliberal" orientation. If this orientation were maintained, it would condemn the country to a "subordinated integration" to global capitalism at a high economic and social cost. The proof of this was the process of "deindustrialisation" and growing unemployment and informality in the labor market.

At its twelfth national encounter, held in December 2001, the PT approved a document preaching a rupture with the "neoliberal model" as a condition for the resumption of development. This rupture would imply "rejection of the agreement with the IMF," an audit of the external public debt, "substitution of the fiscal policy of growing surpluses," and suspension of the privatizations and investigation of those already undertaken. The same document proposed a transition to a new model in which the "internal mass market" would be the major driver of growth.

It should be noted that the "internal mass market" did in fact flourish during the Lula government, but without the "necessary rupture" preached by his party. The Lula government, however, was not to be a simple prolongation of the Cardoso administration. While on the one hand the general lines of the economic policy were maintained, the privatized companies were not renationalised and the external debt was not renegotiated, on the other hand, the state as the self-appointed leader of development certainly re-emerged in theory, and partially, in reality.

7.10 ALTERNATION IN POWER: LULA'S VICTORY

In October 2002, in his fourth consecutive bid for the presidency of the country, Luiz Inácio Lula da Silva was elected president of Brazil. In the second round, he beat the candidate of the PSDB-PMDB alliance, senator José Serra of the PSDB, ex-minister of planning and of health in the Fernando Henrique Cardoso government. Lula obtained 61 percent of the valid votes, against 39 percent for Serra.

The PT candidate managed to add a new contingent of voters to the faithful followers who had supported him in 1989, 1994, and 1998. These new voters consisted of broad sectors of the middle class that had been reluctant to support the PT candidate in the previous elections. This time Lula knew how to attract them. A reduction in the apprehension inspired by the PT candidate was compounded by the low popularity of the Cardoso government at the end of its term in office. In the election year, its approval rate was at around the 30 percent mark.

The Lula government is the result of the democratization of Brazilian politics and society. Social movements, unions, and left-wing parties, in particular the PT, played a crucial albeit sometimes contradictory role in this process. Crucial, because these social forces introduced new players to the political arena. And this broadening of the political arena, with the ingress of leaders, parties, and movements not originating from the traditional elite, was an essential aspect of re-democratization. Contradictory, because frequently these same forces denied the validity of democratic advances. Nothing expresses this more eloquently than the refusal of the PT to approve the final text of the 1988 constitution, declaring at that time that it was "bourgeois and conservative."

However, neither the PT nor the Lula who came to power in 2003 were the same as they had been in 1988. The party had discarded its advocacy of a "workers' government," its rejection of alliances with non-left wing parties, and, in practice, the utopia of a socialist society. It had become a pragmatic reformist party, betting more on the power of the ballot box than on the mobilization of the masses. On its way, it had accumulated valuable administrative experience in a number of municipal governments (in various important state capitals, such as São Paulo, Belo Horizonte, Porto Alegre, and Fortaleza) and in one of the largest states (Rio Grande do Sul, as well as Espírito Santo and Acre), mostly receiving positive assessments. And it had put together a powerful party machine, which mobilized and consumed resources and employed people. Its initial ties with social movements weakened as the movements themselves lost power and autonomy. At the same time, it consolidated its roots in the union movement through the Central Única dos Trabalhadores or CUT, which had close ties with the party.

Although increasingly engaged in "real politics," the PT managed to maintain the image of an "ethical party." Additionally, it had consolidated the image of a party associated with the interests of wage earners and the poor, in spite of the fact that its main factions and leaders either came from or were in the process of ascending to the middle class.

Lula had also changed during this time. It was Lula himself who demanded that the party give him the freedom to form broader alliances to run again in 2002. This was to lead to the choice of the senator from Minas Gerais, José Alencar, a political moderate and proprietor of a major textile business, as vice president on the ticket.

In spite of these changes in the party and, particularly, in the candidate, the PT still preached rupture with the policies implemented by the Cardoso government, a cause that preoccupied broad sectors of the middle class and even workers, not to mention the financial markets. There was concern that a future Lula government would interfere in financial investments in order to reduce the public debt (the trauma caused by the "confiscation" in the first Collar Plan was still very much present), thus compromising monetary stability. To reassure the public, the PT candidate issued his "Letter to Brazilians" in June, 2002. This was at odds with the positions approved in the party's national convention held only a few months previously at the end of 2001 and published in the document "The Necessary Rupture."

Thus the Lula government began with a tough dilemma: on the one hand, the new president had to respond to the expectations for change raised by his election; on the other, he needed to overcome the fears that persisted in society and in the financial markets in relation to maintaining the economic stability achieved with the Real Plan, seen by the public as the main positive legacy of the Fernando Henrique Cardoso government.

7.11 THE FORMATION OF THE NEW GOVERNMENT

The nominations for the key economic posts were indicative of the president's preference for economic stability. The physician Antonio Palocci was put in charge of the ministry of finance. He had gained popularity among the business community as mayor of the city of Ribeirão Preto, in the heart of São Paulo's thriving, modern sugar- and ethanol-producing region. A federal deputy dedicated to tax questions, Palocci headed the elected president's transition team. He was viewed as a PT member with close links to the private sector.

Henrique Meirelles, an executive from the world of finance who had been president of a major American bank, was made president of the central bank. Elected as a PSDB federal deputy, Meirelles had to leave the party in order to assume the post. Lula assured Meirelles that he would not interfere in the central bank's autonomy.

At the same time, Lula nominated as chief of staff of the presidency a typical representative of the PT machine and a symbolic figure for the Brazilian left, José Dirceu. An ex-student leader, Dirceu had been engaged in the armed struggle against the military regime later going into exile in Cuba. With re-democratization, he was elected deputy and was president of the PT from 1995 to 2003. At the beginning of his first term, Lula referred to Dirceu as "the captain of the team," indicating his political weight within the government. Another PT leader, Luiz Gushiken, was nominated secretary of strategic affairs to the presidency. He had entered politics via the bank workers' union movement. Ricardo Berzoini, a PT member with a similar background, who was to be president of the party in 2007, became minister of pensions. The ministry of labor was headed by Luiz Marinho, who had also come up through the union movement, in this case the ABC Steelworkers Union, in which Lula had begun his political career. There could be no doubt that the political reins of the government were firmly in the hands of the PT.

In the remaining ministries, Lula followed the Brazilian presidential system tradition of choosing representatives of social sectors whose interests were divergent, when not completely antagonistic. This is illustrated by the following choices: a well-known agribusiness leader was made minister of agriculture, while a politician from the left-wing of the PT was put in charge of the ministry of agricultural reform; to head the ministry of the environment, the nominee was Marina Silva, a PT senator with a history of militancy in the party and a symbolic figure in social and environmental struggles. The conflicts between these areas of the government were to be frequent and intense.

If on the one hand, this heterogeneity frequently jeopardized the coherence of government policy, on the other, it allowed greater room for maneuver. This may be illustrated by the fact that, while there was no shortage of efforts to support large agricultural producers, public funding for the MST landless movement was increased and the measures adopted by the previous government to contain the movement's invasions were suspended. The government's capacity to absorb these contradictions reduced the range of actions open to opposition parties.

Analysis of the social origin of members of the first (ministries, central bank) and second ranks of government shows a change in the elite in power. Representatives of the bourgeoisie or the professional middle classes did not disappear. However, there was a new prominence of union members, a number of whom were President Lula's old companions in the struggle.

7.12   LULA AND COALITIONAL PRESIDENCY

In addition to gaining the trust of the markets, the new government soon realized it would have to amplify its support base in the congress.

Lula was elected by a coalition comprising the PT, PL, PC do B, and two other minute left-wing parties. The sum of the representatives of these parties did not give the president a majority in congress. To overcome this disadvantage, Lula incorporated into his cabinet representatives of parties that had not supported his election.

Reluctant to become a hostage to the PMDB, Lula decided not to make this party a "preferred partner." To ensure a comfortable majority and preserve the PT from becoming artificially bloated, as had occurred with the PSDB after Cardoso's victory, Lula and his political operators encouraged deputies and senators elected by the opposition to migrate to smaller parties in the government coalition that was being formed. This post-election switchover was to strengthen parties such as the PL and the PTB.

In addition to incorporating the smaller parties and the PMDB, Lula also found places for the various currents of the PT in his cabinet. This accommodation was to result in more than thirty ministerial posts. State companies were submitted to more intense party political allotment than in the previous government, as were the regulatory agencies.

The political crisis known as the "*mensalão*" which we will analyze further ahead, was to show the vulnerability of a political alliance organized around ad hoc support from small parties, akin to "parties for rent." In his second term in office, Lula opted for a preferential alliance with the PMDB, whose quota of ministries and posts in state companies was to expand significantly.

The central axis of the government in his second term, the PT-PMDB alliance served as the basis for launching Chief of Staff Dilma Roussef as candidate to succeed Lula. Thus the PMDB, which had not had its own candidate for president since 1994, confirmed its central role in the operation of the Brazilian presidency, characterized by the need to build broad-based electoral and government coalitions.

While it may have served to protect the government from new political crises and provide a robust alliance for the 2010 presidential election, the alliance with the PMDB did not produce legislation of importance. The reform agenda was paralyzed except for changes in public sector pensions, which were introduced at the beginning of Lula's first term and led to a split with the left-wing of the PT and the formation of the PSOL, and some initiatives on the so-called microeconomic agenda, inherited from the previous government and embraced by Antonio Palocci's team. Critical of the union structure when he headed the São Bernardo steelworkers, Lula kept it intact as president. To seal his alliance with the union confederations, he supported a bill reserving part of the mandatory union membership fees for them, vetoing a rule enabling federal audits of the use of these funds.

7.13 ACCELERATION OF GROWTH

When Lula took over the presidency, inflation was on the rise. The country's fiscal and external accounts had improved since 1999, but were not robust enough to neutralize the uncertainties generated throughout the year by the prospect of Lula's election. Faced with this situation, in the final months of his government president Cardoso negotiated a U.S.$30 billion loan from the IMF. FHC informed all the main presidential candidates of the terms of the loan, obtaining Lula's tacit agreement with the initiative – one of the conditions imposed by the IMF.

Economic Policy in Lula's First Term

Palocci and Meirelles confronted the economic situation with fiscal and monetary adjustment measures that went further than those adopted by president Cardoso. These consisted of simultaneously tightening monetary policy and increasing interest rates until mid-2003, and the adoption of a primary surplus target (the balance of government revenues and expenditures before interest payments) for the period from 2003 to 2006 higher than those fixed by the Cardoso government. The adjustments were successful, reducing inflationary pressure and establishing the government's credibility in the financial markets. Nonetheless, Palocci and Meirelles became the targets of "friendly fire" from the PT and its main representatives in high government offices. The intensity of this "friendly fire" only abated when the results of the economic policy began to become apparent in 2005. Palocci and Meireles survived because they had

Lula's support. Paradoxically, they also had the tacit support of the opposition, who saw them as upholding the economic policy implemented in Cardoso's second term.

From the second half of 2003, there was a sharp decline in inflation, which stood at below 4 percent in 2006. The decline in inflation was followed by a reduction in interest rates and a resumption of growth. Initially the major driver of growth was foreign trade. The cumulative devaluation of the real in 2001 and 2002 impelled Brazilian exports, which grew from approximately U.S.$60 billion to U.S.$100 billion between 2000 and 2004, assisted by the expansion of the world economy and the rise in agricultural and mineral commodity prices, due mainly to accelerated growth in China.

A competitive producer of a broad range of commodities, Brazil was one of the countries that most benefited from the accelerated growth in Chinese demand, which would continue over the following years. Between 2004 and 2008, Brazilian exports almost doubled in value, from U.S.$100 billion to U.S.$200 billion a year, with a growth in the proportion of commodities.

While exports grew, leading to the generation of larger trade balance surpluses, capital inflow resumed the upward trend seen in the 1990s. There was a surplus of available funds in the world, which was enjoying a long period of calm and optimism that would only end in 2007. In fact, between 2003 and 2008 the global economy had its best five years since the period from 1968 to 1973. With growing trade balance surpluses and a strong capital inflow, between 2004 and 2007 Brazil posted surpluses in the current account of the balance of payments, which consists of all the money legally entering and leaving the country. To mitigate the trend toward an appreciation in the exchange rate, the central bank adopted a policy of accumulating reserves. In 2007, twenty years after the moratorium on external debt, Brazil became a net external creditor, that is, the value of its assets (credits receivable plus international reserves) exceeded its liabilities in foreign currency. This led the credit rating agencies to classify the country as "investment grade" at the beginning of 2008.

Progressively, the mainspring of the economy shifted from exports to internal consumption. This was driven by the expansion of formal employment, by the policy of increasing the minimum salary above inflation (in real terms, the minimum salary grew by around 40 percent under the Cardoso government and 60 percent in the Lula government), by expanded access to credit, and by the reinforcement of direct income transfer programs benefiting poorer families.

Access to credit was facilitated by an economic environment with low inflation and reductions in the domestic interest rate. The government also adopted a program of payroll-deductible loans for civil servants and pensioners. Between 2003 and 2008, total credit in the country increased from just over 25 percent to more than 40 percent of GDP, and it continued to grow in the following years, leading to concern about the speed of expansion and the possibility of "credit bubbles." The public banks, in particular the Caixa Econômica Federal, were particularly liberal in the concession of credit to low-income consumers.

No less important was the acceleration in the creation of formal jobs. From 2004, the average net annual creation of work posts exceeded 1.5 million, a trend that was only interrupted in 2009 by the effects of the global financial crisis on the domestic economy. Thus, by the end of Lula's two terms, more than 10 million formal jobs had been created, with the unemployment rate standing at half the figure for the beginning of the period.

The Emergence of a New Middle Class

In the same period there was a significant reduction in poverty with the social ascent of a broad contingent of the population, estimated at more than 30 million people. This so-called new middle class encompasses families with an income between approximately BRL1,200 and BRL4,800. This broad upward social mobility was the result of a combination of low inflation, higher employment, and the expansion of credit. There was also upward social mobility from the very bottom of the pyramid. At the base of the social pyramid, the most important lever for rising was the transfer of funds through the *Bolsa Família* (Family Allowance) program and other government assistance programs. With more income and more credit, popular consumption expanded. Items previously accessible only to higher income groups, such as cars and computers, became incorporated in the consumption repertoire of lower income groups. The use of mobile phones became widespread. And the gateway was opened to the main consumption aspiration for the new "middle class," finance for their own homes.

The emergence of a new middle class was a large-scale phenomenon with major socio-economic and political implications. This "class" now represents more than 50 percent of the Brazilian electorate and its purchasing power exceeded the sum of those groups with higher family income.

The designation "middle class" for this broad contingent of the population is questionable. The middle class cannot be defined only on the basis of income. It is not, however, possible to argue with the fact that "new middle class" consumption was the main driver of GDP growth and a factor attracting and generating new investments in recent years. A similar phenomenon had been apparent in the first years after the Real Plan, until the crises in the late 1990s caused incomes of poorer consumers to decline. From 2004, in the absence of external crises, the phenomenon was repeated more intensely and on a larger scale. This is one of the elements explaining the very favorable international perception Brazil began to enjoy during this period: in addition to a stable, growing economy, with finances in order and a consolidated democratic regime, at least compared with the majority of developing countries, Brazil projected the image of a society with an expanding middle class. This social phenomenon has profound implications. The new "middle classes" generate unprecedented demands on the state. The emergence of these classes has been accompanied by an expansion in the offer of private services in the health and education areas. The number of clients for private health plans doubled in the first decade of the 21st century (the number today is around 50 million people). A similar process, albeit involving more modest numbers, may be seen in higher education, where private institutions account for almost 80 percent of the places on offer. This expansion in the private offer of social services places unprecedented demands on the state in terms of regulation, an issue that has already been incorporated into the political agenda. On the other hand, the rise of an immense new contingent of people into income groups subject to direct taxation in the form of income tax tends to reinforce the notion of what it is to be a tax payer in the electorate and generate greater social discomfort due to the high tax burden, without the corresponding offer of public services deemed acceptable to the "new middle classes."

Economic Policy in Lula's Second Term

In 2006, economic growth exceeded 6 percent and was above 5 percent the following year. With internal consumption high, imports started to outstrip exports, reducing the trade balance surplus from more than U.S.$45 billion in 2005 to less than U.S.$25 billion in 2008. Current account transactions once again showed a small deficit, which would grow in the following years, reaching 2.5 percent of GDP at the end of the period in question. There was, however, no lack of external finance to cover this deficit. On the contrary, except for a short period between the end of 2008 and 2009, the inflow of dollars was consistently higher than the outflow. International reserves kept on growing, as the central bank bought dollars to alleviate the trend toward an appreciation in the exchange rate. Even so, the exchange rate appreciated significantly, more so than in the first months of the Real Plan. Now, however, Brazil had the advantage of a stable economy and enjoyed very favourable terms of trade, given the upsurge in demand for commodities and their higher prices on the international market.

With the perception that the appreciation of the real might be long-lasting – ultimately it was linked with the growing demand for commodities due to China's accelerated growth rate – there was a resumption of the debate about the risks of the deindustrialization of the Brazilian economy, latent since the exchange devaluation in January 1999.

The major novelty in relation to the past was China, a country that was to become Brazil's main trading partner in 2010. A large importer of primary goods, during the course of the first decade of this century, China developed into a major exporter of a wide range of manufactured products. The appreciation of the exchange rate accentuated the difficulties Brazilian industry found in competing with Chinese products, mainly in the domestic market, but also in external markets, in particular the United States. Brazilian exports to the North American market declined greatly, in relative terms, in the first decade of the 21st century. The growth in exports to China and the reduction in exports to the United States were reflected in a significant drop in the proportion of manufactured goods in Brazil's overall external sales, from approximately 50 percent in 2000 to around 30 percent ten years later.

Judging by the past, it would have been natural to expect that the Lula government would react to this situation by adopting measures to close the economy in order to protect Brazilian industry. There was no shortage of demands from business leaders to do precisely this. The government, however, limited itself to maintaining the policy of accumulating international reserves in order to prevent even higher appreciation of the real.

The very favourable international situation allowed the government to maintain accelerated growth, control inflation, and keep the fiscal situation and external accounts relatively well balanced, in spite of the accelerated expansion in government spending and consumer credit. Driven by family consumption and government spending, the accelerated growth generated optimism and a feeling of well-being, in particular among the poorer segments of the population. Between 2002 and 2009, the income of this group grew by over 60 percent, while that of the better-off segments increased by around 12 percent. Everyone's boat was rising on the full tide of economic expansion, but that of the poor was rising faster than the others.

In the second half of 2008, however, Brazil felt the effects of the financial crisis that spread around the world after the Lehman Brothers bank went bust in September. The subprime mortgage crisis, which had been underway in the United States since the previous year, took a dramatic turn and extended its reach.

While the effects were felt globally, the center of the crisis was in the United States and some European countries that were more exposed to the "exotic products" generated by the American financial industry centered on Wall Street. The subprime mortgage-backed derivatives had not penetrated the Brazilian financial system. Even so, the general contraction of loans and investments worldwide produced shocks in the Brazilian economy, particularly in mid-size banks and some large companies that had bought exchange rate derivatives that generated huge financial losses when the real was suddenly devalued. Fearful, industry slammed on the brakes in the last quarter of 2008, cutting production and laying off employees. The government took action to avoid recession. It used international reserves to finance external trade, expanded the liquidity of the financial system, reducing interest rates and compulsory deposits; it increased public spending and granted tax incentives to certain sectors, such as the automobile industry. The measures produced the expected effect: after a strong deceleration at the end of 2008, the economy started to revive in the second quarter of 2009. Brazil, as China and India, emerged from the crisis in comparatively good shape and did so before Europe and the United States.

With the developed countries still in crisis, Brazil reinforced its image as an emerging economic power. With international interest rates very low and reduced growth in the developed nations, Brazil once again became a powerful magnet for external capital, in greater quantities than before. Moreover, commodity prices did not take long to recover on the international market, influenced by the resumption of growth in China. In summary, the external situation rapidly became favorable for Brazil once more. The exchange rate started to appreciate again. Among the currencies of the emerging countries, the real was the one that appreciated the most in the two years following the crisis.

The government, however, decided to prolong the economic stimulation measures in place. It had achieved an economic and political victory and felt confident in sustaining that these measures were necessary, despite warnings that continuing them after the effects of the crisis had been overcome could overheat the economy and accelerate inflation. The opposition identified electoral motivations in the continuation of the stimulus measures, given that the 2010 general elections were drawing near.

In 2010, Brazil grew more than 7 percent and generated 3 million formal jobs. With this, the average growth rate during the eight years of the Lula government topped 4 percent, higher than the 2.5 percent of the Cardoso period, but below the average for a number of other emerging countries. Inflation, however, accelerated, ending the year at close to 6 percent and on an upward trend. Together with spending cuts, which during the Lula government increased far above GDP growth, controlling inflation was to represent the greatest challenge bequeathed to his successor.

7.14 SOCIAL POLICY: MORE CONTINUITY THAN RUPTURE

Given the historical commitments and programs of the PT and the president himself, it is hardly surprising that the Lula government sought to make its mark in the social area.

Nevertheless, instead of a "revolution" what was seen in large part was the continuation of the policies based on the 1988 constitution that had been in place since the previous government. The Lula administration pursued continuity, with more resources – provided by significant gains in revenues – channelled in great part to the social area, indicating a clear political priority.

In education, for example, Fundef was transformed into the Basic Education Maintenance and Teacher Support Fund (Fundeb), encompassing secondary as well as basic education. Two complementary tests and a development index for basic education were added to the basic education assessment system in 2007. The same year, the National Education Plan was launched with growth targets linked with the index. The initiative received widespread approval, even among educators linked with the previous government. There was also a consensus around basic education in society as a whole. The movement *Todos pela Education* (Everyone for Education) was created, receiving support from large companies. Its purpose was not only to monitor and discuss the government's basic education policy, but also to demand results and to offer cooperation in the formulation and execution of policy at the three levels of government.

In spite of increased public funding and broader social engagement, the results in terms of improved teaching quality have been modest. The major problem is in secondary education for adolescents aged 15 to 17 and in the areas of mathematics and science. There has in fact been a reduction in the number of school enrolments and an increase in the drop-out rate in secondary education, a surprising result given the universalisation of basic or primary-level education.

Without a doubt the most important social policy for the government has been the *Bolsa Família* (Family Allowance) program, which resulted from the unification of four conditioned-cash transfer programs created under the Fernando Henrique Cardoso government. The decision to unify them and transform them into the flagship of the government's actions in the social area occurred after the brief and unsuccessful experience of the *Fome Zero* (Zero Hunger) program, based on the idea of encouraging family agriculture through the local distribution of food to needy families, which had been one of the mainstays of Lula's electoral campaign.

By substituting the Family Allowance program for Zero Hunger with, the government relegated to a secondary level a program whose DNA contained the mark of the Christian left, present since the formation of the PT, in order to embrace a program that had come into vogue in Latin America in the 1990s under the auspices of the World Bank and the Inter-American Development Bank.

The changeover was advantageous. In addition to unifying the income transfer programs, the Lula government significantly increased the number of beneficiaries (from approximately 4 million to 12 million families between 2002 and 2009), increased the value of the benefit, and extended support to families with children aged 15 to 17 enrolled in school. With the higher number of beneficiaries and greater volume of funds transferred, the Family Allowance played an important role in reducing poverty, particularly in the northeast of the country, helping to consolidate Lula's broad electoral majority in the region.

The program gained wide support due to its low fiscal cost and robust results. From the opposition there was criticism that the program was creating a new kind of clientelism, buying voter loyalty with benefits. This criticism reflects a prejudice against the poor. Furthermore, it downplays the fact that the benefit, although not immune to electoral manipulation, is the expression of a legally guaranteed right and not a favour granted arbitrarily, as was the norm in the system of oligarchic patronage that marked Brazil's social formation, particularly in the northeast.

In addition to the Family Allowance, there was the policy of real increases in the minimum salary, as mentioned in the section on the economy and economic policy. In addition to its effect on the lowest salaries in the labor market, the minimum salary increase boosted the volume of transfers to poor families via assistance programs created by previous governments. This was because the benefits in these programs are constitutionally indexed to the minimum salary. Data from the 2006 *Pesquisa Nacional por Amostra de Domicílios* (National Household Survey Sample) provide an idea of the impact of programs. According to the survey, almost 30 percent of the Brazilian population received at least one type of benefit from the government, with this percentage reaching 45 percent in poorer regions of the country, such as the northeast.

In terms of political visibility, the Family Allowance greatly overshadowed the agrarian reform program, one of the PT's historical causes. Note that the program was discontinued. On the contrary, with the exhaustion of the stock of land that was available for expropriation at the end of the Cardoso government, the Lula government increasingly resorted to land purchase for agrarian reform, leading to a greater disbursement of funds to settle some 600 thousand families between 2003 and 2010. A lot of money was spent, while the results in fixing these families on the land and making the settlements economically viable were few and far between. This led to greater tension between the government and the MST. In 2009, Lula was to label as "vandalism" the invasion and destruction of orange groves on a property belonging to a large orange exporting group in the state of São Paulo. And his government refused a proposal to raise the productivity levels used to characterize properties as liable for expropriation for purposes of agrarian reform.

The aspirations of the "new middle classes" did not escape the attention of the government. An own-home acquisition program called *Minha Casa, Minha Vida* (My Home, My Life) offering subsidized funding for lower income groups was launched in 2009 and would gain strength in the following years. The government was also sensitive to the aspirations of these classes in terms of higher education. To support students from lower income groups, the government granted fiscal incentives to private institutions, responsible for the majority of places available in higher education, in exchange for the concession of study scholarships for poorer students. Affirmative action, a question that had been raised in the previous government, gained prominence at both the federal and state levels.

Affirmative action policies focused on higher education provoked lively public debate, engaging intellectuals representing all shades of opinion. The debate was heightened when one of the parties in opposition to the government, the Democratas or DEM (the new name for the old PFL) brought a suit in the federal supreme court, alleging the unconstitutionality of the policy of racial quotas adopted by the University of Brasilia, a federal public institution. In their first public manifesto, "Everyone is equal in the Democratic Republic," issued in 2006, intellectuals critical of the adoption of racial quotas used the argument that it injured the republican principle of equality before the law and introduced an artificial racial division in a society characterized by the mixing of races. This action was only heard by the federal supreme court in 2012, when it found for the constitutionality of racial quotas. The public debate, however, continued.

Neither did the Lula government neglect the "old middle classes." There were significant salary increases for federal civil servants, as well as an increase in the number of civil service entry examinations. The base salaries of university lecturers were also readjusted. In fact, the almost complete absence of general salary increases for federal university lecturers had been one of the reasons why a significant number of them had been dissatisfied with the Cardoso government.

If in practice the economic and social policies of the new government represented a continuation of those of the previous one, rhetorically Lula and his party invested heavily in stigmatizing his predecessor from the outset. An example of this was the expression "damned legacy." Another phrase used often in presidential speeches praising the government's achievements was "never before in the history of this country." The expression was designed to underscore the idea that his government was initiating a new stage in Brazilian history.

Among the few positive references to the past, Getúlio Vargas was by far the most important in Lula's speeches. In this manner, the president accentuated the symbolic contrast with the Cardoso government, whose proposal had been to overcome the "Vargas Era."

More than other political leaders of the past, Lula resorted to symbols and linguistic expressions from popular culture to communicate with the public and to reinforce his image as a "man of the people" already inherent in his biography. Along similar lines, he constructed an image of himself as the benevolent father, inclusive and fair in the treatment of his children, but especially attentive to the needier ones. Critics saw in this a regressive populism, which reduced people to an infantile and subordinate position. The presidential rhetoric, however, was well received among broad sections of the population, mostly the poor and those not fully incorporated into the universe of citizenship. This was not only due to the effectiveness of the president's communication, backed by his biography, but also to the concrete fact that the presidential rhetoric corresponded to an effective extension of the income transfer programs and a significant increase in the minimum salary.

This combination of personal attributes and social results achieved by his government explains why Lula was able to survive politically amidst a series of scandals, achieving unprecedented levels of popularity during his second term.

7.15 POLITICAL CRISIS AND THE CRISIS OF POLITICS: THE SUCCESSION OF SCANDALS

During its long years in opposition, the PT had wielded the banner of "ethics in politics," constantly denouncing alleged or proven acts of corruption. Even those who did not identify with the party were convinced that its conduct would be morally differentiated. This conviction was to be roundly disabused.

The Lula government was marked by scandals that caused great repercussions. Although there had been scandals in previous governments, one of which had led to the impeachment of a president, those of the most recent presidential period were distinguished by the involvement of party leaders and high-ranking members of the government.

Of all the scandals that emerged in the Lula government, the so-called *mensalão* was the only one to truly threaten the government and political stability in the country. The scandal was initiated when the deputy Roberto Jefferson (PTB), until then a government ally, made a speech declaring that the Lula government, without the president's knowledge, had been using public and private funds to bribe deputies on a monthly basis to ensure the approval of projects of its interest. The main target of the accusation was the chief of staff of the presidency, José Dirceu.

The government's defense strategy was elaborated on two fronts. On the political front, it consisted of denying the purchase of votes in congress, concentrating the blame and responsibility on the PT's treasurer and characterising the accusations as a fabrication aimed at bringing down the government, the work of an elite unable to digest the success of a working man in the role of president of the republic. In accordance with the official discourse, Lula knew nothing about the alleged scheme. On the judicial front, the government claimed that the financial movements identified by the parliamentary inquiry commission represented the settlement of debts between parties in the government coalition using funds not included in the official accounts presented to the electoral courts. In other words, there was no scheme organized by the office of the chief of staff to purchase deputies' votes with funds diverted from public coffers, but rather isolated operations financed from a "slush fund." This argument was aimed at characterising any wrongdoings as infractions of electoral legislation attributable to party representatives, as opposed to a crime that could lead to impeachment should any indications of the president's involvement emerge.

The government won the political battle. The opposition opted not to fight to oust the president, fearing that it might come off worse in an eventual political polarization and concerned about the long-term effects of such a split on democracy. It imagined that the political scandal would be enough to blemish Lula's image and ensure his defeat in the October 2006 elections. The reality, however, would prove to be different.

In fact, the president did suffer a significant decrease in popularity during the course of 2005. However, this did not extend beyond higher income and better educated social segments and proved to be transitory. At the beginning of the 2006 electoral race, the president had recovered his lost popularity and was the outright favorite for re-election, in spite of a new scandal of a different nature that had led to the fall of his minister of finance. The material gains resulting from the ongoing expansion of income, credit, employment, and government income transfers through programs such as the Family Allowance held sway over the poorer sections of society, eclipsing the damage caused by the scandal. While Lula might have lost the middle class momentarily, he consolidated his support at the base of the social pyramid.

Within the PT, a minority who had insisted on "re-founding" the party went quiet. Moralisation measures were limited to expelling the treasurer from the party and substituting its president.

The federal public prosecutor, however, brought before the federal supreme court charges accusing a number of government ministers of involvement in the scheme. The case was only heard in 2012, and it resulted in the condemnation of 25 people, including members of parliament, ex-ministers, bankers, and an advertising executive, as responsible for the financial orchestration of the scheme. These included two leaders of the PT: José Dirceu and José Genoíno, president of the party at the time, as well as the party treasurer, the self-confessed main operator of the financial transactions.

Lula emerged from these episodes with some damage to his image and without two important cabinet members, Dirceu and Palocci, replaced respectively by Dilma Rousseff, until then minister of Mines and Energy, and Guido Mantega, president of the BNDES, and prior to this minister of planning. Lula's personal image suffered less than that of the party. This situation merely underscored what had already become evident: Lula had risen above and become greater than the PT. The party, however, continued to be the most popular among the electorate. Party identity surveys show that, throughout the last decade, the PT regularly had the support of around 15 percent of the electorate, twice as much as the party in second place, the PMDB, and three times that of the PSDB, which came in third.

The main opposition parties were unable to capitalize on the momentary damage suffered by the PT. This was due in part to accusations involving opposition parties. During the investigation of the "*mensalão*," there emerged signs of the existence of a similar, although much smaller, scheme in Minas Gerais in 1998, which used public company contracts with an advertising agency to illegally finance the re-election campaign of the then-governor of the state, Eduardo Azeredo, of the PSDB. At the end of 2009, during Lula's second term, the "DEM mensalão" also came to light, with accusations against the only governor of the old PFL, elected in October 2006.

The main victim of this sequence of scandals was the already blemished image of politics in general and of congress in particular, although, paradoxically, a striking characteristic in all of them had been the involvement of members of the first rank of the executive.

In reaction to this state of affairs, civil society organizations presented congress with a bill based on a mass initiative – for which two million signatures had been collected – demanding the alteration of electoral legislation to prevent politicians with criminal records from running for office. The bill was approved in the first half of 2010, just under six months before the October general elections. The version approved affected candidates who had been condemned in court, even if the sentence was subject to appeal in a higher court.

7.16 A "NEW DEVELOPMENT MODEL"?

With Antonio Palocci no longer in office, the government distanced itself from the more liberal line pursued in Lula's first term.

The change occurred less in the management of economic policy and more in the role attributed to the state in regulating and stimulating the economy. Thus a trend already evident since the beginning of the government was accentuated, with the weakening of the regulatory agencies created by Cardoso.

In Lula's second term, the conviction grew that the key to economic development lay in alliances between state-owned companies and some large private Brazilian companies with the size to compete in the global market. New state companies were created and old ones resuscitated. The proportion of shares held by the BNDES and state-companies pension funds in private companies increased. State participation in greenfield investments in the infrastructure and other sectors, such as petrochemicals, also increased, and, with financial support from the BNDES, mergers were promoted between private companies to form large companies controlled by Brazilian private capital.

The Growth Acceleration Program or PAC (Programa de Aceleração do Crescimento) was created to drive investment. Launched in 2007, the PAC was one of the government's main flagships in Lula's second term. Dilma Roussef, who was to be the candidate to succeed Lula, was given responsibility for coordinating the program, being hailed as "mother of the PAC" by the president.

The swing of the pendulum toward a more "statist" position represented a re-encounter between the government and dominant thinking in the PT about the role of the state in economic development. During Lula's first term, this line of thinking had not been reflected in the actions of the central bank under Henrique Meirelles, nor in the ministry of finance, where the minister Antônio Palocci commanded a team in large part left over from the previous government or at least attuned with its policy. These two areas had been subjects of open criticism from high ranking leaders of the PT. The criticisms against them revolved around Palocci and Meirelles' insistence on fiscal and monetary rigour and emphasis on reforms to improve economic efficiency and productivity through the more effective functioning of the markets, rather than by direct state action.

This swing of the pendulum was made possible because the economic policy in Lula's first term had produced results and because Brazil, as we have seen, had benefited from the growth of the international economy and from the expansion in world trade. With resources available, through higher tax revenue and the capacity to raise funds internally and externally, the Lula government gained greater freedom of action to put into practice what, with some exaggeration, it termed "a new development model," based on the internal mass market and state leadership of investment.

The "new model" was already clearly taking shape when the global financial crisis exploded, reaching Brazil in the second half of 2008. The Lula government used the new global ideological climate to reinforce the legitimacy of the reorientation of Brazil's development model and highlight the contrast with the "neoliberalism" attributed to the Cardoso government.

The opposition to Lula responded with two types of criticism, voiced mainly by his predecessor. The first consisted in pointing out the economic and political risks of regression to General Geisel's national-statist development model when, under that authoritarian regime, the state greatly expanded its direct participation in the economy. In addition to state expansion, there was also criticism of the use of treasury-subsidized funds to provide loans to a restricted group of companies through the BNDES. The second type of criticism was aimed at the acceleration in the federal government's current account spending, a trend that was increased after the global financial crisis. With the electoral race just beginning, the opposition saw this acceleration in current expenditures as being more politically than economically motivated.

The government's efforts to mobilize funding and promote investment proved to be greater than the results obtained. In aggregate, there was an upward trend in the investment rate, but at the end of Lula's second term it stood at around 20 percent, a level insufficient to sustain growth at 5 percent a year without greater inflationary pressure or external imbalance. As a result of economic growth, infrastructure bottlenecks became tighter, leading to saturation of the country's ports and airports and deterioration of the highway network. The government was hesitant about mobilizing private capital to invest in these sectors and experienced difficulty in executing planned public investment, which was reflected in the disappointing performance of the PAC.

7.17 THE PRE-SALT CONTROVERSY

Because of what it represented and its possible future implications, no other initiative marked the effort to introduce a "new development model" as much as the proposal to change the regulatory framework for the oil and natural gas sector.

This was presented to congress as if it were an urgent measure at the end of 2009, on the eve of the start-up of the presidential race. It was related to the exploitation of the so-called "pre-salt" oil reserves, discovered in 2006 in the ultra-deep waters of the Brazilian continental shelf, some 300 km off the coast of the states of São Paulo, Rio de Janeiro, and Espírito Santo in the southeast of the country. Petrobras's initial estimates indicated oil reserves two times bigger than the country's existing reserves. Should these be confirmed, Brazil will rank among the top ten countries in oil and gas reserves.

Since confirmation of the first pre-salt reserves, the discovery was used repeatedly by the government to reinforce the idea that Brazil was finally becoming a world power.

To exploit the reserves, the government proposed changing the concession regime in place since the approval of the petroleum law in 1997. As an alternative, it presented a production-sharing regime, whereby the state would receive its part in barrels of oil rather than in taxes. For the government, this proposal was the only one capable of ensuring the nation's control over the exploitation of this natural wealth.

For critics, the only justification for the proposal was ideological and political in nature. They argued that the concession regime, whose positive results the government did not deny, already incorporated mechanisms that would allow the state to appropriate a larger share of the oil revenues. In addition to being unnecessary, the change in regime would be prejudicial, since it included rules that inhibited competition and the attraction of more investments to the sector. The government proposal determined that Petrobras would be the exclusive operator of the pre-salt fields and would have a minimum share of 30 percent in all projects in the area.

The change in the sector regulatory framework was approved in a rush by congress at the beginning of 2010, with the presidential race already underway. The framework, however, led to a major conflict over the distribution of royalties between the states that produced oil and gas and those that did not. These and other factors led to the virtual paralysis of investment in the sector. Instead of the much vaunted self-sufficiency, Brazil actually increased its oil imports in the following years.

7.18 GROWTH AND THE ENVIRONMENT

Impacts on the environment attracted increasing attention as economic growth accelerated and the Lula government placed greater emphasis on major investments in the energy and transportation sectors. Another growing source of tension was the environmental impact caused by agribusiness, given increased global demand for food and pressures to bring more land under cultivation for agriculture and livestock.

The environmental question extended beyond national borders, becoming a major item on the country's external agenda, in line with the growing perception of Brazil as a world power in agriculture and energy, in particular due to the development of its ethanol industry and the discovery of the pre-salt reserves.

It was within this broader context that the Lula government's decisions were made – or not made – about the ever wider and more complex range of issues concerning the use of the country's abundant natural resources to drive Brazil's development. Evident in society, the conflicts surrounding these issues were also reflected within the government. On the one hand there were the ministries of agriculture, transport and energy, which were more attuned to the needs and benefits of economic growth than concerns about potential environmental impacts, and on the other hand, the ministry of the environment, in particular when the Senator Marina Silva was in charge. Lula sought to arbitrate this conflict, tending more to the side that was in favor of accelerated growth and frequently found environmental precautions excessive.

The main figures in this struggle were Marina Silva and Dilma Rousseff. The latter was first minister of mines and energy and later chief of staff to the presidency, acquiring command of the PAC. Both were to be candidates to succeed Lula.

Rousseff adopted a position aligned with most of the business community – in particular heavy construction – governors, mayors, and large parliamentary interest groups, such as agribusiness. From their standpoint, IBAMA (the Brazilian Institute for the Environment and Renewable Natural Resources) and the public prosecution service, which had become intensely involved in the environmental question since the 1998 constitution, created barriers to the country's development under the pretext of protecting diffuse collective rights. It was not long before conflicts arose around the concession of environmental licenses for transportation and energy projects. Marina Silva was criticised for the length of time IBAMA, which was subordinated to her ministry, took in issuing these licenses. Her critics accused her of wanting to maintain the legally delineated Amazon region, which included parts of the Cerrado biome, as an "ecological sanctuary." They also disapproved of her resistance to the use of transgenic varieties in agriculture, a criticism in which agribusiness was supported by members of the scientific community. She did, however, have the support of Brazilian and international NGOs, which had gained space and influence in the country throughout the 1990s. She also enjoyed a high degree of international prestige as a result of her engagement in socio-environmental causes.

Successive shocks led Marina Silva to resign her post in 2008. Attentive to the balance between the political and social forces in his government, Lula chose Carlos Minc, at that time secretary of the environment of the state of Rio de Janeiro, to substitute for Marina Silva. With the new minister, considered to be more pragmatic, the conflicts with the office of the chief of staff decreased.

However, the struggle over the environmental issue did not disappear altogether. Rather there was a change in some of the key figures involved. The next battle was to take place, both inside and outside congress, over the proposal to change the Brazilian forestry code. On one side were the representatives of agribusiness, and on the other, the environmentalists, both of whom were represented in the government coalition. The former enjoyed a distinct majority, especially in the government's parliamentary support base.

Created initially in 1934, the code had undergone a series of modifications in the following decades, particularly under the Cardoso government, when more rigorous rules for protecting vegetation cover were introduced. For the representatives of agribusiness, such rules, which they believed were applied arbitrarily by public prosecutors, created a generalized legal uncertainty for agricultural producers. In some cases, they made agricultural activity impracticable in areas in which it had already been consolidated, in addition to impeding expansion to new areas. From the viewpoint of the environmentalists, the code represented a boundary that had to be defended, and the attempt to change it a manoeuvre to open the gates to further deforestation. When the Lula government ended, the bill on the forestry code was in line to be voted in the Chamber of Deputies.

While unable to implement integrated policies to ensure socially and environmentally sustainable development, the Lula government did significantly reduce the rate of deforestation in the Amazon, the administration's main triumph in the environmental area both internally and externally. Similarly, under this government Brazil created more environmental protection areas than any other country worldwide.

This brings us to Brazil's participation in the negotiations of the global convention on climate change.

7.19   BRAZIL'S POSITION IN THE NEGOTIATIONS ON CLIMATE CHANGE

From 2007 on, there was an intensification of the global negotiations on a new framework for mitigating global warming and adapting to its effects. Signed ten years previously, the Kyoto Protocol would be in effect until 2012.

The negotiations took place under the influence of the third assessment report published by the Inter-Governmental Panel on Climate Change in 2007 with a view to the 15th conference of the parties to the United Nations Convention on Climate Change, to be held in Copenhagen at the end of 2009. In the report, the IPCC indicated the increased probability of critical scenarios resulting from rising temperatures and urged governments to improve on the targets and measures established in the Kyoto Protocol. The Copenhagen Summit was to be decisive toward this end.

Reflecting changes in domestic and international opinion, Brazil adjusted its position on this question. Since the first summit, Rio-92, held in the city of Rio de Janeiro in 1992, the Brazilian government had advocated the concept of shared but differentiated responsibilities among members of the United Nations Convention on Climate Change. A central element of the convention, this concept maintains that only the developed countries would be obliged to fulfil international emission reduction targets, because historically they were responsible for most of the greenhouse gases in the atmosphere. These countries should also provide technical and financial assistance to the developing nations, enabling them to move voluntarily toward a low-carbon economy at their convenience and in accordance with their economic and social abilities. The developing countries would not be obliged to meet the targets established by the international convention on climate change. The Kyoto Protocol endorsed the concept of shared but differentiated responsibility.

However, the division of the world between developed and developing countries became more problematic with the generalized acceptance of the category of "emerging countries" in the course of the first decade of this century. This category came to be confused with an acronym comprising the initials of Brazil, Russia, India and China: BRIC. Recognized for the dynamism of their economies and external trade, these counties came under pressure to assume new responsibilities in questions related to global governance. With respect to the convention on climate change, this implied submitting to measurable and verifiable emission reduction targets.

With the fourth highest greenhouse gas emissions worldwide in absolute volume, Brazil did not escape from these pressures, although the main target of the developed countries, in particular the United States, was China. However, internal pressures had greater influence on the change in the Brazilian government's position on this question. The question gained greater political relevance with increased sensitivity about the main source of greenhouse gas emissions in the country: deforestation in the Amazon. This sensitivity was heightened by government programs to monitor and control burning and the illegal extraction of timber from the region.

Just before the Copenhagen Summit in 2009, the government presented an amendment to the national climate change plan that was passing through Congress, assuming quantitative greenhouse gas emission reduction targets. Targets were also established to reduce deforestation in the Amazon. In other words, Brazil maintained its position of not assuming international obligations in this area, but voluntarily established verifiable domestic greenhouse gas emission reduction targets.

By doing this, the government forestalled an initiative announced by Senator Marina Silva. After resigning from the government she had left the PT and joined the small Brazilian Green Party, immediately being singled out as probable candidate for the presidency and adversary to Dilma Rousseff, who had already been informally designated as the candidate to succeed Lula. For its critics, this change represented too little and too late, the result of an adaptation to accommodate public opinion, rather than a consistent strategy to combat the problem of climate change. Whatever the case, the change did differentiate Brazil from its traditional allies in the climate-change negotiations, such as China and India, who arrived in Copenhagen with more defensive positions. Symptomatically, Dilma Rousseff was chosen to head the Brazilian delegation to the Danish capital.

With the Summit already underway, the government introduced another change. Unexpectedly, two days after the head of the Brazilian delegation had made a speech to the opposite effect, president Lula arrived in Copenhagen and announced publicly that Brazil would contribute to a global fund to help lower-income countries adopt climate change mitigation and adaptation measures.

The three main candidates for president in the elections to be held the following year were present in Copenhagen. In addition to Dilma and Marina, José Serra attended the meeting in his capacity as governor of São Paulo, a state that had adopted its own program incorporating greenhouse gas emission reduction targets. This was a clear indication that climate change had moved up on the national political agenda.

The failure of the Copenhagen Summit and the enduring impasses in the negotiations on climate change reduced the political priority attributed to the issue in the following years. There can be no doubt, however, that there was a sharp change in perception of the seriousness of the problem in Brazil.

7.20   THE IDENTITY OF FOREIGN POLICY

Foreign policy made a significant contribution to defining the identity of the Lula government. In addition to enhancing the government's image overseas, it represented a significant element in the dispute with the opposition inside the country.

During Lula's first term in office, foreign policy was seen as a compensation for economic policy. While in economic policy, continuity of the previous government's policy had prevailed, foreign policy was marked by changes. On the one hand, the government focused on tranquilizing the "markets," on the other, it made a point of meeting the ideological demands of the left in general, and the PT in particular.

In Lula's second term, with a less orthodox macroeconomic policy and a more "statist" development policy, the initial distance or divergence disappeared. Instead of compensation, there was a convergence between economic policy and foreign policy around the idea of the "developmentalist" state and a nation that was "powerful" on the international scene. With this, the defense area gained an importance not seen since the time of the military government. The 2008 National Defence Strategy, without relinquishing the country's pacific tradition, projected a vision of a Brazil that had reached a stage of development which increased its international projection, requiring that its armed forces be strengthened. The document underscored the need for military protection of the country's natural resources, in particular the newly discovered pre-salt oil reserves, a theme which was dear to the statist-developmentalist mindset and to the armed forces.

The overall diagnosis that oriented the Lula government's foreign policy may be summarized as follows: with the relative decline of the United States, except in the military sphere, and the emergence of new poles of political and economic power, there was more room for Brazil to participate in the global economy and in the international system. This phenomenon was reinforced by the new global terms of trade, favorable to the commodity-producing countries. In general, the diagnosis did not generate political discord. The divergences would become apparent when it came to concrete action.

Based on its vision of the new balance of power emerging in the world, the Lula government sought to accentuate the contrast between Brazilian interests and those of the dominant countries in the northern hemisphere. Brazil's interests would be much better served by alliances with the emerging nations in the southern hemisphere, on the diverse levels of international interaction, from trade to the environment. First, this would give the country more bargaining power in international forums. Second, the emergence of the South would increase the pressure to redistribute power in global governance bodies, in particular in the areas of finance (IMF) and security (UN).

Known as South-South, this policy did not result in systematic antagonism toward the north on the part of Brazil. Rather it sought diversification in the country's economic and political relations.

For defenders of the policy, executed by Celso Amorim, external relations minister during the eight years of the Lula government, it enabled Brazil to affirm itself in the new multi-polar configuration of the international order, with just the right dose of daring, without which these spaces would not have been conquered. For critics, the foreign policy was characterized by a striving for circumstantial prestige and, not infrequently, an unrealistic assessment of the country's effective capacity to participate in the great global power game. An example of this would be the country's efforts to obtain a permanent seat on the UN Security Council, an aspiration that was not new, but which became a priority in the Lula government. Brazil was accused of turning a blind eye to human rights violations in Arab and African countries with a view to obtaining this seat.

Nonetheless, even the critics would recognize Brazil's positive participation in multilateral forums, starting with the WTO. Even though the Doha Round did not prosper and produce concrete results, Brazil's performance leading the commercial G-20, constituted in 2003 in response to a proposal from the developed nations, strengthened perception of the effectiveness of Brazilian "soft power." There was an equally positive perception both internally and externally of the country's significant participation in the financial G-20, reactivated in the wake of the 2008 global financial crisis. The country's performance in the first group demonstrated its capacity to build alliances among the developing countries, while its participation in the second indicated recognition of Brazil's new status on the part of the developed countries.

More controversial both internally and externally were the foreign policies measures adopted for South America.

South America at the Center of the Agenda

South America has been the focus of Brazilian foreign policy for decades. The novelty in the Lula government was the emphasis on the political dimension of the country's relations with neighbouring countries.

Those directly involved in formulating foreign policy for the region were the diplomat Samuel Pinheiro Guimarães and the presidential special aide for international affairs, Marco Aurélio

Garcia. Pinheiro Guimarães hailed from the nationalistic wing of the Itamaraty, Brazil's diplomatic service. Garcia had a long history of left-wing activity, first in the clandestine opposition to the military dictatorship and later in the PT.

At the very beginning, it became clear that the government viewed South American integration in opposition to hemispheric integration. It was not long before negotiations for the formation of the Free Trade Area of the Americas were interrupted. The Brazilian viewpoint was that the FTAA would only serve to consolidate trade consolidate economic asymmetries unfavorable for the country's development. The initiative was definitively laid to rest at the Americas Summit held in Mar del Plata in 2005.

The controversy around foreign policy for South America heightened with the election of Evo Morales as president of Bolivia and as the Venezuelan president, Hugo Chávez, started to radicalize his "Bolivarian revolution," both internally and regionally. The crucial episode with Bolivia occurred in May 2006, when Morales issued a decree nationalising the oil and gas sector, accompanied by the military occupation of the facilities of foreign companies with operations in Bolivia, including Petrobras. The diplomatic reaction from the Brazilian government was considered tepid in Brazil. From the Brazilian government viewpoint, the mild reaction was meant to demonstrate two things: Brazil was not an arrogant regional leader; Brazil did understand the developmental aspirations of its poorer neighbors.

The radicalisation of the Chavist regime from 2005, when Chávez raised the banner of "21st century socialism," and his push for regional leadership, explicit in the creation of the Bolivarian Alliance for the Americas, ALBA, in 2004, presented a greater political threat to Brazil than did the Bolivian nationalization of oil and gas. Instead of confrontation, the Brazilian government opted to contain within certain limits the impact of Chávez's regional initiatives and with it the Venezuelan president's leadership in South America.

For Chávez, South American integration represented an updating of the dream of "La Patria Grande" nurtured by Simon Bolívar in the 19th century, in the wake of the independence wars against Spain. In the Venezuelan president's vision, it was up to him as

Bolívar's heir to lead this project forward. It consisted of integrating the South American countries under the aegis of the Bolivarian Republic of Venezuela, in opposition to the United States. This prospect was contrary to the interests of Brazil, even if some members of the Brazilian government were sympathetic to Chávez and mildly anti-American.

In the creation of the Union of South American Nations (UNASUR) concluded in 2008, Brazil worked toward ensuring that the new institution would not have the characteristics desired by the Venezuelan president. This became clear with the definition of the goals of the South American Defence Council, which Chávez saw as a body that would coordinate the member-countries' armed forces. Through the action of the Brazilian government, the council was given more limited scope, as a result of which even Colombia, with its special relations with the United States, accepted a seat on the council.

UNASUR was an expression of the Brazilian strategy of affirming its influence in the region through institutions whose rules did not imply a major surrender of the member-countries' sovereignty. Within this strategy, the economic agenda was subordinated to the political-integration agenda. This reflected the growing divergence between the economic strategies of the countries that had maintained a liberal orientation since the 1990s, such as Chile, Peru, and Colombia, and those that had turned in the opposite direction, Venezuela, Bolivia, and Ecuador.

Brazil preferred to bet on the incorporation of the "Bolivarian countries" into Mercosur. For many, the incorporation of Venezuela represented the last nail in the coffin of the already faltering customs union, debilitated by Argentina's growing protectionism under the successive presidencies of Nestor and Cristina Kirchner. Ratified by the senates of the other member-countries, Venezuela's official entry into Mercosur was stalled, pending approval by the Paraguayan senate, and was only to come about in 2012 under heavy political pressure from Brazil and Argentina.

In favor of the Brazilian strategy, it may be argued that it increased Brazil's soft influence amidst the political tensions latent in the region and favored increased investments by Brazilian companies neighbouring countries, both liberal and anti-liberal. Thus, the country strengthened its political position as a moderating power and, in parallel, its economic presence in the region. For critics of the foreign policy, however, the Brazilian government was complacent toward the exportation of the Bolivarian revolution to other countries in the region (Chávez's intrusion in the domestic affairs of a number of Latin American countries) and the importation of global tensions into South America via Chávez's international alliances (in particular with Iran). Critics also believed that the potential amplification of Mercosur would tie Brazil into integration processes offering limited economic gains.

Relations with the United States

In 2010, UNASUR was followed by the creation of yet another regional institution, broader in scope although even more fragile in institutional terms: the Community of Latin American and Caribbean States (CELAC), which was an organisation of American states that excluded the United States. The initiative came about amidst divergences in the OAS over the readmission of Cuba to the organisation and diplomatic initiatives following the coup in Honduras. Despite the fact that Brazil and the United States were not on the same side in these two episodes, there was no significant impact on a bilateral relationship that remained normal for seven of the eight years of Lula's administration. In truth, the PT's rise to power did not alter the United States' positive perception of Brazil's leadership in South America. The picture changed in 2010, when the two countries went at loggerheads over a very sensitive global security issue: the Iranian nuclear program. Some context will help to explain why.

Signed by Brazil during the Cardoso government, the Nuclear Non-Proliferation Treaty (NPT) was to become a controversial item on the Lula government's external-relations agenda. Criticisms of the asymmetry of the NPT were raised in the first months of the government. Samuel Pinheiro Guimarães, the number two man in the Itamaraty, declared that Brazil might consider withdrawing from the treaty. The government never endorsed this position, but neither did it deny it. The National Defence Strategy launched at the end of 2008, established Brazil's official refusal to sign the additional NPT protocol.

The following year, the recently elected Barak Obama stepped up the isolation of Iran in the light of new evidence that the country's nuclear program was producing increasingly higher grades of uranium. At the same time, Brazil was showing signs of forging closer relations with Iran, with reciprocal visits by the countries' presidents and foreign ministers in a short interval of time and Brazil's immediate recognition of Ahmadinejad's re-election as president, in a ballot rife with suspicions of fraud.

The Brazilian president and foreign minister justified the closeness with Iran as a question of commercial interests and pointed out the risks involved in the imposition of sanctions on the country. They cited the example of Iraq, where the suspicion, later disproved, of the existence of weapons of mass destruction had been used to justify the American invasion.

In the weeks prior to the expected vote by the UN Security Council on the imposition of sanctions against Iran, Lula and Celso Amorim initiated the most daring Brazilian diplomatic initiative during the period. Feeling it had been authorized by the United States and counting on the cooperation of Turkey, Brazil brokered an agreement based on a proposal put forward months before by the group of countries led by the United States and the European community. In April 2010, this agreement was announced in Teheran as a great triumph of Brazilian and Turkish diplomacy. Newspapers around the world carried a photograph of Lula raising Ahmadinejad's arm in celebration.

The illusion of a great victory lasted only a few hours. The following morning, Hillary Clinton, U.S. secretary of state, declared the terms of the agreement unacceptable, stating that they were outdated, given that Iran's production of enriched uranium had increased since the initial proposal had been presented. Simultaneously, Hillary Clinton announced that the five permanent members of the UN Security Council (United States, France, England, Russia, and China) had developed a joint proposal for the imposition of sanctions against Iran. This frustrated the expectation nurtured by Brazilian diplomacy that Russia and China would support the agreement brokered by Brazil and Turkey.

In spite of Brazil's arguments that negotiation was preferable to sanctions, which had proved counterproductive in the past, the United States' capacity to impose its interests and its vision of the problem prevailed.

For the government, in spite of the paucity of results, the diplomatic initiative reinforced Brazil's image as a relevant new actor in the resolution of crucial questions of global governance. For critics both inside and outside the country, it confirmed one of the major defects of the Lula government's foreign policy: over-estimation of Brazil's capacity for action in highly complex regions of the world where the country's real influence was limited or inexistent and a propensity to seek opportunities for circumstantial prestige, without properly assessing the country's interests.

7.21 LULA'S SUCCESSION

The map emerging from the October 2006 presidential elections – when Lula was re-elected after defeating the PSDB candidate and ex-governor of São Paulo, Geraldo Alckmin, in the second round, with a percentage of votes practically identical to that in the previous election – showed a country divided socially and geographically. Opposition votes were concentrated among the higher-income and more educated segments of society and in the south and southeast of the country (in particular the state of São Paulo). Lula won by a broad margin among the poorer social segments and in the north and northeast regions. The political scientist André Singer, spokesman for the presidency in Lula's first term, saw the 2006 presidential election as an electoral realignment around the phenomenon of "Lulism": in the previous elections, most of Lula's votes had come from the social bases of his party, that is, the industrial proletariat and sectors of the urban middle class; however, in the 2006 election, the bulk of the votes came from the poorer sectors of the population, principally those tied to the informal economy.

It is worth noting, however, that instead of accentuating the geographical and social polarization evident in the electorate, a possibility it had flirted with during the "*mensalão*" crisis, the government sought to overcome it, with its sights on 2010. It adopted a series of programs that, in addition to meeting basic needs, sought to satisfy the demands of the urban middle classes, both traditional members with their roots in public service and the "emerging" urban citizens aspiring to higher education and their own homes.

After the dismissal of a proposal by members of the PT to change the constitution to permit another re-election for Lula, a cause which he himself never embraced, Lula anointed his chief of staff as his successor. Never having disputed an elected position and with a relatively short history in the PT, which she had joined in 2001, Dilma Rousseff was Lula's personal choice. The president was confident he could transfer his immense political and electoral cachet to her. After overcoming the damage caused by the *"mensalão"* scandal, Lula's popularity soared during his second term, reaching unprecedented levels. What appeared to be a risky bet – his candidate would face José Serra, the PSDB governor of the state of São Paulo, an opponent with broad political and administrative experience who was well known to the voters – eventually proved successful.

To strengthen her candidacy, Lula sought to install a member of the PMDB in the vice-presidency, in the person of the São Paulo deputy Michel Temer. While putting together a broad-based electoral alliance, the president started to promote Dilma Rousseff long before the official campaign launch, taking advantages of ambiguities and loopholes in the legislation governing the participation of the heads of state in electoral campaigns.

Lula's strategy was successful, and his candidate won, but not in the first round. The second round occurred because of the growth of Marina Silva's popularity in the run-up to the election. As a candidate for the Green Party, she garnered votes among middle-class voters, who identified with her biography and her platform favoring a "new vision of development," emphasising the environment. She also received a significant portion of the religious vote, especially from evangelical groups, who were wary of the shifts in Rousseff's position on abortion. The Green Party candidate, herself evangelical, received a surprising 20 percent of the valid votes. With 33 percent of the vote going to the PSDB candidate José Serra, there was a second round, which Dilma Rousseff won with 56 percent of the valid votes. Thus, for the first time in its history, Brazil elected a woman as president.

In spite of the victory of the government candidate and a reduction in opposition representation in Congress, where Dilma Rousseff's coalition obtained more than two-thirds of the votes in the Chamber and the Senate, the electoral map resulting from the October 2010 elections once again revealed a politically plural country. The opposition parties won in ten states, including the two most important ones, São Paulo and Minas Gerais. Compared with the situation after the 2006 election, analysis of the geographical and social distribution of the votes for the PT and PSDB candidates in the second round shows relative stability, with some slight modifications: the PT increased its votes in sectors of the middle class, reducing the difference in relation to the PSDB in the south of the country. In other words, the clear social and geographical divisions seen in 2006 gained a number of nuances in 2010.

7.22   DEMOCRACY UNDER LULA

The Lula government observed the formal rules of the democratic game. Even with popularity ratings unprecedented in the country, the president did not support the constitutional amendment presented by a PT deputy, his personal friend, which would have enabled him to pursue (and probably win) a third consecutive term. The "re-election" amendment was quashed by the congressional committee responsible for its initial assessment, in an opinion issued by José Genoíno, also from the PT, considering it incompatible with Brazilian democracy.

Nonetheless, the Lula government was seen by part of the opposition and public opinion as a threat to democracy in the country. Not because it had adopted a deliberate anti-democratic strategy, but due to a series of actions that some thought capable of undermining democratic institutions, in particular freedom of expression and the balance of power.

In part this fear expressed a certain prejudice against the social origins of the president and the "new elite" in power. It also revealed the difficulty of co-existing in the political system with a party like the PT, the first and only party with deep roots in society among the rank and file and a broad base of activists to enter the political power game since the country's return to democracy.

This fear, however, was based on a plausible interpretation of facts. This diagnosis was best put forth by the ex-president Cardoso, the voice who had the most credibility among the opposition parties. For him, under the auspices of the state and supported by public funds, the Lula government represented the embryo of a power block with the appetite and capacity to throw the political game off balance and perpetuate itself in power. In this process, the external forms of democracy would be preserved – with periodic elections, including those for president – but with the risk of these electoral procedures loosing much of its real meaning due to the domination of the state by the new power block and the corresponding limitation of effective public debate.

Such a power block would be commanded by the PT in alliance with the union confederations benefiting from compulsory union fees, and with large private groups favoured by subsidized BNDES loans. The block would also include state company pension funds, the link between business and the unions, given the CUT's growing dominion over these entities and their expanding presence in business ventures and other companies associated with large private groups.

It was along these lines that the sociologist Francisco de Oliveira, a founder of the PT who split with the party during the Lula government, elaborated the idea of the emergence of a "new class," formed at the intersection of the party, unions, and state company pension funds. A typical representative of this "new class" would be a union or party leader placed in command of state funds, in particular pension funds, organisations that have achieved a key role in Brazilian capitalism.

The fear about the medium-term effects the Lula government would have on democracy was also fuelled by facts not requiring elaborate sociological interpretation. Relations between the government and media were characterized by tension, in particular after the "*mensalão*," although they never came anywhere near the degree of confrontation seen in neighbouring countries.

The government, and the president in particular, formed the notion that they were victims of a media campaign. This perception was reinforced by a position sustained historically by the PT according to which democratization had never reached the country's communications sector, which lacked rules to prevent the concentration of diverse media (TV, radio, and newspapers) into the hands of one business group. Under the dubious heading of "social control of the media," the government elaborated an agenda that, in spirit, if not in word, confused legitimate public regulation of media operated under concession by private initiative (TV channels and radio stations) with control of the content transmitted by the diverse communication media, including newspapers.

While never implemented, this ambiguous "social control of media" agenda did not entirely disappear or receive a clearer definition. It was only directly rejected by the candidate and President-Elect Dilma Rousseff after causing her a certain amount of discomfort during the election.

7.23 CONCLUSION

At the beginning of this chapter I said that an observer at the end of the 1980s would have had difficulty in foreseeing the advances achieved by Brazil in the following twenty years, in particular after the Real Plan in 1994. In the course of the chapter we underscored some of the limitations to these advances. Here we return to the theme to add some comments on the challenges the country faces, if it is to become a more prosperous and fairer society.

The liberalization of the economy, the stabilization of the currency, and the strengthening of public policy, particularly in the social area, are at the root of the robust performance in the majority of Brazil's economic and social indicators in the last two decades. Will it be possible to maintain this trajectory without new reforms? Will it be sufficient to maintain the status quo to make Brazil a more prosperous and fairer society in the next twenty years?

Time is important. The country is currently experiencing what is known as a "demographic window of opportunity," which should begin to close in 2030. The birth rate of the Brazilian population has decelerated rapidly in the last two decades, and the breakdown by age group is changing rapidly: the proportion of adults compared with children is growing, as is the proportion of the elderly, though more slowly than that of adults at an economically active age. While this process lasts, Brazil will be best positioned to generate greater wealth (and distribute it more fairly). What is lacking for Brazil to take advantage of this opportunity is an increase in the country's rate of investment in physical and human capital.

Under the military regime, the country achieved high investment rates (more than 25 percent of GDP) in equipment, machinery, and infrastructure. The public sector was the main driver of these investments. It took these funds from society by forced-savings mechanisms – such as the FGTS fund and Social Security (at that time in surplus) – and channelled them through state companies. Inflation also functioned as a mechanism for transferring resources from society to the "developmentalist" state. Since the regime was authoritarian, there was little pressure for social spending. GDP grew vigorously (running at an average rate of almost 10 percent a year between 1968 and 1973); however, income was increasingly concentrated, and there were virtually no universal social policies. This model entered into progressive collapse with the external debt crisis and the return to democracy in the first half of the 1980s. The most evident symptom of this was the latent hyperinflation, which would only be brought under control with the Real Plan.

The opening of the economy, the stabilization of the currency and the reforms introduced in the 1990s, including the privatizations, presaged the resumption of investments, this time undertaken mainly by the private sector. The reality, however, proved to be more complex. The drastic reduction in inflation drove an increase in family and individual consumption, with simultaneous growth in public spending, especially in the social area. The state could no longer count on inflation to deal with the pressures of a democratic society, in which various actors and social groups sought to increase their share from the public coffers. Since resistance from the sectors already benefiting from public funding made redistribution difficult, the new priorities in favor of previously neglected groups implied a heavy increase in the tax load. To cover the growth in social spending and interest on the public debt, the total tax load increased from 26 percent to 35 percent of GDP between 1993 and 2002. Brazil became the country with the highest tax load among the middle-income countries. Even so, the public sector continued to transform savings into consumption, because of the rigidity of government expenditures, including interest payments, which are still abnormally high sixteen years after the end of hyperinflation.

Because of the lack of internal savings, investment was dependent on external savings, which the country started to attract in quantity after the Real Plan. But it did this at the expense of the long-term sustainability of the balance of payments, leading to the exchange crisis at the end of the 1990s. Inflation did not return, but investment, which had increased, declined once again, compromising the potential for sustained growth.

In the Lula government, with the commodities boom, external accounts stopped being an obstacle to growth. But the knot in investment was not undone. Growth accelerated, driven by family and government consumption. Total investment did not exceed 20 percent of GDP. This dearth of investment is felt most clearly in the infrastructure sectors (ports, railways, roads).

Investing more in physical capital, however, is not sufficient. It is necessary to invest in human capital. Social spending has grown, but in addition to problems in efficiency, it is less progressive than it should be in order to further reduce social inequalities and lift the base of the Brazilian social pyramid. A significant portion of this spending ends up benefiting the middle-income groups. This may be seen in the education area, for example, where higher education, to which the poorer segments do not have access, absorbs a disproportionate amount of funds to the detriment of basic education. This may also be seen in the pensions area, upon which Brazil spends an abnormally high percentage for a country that is still so young (12 percent of GDP, compared with less than half of that on education), and the state transfers copious public funds to maintain the special retirement plans of civil servants. This situation imposes restrictions on productivity and efficiency in the economy and on the more socially progressive allocation of public funds.

The insufficient amount of available qualified labour, a business environment which still inhibits the assumption of risk, the high cost of money, and the elevated tax load limit Brazil's capacity to promote innovation. In spite of incentive programs and policies adopted in recent years, investments by Brazilian companies in innovation are relatively stagnant and inferior to those in developed countries or other emerging nations, such as China or India.

The efficient production of a broad range of commodities, which has been advantageous for Brazil in recent years, is not enough (the future of industry is a concern). Growth driven by consumption is showing its limitations, making a sustainable increase in investment urgent. This should not come exclusively from either the state or from the private sector. It requires cooperation between the two. And, more than ever, the environmental variable will have to be taken into account. There are also evident limits to the continuity of income distribution undertaken without a significant increase in productivity, which will not occur without a great change in the quality of workforce education and further opening of the Brazilian market to competition. The adaptation of the health and pension systems to demographic change is equally essential. In all, this represents a complex set of challenges, in terms of political choices, ideological and technical debates, and the implementation of public policy.

Just how prepared are the elites, the state, and the Brazilian political system to meet these challenges? Judging from the last twenty years, there are reasons for cautious optimism. In spite of the fragility of the parties, the provincialism of most of the country's politicians, excessive state protection of a handful of large business groups, and the allotment of part of the state among the government majority parties, the country has advanced. Moreover, two robust long-term trends conspire in Brazil's favor: the demographic dividend and the growing global demand for food. The recent relative bonanza, however, has dampened the momentum of change necessary to ensure maintenance of the positive course the country has pursued since the mid-1990s. If Brazil gives in to the temptation to "lie down in its splendid cradle," as one of the verses of the national anthem puts it, the country runs the risk of not realizing its potential, not to mention the expectations of the Brazilian people.

BIBLIOGRAPHY

I COLONIAL BRAZIL (1500–1822)

The description of European socioeconomic transformations prior to Portuguese overseas expansion comes from Immanuel Wallerstein, *The Modern World-System* (London: Academic Press, 1974), and from Fernand Braudel, *Civilisation matérielle, économie et capitalisme* (Paris: Armand Colin, 1979). For a description and analysis of Portuguese overseas expansion, see José Hermano Saraiva, *História concisa de Portugal*, 2d. ed. (Lisbon: Publicações Europa-América, 1984).

The section dealing with Indians is based on Carlos Fausto, "Fragmentos de história e cultura tupinambá: da etnologia como instrumento crítico de conhecimento etno-histórico," in Manuela Carneiro da Cunha, *História dos índios do Brasil* (São Paulo: Companhia das Letras, 1992).

Several parts of this chapter echo consistent observations from works included in Leslie Bethell, ed., *The Cambridge History of Latin America*, vols. 1–3 (Cambridge University Press, 1984). Pertinent essays in vol. 1 are: Frédéric Mauro, "Portugal and Brazil, Political and Economic Structures of Empire, 1580–1750," 441–468; and Andrée Mansuy-Diniz Silva, "Portugal and Brazil: Imperial Re-organization, 1750–1808," 469–508. Those from vol. 2 are: Stuart B. Schwartz, "Colonial Brazil, 1580–1750: Plantations and Peripheries," 423–500; A. J. R. Russell-Wood, "Colonial Brazil: the Golden Cycle, 1690–1750," 547–600; and Dauril Alden, "Late Colonial Brazil, 1750–1808."

For a discussion of the functioning and the crisis in the colonial system, see Caio Prado Júnior, *Formação do Brasil contemporâneo* (colônia), 6th ed. (São Paulo: Brasiliense, 1961); and Fernando A. Novais, *Portugal e Brasil na crise do antigo sistema colonial, 1777–1808* (São Paulo: Hucitec, 1979).

For a classical interpretation of (colonial and post-colonial) Brazil, see Sérgio Buarque de Holanda, *Raízes do Brasil*, 5th ed. (Rio de Janeiro: José Olympio, 1969).

My description and analysis of the sugar economy is based, in essence, on Stuart B. Schwartz, *Sugar Plantations in the Formation of Brazilian Society* (Bahia 1550–1835) (Cambridge University Press, 1985). The references to the 17th-century economy of São Paulo come from a 1985 University of Chicago Ph.D. dissertation: John M. Monteiro, "São Paulo in the Seventeenth Century: Economy and Society." My sources of information on the wars with the Dutch and on Pernambucan nationalism were, respectively: Evaldo Cabral de Mello, *Olinda restaurada. Guerra e açúcar no nordeste, 1630–1654* (São Paulo: Forense/ EDUSP, 1975); and Cabral de Mello, *Rubro veto: o imaginário da restauração pernambucana* (Rio de Janeiro: Nova Fronteira, 1976).

For background on Minas Gerais society during the gold rush, see Laura de Mello e Souza, *Desclassificados do ouro* (Rio de Janeiro: Graal, 1982). My section on the Inconfidência Mineira relied on considerable data and observations from Kenneth Maxwell, *Conflicts and Conspiracies: Brazil and Portugal, 1750–1808* (Cambridge University Press, 1973). For information on the symbolic value of the Inconfidência, see José Murilo de Carvalho, *A formção das almas. O imaginário da República no Brasil* (São Paulo: Companhia das Letras, 1990). My information on the economy of Minas Gerais after the high point of the gold mining period is based on Roberto Borges Martins, "Minas Gerais, século 19: Tráfico e apego à escravidão numa economia não-exportadora," *Estudos econômics* 13 (1983) FEA-USP.

In the controversy concerning the basic form of Portuguese colonization, Caio Prado Júnior and Fernando A. Novais are on one side: they maintain that Brazil's colonization was based on the production of raw materials for export. Authors such as Capitstrano de Abreu (*Capítulos de história colonial: 1500–1800*, 5th ed. [Rio de Janeiro: Livraria Briguet, 1969]) and Ciro Flamarion Santana Cardoso emphasize the amount of rural products destined for local consumption. A synthesis of this point of view can be found in the chapter titled "O trabalho da colônia" which Ciro F. S. Cardoso contributed to Maria Yedda Linhares, ed., *História geral do Brasil* (Rio de Janeiro: Campus, 1988).

Concerning the different interpretations of the relationships between state and society, see Raymundo Faoro, *Os donos do poder. Formação do patronato político brasileiro*, 2 vols., 2d. ed. (São Paulo: Globo/EDUSP, 1975); Oliveira Viana, *Instituições políticas brasileiras*, 2 vols., 2d. ed. (Rio de Janeiro: José Olympio, 1949); Nestor Duarte, *A ordem privada e a organização política nacional* (São Paulo: Editora Nacional, 1930).

For more on the political process between the opening of Brazil's ports to independence, see Leslie Bethell, "The Independence of Brazil," in *Cambridge History of Latin America*, vol. 3; and Emília Viotti da Costa, "Introdução ao estudo da emancipação política," in *Brasil em perspectiva* (São Paulo: Difel, 1968).

I should also mention the more general works used for this book: Antônio Mendes Júnior et al., *Brasil história, colônia* (São Paulo: Brasiliense, 1976), and *História geral do Brasil*, which I have already mentioned, edited by Maria Yedda Linhares.

2 IMPERIAL BRAZIL (1822–1889)

To begin with, see several essays included in Sérgio Buarque de Holanda, ed., *História geral da civilização brasileira* (São Paulo: Difel, 1963–1984). Especially pertinent are Amaro Quintas, "Agitação republicana no nordeste" (tome 2, vol. 3); Teresa Shorer Petrone, "Imigração assalariada" (vol. 4); Odilon Nogueira de Matos, "Vias de comunicação"; Alice P. Canabrava, "A grande lavoura"; and John Schulz, "O Exército e o Império" (vol. 6).

See vol. 4 of *The Cambridge History of Latin America* for Leslie Bethell and Murilo de Carvalho, "Brazil from Independence to the Middle of the Nineteenth Century," and Richard Graham, "Brazil from the Middle of the Nineteenth Century to the Paraguayan War." In vol. 5, see Emília Viotti da Costa, "Brazil, the Age of Reform 1870–1889."

The description and analysis of the imperial political process derive in large part from Murilo de Carvalho, *A construção da ordem* (Rio de Janeiro: Campus, 1980). See also Richard Graham, *Patronage and Politics in Nineteenth-Century Brazil* (Stanford: Stanford University Press, 1990). Electoral data were taken from Walter Costa Porto, *O voto no Brasil da Colônia a Quinta República* (Brasília: Gráfica do Senado Federal, 1989).

For information on the Farrapos War, see Spencer Leitman, *Raízes sócio-econômicas da Guerra dos Farrapos* (Rio de Janeiro: Graal, 1979). For details on the Malê Uprising in Bahia, see João José Reis, *Slave Rebellion in Brazil*, trans. Arthur Brakel (Baltimore: Johns Hopkins University Press, 1993). My interpretation of the Paraguayan War relies on Ricardo Salles, *Guerra do Paraguai: escravidão e cidadania na formação do exército* (Rio de Janeiro: Paz e Terra, 1990); and, especially, on the work of Francisco Doratioto, *A Guerra do Paraguai* (São Paulo: Editora Brasiliense, 1991). My observations on the National Guard and the army are based on Wilma Peres Costa, *A espada de Dâmocles: o Exército, a guerra de Paraguai e a crise do Império* (São Paulo: HUCITEC-UNI-CAMP, 1996).

For more on the last years of slavery, see Robert Conrad, *Os últimos anos da escravatura no Brasil*, 2d ed. (Rio de Janeiro: Civilização Brasileira, 1978). Some information on slavery came from *Estatísticas históricas do Brasil*, vol. 3 (Rio de Janeiro: IBGE, 1987).

Population data for the period 1822–1890 come from Maria Luiza Marcílio et al., *Crescimento populacional e componentes do crescimento* (Cadernos CEBRAP, 16 São Paulo, 1973). References to coffee, sugar, and rubber are based respectively on: Antônio Delfim Neto, O *problema do café no Brasil* (Rio de Janeiro: FGV, 1979); Peter L. Eisenberg, *Modernização sem mudança*, A *indústria açucareira em Pernambuco – 1840–1910* (Rio de Janeiro: Paz e Terra, 1977); and Barbara Weinstein, *The Amazon Rubber Boom 1850–1920* (Stanford: Stanford University Press, 1983). For more on railways, see Flávio A.M. de Saes, *A grande empresa de serviços públicos na economia cafeeira* (São Paulo: Hucitec, 1986).

Differing interpretations for why Brazil did not break up after independence can be found in José Murilo de Carvalho, *A construção da ordem;* and Luiz Felipe de Alencastro, "La Traite négrière et l'unité nationale brésilienne," *Revue française d'histoire d'Outre-Mer 64* (1979): 244–245.

On one side of the debate on the brecha camponesa sit Luiz Felipe de Alencastro, mentioned above, and Jacob Gorender (*A escravidão reabilitada* [São Paulo: Atica, 1990]). They are not in complete agreement, however. On the other side one finds Ciro Flamarion Santana Cardoso, *Escravo ou camponês; o protocampesinato negro nas Américas* (São Paulo: Brasiliense, 1987).

For an overall interpretation of the Brazilian empire, see Ilmar Rohloff de Matos, *O tempo saquarema* (São Paulo: Editora Hucitec, 1987).

A synthesis of Brazilian foreign policy from the empire to the present can be found in Amado Luiz Cervo and Clodoaldo Bueno, *História da política exterior do Brasil* (São Paulo: Editora Atica, 1982).

3 THE FIRST REPUBLIC (1889–1930)

Most of the economic data for the period from 1889 to 1945 come from Anníbal Villanova Villela and Wilson Suzigan, *Política do governo e crescimento da economia brasileira: 1889–1945* (Rio de Janeiro: IPEA/INPES, 1973). My discussion of economic policy and the oligarchical alliances uses the analyses of Eduardo Kugelmas, "Difícil hegemonia. Um estudo sobre São Paulo na Primeira República" (1986), a doctoral dissertation defended at the Universidade de São Paulo. Comparative data on elections during the empire and during the republic come from Joseph L. Love, "Political Participation in Brazil, 1881–1896." *Luso-Brazilian Review 9* (1970): 3–24. Love has also worked on the presence of Rio Grande do Sul in federal politics. See his *Rio Grande do Sul and Brazilian Regionalism, 1882–1930* (Stanford: Stanford University Press, 1971).

For an overall analysis of the First Republic, I have used parts of my *Pequenos ensaios de história da República* (*Cadernos Cebrap* 10, 1975).

The part on immigration owes much to Thomas Holloway, *Immigrants on the Land: Coffee and Society in São Paulo, 1886–1934* (Chapel Hill: University of North Carolina Press); Maria Stella Ferreira Levy, "O papel da imigração internacional na evolução da população Brasileira (1872–1972)," *Revista de saúde pública 8* (1974): 49–90; Herbert S. Klein, "A integração social e econômica dos imigrantes espanhóis no Brasil,"

Estudos econômicos 19(3) (1989): 443–456; Herbert S. Klein, "The Social and Economic Integration of Portuguese Immigrants in Brazil in the Late Nineteenth and Early Twentieth Centuries," *Journal of Latin American Studies* 23 (1991): 309–337; Maria Tereza Schorer Petrone, "Imigração," in Boris Fausto, ed., *História geral da civilização brasileira. O Brasil republicano*, tome 3, vol. 9 (São Paulo: Difel, 1977), 95–133.

For more on industrialization, see Wilson Suzigan, *Indústria brasileira. Origem e desenvolvimento* (São Paulo: Brasiliense, 1986); and Paulo Singer, *Desenvolvimento econômico e evolução urbana* (São Paulo: Companhia Editora Nacional, 1968). My observations on the industrial bourgeoisie that go beyond the First Republic are based on Maria Antonieta P. Leopoldi's Ph.D. dissertation, "Industrial Associations and Politics in Contemporary Brazil," defended at Oxford University, 1984.

Data on the economy of Rio Grande do Sul come from Pedro Cézar Dutra Fonseca, "A transição capitalista no Rio Grande do Sul: a economia gaúcha na Primeira República," *Estudos econômicos* 15(2) (1985), FEA-USP. Concerning internal migration, see Douglas H. Graham and Sérgio Buarque de Holanda Filho, *Migration, Regional and Urban Growth and Development in Brazil: A Selective Analysis of the Historical Record, 1872–1970* (São Paulo: IPE-USP, 1971).

My observations concerning the rise of agricultural activities linked to the São Paulo internal market are based on Maurício A. Font, *Coffee, Contention, and Change* (Basil Blackwell, 1990).

For information on foreign investment and the external debt, see Flávio A. M. de Saes and Tamás Szmrecsányi, "O capital estrangeiro no Brasil, 1880–1930," *Estudos econômicos* 15(2) (1985); Warren Dean, "The Brazilian Economy, 1870–1930," in *Cambridge History of Latin America*, vol. 5, 685–725; and Steven Topik, *The Political Economy of the Brazilian State 1889–1930* (Austin: University of Texas Press, 1987).

4 THE VARGAS STATE (1930–1945)

My description of revolutionary movements draws on Edgard Carone, *Revoluções do Brasil contemporâneo* (São Paulo: Buriti, 1965). My description of the political process comes even more directly from my *Pequenos ensaios de história da república* and Robert M. Levine, *The Vargas Regime: The Critical Years, 1934–1938* (New York: Columbia University Press, 1970). Much information on the period from 1930 to 1983 was obtained from Israel Bloch and Alzira Alves de Abreu, eds., *Dicionário histórico-biográfico brasileiro, 1930–1983*, 4 vols. (Rio de Janeiro: FGV-CPDOC-Forense, 1984).

The analysis of Integralism is based on Hélgio Trindade, *Integralismo. O fascismo brasileiro na década de 30* (São Paulo: Difel, 1974). For more on the role of industrialists, see Ely Diniz, *Empresário, Estado e capitalismo no Brasil: 1930–1945* (Rio de Janeiro: Paz e Terra, 1978).

My analysis of foreign policy is mainly based on Gerson Moura, "A Revolução de 1930 e a política externa brasileira: ruptura ou continuidade," in *A Revolução de 30. Seminário internacional* (Brasília: Universidade de Brasília, 1982). For more on the armed forces, see José Murilo de Carvalho, "Forças Armadas e política, 1930–1945," in *A Revolução de 30. Seminário internacional*. My information concerning the formation of public opinion during the Vargas government is based on Angela Castro Gomes, *A invenção do trabalhismo* (Rio de Janeiro: Vértice-IUPERJ, 1988). On the matter of education and the foundation of the University of São Paulo, see, respectively, Otaiza de Oliveira Rommanelli, *História da educação no Brasil*, 4th ed. (Petrópolis: Vozes, 1978); and Fernando Limongi, "Mentores das ciências sociais no Brasil," in Sérgio Miceli, ed., *História das ciências sociais no Brasil*, vol. 1 (São Paulo: Vértice/IDESP, 1989). Concerning financial policy and the foreign market, see Marcelo de Paiva Abreu, "O Brasil e a economia mundial, 1929–1945," in Boris Fausto, ed., *História geral*, tome 3 (São Paulo: Difel, 1984).

5 THE DEMOCRATIC EXPERIMENT (1945–1964)

My overall analysis of the process is based on Thomas Skidmore, *Politics in Brazil. An Experiment in Democracy, 1930–1964* (Oxford: Oxford University Press, 1969). For more on the Kubitschek government, see Maria Victória de Mesquita Benevides, *O governo Kubitschek. Desenvolvimento econômico e estabilidade política, 1956–1961*, 3d. ed. (Rio de Janeiro: Paz e Terra, 1979). My references to the UDN are largely based on Mesquita Benevides, *A UDN e o udenismo. Ambiguidades do liberalismo brasileiro, 1945–1965* (Rio de Janeiro: Paz e Terra, 1981). My main source for the analysis of the army is Alfred Stepan, *The Military in Politics: Changing Patterns in Brazil* (Princeton: Princeton University Press, 1971).

The analysis of the workers' movement is based on Leôncio Martins Rodrigues, "Sindicalismo e classe operária, 1930–1964," in Boris Fausto, *História geral*, tome 3, vol. 10; and Francisco C. Weffort, "Sindicatos e política," a *livre docência* thesis presented at the Universidade de São Paulo, n.d.

Concerning international economic relations, see Pedro Sampaio Malan, "Relações econômicas internacionais do Brasil 1945–1964," in Boris Fausto, *História geral*, tome 3, vol. 2. My data on the automobile industry were obtained from Benedicto Heloiz Nascimento, *Formação da indústria automobilística brasileira* (São Paulo: Instituto de Geografia USP, 1976).

6 THE MILITARY GOVERNMENT AND THE TRANSITION TO DEMOCRACY (1964–1984)

My description of the political process is based on Maria Helena Moreira Alves, *Estado e oposição no Brasil, 1964–1984* (Petrópolis: Vozes, 1984);

and, mainly, Thomas Skidmore, *The Politics of Military Rule in Brazil, 1964–1985* (New York: Oxford University Press, 1988). For more on the analysis of the political model, see Fernando Henrique Cardoso, *O modelo político brasileiro* (São Paulo: Difel, 1979). See also Cardoso, "Associated-Dependent Development and Democratic Theory," in Alfred Stepan, ed., *Democratizing Brazil (Problems of Transition and Consolidation)* (New York: Oxford University Press, 1989), 299–326. Cardoso analyzes the relationship between economics and politics. Concerning the military, see Alfred Stepan, *Os militares: da abertura à Nova República* (Rio de Janeiro: Paz e Terra, 1986). Election results and an analysis of the MDB can be found in Maria D'Alva Gil Kinzo, *Oposição e autoritarismo. Gênese e trajetória do MDB, 1966–1979* (São Paulo: IDESP/Vértice, 1988).

Data on auto workers in the ABC triangle of São Paulo come from John Humphrey, *Fazendo o "milagre": controle capitalista e luta operária na indústria automobilística brasileira* (Petrópolis: Vozes, 1982).

I have used several essays contained in Edmar Bacha and Herbert S. Klein, eds., *Social Change in Brazil: The Incomplete Transition* (Albuquerque: University of New Mexico Press, 1989). See especially Thomas W. Merrick, "Population Since 1945," 15–48, for data on population. For the agrarian issue, see David Goodman, "Economia e sociedades rurais a partir de 1945." For education, see Cláudio de Moura Castro, "O que está acontecendo com a educação no Brasil?" On the controversy over the consequences of Geisel's Second National Development Plan, see, for a negative interpretation, Albert Fishlow, "Uma história de dois presidentes: a economia política da gestao da crise," in Alfred Stepan, ed., *Democratizing Brazil*; and Alkimar R. Moura, "Rumo à entropia: a política econômica de Geisel a Collor," in Bolivar Lamounier, ed., *De Geisel a Collor: o balanço da transição* (São Paulo: IDESP, 1980). For a positive interpretation of the PND II, see Antônio Barros de Castro and Francisco Eduardo Pires de Sousa, *A economia brasileira em marcha forçada* (Rio de Janeiro: Paz e Terra, 1985). For the structure of the countryside and agrarian reform, see Francisco Graziano, *A tragédia de terra: o fracasso da reforma agrária no Brasil* (São Paulo: Iglu-Funep-Unesp, 1991).

7 MODERNIZATION UNDER DEMOCRACY (1985–2010)

For a comprehensive view of the political process from the transition to democracy until Lula's first term in office, see Melo, Carlos Ranulfo e Saez Manuel Alcântara (orgs), *A Democracia Brasileira: balanço e perspectivas para o século XXI*, UFMG, 2007.

For an analysis of constitutional reforms under Fernando Henrique Cardoso government, see Melo, Marcus Andre, *Reformas Constitucionais no Brasil: Instituições Políticas e Processos Decisórios*, Editora Renavan, 2002.

For an analysis of Lula and "Lulismo," see Singer, André, *Os Sentidos do Lulismo: reforma gradual e pacto conservador*, Companhia das Letras, 2012.

For a comprehensive view of economic and social changes during the decade of 1990, see Baumann, Renato (org), *Brasil, Uma Década em Transição*, Editora Campus, 1999.

For a comprehensive view of demographic transition in Brazil, see Giambiagi, Fábio e Tafner, Paulo, *Demografia: a ameaça invisível*, Campus Elsevier, 2009.

About the privatization process, see Castellar, Armando e Giambiagi, Fabio, *A Privatização no Brasil: os antecedentes macroeconômicos e a estrutura institucional*, BNDES, 2000.

For a critical appraisal of the opening up and privatization processes, see Coutinho, Luciano et alli, *Internacionalização e Desenvolvimento da Indústria no Brasil*, Editora da UNESP, 2004.

For a brief historical view of a limited welfare state in Brazil, from 1980 to 2000, see Draibe, Sônia, *Proteção e Insegrança Sociais em Tempos Difíceis, Report presented at Taller Inter-Regional "Protección Social en una Era Insegura,"* Santiago, 2002.

For a hard data-based analysis of the evolution of social indicators in Brazil in the decades of 1990's and 2000's, see Neri, Marcelo, *Desigualdade, Estabilidade e Bem-Estar Social*, FGV, 2006.

For an economic analysis of the emergence of the "new middle class," see Neri, Marcelo, *A Emergência da Nova Classe Média: Lado Brilhante da Pirâmide*, Saraiva, 2011.

For an analysis of Brazilian Foreign Policy under Fernando Henrique Cardoso government, see Lafer, Celso, *A Identidade Internacional do Brasil e a Política Externa Brasileira: passado, presente e futuro, Perspectiva*, 2ª edição revista e ampliada, Editora Perspectiva, 2004.

For an analysis of Brazilian Foreign Policy from Sarney government to Lula government, see Vigevani, Tulo and Cepaluni, Gabriel, *Política Externa Brasileira – Em busca da autonomia, de Sarney a Lula*, Unesp, 2011.

INDEX